ASIA
AFTER THE "MIRACLE"
REDEFINING U.S. ECONOMIC AND SECURITY PRIORITIES

EDITED BY
SELIG S. HARRISON
CLYDE V. PRESTOWITZ, JR.

ECONOMIC STRATEGY INSTITUTE

1401 H Street, N.W., Suite 750
Washington, D.C. 20005
Tel. (202) 289-1288
Fax. (202) 289-1319

The views expressed in the recommendations and chapters in this publication are those of the members who are their signatories or authors, respectively, and not necessarily those of the Economic Strategy Institute, its board of directors, or its member organizations.

Please order ***Asia After the "Miracle": Redefining U.S. Economic and Strategic Priorities***
($22.95 paperback: ISBN 0-8157-3487-5)
directly from the Economic Strategy Institute's distributor:
Brookings Institution Press
Dept. 029, Washington, D.C. 20042-0029
Tel. 1-800-275-1447 (toll-free in U.S.) or 202-797-6258.
Fax 202-797-6004.

Produced by Kallab Communications, Inc.
Cover and design by Paddy McLaughlin, Concepts & Design.
Printed by Automated Graphic Systems.

CONTENTS

FOREWORD

American policy in Asia rests on the premise that the United States does not have to choose between economic and security priorities because the American military presence is valued by regional powers in its own right. For example, the former Assistant Secretary of State for East Asian and Pacific Affairs, Winston Lord, assured Congress that "we have insulated our security ties from our trade frictions."

But is this premise justified?

In 1990, we argued in a *Foreign Policy* article that American domestic political support for current levels of the U.S. security posture in Asia would gradually erode in the absence of significant movement toward greater equity and reciprocity in U.S.–Asian economic relations. At the same time, we questioned the need for a paramount U.S. military role in Asia in the aftermath of the Cold War, pointed to changing Asian attitudes toward the American military presence, and called for efforts to reduce U.S. forces in Asia as part of a regional arms control bargain embracing Russia and China. Now, eight years later, much has changed in the Asian environment, but the issues we raised in 1990 remain the pivotal issues in the U.S. debate over Asia policy.

In an effort to focus and shape the debate with a new emphasis on the relationship between economic and security priorities, we invited thirty-four distinguished Americans with diplomatic, military, business, journalistic, and academic experience in Asia to join with us in examining emerging trends in the region and considering what changes in U.S. policy might be necessary to harmonize the promotion of American economic and security interests. A Study Group on "American Interests in Asia: Economic and Security Priorities" under our co-chairmanship was established by the Economic Strategy Institute and met nine times during 1996 and 1997 (see list of members, p. 7).

By design, the Study Group brought together a heterogeneous array of specialists representing a broad diversity of experience and the full spectrum of contending views on the most sensitive issues of Asia policy. Given such heterogeneity, we did not attempt to produce a report reflecting the least common denominator of the widely divergent views within the Study Group on all aspects of the emerging Asian environment and future U.S. policy options. Instead, we have divided this report into three parts. First, drawing on the rich insights provided by the papers prepared for the Study Group and by the Study Group discussions, we have presented our own assessment of the factors that we believe should govern U.S. policy choices in Asia. We alone are responsible for this Overview.

This assessment is followed by the specific recommendations of the Study Group in ten key areas of the Asia policy debate. These recommendations represent a consensus of the signatories whose names appear at the end of each of ten statements on the key areas of the debate. Representatives of the White House, the State Department, the Department of Defense, the Department of Commerce, and the Central Intelligence Agency participated in the discussions but were not invited to join in the report.

Finally, the bulk of this volume consists of the sixteen papers prepared for the Study Group meetings held in 1996 and 1997. The papers are presented here in the form of mini-debates covering each of the major policy areas addressed by the Group. In commissioning the papers, we asked for a policy argument, not for expository background papers, selecting authors who were qualified to provide authoritative statements of conflicting policy approaches. The last chapter in the book is a background paper providing a factual overview and expert assessment of the military environment in Asia.

We would like to express our thanks to the following donors: the Starr Foundation, the Henry R. Luce Foundation, Federal Express, the Cotsen Family Foundation, and the Kearney Foundation. Without their support, we could not have conducted the Study Group and published this book.

Selig S. Harrison and Clyde V. Prestowitz, Jr.
April 1998

MEMBERS OF THE STUDY GROUP

The following members support all or parts of the recommendations of the ESI *Study Group on "American Interests in Asia: Economic and Security Priorities," as indicated in the list of signatories of each recommendation on pp.* 43-77.

Co-Chairmen

Selig S. Harrison
Senior Scholar, Woodrow Wilson International Center for Scholars and Fellow, The Century Foundation

Clyde V. Prestowitz, Jr.
President, Economic Strategy Institute, and former Counselor to the Secretary of Commerce

Doug Bandow
Syndicated Columnist, Copley News Service; former Special Assistant for Policy Development to President Ronald Reagan

Ted Galen Carpenter
Vice President for Defense and Foreign Policy Studies, Cato Institute

Rear Admiral Eugene Carroll, Jr.
Deputy Director, Center for Defense Information

Lawrence Clarkson
Senior Vice President, Boeing Corporation

Steven C. Clemons
Senior Policy Advisor to Senator Jeff Bingaman, Ranking Member, Joint Economic Committee

Bruce Cumings
Professor of History, University of Chicago

David D.H. Denoon
Professor of Politics and Economics, New York University

Susan Dentzer
former Economics Editor, U.S. *News and World Report*

Richard Elkus
Vice-Chairman, Tencor Instruments

Charles W. Freeman, Jr.
former Ambassador to Saudi Arabia and Assistant Secretary of Defense for International Security Affairs

Maurice Greenberg
President and Chairman of the Board, American International Group; Chairman of the Board, Asia Society

Donald C. Hellmann
Professor of International Studies and Political Science, University of Washington

Gary Hufbauer
Director of Studies, Council on Foreign Relations

Chalmers Johnson
President, Japan Policy Research Institute

Nicholas Lardy
Senior Fellow, Brookings Institution

Charles William Maynes
President, Eurasia Foundation; former editor of *Foreign Policy*

Rear Admiral Michael A. McDevitt
Senior Fellow, Center for Naval Analysis; former Commandant, National War College

Walter Russell Mead
Senior Fellow, Council on Foreign Relations

Mike Masato Mochizuki
Senior Fellow, Brookings Institution

Marvin C. Ott
Professor of National Security Policy, National War College; former Deputy Director, Senate Intelligence Committee

Robert Perkins
former Vice President, Chrysler Corporation

Harold A. Poling
former Chief Executive, Ford Motor Company

Richard J. Samuels
Ford International Professor and Chairman, Department of Political Science, Massachusetts Institute of Technology

Susan Schwab
Dean, School of Public Affairs, University of Maryland

Edson W. Spencer
former President, Honeywell Corporation

Ronald Steel
Professor of International Relations, University of Southern California

John Steinbruner
Senior Fellow and former Director of Foreign Policy Studies, Brookings Institution

William J. Taylor
Senior Vice President for International Security Affairs, Center for Strategic and International Studies

Allen S. Whiting
Regents Professor of Political Science, University of Arizona

Jeffrey Winters
Professor of Political Science, Northwestern University

The following participants did not join in the report:

Harry Harding
Dean, Elliott School of International Affairs, George Washington University

Kenneth Lieberthal
Professor of Chinese Studies, University of Michigan

Robert Manning
Senior Fellow, Council on Foreign Relations

Don Oberdorfer
former Diplomatic Correspondent, *The Washington Post*

Representatives of the White House, the State Department, the Defense Department, the Commerce Department, and the Central Intelligence Agency participated in the discussions but were not invited to join in the report.

I. OVERVIEW: NEW PRIORITIES FOR U.S. ASIA POLICY

Selig S. Harrison and Clyde V. Prestowitz, Jr.

The Asian economic meltdown of 1997 has dramatically underlined the need for a new emphasis on economic priorities in U.S. Asia policy, reflecting a new recognition that the basic threats to American security interests in this critical region are economic, not military, in character. Indeed, in the emerging Asian environment, economic policy ***is*** security policy.

During the Cold War, successive U.S. presidents consciously subordinated American economic interests in Asia to perceived geopolitical priorities. The United States actively promoted and subsidized the economic development of Japan, South Korea, and Taiwan in order to obtain their military and political support, and it sponsored Japan's role as the organizer and driving force of economic growth elsewhere in Asia under its aegis.

Washington struck an expedient bargain with governments from Seoul to Bangkok. In exchange for Cold War cooperation, the American market would be relatively open, while the markets of its partners could be much more restrictive, subject to cartelization, government guidance, and non-transparent administrative procedures. As part of this bargain, the United States acquiesced in the development of a mercantilist, export-oriented Asian model of capitalism that initially produced high growth rates but contained the seeds of its own destruction. U.S. leaders were reluctant to acknowledge the built-in defects of this model and its inherent incompatibility with the concept of free trade based on equity and reciprocity. "Allies," they argued, could not become economic adversaries. It was not until the 1997 crisis, leading to Asian pleas for U.S. economic help, that Washington belatedly began to insist on the basic structural reforms needed to rebuild Asian economies on more solid foundations as the precondition for establishing equitable trade and investment relations.

Was this preoccupation with security priorities unavoidable in the context of the superpower rivalry? Whatever the ultimate verdict of history, it is clear that the legacy of the Cold War decades haunts the United States today as it seeks to shape new policies relevant to a radically changed Asian environment. In this new Asia, marked by the absence of any clear and present threat to U.S. security, the principal challenge facing Washington is no longer how to project its power in the region militarily but rather how to get Asian countries to restructure their economies. Ironically, in the two countries with which the United States has military alliances, Japan and South Korea, the American military presence does not enhance U.S. leverage in pressing for economic reforms. On the contrary, Tokyo and Seoul, exploiting the American desire to keep forces in Asia, use the implicit threat of a rupture in security relations to strengthen their own bargaining positions on economic issues.

The need for a new focus on economic priorities is enhanced by the rising economic power of China, India, and Southeast Asia. Increasingly, however, the U.S. debate on Asia policy has been diverted from economic issues by greatly exaggerated fears of Chinese military expansionism.

A "MIRACLE" MADE IN AMERICA

The starting point for a reappraisal of U.S. policy options is a recognition that the high growth rates achieved by many Asian countries have been a "miracle" made in America. The United States has directly promoted this explosion of growth by accommodating to mercantilist, export-oriented Asian economic models despite their adverse impact on American economic interests. This tacit collusion in Asian mercantilism has been central to a pattern of direct and indirect U.S. subsidies that have artificially accelerated and inflated Asian economic expansion. To be sure, indigenous factors have also been critical to Asian economic progress. In the cases of Japan, South Korea, and Taiwan, a disciplinarian work ethic rooted in Confucian values is shared by all three of these societies. But without a variety of Cold War American subsidies dictated by security considerations, the economic rise of these countries would have been much less spectacular, and its multiplier effect in Southeast Asia would have been greatly reduced.

The Trade Subsidy. The most important of these subsidies have been the built-in trade surpluses resulting from inequitable trade relationships. "Japan, Inc.," and similar Asian economic models inspired by the Japanese example were deliberately designed to generate trade surpluses that can be plowed back into national economic expansion. The objective of these models was to catch up with the West and then, having caught up, to shift from a production to a consumption model. In practice, however, the vested interests that have profited from this model have resisted change, and trade surpluses have become chronic. Moreover, by its nature, a government-directed model of capitalism with its web of insider relationships, bureaucratic guidance, and subsidies has encouraged corruption and speculation. In South Korea and Thailand, in particular, U.S. support for military dictatorships directly contributed to the growth of an extreme form of crony capitalism.

By the late 1980s, with most of Asia pursuing an export-oriented strategy, Asian exporters began competing among themselves for markets. To reduce the costs of production and keep ahead of its new competitors, Japan reduced interest rates, thus fostering the speculative bubble that finally burst in 1991. In 1994, China devalued the yuan, thereby putting pressure on other producers of the textiles, toys, and electronic goods that dominate Chinese exports. Since 1995, Japan has periodically intervened in the foreign exchange markets and taken other steps to drive its yen down in an effort to jump-start its languishing economy. This has put enormous additional pressure on other Asian exporters. The strong bias against consumption in Japan's export-focused policies was epitomized by the increase in the sales tax from 3 percent to 5 percent in April 1997. In retrospect, it is apparent that Japanese policies directly triggered the series of competitive Asian currency devaluations that led to the crash of late 1997.

Even before the crash, out of a global U.S. trade deficit of $181.6 billion in 1997, Japan, China, and Taiwan accounted for $117.5 billion, and fifteen other Asian countries accounted for an additional $19.2 billion. Asian markets remain relatively closed compared to the transparent and relatively open U.S. market. Thus, several authoritative estimates suggest that the U.S. trade deficit would be reduced by as much as $55 billion a year if Japan removed existing import barriers. An additional $55 billion of Japanese imports from the United States would raise the U.S. GNP by $115 billion, add 1.5 million jobs, and reduce the federal budget deficit by $25 billion. Estimates for Asia as a whole suggest that the current impact of lost exports to the region on the U.S. economy could well amount to $150 billion of GNP, 1.9 million jobs, and an addition of $45 billion to the projected U.S. budget surplus.[1]

Ironically, the United States actively helped Asian allies during the Cold War to promote their exports and to get special tariff reductions for their imports. To offset China, the United States not only pumped massive economic and military aid grants into Taiwan but also sought to discourage its natural economic tilt to the mainland by reorienting its exports to the United States, actively fostering U.S. investment in Taiwanese industries geared to the U.S. market. In both Taiwan and South Korea, the United States misused the Generalized System of Preferences (GSP), an international arrangement designed to provide low tariffs for developing countries. Taipei, like Seoul, continued to receive GSP trade concessions until 1989, long after it merited such support. By November 1997, Taiwan had piled up $82.9 billion in foreign exchange reserves—an amount surpassed only by Japan and China.

The Currency Subsidy. Directly related to the subsidy provided by U.S. acceptance of unequal trade relationships has been the substantial overvaluation of the dollar in relation to East Asian currencies. For most of the past forty-five years, the dollar has been chronically overvalued in relation to the yen. From 1960 to 1985, this overvaluation amounted to an effective subsidy of slightly more than $300 billion. The same story has been repeated in other Asian economies. A World Bank study shows that real per capita GNP in Asia grew by more than 5 percent a year from 1965 to 1990 compared to U.S. growth of 2 percent per year.[2] Yet, despite this productivity differential and the enormity of the Asian trade surpluses with the United States, there has been relatively little adjustment in the inflation-adjusted exchange rates of most Asian currencies, and the competitive devaluations touched off by the 1997 crisis have aggravated the problem.

The Technology Subsidy. The United States has also provided a research and development subsidy by acquiescing in Asian policies designed to force the transfer of U.S. technology at little or no cost. Japan made technology transfer a condition for entering its market, imposing terms it is not willing to reciprocate when it invests in the United States. James Abegglen's analysis of 42,000 licensing agreements shows that Japan acquired the technology for some 20 percent of its manufactured products at politically influenced bargain-basement prices, saving at least $65 billion that U.S. firms would have received through royalties of only 3 percent.[3]

The Defense Subsidy. The United States channeled billions in procurement and supply contracts to Japan during the Korean War and billions more to both Japan and South Korea during the Vietnam War.

More important, by maintaining security treaties with Japan, South Korea, and (until 1979) Taiwan, the United States has provided large indirect subsidies, over and above the direct costs of maintaining U.S. forces in Asia. While the direct cost of the U.S. force presence in Asia is about $42 billion,[4] the indirect value of the resulting economic subsidy to Japan and South Korea is much greater. For example, without the U.S. subsidy, Tokyo and Seoul, which spent $48 billion and $13 billion respectively on defense in 1997, would have to double or triple their military budgets to replace the conventional forces deployed for their defense by the United States—not to mention the much higher outlays that independent nuclear forces would require.

In reality, neither Japan nor South Korea would be likely to make such massive increases in defense spending if the United States withdrew its forces, given the relaxation of military tensions in Asia since the end of the Cold War and the current climate of economic stringency in both countries. Nevertheless, the U.S. defense subsidy has had an incalculable economic value. It has enabled Tokyo and Seoul to defer difficult choices concerning their defense needs, thus reducing their immediate defense burden and freeing them to concentrate resources on their export offensives.

Although the United States has exacted "burden-sharing" contributions to help offset the costs of the U.S. presence, the size of these offset payments is modest compared to the direct and indirect costs of the U.S. presence ($4 billion from Japan in 1996 and $226 million from South Korea).

THE PERCEPTION GAP

The American response to the challenges and problems of the East Asian economies should come in the economic arena. Instead, the United States has linked economic and security priorities, attempting to obtain a price in the security sphere for its acquiescence in unbalanced trade relations. Successive administrations have continued to press for greater burden-sharing, not only in the form of larger offset payments but also through expanded commitments to cooperate militarily in the event of a security crisis in Asia. This approach only serves to exacerbate frictions, because it ignores basic differences in how Washington and its Asian allies perceive their relations and, above all, how they perceive the post–Cold War Asian security environment.

For example, Americans generally believe that South Korea should feel indebted to the United States for its economic and military help. Most South Koreans, however, rejecting the idea of such a debt, think of themselves as the victims of a partition imposed by the superpowers. While they are grateful for American support, especially in the Korean War, they feel that the United States owes them continued military protection and special economic treatment until unification is achieved.

Similarly, as many Americans see it, the United States showed a rare benevolence in helping a defeated Japan to its feet, and the affluent Tokyo of the 1990s should feel indebted for the multifaceted economic subsidies it has received as well as for its military "free ride." This concept of a "debt" is flatly rejected in Japan, however, because most Japanese recognize that the United States rebuilt Japan for its own strategic reasons. While they acknowledge that the Cold War was a bonanza, greatly speeding their recovery, this bonanza is seen as an incidental byproduct of American policies conceived with American purposes uppermost, and as a natural outgrowth of the progress that Japan had achieved on its own before the war. Thus, they point out that during the Korean War, Japanese technical know-how made Japan an indispensable logistical base for U.S. forces, and the rebirth of Japanese industry generated by Korea-related contracts was the product not of U.S. magnanimity, but of sheer necessity.

Far from feeling indebted for the U.S. military presence, many Japanese resent American military bases. In a 1996 referendum on Okinawa, where more than half of the 47,000 U.S. forces in Japan are stationed, 53 percent of those polled wanted a reduction of the American presence on the island. In November 1997, a Gallup poll commissioned by *Yomiuri*, Japan's leading newspaper, found that 40 percent of the Japanese people favored U.S. force reductions in Japan as a whole.[5]

In part, the sentiment against U.S. bases can be explained by their location in or near congested urban areas, where they occupy valuable real estate and inflict noise and other inconveniences on local residents. But a deeper reason for their unpopularity is that they serve as a reminder of Japan's defeat in World War II and of a continuing dependence on the United States that conflicts with rising nationalist feelings. In March 1990, the U.S. Marine Commander in Japan, Major General Henry Stackpole III, stirred up a storm when he said that the U.S. force presence is "a cap in the bottle" to prevent a resurgence of Japanese military power. This was a diplomatically damaging but honest acknowledgment of the governing reason why the Pentagon wants to keep U.S. forces in Japan indefinitely despite the end of the Cold War. To be sure, many other explanations are frequently offered. U.S. forces serve as a "balancer" and "stabilizer," it is said, preventing an arms race and an inevitable confrontation between China and Japan. In pressing Japan to accept new Defense Cooperation Guidelines in 1997, U.S. negotiators were more specific, warning that China poses a growing military threat to the region and that an economically destitute North Korea might launch an invasion of the South. When challenged to elaborate, however, U.S. officials find it difficult to specify precisely what obligations a "balancing" and "stabilizing" role might entail in specific contingencies, such as a Sino-Japanese conflict. Most often they fall back on the "cap in the bottle" argument that if U.S. forces leave, Japan will compensate for their loss by building up its own independent military capabilities, including nuclear weapons.

The central reason for the steady growth in anti-base sentiment is the difference in U.S. and Japanese perceptions of the security environment in Asia. During the Vietnam War, Japan cooperated with the United States because it was economically profitable to do so, even though the majority of Japanese disliked the U.S. role in the war and the use of U.S. bases in Japan for operations in Vietnam. Similarly, in the present context, there is a sharp contrast between the image of a militarily menacing China projected by many American analysts and the low-key prediction in the 1997 Japanese Defense White Paper that "the modernization of Chinese military power in the future will proceed gradually." Polling evidence in Japan suggests an undercurrent of public uneasiness over the long-term implications of a powerful China and a significant hawkish minority view favoring closer military cooperation with the United States to contain Beijing. However, most polls indicate that a substantial majority of the Japanese people do not see China as a military threat in the foreseeable future and are opposed to Japanese involvement in a U.S. war with China over Taiwan. In the case of Korea, most Japanese do not share Pentagon concerns that the North might invade the South. In the dominant Japanese view, Pyongyang is unlikely to commit *hara-kiri* by giving Seoul and Washington an excuse to march North. Japanese attitudes toward Korea are dominated by fears that Korean unification would create a strong economic and military rival and thus by a desire to stabilize the division of the peninsula economically and militarily.

Despite this growing perception gap and significant popular opposition to the Japan–U.S. Security Treaty, conservative Japanese governments have been able to sustain the treaty because the public understands that it is part of a tacit trade-off in which Tokyo provides military privileges and foreign policy support in exchange for U.S. solicitude in economic matters. For many conservative politicians and Defense Agency bureaucrats, the treaty has a specifically military rationale. But for the broader Japanese public, with its diversity of views on security and foreign policy issues, the alliance has been politically sustainable primarily in terms of its economic benefits. Most Japanese have viewed the treaty as a tacit precondition for assuring access to the American market as well as for securing stable supplies of food grains and a variety of American, or American-controlled, natural resources—notably enriched uranium and coking coal.

The Clinton-Hashimoto summit of April 1996 marked an attempt to preserve the trade-off that continues to underlie U.S.–Japan relations despite the growth of trade tensions. Prime Minister Ryutaro Hashimoto promised to negotiate the Defense Cooperation Guidelines in order to paper over differences with President Bill Clinton on trade and the future of U.S. bases in Okinawa. But it would be a mistake to assume that the trade-off can continue indefinitely in the face of changing public attitudes in the United States and Japan alike. In Washington pressures have long been building up for more equitable trade and investment relations, and in Tokyo it is clear that the Guidelines, which were formally adopted in September 1997, are likely to have little practical meaning. The *Yomiuri* poll cited earlier found that only 4 percent of the Japanese respondents would approve Japanese participation in military action if a war should occur in Korea. Only 11 percent favored Japanese support for refueling and repairing U.S. ships and aircraft in a Korean conflict, even though such support is explicitly envisaged in the Guidelines. Still smaller percentages favored comparable Japanese help to U.S. forces in the event of a Taiwan conflict.

IS CHINA A THREAT?

The controversy within Japan over the Guidelines has paralleled a broader debate over whether Japan should amend its "No War" Constitution to permit the development of military power projection capabilities and the overseas deployment of military forces.

The hawkish minority of Japanese who support the Guidelines are also the leading advocates of a major expansion of Japanese forces focused on what they perceive to be a Chinese military threat. In Tokyo and Washington alike, proponents of the Guidelines see them as the first step in a growing program of U.S.–Japan military cooperation to counter this threat. In their controversial book, *The Coming Conflict With China*, Ross H. Munro and Richard Bernstein explicitly advocate converting the U.S.–Japan alliance into an anti-China alliance. "The primary American objective in Asia," they argue, "must be to prevent China's size, power and ambition from making it a regional hegemon. . . . The United States cannot block Chinese hegemony in Asia unless Japan is an equal and willing partner in the process." China has set goals for itself, they warn, "that are directly contrary to American interests, the most important of those being to replace the United States as the preeminent power in Asia."[6]

In reassessing its post–Cold War security role in Asia, the United States must consider first whether China does indeed pose the military threat assumed by American and Japanese hawks. Against this background, it will then be possible to judge: whether it is in the U.S. interest to take sides in Sino-Japanese relations; whether it is possible or desirable for the United States, a non-Asian power, to orchestrate the balance of power between China and its smaller neighbors, claiming the right to preeminence in Asia in the face of China's "size, power and ambition"; and, finally, whether such an ambitious U.S. security role in Asia would be compatible with the pursuit of U.S. economic interests.

In alarmist assessments of Chinese military power, it is argued that official defense budget figures are understated and that substantial defense spending is hidden in other budget categories, including spending on military purchases abroad that will enhance China's ability to project power. There is an element of truth in this argument, but extremely misleading numbers are frequently advanced.

Munro and Bernstein, for example, contend that a "conservative" estimate of Chinese military spending would be at least $87 billion per year, not the $8.7 billion figure reported in 1996. A more widely accepted consensus of government and academic experts suggests an annual figure of $30-$35 billion a year, which is about 1.5 percent of gross domestic product, in contrast to U.S. expenditures in the 3-4 percent range. Moreover, it is argued that, when Munro and Bernstein point to increases during recent years in announced defense spending levels, they ignore or minimize the extent to which these increases reflect higher outlays for pay raises and other benefits for the armed forces as well as for defensive systems such as air defense radar and anti-aircraft systems on ships.

Recent reports of projected Chinese weapons acquisitions from Russia impart an element of uncertainty to assessments of Chinese military capabilities. However, these acquisitions should be evaluated in relation to the overall decrease in Chinese military power that has taken place in recent years.

Military modernization is slower in China than in Japan, South Korea, or Taiwan. In terms of personnel and hardware, it is in decline, and Chinese plans for projecting power are still at the drawing-board stage. The most striking example of this decline is the drop in combat aircraft from 6,000 in 1980 to some 5,000 today; most of these are MIG-17s, MIG-19s, MIG-21s, and their Chinese clones. It is because almost all of those fighters are retiring or have to be retired soon that China is importing SU-27s from Russia. Japanese defense analyst Shunji Taoka of the *Asahi* cites official Japanese estimates that the number of SU-27s imported from Russia or produced under license is not likely to exceed two hundred. Dwight Perkins, a leading expert on the Chinese economy, observed that the number of military aircraft and submarines purchased from Russia to date has been "modest" because China "distrusts dependence on the outside world."[7]

China's indigenously produced fighter plane, the F8-2, is comparable to military aircraft produced in the United States three decades ago. With Japan now producing the U.S. F-2 fighter jet, equipped with air-to-air missiles more advanced than those deployed by Beijing, Tokyo will enjoy air superiority for the next decade in areas within reach of Japan, such as the East China Sea. Similarly, although China is buying four diesel submarines and two destroyers from Russia, its naval capabilities are still limited. The Chinese surface fleet, with 58 major surface combatants, is not growing numerically, and Chinese submarines, which numbered more than 100 a decade ago, are now down to 60 at most—with almost 40 of them Romeo-class boats based on obsolete German-model U-boats.

Within five to seven years, China is expected to acquire the amphibious and airlift capability that would be needed to overcome Taiwan. It is capable even now of short-range missile attacks and of blockading Taiwan's ports, which would inflict crippling economic damage. Most observers agree, however, that Beijing wants to avoid a military conflict with Taiwan and is likely to risk one only if faced with a declaration of independence or steps clearly foreshadowing such a declaration.

Apart from the overwhelming U.S. superiority over China in air and naval power projection, some other Asian countries already have or soon will get air and naval capabilities that equal or surpass what China will be able to deploy in the foreseeable future. South Korea has six German-designed diesel submarines more advanced than the Romeo-class Chinese fleet, and Malaysia has several MIG-29 fighters. Japan has acquired Aegis-class destroyers that will permit maritime operations beyond land-based air cover, and the projected SSM-IB missile will give the Maritime Self-Defense Forces (MSDF) a significant anti-ship capability. China has watched warily as the mission of the MSDF has evolved from one of limited coastal defense two decades ago to one now encompassing a 1,000 nautical-mile defense perimeter reaching close to Guam and the Philippines. Japan's National Defense Program Outline authorizes the use of the MSDF to build up to 60 surface combatant ships, 16 submarines, and 200 combat aircraft. At present, the Japanese naval forces number 34 surface combatant ships in operation or under construction. But with its new ocean-going replenishment ships, one for each of its four flotillas, the MSDF will have a much greater ability to operate on the high seas for sustained periods than the Chinese navy.

During the next two decades, China will be able to project conventional military power effectively only in areas reachable by its land-based aircraft, notably the northern part of the South China Sea adjacent to Vietnam. Thus, it will be able to defend its territorial claims to the Paracel Islands and to petroleum-rich seabed areas contested by Vietnam. In order to project power over greater distances where it might come into conflict with U.S. interests, Beijing would have to acquire aircraft carriers. Although one carrier could conceivably be purchased or built within a decade, a rotating fleet of three would be necessary so that one could be kept regularly on station. That would require another decade, assuming that Beijing decided to sacrifice civilian economic needs to a carrier program—an assumption that many experts consider unlikely.

To assess whether China poses a military threat to its neighbors or is likely to do so in future decades, it is necessary to distinguish sharply between its conventional and its nuclear capabilities.

Hypothetically, China could pose a conventional threat in future decades that it does not pose today, but only if one makes a series of assumptions that are highly questionable. One such assumption is that it will be able to sustain indefinitely such high levels of economic development that it will be free to channel increased resources into defense spending. Another is that it will make much more rapid progress in developing its defense industries than it has been able to do so far, and that it will thus be able to produce advanced weapons systems on its own that it does not now possess or has been reluctant to purchase from others. Still another questionable assumption is that China will shift from its present inward posture, with its focus on economic development, to an expansionist posture. The Chinese goals most often cited as evidence of expansionist intentions are the reincorporation of Taiwan in some form into a "One China" framework and the restoration of sovereignty over the Spratlys, Paracels, and Senkakus. But these goals do not reflect a desire to expand beyond what China sees as its historic borders. In the case of Taiwan, they reflect a determination to reestablish what is seen as China's legitimate national identity and to erase the humiliation of Japan's annexation of the islands as its prize for winning the Sino-Japanese War. In the case of the Spratlys, Paracels, and Senkakus, Beijing has implicitly acknowledged that its claims are arguable by signaling a readiness to cooperate in jointly developing seabed petroleum resources while deferring the issue of sovereignty.

Citing the seven tasks assigned to the People's Liberation Army, Charles W. Freeman, Jr., states in his chapter in this volume (see p. 172):

> Notably absent from this list are many of the aspirations and objectives that made the rise of other great powers, such as the United States, Japan, Germany, or the Soviet Union, so disruptive of international peace and security. China asserts no doctrine of "manifest destiny" or hemispheric exclusion. It has no ideology of Lebensraum to motivate territorial expansion. Its revanchism does not extend to areas inhabited and claimed by non-Chinese. China does not seek to bring additional minority (non-Han peoples) within its borders. China appears to believe that access to distant resources is best guaranteed by an open international trading system, rather than by power projection. It has no colonies or satellites and no apparent impulse to establish them.

In contrast to the limitations of its indigenous capabilities in producing conventional weaponry, Beijing already possesses the ability to make its own nuclear weapons, including short-range ballistic and cruise missiles that are viewed as a potential threat by neighboring countries. China's estimated 272 nuclear warheads include not only intercontinental ballistic missiles but also 50 DF-3 intermediate-range missiles and 36 DF-21 mobile intermediate-range ballistic missiles (IRBMs) capable of reaching nearby targets in Asia. According to Western intelligence reports shared with Japan, most of the DF-3s, with a range of 1,689 miles, are deployed in northern China—some near Tianjin opposite Korea and the rest at Xuanhua west of Beijing, Liujihou south of Tianjin, Yidu in Shangdong province, and Dalong in Hubei province, all close to Japan.

China argues that these deployments are not directed at its neighbors but are necessary to have a balanced deterrent posture in the face of U.S. and Russian nuclear deployments that are still maintained in Asia despite the end of the Cold War. Moreover, Beijing correctly points out that Japan's sophisticated civilian nuclear and space capabilities could be transformed quickly into a formidable nuclear weapons program, complete with missiles comparable in thrust and range to the most advanced American missiles. Beijing would only intensify its nuclear buildup if Tokyo were to undertake the major expansion of its conventional military capabilities urged by Munro and Bernstein, commit itself under the Japan–U.S. Guidelines to support intervention in Taiwan, and continue to accumulate stockpiles of nuclear materials in its civilian nuclear program. In particular, if Japan and the United States create the Theater Missile Defense system now under discussion, China would conclude that Tokyo does indeed intend to develop a nuclear weapons program, using the projected missile defense system as a shield behind which it could mount a first strike.

The danger of a Sino-Japanese nuclear arms race is directly linked to whether or not the United States and Russia take meaningful steps leading to a global process of nuclear disarmament embracing China. In a world moving toward denuclearization, however gradually, Japan's anti-nuclear consensus is likely to hold firm, and China is likely to join in de-nuclearization measures. In a world with a frozen power structure in which Washington and Moscow seek to keep a margin of overwhelming nuclear superiority, China will undoubtedly attempt to catch up with them, and the pro-nuclear hawks in Japan will become progressively stronger as China's nuclear capabilities grow.

The U.S. nuclear umbrella over Japan will not, in itself, assure a non-nuclear Japan in the absence of global nuclear arms reductions that curb China's nuclear expansion. Would the United States actually risk a nuclear exchange with China to defend Japan against nuclear blackmail or a nuclear attack? Most Japanese do not really expect nuclear protection from Washington. Even during the Cold War, a panel of Japanese security experts convened by *Yomiuri* in 1966 declared that it would be "highly unthinkable" for the United States to use nuclear weapons or any other form of military pressure to protect Japan from nuclear blackmail by the Soviet Union or China. The communist powers could use Japan as a hostage to deter a U.S. attack, the panel concluded, and there would be "little practical meaning" in the destruction of communist cities after "Tokyo and Osaka had been turned into a second Hiroshima and Nagasaki."[8]

Although its credibility is questionable, the U.S. pledge of nuclear protection for Japan contained in the Security Treaty serves a useful purpose by making it difficult for pro-nuclear hawks in Japan to justify a Japanese nuclear capability. This is recognized by the anti-nuclear forces in Japan, who resent the "cap in the bottle" concept, like other Japanese, but are well aware that the U.S. nuclear commitment helps to undercut the case for Japanese nuclear weapons. Significantly, many of those who welcome a symbolic U.S. nuclear commitment also call for the reduction or complete removal of U.S. conventional combat forces. Their argument is that a U.S. combat force presence exacerbates tensions with China, especially in the context of the Guidelines. Like other neighbors of Japan, Beijing, for its part, has until recently been ambivalent about the U.S. presence. While opposed in principle to foreign forces in Asia, China has acknowledged the expedient value of the U.S. role as a "cap in the bottle" in Japan. But the Guidelines have radically changed Chinese attitudes. Expressing "serious concern" about the Guidelines, *People's Daily* called them "a signal of the Japanese intention to undertake military intervention on the Taiwan issue."

IS NORTH KOREA A THREAT?

Forty-three years after the Korean War Armistice, U.S. policy in Korea continues to rest on obsolete Cold War assumptions despite the radical changes in the roles played by Russia and China in the peninsula and despite major changes in North Korea since the death of Kim Il-sung.

The U.S. military alliance with South Korea was a response to Soviet and Chinese military alliances with the North. Now Moscow has nullified its security treaty with Pyongyang and is selling its most advanced military equipment and technology to Seoul. Beijing, while retaining its nominal security commitment, has progressively downgraded its relations with Pyongyang in most spheres. North Korea can no longer count on either Russian or Chinese help in the event of a conflict with the South. Indeed, Pyongyang is continually urged by both Moscow and Beijing to moderate tensions with Seoul. Equally important, Russia and China have forged much more significant economic links with South Korea than with the North.

Impelled in large part by the loss of its Russian and Chinese patrons, Pyongyang has radically reoriented its posture toward the United States and Japan. The 1994 nuclear freeze agreement with Washington marked the start of a continuing effort to open up not only economic and diplomatic relations but also military relations with Washington. Since 1995, Pyongyang has attempted to initiate a security dialogue between U.S. and North Korean generals to set the stage for replacement of the Armistice with a new peacekeeping structure. In such a structure, U.S. forces would remain in Korea for an agreed transition period. Their mission would no longer be restricted to the defense of the South but would focus on stabilizing North-South relations, helping "to prevent any threat to the peace, whether from the South against the North or the North against the South."[9]

The underlying premise of the North Korean peacekeeping proposal is that the nuclear freeze agreement envisages a normalization of relations with the United States that is incompatible with the adversarial relationship enshrined in the Armistice. In the North's view, since a U.S. general heads the U.S.–South Korea Combined Forces Command and the United States would have operational control over South Korean forces in time of war, the United States is its major adversary. Thus, it would be appropriate for the United States and North Korea alone to negotiate the formal decision that the Armistice is to be replaced, especially since the South did not sign the Armistice in the first place. In this initial, symbolic stage of the security dialogue, the South would be restricted to the role of an observer, but substantive negotiations on the modalities of a peacekeeping structure and related arms control measures would include the South as an equal participant.

To a great extent, the United States has ignored post–Cold War changes in the Korean security environment, continuing to equate its interests with those of South Korea. Thus, Washington has continued to impose economic sanctions on North Korea dating back to the Korean War, notwithstanding Article Two of the nuclear freeze agreement, in which both sides pledge to "take steps to reduce barriers to trade and investment." Rejecting the North Korean offer of a security dialogue, under pressure from Seoul, the United States accepted a South Korean suggestion for a four-party peace process instead.

The Clinton Administration has pursued what can be described as a policy of "limited engagement" toward the North that is more flexible than the policies of its predecessors. But the Administration has been deeply divided over the nature of U.S. interests and goals in Korea and has thus pursued *ad hoc* policies reflecting the shifting tides in an unresolved debate. Is North Korea on the verge of collapse, or is it capable of surviving by moving toward a liberalization of its economy broadly similar to what has been happening in China since the death of Mao? Would its collapse and absorption by South Korea be desirable? Or would American interests be better served by a "soft landing"—a gradual process of unification in which neither side is swallowed up by the other and Washington helps Pyongyang to achieve a China-style economic transformation?

Three years ago, General Gary Luck, then the Commander of U.S. and United Nations forces in South Korea, said in congressional testimony that "the question is not will this country disintegrate but rather how will it disintegrate, by implosion or explosion and when."[10] Since then, the Kim Jong-Il regime has displayed remarkable resilience and staying power in the face of continuing food shortages. Nevertheless, while the North Korean system appears unlikely to "implode" or "explode" in the foreseeable future, it could well erode over a period of five to ten years if the United States and its allies remain wedded to policies that exacerbate the economic problems facing the regime.

The United States should not seek to assure the survival of the North Korean regime. At the same time, it should not block the efforts being made by the regime to open up its economy to the outside world, notably its creation of free trade and investment zones in which the terms for foreign investors compare favorably with those in other parts of Asia. Given the low cost of North Korean labor, many Japanese, South Korean, and Chinese firms have shown interest in using these zones as a base for exports to the U.S. market. But such exports are barred as long as U.S. economic sanctions continue. The effect of U.S. policy thus is to undermine the efforts of the reform-minded elements in Pyongyang who have established the zones as a step toward the broader liberalization of foreign economic policy. More important, by impeding the North's efforts to deal with its economic problems, U.S. policy adds to the danger of instability there that could lead to mass refugee flows, "boat people" attempting to enter Japan, and civil strife that could spill over into North-South military encounters, drawing in U.S. forces. In the unlikely event of a complete breakdown in Pyongyang, the costs of economic reconstruction in an absorption scenario could greatly exceed those experienced in Germany since 1989, and the United States would undoubtedly be called upon to bear a disproportionate share of what could be a staggering burden. East Germany had a population and per capita income one-fourth as large as West Germany's, whereas the North, with a population half that of the South, has a per capita income at most one-fifth as large.

In short, the danger of a North Korean invasion of the South envisaged by William J. Taylor in his chapter in this volume (see p. 141) is no longer the principal threat to the U.S. interest in a stable Korea. Rather, the threat lies in the possibility of a disorderly transition to a unified Korea in which U.S. forces could become involved. Such a possibility has been reduced by the election of South Korean President Kim Dae-jung, a longtime advocate of a "soft landing" approach by Seoul and Washington. Nevertheless, given the entrenched power of hard-line political and military leaders in Seoul and Pyongyang alike, the future of North-South relations remains uncertain.

The American presence in the South provides an economic subsidy that postpones a stabilization of North-South relations by enabling the South to have a maximum of security with a minimum of sacrifice. The South's upper- and middle-income minority, in particular, has acquired a vested interest in the status quo. As long as the South has the U.S. military presence as an economic cushion, it is under no compulsion to explore a *modus vivendi* with the North. A former U.S. Ambassador to South Korea, the late William Porter—who during his tenure (1967-1971) had unsuccessfully pressed Seoul to help pay for the American presence—summed up the situation pithily during a conversation with one of the writers in April 1970, saying: "they've got hold of our big fat udder, and they won't let go."[11]

In contrast to 1971, South Korean "burden-sharing" in support of the U.S. presence should be a less pressing issue between the two countries in the post–Cold War context, given the decline of the North Korean military threat. Indeed, South Korea should seek to reduce its defense burden and facilitate a gradual withdrawal of U.S. forces by pursuing mutual North-South force reductions as the North has proposed. Pyongyang, with half the population of the South, must spend four to five times more of its GNP on defense than the South does to maintain what it considers adequate defenses against the U.S.–South Korea Combined Forces Command. Thus the pressures for force reductions in the North are real. By contrast, rapid economic growth and the subsidy provided by the U.S. presence have enabled past regimes in Seoul to avoid increasing the proportion of GNP allocated to defense while at the same time steadily raising the actual level of defense expenditures.

A striking illustration of the obsolete Cold War mindset in U.S. policy came when U.S. officials invoked the supposed North Korean military threat to overcome congressional doubt about the wisdom of direct U.S. financial participation in the South Korean bailout of January 1998. Skeptics in Congress and elsewhere have understandably asked a series of obvious questions about the bailout. Why should U.S. taxpayers pay for the mistakes made by private investors who have ignored the reckless, skyrocketing growth of government-backed South Korean borrowing? More broadly, why should U.S. taxpayers help a country that has pursued mercantilist trade policies and blocked U.S. investment access for decades while the United States has at the same time been subsidizing its military defense, putting the lives of U.S. soldiers at risk?

Doug Bandow in his chapter in this book (see p. 155) argues that the goal of U.S. policy should be to disengage from an open-ended military commitment that carries with it open-ended economic burdens. His proposal fails to distinguish, however, between the withdrawal of U.S. combat forces and the termination of the U.S. mutual security treaty with the South. In our view, unless and until Beijing ends its security treaty with Pyongyang, and until Moscow and Beijing both pledge not to intervene in the event of a new Korean War, the U.S. security treaty with the South should remain intact, giving Washington the option to intervene after its combat force presence has been withdrawn. We agree with Bandow, however, that the United States should set a definite time limit for its withdrawal. While U.S. forces could remain for a transitional period as part of peacekeeping arrangements, such a period should be finite. A commitment to remain until tensions are reduced could become a commitment to stay indefinitely. An open-ended U.S. presence is more likely to result in continued tensions than would a U.S. departure preceded by ample notice and serious mediation efforts.

In 1989, William J. Taylor proposed a seven-year withdrawal process that would have left only one U.S. battalion in Korea by 1996 as a "tripwire."[12] His paper for the Study Group completely reversed this position, even though North Korea's military readiness has markedly declined in the face of petroleum shortages resulting from its loss of Soviet and Chinese support and the economic crisis dramatized by its serious food shortages. Ironically, Taylor and like-minded observers argue that the case for the U.S. presence is strengthened by the North's economic problems, since Pyongyang might seek to lash out militarily in desperation. Such a contingency cannot be categorically ruled out, but it appears most unlikely, since the North recognizes that an invasion of the South would give Washington and Seoul a pretext for all-out military action to oust the communist regime.

North Korea has scrupulously honored the 1994 freeze agreement, while the United States has failed to fulfill its pledge in Article 2 of the agreement to phase out economic sanctions and has fallen behind in promised oil deliveries. Nevertheless, critics of the agreement charge that Pyongyang may be secretly developing nuclear weapons and point to its growing missile capabilities. Even if it turns out that North Korea has more plutonium than it declared in 1994, there is a big difference between acquiring a small amount of plutonium and developing the accurate targeting and miniaturization of warheads needed for a meaningful nuclear weapons capability. Moreover, Pyongyang explicitly offered on June 16, 1998, to end its missile exports in return for economic compensation and to discontinue missile development altogether as part of a peace agreement with the United States.

Ridiculing the idea of a North Korean conventional threat to the South, Japanese defense analyst Shunji Taoka of the *Asahi* points out that the South has 400 first-line fighter planes, plus 280 U.S. planes, based in South Korea, while the North has at most some 100 operational first-line combat aircraft. Above all, he contends, pointing to the impact of its limited petroleum reserves, Pyongyang is no longer in a position to wage a sustained, protracted war.

What the North clearly does have is the ability to inflict horrendous damage on Seoul with its forward-deployed heavy artillery and multiple rocket launchers. Pyongyang argues that the forward deployment of so much of its forces and weaponry is a defensive response to the combined superiority of U.S. and South Korean forces, especially in air power. Only when U.S. forces are withdrawn from the peninsula, the North says, will Seoul and Pyongyang be able to conduct meaningful negotiations leading to the pullback of forces and weaponry and other arms control and confidence-building measures. Significantly, a key South Korean official, retired Major General Lim Dong-won, one of President Kim Dae-jung's advisors, has also argued that the current form of U.S. military intervention in Korea obstructs a North-South accommodation. General Lim, who directed negotiations with the North during the Roh Tae Woo period, has urged the United States to relinquish its operational control over South Korean forces. "Only with the reversion of operational control will North Korea respect and fear the South," Lim declared in 1996. "Unless operational control is returned to us, the North will continue to confine its approaches to the United States alone and sidestep or bypass the South."[13] But the South Korean armed forces suspect that the surrender of operational control would presage a U.S. withdrawal, and the United States, for its part, fears that the South might drag the United States into a needless conflict unless it is kept on a tight leash.

STRATEGIC MOBILITY AND THE U.S. PRESENCE IN ASIA

The United States finds itself committed in Korea to one side in an unfinished civil war in which both sides now want to be its friends and in which no other outside power is militarily involved. The Taiwan conflict, too, is the final chapter in an unfinished civil war that has been prolonged by the Cold War U.S. role in Asia. In the case of Taiwan, however, the United States has not had an obligation to intervene with its military forces since it terminated its mutual security treaty with Taipei in 1979. The Taiwan Relations Act requires only that the U.S. president decide what he considers a level of military assistance "sufficient" to enable the island to defend itself.

It is striking that the two contingencies most often cited to justify the forward deployment of U.S. combat forces in Asia involve unfinished civil wars. Neither case fits the standard argument that

U.S. forces are needed to play a "stabilizing" and "balancing" role. What would make Asia more stable is a resolution of the civil wars left over from World War II and the Cold War, not their perpetuation. When North Korea was a projection of Soviet and Chinese military power, the U.S. presence in the South did play a stabilizing, deterrent role, balancing the foreign forces available to the North. In the post–Cold War context, however, the open-ended presence of U.S. forces decades after the departure of Soviet and Chinese forces has been destabilizing, adding to the North's sense of insecurity and to the South's desire to impose a settlement of the civil war on its own terms. In Korea and Taiwan alike, U.S. policy strengthens the vested interests that are opposed to accommodation. The failure of the United States to make progressive reductions of its sales of weaponry to Taiwan, as pledged in the 1982 "Second Shanghai Communiqué," emboldens pro-independence forces to resist an accommodation with Beijing short of *de jure* independence and encourages their belief that the United States would send forces to help defend them in the event that a declaration of independence should provoke Chinese military pressures.

The "balancing" argument takes various forms. Thus it is said that the U.S. presence deters aggressive Chinese behavior toward Japan and other neighbors. Applied to specific contingencies, however, this formulation quickly loses its plausibility. In the case of Taiwan, it is most unlikely that a Chinese military response would be deterred by the possibility of U.S. intervention in the event of a declaration of independence; and, in other cases, Beijing is not likely to take the possibility of U.S. intervention very seriously. For example, are the issues in the Sino-Japanese dispute over the Senkaku Islands in the East China Sea so unambiguous and so momentous that the United States would intervene on the side of Japan in the event of a military conflict resulting from unilateral Chinese seabed petroleum exploration in the Senkaku area? Is China deterred from such exploration by the fear of the U.S. Marines in Okinawa or by its interest in expanding a wide range of beneficial economic relations with Japan? Another version of the argument is that the U.S. presence discourages a Sino-Japanese arms race. But this formulation, too, dissolves under close scrutiny. The dispatch of U.S. carriers to the Taiwan area in 1996 and the U.S.–Japan Guidelines in 1997 have exacerbated Sino-Japanese tensions, strengthening the forces in China favoring military expansion.

The U.S. interest lies in a scrupulously neutral stance in the Sino-Japanese rivalry as part of a broader shift to a more detached military posture in Asia designed to avoid embroilment in a U.S. conflict with Beijing. The need to avoid a collision with Beijing is of particular importance in Taiwan, where a military confrontation could escalate to the nuclear level. In Korea, too, there is potential for a dangerous conflict of interest with China if U.S. forces remain in the peninsula indefinitely, especially after unification. Yet moving to a more detached posture need not and should not mean a complete U.S. military disengagement from Asia that would make it difficult for the United States to intervene with sufficient force at some point in the future if it should ever become necessary. The continuing improvement in U.S. strategic mobility capabilities makes it possible to bring forces to Asia quickly and effectively and thus to reduce or eliminate the ongoing forward deployment of combat forces in Japan and Korea.

In defining the precise character of a more detached posture, it is essential to distinguish between the forward basing of Army, Marine, and Air Force combat forces, which no longer serves U.S. interests, and the continuing deployment of U.S.–based naval forces, including aircraft carriers, on regular patrols in the Pacific Ocean, the South China Sea, and the Indian Ocean, which is still desirable. Continuing naval deployments would go together with the continued forward basing of the logistics and communications forces that would be needed to serve peacetime Seventh Fleet patrols and to facilitate any future wartime intervention. This distinction is closely linked to the distinction between a "tripwire" role for U.S. forces and the new U.S. role defined by Ted Galen Carpenter in his chapter in this volume (see p. 293) as that of "the balancer of last resort, not the intervenor of first resort."

The "tripwire" role is exemplified in its most extreme form by current U.S. strategy in Korea, in which U.S. forces are so positioned that some of them would be involved from the first moment of hostilities. During a transition to a U.S. withdrawal, as envisaged in the recommendations that follow, U.S. ground forces would be reduced and repositioned so that South Korean forces would bear the brunt of the initial fighting, with the U.S. role limited to air and naval support. It is the U.S. "tripwire" role in Korea that provides the principal rationale for keeping U.S. forces and bases in Japan to assure rapid support for any U.S. military action in Korea.

The "tripwire" concept arose as a Cold War response to U.S. fears of communist "human wave" offensives in Europe and Korea. In the post–Cold War Asian environment, it exposes the United

States to excessive risks of precipitate military involvement that can no longer be justified. As the "balancer of last resort," the United States would seek to maximize its freedom of action, keeping out of internecine conflicts over the terms of power relationships within and between Asian countries. The rise of China to the "preeminent" position envisaged by Munro and Bernstein would not in itself be regarded as a threat to the United States if it occurred in a peaceful context. This concept of a balancing role would differ fundamentally from the loosely defined traditional concept that the U.S. interest lies in preventing the emergence of any one "dominant" power in the region.

In the event of unforeseeable developments that pose a clear threat to the United States or to vital American interests, an effective U.S. response would not require forward-deployed U.S. combat forces. The presence of the Seventh Fleet, combined with increasingly sophisticated strategic mobility capabilities, would enable the United States to defend its interests and to join in multilateral action, if necessary, to maintain international order.

The massive emergency movement of U.S. forces to Saudi Arabia and Kuwait during the Gulf War provided a dramatic demonstration of American airlift and sealift capabilities. Drawing on its experiences in Desert Shield and Desert Storm, the United States has subsequently stepped up its strategic mobility buildup, focusing on Korea and the Gulf as the most likely theaters of future crisis.

The centerpiece of this ongoing expansion is the augmentation and eventual replacement of 214 C-141 and 109 C-5 transport aircraft with 120 C-17s capable of carrying much bigger loads. Forty-eight of the C-17s were already in service by 1997. This substantial airlift capacity operates in close coordination with a sealift capability now consisting of 197 ships, including 58 giant "roll-on, roll-off" container ships of varying sizes, most of them laden with pre-positioned equipment and supplies for the Army, Navy, and Marine Corps. Significantly, 33 of these ships are based in Diego Garcia (19) and Guam (14), relatively close to potential crisis areas in Asia. Thirteen of these 33, assigned to the Army, carry enough equipment, food, water, and other supplies to support elements of two Army heavy divisions numbering some 34,000 personnel for up to 30 days.

Even in 1978, when airlift capabilities were limited to C-141s and C-5s, and when "roll-on, roll-off" ships were still on the drawing board, a Brookings Institution analyst cited Pentagon data showing that an airborne division and its equipment could be deployed to Korea from Guam and continental U.S. bases in 1.4 days and that two Guam-based infantry divisions could be deployed there in 3.7 days. With equipment pre-positioned in Korea, an infantry brigade could be deployed there in 24 hours and an airborne brigade in 17 hours.[14]

A Congressional Budget Office (CBO) study, *Moving United States Forces: Options for Strategic Mobility*, reveals that, since 1996, the Army has prepositioned 120 M-1 tanks and 68 Bradley armored fighting vehicles in Korea—enough to equip one heavy brigade[15]—over and above the 37,000 troops stationed there. This could be rapidly augmented by airlift and by the equipment and supplies prepositioned aboard ships at Guam and Diego Garcia. The CBO study estimated that the volume of airlift deliveries to Korea in any future crisis would nearly triple the average of 1,700 tons per day achieved during the first months of Desert Shield. Moreover, as C-17s (with their greater load capacity) are put into operation, airlift operations to Korea would become progressively easier, since a smaller number of planes would be required, relieving airport congestion. The use of large "roll-on, roll-off" ships would be easier in South Korea than in many less developed Asian countries, the study points out, since it has modern port facilities with berthing areas long enough and deep enough to accommodate these large vessels.

Ironically, many of the same members of Congress who have resisted the $54.2 billion that would be needed for the full implementation of the Pentagon's strategic mobility plans give uncritical support to a much more expensive—and much more risky—Pacific defense posture that now costs an estimated $42 billion ***every year***. The armed forces want strategic mobility in addition to their existing force levels, which would be difficult to justify in the absence of exaggerated Chinese and North Korean threats. North Korea alone has provided the rationale for at least four of the twelve carrier battle groups maintained by the Navy. Similarly, the case for a ten-division Army is buttressed by the purported need to station 37,000 Army men in Korea, including two combat infantry brigades, and to maintain another five active Army divisions to be sent there as reinforcements in the event of war.[16]

In April 1991, following the Gulf War, General Colin Powell came close to acknowledging the importance of Korea to the Army's budget when he commented wryly, "now that the Cold War is over, I'm running out of villains. I'm down to Castro and Kim Il-sung."[17]

THE ECONOMIC ARENA

The recommendations that follow envisage a very gradual transition to a more detached U.S. military posture in Asia. Behind the military rationale for these recommendations lies the basic conviction that the present U.S. security posture directly conflicts with U.S. economic interests. This conviction runs counter to the conventional assumption that the U.S. security posture has had and continues to have a positive impact on U.S. economic interests. The Clinton Administration reaffirmed the view that the impact has been positive in its February 1995 policy review, *Security Strategy for the East Asia–Pacific Region*, which remained the most authoritative statement of Administration policy in Asia during 1997. "The stable and prosperous East Asia of 1995," stated the review, has resulted in critical measure from "American alliances in the region and the continued presence of substantial United States forces. Security is like oxygen: you do not tend to notice it until you lose it. The American security presence has helped provide this 'oxygen' for East Asian development." Asian economic prosperity is beneficial to the United States, this argument runs, because it brings with it growing opportunities for American exports and investment. Moreover, the U.S. presence guarantees the security of sea lanes vital to the flow of Middle Eastern oil and, most important, prevents "a rival, hostile power or coalition of powers . . . from having command over the vast resources, enormous wealth and advanced technology of the Asia-Pacific region." Elaborating this view, the principal author of the policy review, Joseph Nye, Assistant Secretary of Defense for International Security Affairs, added in *Foreign Affairs* (July 1995) that the U.S. security presence helps to assure U.S. economic access to Asia because Asian leaders "realize that if they excluded the United States from the region economically, the United States would probably withdraw its security presence, and they would therefore lose the basis for stability and prosperity in the region."

Significantly, the 1995 policy review differs in one crucial respect from other Clinton Administration pronouncements on U.S.–Asia and global objectives. In other pronouncements, economic, security, and political interests have been treated as equal in importance. For example, in *A National Security Strategy of Engagement and Enlargement* (July 1994), the White House carefully avoided giving priority to any one of three declared goals of U.S. policy: "to promote cooperative security measures, to open foreign markets and spur global economic growth and to promote democracy abroad."

By contrast, *Security Strategy for the East Asia–Pacific Region* states that "in thinking about the Asia-Pacific region, *security comes first* [italics added] . . . nowhere are the strands of our three-part strategy more intertwined; nowhere is the need for continued engagement more evident."

Chalmers Johnson points out in a rebuttal to Nye in *Foreign Affairs* (July 1995) that "East Asia's own invention of state-guided capitalism did more to overcome communist militancy and wars of national liberation in the region than any military role played by the United States." Moreover, the Administration position ignores the devastating evidence set forth earlier indicating the enormity of the economic costs incurred by the United States in its bilateral economic relations with Asian countries during the Cold War decades—costs far outweighing the purely economic benefits. More important, it fails to take into account the magnitude of the U.S.–sponsored expansion of Japanese economic influence in Asia during these decades and the resulting diminution of the competitive position that U.S. companies would otherwise have had in Asian markets today. In reality, a significant result of the U.S. security role has been to lessen the U.S. economic presence in Asia.

By the end of 1996, Japanese companies had invested a total of $101.5 billion in Asia, in contrast to $66.4 billion invested by their American counterparts. Japanese exports to Asia in 1996 ($184.1 billion) were 53.8 percent higher than U.S. exports to the region ($119.7 billion). To add insult to injury, while Japan, with its barriers to equitable trade, had a surplus of $52.4 billion with other Asian countries, the United States had a deficit of $71.8 billion with these countries. This dominance has been achieved in substantial measure through conscious policies of regional integration in which Japan's *keiretsu* conglomerates turn to Japanese subcontractors based in Asia, not to the open market. Production is distributed on a regional basis, with only the final assembly of more technologically sophisticated products taking place in Japan. As New Zealand economist Rob Steven has observed, "when buying and selling across national boundaries is not just between different firms, but between different branches of the same firm, the notion of trade becomes quite meaningless."[18]

The full import of Japanese economic dominance in Asia has become increasingly apparent following the 1997 economic crisis. Japan is uniquely situated to be the driving force of Asian recovery by strengthening the yen, shifting to a domestic demand-led model, absorbing an ever larger flow of exports from its Asian neighbors, and facilitating Asian exports to other markets by reducing its trade surplus. By the same token, however, Tokyo can make matters worse if it continues the policies that helped trigger the 1997 crisis: competing with other Asian countries and crowding them out of the world's export markets.

Despite the expansion of Japanese economic influence in Asia under the American aegis, the United States nonetheless has powerful economic assets of its own in dealing with the region that are not adequately reflected in comparative trade and investment statistics. Asian countries need American agricultural exports, American support for their financial stability, a wide range of American technology, and, above all, access to the American market. For this reason, the United States has the leverage necessary to promote the economic restructuring necessary for Asian recovery, including the restructuring of the Japanese economic system.

It is often argued that Japanese holdings of U.S. Treasury securities, which totaled $271.7 billion in June 1997—8 percent of U.S. foreign indebtedness—rob the United States of any leverage in economic dealings with Tokyo. This argument was strengthened when Prime Minister Hashimoto declared that "on several occasions we've had the feeling that we should try to sell off U.S. Treasury bills and bonds. For example, when I was fighting Mickey Kantor over automobiles and when we have been faced with currency volatility."[19] However, as Martin Feldstein has observed, "a decision by Japanese investors to sell dollar bonds and shift the funds to other countries would put downward pressure on the U.S. dollar relative to the yen and to the currencies in which the Japanese invested, and upward pressure on our interest rates relative to other interest rates in the world financial markets. The combination of a depressed dollar and higher U.S. interest rates would induce the funds displaced elsewhere by the shift of Japanese investments to flow to the United States." Moreover, if push came to shove, he warns, Japan would be vulnerable to a shift in U.S. policies, given its dependence on imports of food and energy, and "the large amount of foreign direct investment that Japan has in the U.S. is a hostage that is not matched by comparable U.S. investment in Japan." Beyond this, he adds, "the hundreds of billions of dollars of portfolio investments that Japanese companies have in U.S. securities are a further hostage that could be effectively destroyed by a change in U.S. tax policy." Finally, "closing the U.S. market to the nearly $100 billion a year that the U.S. imports from Japan would do substantial damage to Japanese industry."[20]

In reality, there is little likelihood of such a confrontation, because both Japan and the United States are well aware that they need each other economically. The 1997 crisis has underscored this interdependence and, more broadly, the growing economic interdependence between the United States and Asia as a whole. The U.S. interest clearly lies in promoting Asian economic recovery through the restructuring and reform of mercantilist economic models, since only thriving, open Asian economies will provide expanding opportunities for U.S. trade and investment on equitable terms. But the United States can pursue this interest effectively only if it brings to bear its full bargaining leverage in dealing with Asian trading and investment partners, which will require, in turn, getting rid of its Cold War mindset.

The absence of clear and present military threats to the United States and the diminished need for a forward-based combat force presence now make it possible for the United States to take the risks inherent in giving overriding priority to economic goals. Washington need no longer pull its punches in promoting its economic interests as it did during the Cold War decades. As we have seen, two key trading partners who are also military allies, Japan and South Korea, often act as if they are doing the United States a favor by maintaining their alliances, using the threat of a rupture in security links to get their way in economic disputes. The United States can achieve its economic goals only if it can change the bidding, making clear that it no longer considers its military links as important as its economic interests. This is the underlying rationale for our recommendation that the United States offer to phase out the combat force component of its military presence within five years if Japan wishes us to do so, while keeping the Security Treaty and the nuclear umbrella intact.

The United States should be prepared for the possibility that Japan or South Korea might adopt a more independent military posture in response to a determined U.S. stance on economic issues. Such an independent posture would not threaten American interests if the United States adapts gracefully to the changes, accepting a new political and security relationship on a basis of greater equality.

In charting a new economic relationship with Asia, the United States should give a heightened importance to Asia's two giants—China, with 1.2 billion people, and India, with 937 million—which together constitute 37 percent of the world's population. Securing equitable economic relations with China will be a formidable task that should not be compromised by a confrontational posture on the Taiwan issue. A determined U.S. approach in contentious economic disputes would not, in itself, lead to dangerous tensions with China in the security arena, but U.S. military intervention in Taiwan, or the threat of such intervention, combined with a firm line on economic issues, would overload the circuits.

As Geoffrey Kemp and Paul Kreisberg point out in their chapter in this volume (see pp. 257 and 277, respectively), India is growing at a rate of 5-7 percent annually, shows an increasingly hospitable attitude to U.S. investment, and is acquiring a growing military power projection capability that could affect U.S. access to the Indian Ocean. The United States should therefore give priority to the achievement of more positive economic and political relations with New Delhi, de-emphasizing rigid nuclear non-proliferation goals. As in the case of the Japanese nuclear option discussed earlier, the United States is not likely to forestall the possibility of a nuclear India in the absence of a global process of nuclear arms reductions that embraces China. With a more flexible non-proliferation policy, however, the United States might be able to get India to cap its nuclear weapons potential at present levels. For this reason, one of our recommendations calls for a trade-off with India in which the United States would relax its ban on the sale of U.S. nuclear reactors, as it is doing in the case of China, in exchange for non-proliferation concessions comparable to those China made when President Jiang Zemin visited the White House in 1997. In both China and India, with their burgeoning energy needs, it is in the U.S. interest to promote a diversified expansion of energy supplies embracing nuclear power as well as petroleum pipelines from Central Asia. In the absence of such expansion, mounting Indian and Chinese petroleum imports from the Persian Gulf and other U.S. petroleum sources will put a growing strain on global petroleum supplies and prices.

The recommendations that follow propose specific steps by the United States to promote Asian recovery and expand U.S. trade and investment relations with Asian countries big and small, based on economic restructuring, where necessary, and a consequent shift from mercantilist, export-oriented policies.

Initially, the United States should focus on stabilizing financial markets and re-establishing the foundations for growth and sound future development. The bailout programs of the IMF, the United

States, and private creditors have been unavoidable. But it is critical to set precedents during this emergency period that will ensure against a perpetuation of the unsound practices and institutions that led to the 1997 crisis. This means first of all that those who loaned and invested unwisely must share in the pain of reconstruction. Looking ahead, it means that help should be conditioned on fundamental restructuring programs.

In reform programs, emphasis should be given to strengthening the rule of law. In the absence of effective legal procedures and institutions, government officials can intervene arbitrarily in economic affairs to suppress consumption and compel high levels of savings that are allocated to favored, often cartelized, industries, resulting in excess production capacity that can only be sustained by continual export drives.

Many Asian economies have become so organized around exports that it is extremely difficult for them to restructure. In the attempt to keep the export machine going in the face of the inevitable upward pressure on exchange rates that excessive investment creates, national leaders engage in maneuvers that result in "bubbles," financial crises, and serious distortions of the world economy. At the moment, for example, many Asian countries are looking to the United States as a perpetual export market. Some are lending the United States money to enable it to continue to purchase their excess goods, while their high savings and investment rates create more capacity to export more goods. This is not a stable situation, and there is now a danger that the IMF may exacerbate the problem by further reducing domestic consumption and emphasizing even greater savings. Most Asian countries did not have big budget deficits before the crisis. Indeed, Thailand and Indonesia had surpluses in 1996. By imposing the austerity model that it has used in situations in which government spending was out of control, the IMF may perpetuate the very problem it is trying to solve.

In place of austerity, the IMF, the United States, and private creditors should go back to fundamentals. A condition of IMF assistance should be the breakup of cartels, the introduction of transparent administrative regulations, and the deregulation and removal from informal government guidance of distribution, shipping, aviation, telecommunications, and land use activities. In addition, tax laws should be revamped to encourage consumption while providing less incentive for over-saving.

Barry Bosworth, in his chapter in this volume (see p. 101), reflects the view of some economists who believe that the benefits to the U.S. consumer outweigh the damage to affected U.S. industries in cases where a foreign competitor can undercut American firms by selling at a price lower than the cost of production. Taking into account its long-term interest in a stable Asia, the United States has no choice but to act as the buyer of last resort and should be prepared to accept what is likely to be a flood of Asian imports. But in our view, it should not be necessary to make an either-or choice between welcoming low-priced imports and enforcing a level playing field.

The United States should offer to negotiate the timing of specific steps on the part of each of its trading partners in Asia that would enable them to reduce excessive dependence on exports and would lead to greater equity and reciprocity in trade and investment relations with the United States. If timetables can be agreed upon and Asian countries honor their commitments, the United States should be prepared to live with large trade imbalances with Asia while seeking to narrow these imbalances through more aggressive marketing and investment-promotion efforts, accompanied by appropriate domestic fiscal and monetary policies. Conversely, the United States should make it clear that, unless adequate reforms are forthcoming, it is ready to impose penalties under its existing laws as well as new ground rules that would make trade and investment access to the United States conditional on U.S. access to other markets on equal terms.

Until now, the United States has failed to face reality in Asia, operating on the naive assumption expressed by former Assistant Secretary of State Winston Lord in congressional testimony that "we have insulated our security ties from our trade tensions." In *Strategic Assessments*: 1996, the Institute for National Strategic Studies of the National Defense University made a more straightforward judgment. "During the cold war," the Institute said, "the U.S. government built a firewall between trade and security issues that prevented trade disputes from interfering with critical security relationships. That firewall has disappeared."[21]

NOTES

[1] Clyde V. Prestowitz, Jr., Lawrence Chimerine, and Paul Willen, *Closing the Trade Gap with Japan* (Washington, D.C.: Economic Strategy Institute, 1993), pp. 15-18. See also: Robert Z. Lawrence, "Closed Markets or Closed Minds?" *Brookings Papers on Economic Activity* 2, pp. 517-54; Robert Z. Lawrence, "How Open is Japan?" in Paul Krugman, ed., *Trade With Japan* (Chicago: University of Chicago Press, 1991), pp. 9-50; Peter A. Petri, "Japanese Trade in Transition: Hypotheses and Recent Evidence" in Paul Krugman, ed., *Trade With Japan, op. cit.*, pp. 51-84.

[2] *The East Asia Miracle: Economic Growth and Public Policy* (Washington, D.C.: The World Bank, 1993), p. 2.

[3] James C. Abegglen and George Stalk, Jr., *Kaisha: The Japanese Corporation* (New York: Basic Books, 1985), pp. 126-28.

[4] "Cutting Unnecessary Military Spending: Going Further and Faster," *The Defense Monitor*, published by the Center for Defense Information, Vol. XXI, No. 3, 1993. This estimate is based on unit cost data in William Kaufmann, *Glasnost, Perestroika, and U.S. Defense Spending* (Washington, D.C.: The Brookings Institution, 1990). Pentagon estimates are much lower but include only the direct pay and operating costs of U.S. forces deployed in Asia. The Center for Defense Information estimate includes total costs, including prorated shares of weapons acquisition, overhead and indirect support, and the cost of supporting U.S.–based forces earmarked for use in Asian contingencies. Earl C. Ravenal, using a different methodology, arrived at a $39 billion estimate for the cost of U.S. defense commitments in Asia in 1992. (*Designing Defense for a New World Order*, Cato Institute, Washington, D.C., p. 51).

[5] JPRI *Critique*, Japan Policy Research Institute, January 1998, p. 1.

[6] Alfred A. Knopf, New York, 1997, p. 11. See also "The Coming Conflict with America," *Foreign Affairs*, March/April 1997, pp. 31-32.

[7] Dwight Perkins, *Trade, Security, and National Strategy in the Asia-Pacific*, Vol. 7, No. 3 (Seattle: National Bureau of Asian Research, October 1996), p. 19.

[8] Kobayashi Yosaji, ed., *An Approach to Revision of the Security Treaty* (Tokyo: Yomiuri Shimbun, 1970), pp. 109-10.

[9] Kang Sok Ju, First Deputy Foreign Minister of the Democratic People's Republic of Korea, in a meeting with Selig S. Harrison in Pyongyang, September 29, 1995.

[10] Selig S. Harrison, "Promoting a Soft Landing in Korea," *Foreign Policy*, Spring 1997, p. 57.

[11] Ibid., p. 73. This meeting occurred in Seoul on April 16, 1970, when Selig S. Harrison was Northeast Asia Bureau Chief of *The Washington Post* and responsible for coverage of South Korea.

[12] Taylor and Michael Mazarr, "Strategic Opportunities in Northeast Asia," *Korean Journal of Defense Analysis*, Winter 1989, p. 117.

[13] Selig S. Harrison, "Promoting a Soft Landing in Korea," op. cit., p. 72.

[14] Selig S. Harrison, *The Widening Gulf: Asian Nationalism and American Policy* (New York: The Free Press, 1978), pp. 377-78.

[15] The Congress of the United States, *Moving United States Forces: Options for Strategic Mobility* (Washington, D.C.: Congressional Budget Office, February 1997), p. 33.

[16] For an extended discussion of the use of Korea as a rationale for U.S. military budgeting, see Leon V. Sigal, *Disarming Strangers: Nuclear Diplomacy With North Korea* (Princeton, N.J.: Princeton University Press, 1998), p. 233.

[17] *Bulletin of the Atomic Scientists* Vol. 48, No. 8, October 1992, p. 14.

[18] *Japan's New Imperialism* (Armonk, N.Y.: M. E. Sharpe, Inc., 1991), p. 244.

[19] *Austin American Statesman*, June 28, 1997, p. 1.

[20] Martin Feldstein, "National Security Aspects of United States-Japan Economic Relations in the Pacific Asian Region," in *Regionalism and Rivalry: Japan and the United States in Pacific Asia*, eds. Jeffrey A. Frankel and Miles Kahler (Chicago: The University of Chicago Press, 1993).

[21] Institute for National Strategic Studies, National Defense University, *Strategic Assessments 1996: Instruments of U.S. Power*, January 1996, p. 114.

II. RECOMMENDATIONS OF THE STUDY GROUP ON U.S. ASIA POLICY

1.
After the Meltdown: A New Approach to U.S.–Asian Economic Relations

2.
The Restructuring of the Japanese Economy

3.
The Restructuring of the South Korean Economy

4.
China and the World Trade Organization

5.
The Future of the U.S. Presence in Japan

6.
The Future of the U.S. Presence in Korea

7.
U.S. Intervention in Taiwan

8.
Japan, China, and Theater Missile Defense

9.
Indonesian Democracy and Labor Rights

10.
A Nuclear Bargain with India

1.
AFTER THE MELTDOWN: A NEW APPROACH TO U.S.–ASIAN ECONOMIC RELATIONS

In responding to the unstable economic environment in Asia resulting from the financial crisis of 1997, the United States should set different criteria for its short-term and long-term policies, insisting on needed reforms in the troubled Asian economies while avoiding exploitative terms for their bailout that could provoke a dangerous nationalist backlash.

Initially, the United States should focus on stabilizing financial markets and reestablishing the foundations for growth and sound future development. During this emergency stabilization period, it would be risky to let matters take their course, as some experts have advocated. The danger is real that protracted instability in one of the larger Asian economies could cause a chain reaction that would cause serious harm to the United States and the rest of the global economy. Thus, it has been prudent to proceed with the recovery programs of the International Monetary Fund, the United States, and the private creditors rather than test the chain-reaction theory. But it is critical to set precedents during this emergency period that will ensure against a repetition of the very practices that contributed to the onset of the crisis.

This means first of all that those who lent and invested unwisely must share in the pain of reconstruction. The bailout must not be open-ended and indiscriminate, and it must not result in those who acted unwisely being made whole while workers and ordinary citizens absorb all of the pain. The United States should support the provision of IMF funds as a bridging mechanism that will enable governments to keep large parts of their economies from closing down for lack of hard currency to pay for imports or to make other essential payments. However, these funds should only be provided in cases in which governments make credible commitments to halt the practice of guiding bank lending, to break up cartels, to privatize most government-owned corporations, to initiate broad-scale deregulation, to assure the freedom of labor to organize, and to establish a true rule of law under which bureaucrats lose the discretionary authority that has long enabled them to administer informal "guidance."

To avoid the danger of a severe backlash, the IMF, the United States, and the private creditors should seek to avoid giving the impression that they are trying to exploit the situation for their own financial ends. Public funds should only be made available to private creditors on the condition that banks and investors restructure their investments and extend existing loans on terms that enable the debtors to restore their economic viability and do not add to their burdens. In the restructuring of debt, the debtor country should not be forced to pay exorbitant additional interest.

To cushion the impact of austerity on workers and ordinary citizens, private creditors should not be protected from loss on obligations already outstanding unless they agree to roll over a specified percentage of obligations coming due over an agreed future period. The long-term interests of the creditors will be furthered if they treat their debtors as partners by building performance initiatives into their debt restructuring programs. For example, the rate of interest charged might be progressively lowered if agreed financial targets are achieved.

As Nobel Prize winner economist James Tobin and others have argued, the 1997 crisis has demonstrated the need for new measures to stabilize the international currency exchange system, such as a tax on currency transactions, which would be the same whether the funds were moving on a round trip of hours or years and would thus reduce short-horizon speculation and dampen volatility in exchange rates.

The United States should give continuing attention to the terms being negotiated by the IMF with countries being bailed out, working to prevent the IMF from imposing unnecessarily stringent levels of austerity. In contrast to past cases in Latin America, the Asian economies now experiencing difficulty were in most instances not running budget deficits or engaging in excessive consumption. Indeed, on the contrary, several were running budget surpluses, and all of them had savings rates over 30 percent of GDP.

To ensure that the contagion spreads no further, it is critical that Hong Kong and China not devalue their currencies. The United States should work with the authorities of both governments to help them hold the line.

Taking into account its long-term interest in a stable Asia, the United States has no choice but to act as the buyer of last resort and should be prepared to accept what is likely to be a flood of Asian imports. At the same time, as a condition for adopting a cooperative attitude toward its trading partners, it must insist that others take measures to rectify inequitable aspects of their trade and investment policies toward the United States and to move from export-oriented to consumption-oriented economic models. This is particularly important in the case of Japan.

As the world's largest creditor nation with a chronic trade surplus, huge foreign currency reserves, and one of the world's highest rates of saving, Japan would be expected to have a strong currency and should be acting as a locomotive for the other Asian economies by becoming a major importer and shifting from trade surplus to trade balance. That Japan is not doing this greatly exacerbates the difficulties of the rest of Asia, because Japan effectively competes with and crowds them out of the world's export markets. The United States should orchestrate worldwide pressure on Japan to take steps immediately to clean up the bad debts of its banks, to cut the regulatory stranglehold of the bureaucracy on the economy, to enforce its anti-monopoly laws, and to implement a complementary program of consumption tax cuts and targeted public works measures.

To prevent U.S. industries from being unfairly harmed by the fallout of the Asian turmoil, the U.S. government should closely monitor trade to detect illegal dumping in U.S. markets and should self-initiate anti-dumping actions when violations occur rather than wait for complaints to be filed by private industry. The President should also direct the Federal Trade Commission to use its authority to act against international cartels that burden U.S. commerce by actively investigating and monitoring for possible cartel activity and issuing cease-and-desist orders when warranted by the results of investigation. The U.S. government should also review the provisions of its various treaties of friendship and commerce in the region to assure that they are being implemented completely, along with the conditions of all World Trade Organization (WTO) and other multilateral agreements.

For the past several years, the Asia Pacific Economic Cooperation forum (APEC) has been moving slowly toward a goal of realizing free trade in the region by the year 2020 for developing countries and 2010 for developed countries. In the wake of the current crisis, this timetable is no longer applicable. There is now an overwhelming consensus that what Asia needs as quickly as possible is a big dose of more openness, both domestically and internationally. Therefore, why wait until 2010 or 2020? The U.S.

government should begin pressing APEC to implement free trade immediately.

Finally, the United States must substantially upgrade its resources and capabilities to deal with Asia. While we have an ambassador to the European Union, there is no exclusively economic high-level representation to and resident in Asia. To remedy this, the position of Ambassador to Asia for Economic Affairs should be created. The Ambassador would be based in a major Asian city and be responsible for overseeing all aspects of U.S. economic activities in Asia. At the same time, the commercial and economic staffs of U.S. embassies in Asia should be strengthened, and AID funds for the region increased, perhaps by shifting funds from other areas. In addition, Export-Import Bank capabilities in Asia should be greatly enhanced. Only by giving Asia a truly high priority can the United States ensure that the long-term future of Asia will be healthy and congenial to our interests.

In retrospect, it is clear that U.S. security and geopolitical concerns conditioned economic policies toward Asia that directly contributed to the debacle of 1997. Motivated by fears of a global communist threat, the United States subordinated its economic interests to its security objectives during the Cold War decades, providing non-reciprocal access to the U.S. market in exchange for diplomatic and military cooperation. To avoid disturbing security ties, Washington pulled its punches in disputes over trade and investment and acquiesced in the development of unsustainable economic systems based on crony capitalism, excessive levels of foreign borrowing, and an unbalanced reliance on exports at the expense of domestic consumption. Thus, the precondition for an effective U.S. response to the new economic environment in Asia is to discard the Cold War mentality in formulating U.S. policies in the region.

Stability in Asia remains an important U.S. interest, but in the absence of a direct military threat to the United States in Asia, this interest can now be pursued effectively only by giving priority to economic concerns. Indeed, it is clear that unsustainable economic systems, aided and abetted by the United States, can prove to be more of a threat to stability in the long run than firm insistence on the establishment of economic restructuring, open systems, and equitable U.S.–Asian economic relations.

Recommendation 1 represents the consensus of the signatories. Individual signatories do not necessarily endorse every aspect of the statement. The signatories participated in the Study Group in their personal capacity, not as representatives of the institutions with which they are affiliated.

Selig S. Harrison
Clyde V. Prestowitz, Jr.
Co-Chairmen

Rear Adm. Eugene Carroll, Jr.
Lawrence Clarkson
Steven C. Clemons
Bruce Cumings
Susan Dentzer
Richard Elkus
Charles W. Freeman, Jr.
Maurice Greenberg
Donald C. Hellmann
Chalmers Johnson
Charles William Maynes
Rear Adm. Michael A. McDevitt
Walter Russell Mead
Mike Masato Mochizuki
Marvin C. Ott
Robert Perkins
Harold A. Poling
Susan Schwab
Edson W. Spencer
Ronald Steel
John Steinbruner
William Taylor
Allen S. Whiting
Jeffrey Winters

2.
THE RESTRUCTURING OF THE JAPANESE ECONOMY

By almost any measure, the Japanese economy remains the most closed among the major industrial countries. It has long been the case that competitive U.S. and other foreign producers have been unable to realize the benefits of their comparative advantages because of their inability to participate fully in the world's second largest market. Japan's persistent failure to consume more of what the rest of the world produces has been a brake on global economic growth and has put most of its trading partners at a disadvantage.

Over the years, when Japan was doing well economically, it could easily dismiss the complaints of foreign competitors and trading partners as the protectionist whining of incompetent managers and political leaders who were avoiding the difficult decisions necessary to become competitive. During the past seven years, however, Japan has continued to resist meaningful deregulation and structural change despite the fact that it has not been doing well. Most observers now agree that the Japanese economic system is not only a drag on the world economy but also has become a huge millstone on Japan itself.

This situation might not compel a response by the United States and other countries if Japan were only a minor player. But because Japan is the world's second largest economy and accounts for nearly 75 percent of total Asian GDP all by itself, its inability to come to grips with its problems is harmful not only to Japan but also to the rest of Asia and to the entire global economy. In the current crisis situation in Asia, Japan should be a locomotive for growth with a strong currency and a program of economic stimulus that absorbs imports from the rest of Asia. Instead, the yen has been allowed to fall to stimulate Japanese exports by making them more competitive with the exports of the rest of Asia.

The United States must do all in its power to bring about a fundamental deregulation and restructuring of the Japanese economy. As a creditor country with a chronic current-account surplus, a high rate of saving, and enormous foreign reserves, Japan would be expected to have a strong currency. Instead the yen is weak and falling, because Japanese banks are saddled with bad loans, and the anemic economy has kept interest rates at virtually zero for years. It is imperative that Japan devote public funds to insure bank depositors against losses while taking measures to close failed banks and strengthen those that are viable. At the same time, Japan should undertake a two-pronged effort to regenerate significant domestic demand-led growth.

At the macroeconomic level, a reduction of taxes on consumption is desirable, but classical fiscal stimulus measures such as public works spending and income tax cuts are unlikely to be effective. Prices for consumers should also be lowered by removing the bottlenecks and hidden barriers in the Japanese system. In order to reduce the price of land and create a meaningful market in real estate, the land value tax should be abolished and the land transaction tax cut. In addition, subsidies that keep land in uncompetitive agricultural production (even in downtown Tokyo) should be cut and land-use laws that restrict commercial and residential development revamped.

Furthermore, a whole series of deregulatory measures is critical. Japan has the world's highest electricity prices. These could be reduced by separating the generating and distribution sides of the electricity business and allowing open entry into the generation market. Unloading costs are higher in Japanese ports than anywhere else in the world. These could be dramatically lowered by deregulating port practices and removing the cartels that currently dominate the ports. By the same token, conditions on entry into the truck, bus, taxi, airline, and railroad businesses should be drastically relaxed, and rate-setting should be made transparent. Private firms should be allowed to enter the business of carrying parcels and packages, and the hospital business should be opened to private corporations.

Japan's distribution system is complex, inefficient, and costly. This is largely because a number of important Japanese markets are effectively cartelized and the distributors are owned or controlled by the producers or service providers. De-cartelization should be a major part of any Japanese reform program. This means strengthening Japan's anti-monopoly laws and aggressively enforcing them. In particular, the practice of sealing business arrangements with cross share-holding deals should be strongly discouraged. As part of the revitalization of Japan's banks and financial institutions, the so called "Big Bang" reform program should be fully implemented and even extended. Finally, steps should be taken to get Japan's bureaucrats out of the business of micro-managing the economy. The Administrative Procedures Act should be strengthened to prevent unreasonable refusal or sabotage of permission and acceptance notifications, and the number of necessary notifications should be drastically reduced. Establishment of an Administrative Court and a General Accounting Office to keep an eye on the bureaucrats would be important parts of this program.

Announcement of a program like this would quickly change the direction of the Japanese economy. In particular, it is likely that the yen would begin to strengthen. If this happens, the U.S. Treasury and the Bank of Japan should jointly intervene in the currency markets to buy yen and thus lean with the wind in the direction of a stronger yen.

To press the Japanese government in this direction, the U.S. government should enunciate a list of measures such as the above that it recommends for Japan's consideration. The United States should then ask for emergency consultations in the World Trade Organization (WTO), the Organisation for Economic Co-operation and Development (OECD), and the Asia Pacific Economic Cooperation forum (APEC) on how to deal with the Asian crisis. These proposals to Japan should be part of any crisis discussion. The U.S. government should also coordinate with the European Union, the North American Free Trade Agreement (NAFTA), and MERCOSUR (the customs union between Argentina, Brazil, Paraguay, and Uruguay), and with other Asian nations, to persuade them to convey the same message to Japan. The message should also be carried to the Japanese private sector by organizations such as the U.S.–Japan Businessmen's Council, the Pacific Basin Economic Council, and the Pacific Economic Cooperation Council.

All of these measures would be part of a concerted campaign to open up Japan's markets. In addition, in the context of the Asian crisis, it will become increasingly important that Japanese exports to the United States not unfairly crowd out exports from less well off Asian countries. Moreover, to maintain support in the United States for free trade in the face of a dramatically rising trade deficit, it will be important to assure that U.S. industries are not unnecessarily harmed. Therefore the U.S. government should carefully monitor trade with Japan. The United States should not hesitate to initiate anti-dumping cases where the monitoring evidence suggests possible dumping, and it should be especially vigilant for anti-competitive practices that may harm U.S. competitors. The Federal Trade Commission (FTC) should be directed to review carefully any possible instances of such behavior, and Congress should pass legislation giving the U.S. Trade Representative authority to act jointly with the FTC in pursuing such cases. In general, efforts should be made to ensure that trade with Japan occurs in accordance with all applicable rules, both domestic and international, and in particular that Japanese corporations do not gain benefits from collusive practices either at home or abroad. As part of this effort, the United States should promote adoption by the WTO of rules that will prevent anticompetitive business practices and domestic regulatory procedures from nullifying the effects of free trade agreements.

In past decades the United States has often pressured Japan with threats of sanctions and trade litigation. Now, as Japan struggles with the rigidities of its own system, a more positive way for the United States to attempt to bring about reform would be through the negotiation of an economic treaty aimed at achieving deep integration of the two economies. Such a Comprehensive Market Agreement would include all aspects of a standard free trade agreement, but would also go beyond such a pact by creating agreed-upon procedures and rules with regard to investment, anti-trust policies, administrative practices, and a range of other sectoral matters often identified as structural trade and investment barriers. Just as it attempted to achieve structural and systemic change in Mexico through NAFTA, the United States could try to bring about such change in Japan through such an economic treaty.

It might be objected that Japan, which already has open access to the U.S. market, would have little to gain from such a treaty. But this view misses the point. In the past, when Japan was doing well, there was little reason to accede to U.S. requests beyond humoring an ally. Now that Japan is doing poorly, however, there are many in Japan who want reform but need a mechanism that will enable them to drive the reform over the barriers of the Japanese political system. Such a treaty would provide a framework for implementation of the reforms outlined above, which would revitalize the Japanese economy, facilitate Japanese economic relations with the rest of Asia, and forestall growing tensions with the United States while greatly improving the life of the ordinary Japanese citizen. In short, such a treaty would be a good deal for Japan as well as the United States.

Recommendation 2 represents the consensus of the signatories. Individual signatories do not necessarily endorse every aspect of the statement. The signatories participated in the Study Group in their personal capacity, not as representatives of the institutions with which they are affiliated.

Selig S. Harrison
Clyde V. Prestowitz, Jr.
Co-Chairmen

Doug Bandow
Ted Galen Carpenter
Rear Adm. Eugene Carroll, Jr.
Lawrence Clarkson
Steven C. Clemons
Bruce Cumings
David D. H. Denoon
Susan Dentzer
Richard Elkus
Charles W. Freeman, Jr.
Maurice Greenberg
Donald C. Hellmann
Gary Hufbauer
Chalmers Johnson
Charles William Maynes
Rear Adm. Michael A. McDevitt
Walter Russell Mead
Mike Masato Mochizuki
Marvin C. Ott
Robert Perkins
Harold A. Poling
Richard J. Samuels
Susan Schwab
Edson W. Spencer
Ronald Steel
John Steinbruner
William Taylor
Allen S. Whiting
Jeffrey Winters

3.
THE RESTRUCTURING OF THE SOUTH KOREAN ECONOMY

Of all the countries that imitated the Japanese economic model, none did so more diligently than South Korea, and none is now paying a higher price. Accounting for over 80 percent of its GDP, Seoul's giant *chaebol* industrial combines such as Hyundai, Daewoo, and Samsung came to surpass Japan's *keiretsu* conglomerates like Mitsubishi and Sumitomo in terms of their relative importance to the national economy. The *chaebol* focused on industries such as steel, shipbuilding, autos, consumer electronics, and semiconductors because government policies assured them of protected domestic markets and kept foreign investors at bay. Most important, they were able to invest with enormous sums of borrowed money at preferred rates of interest and with an implicit if not explicit government guarantee.

Many South Korean businessmen leveraged their companies to the hilt, often carrying loans equivalent to four times the equity capital in their companies. They built ever-expanding production capacity linked to ambitious export offensives. The South Korean auto industry developed enough capacity to produce 5 million cars in a market with demand for less than 1 million, while the semiconductor makers installed enough capacity to supply over half the world's demand for memory chips. Now this overcapacity and the high debt levels required to achieve it have become a huge drag on the South Korean economy. The good news, however, is that South Korea, unlike Japan, is being forced to face up to the need for structural change and deregulation. With a new, more democratic government and the intervention of the IMF, South Korea has a very good chance to restructure and revitalize itself in the context of a more open political and bureaucratic system and a more market-based economy. It is important that the United States act to help South Korea seize this chance and avoid reversion to old, failed ways.

The United States should continue to support the IMF bailout program. But how the bailout is structured has important implications—both economic and political. Neither the international banks nor the South Korean banks that made bad loans should be able to avoid all the consequences of their business mistakes. The United States should seek to ensure that depositors in South Korean banks are insured against loss but that the banks themselves are not kept alive if they have clearly failed. By the same token, the international banks should be pressured to roll over and extend their loans and to do so at reasonable interest rates consistent with U.S., IMF, and European policies designed to help, not exploit, South Korea.

The IMF has already set a number of steps as a condition of the bailout. These include a halt to government-backed lending and guidance of the banking system and a decision to let failing banks and *chaebol* go bankrupt if necessary. The IMF has also called for a more open environment for foreign investment. In addition to these requirements, the United States should work with the new South Korean government to insist that thorough deregulation be implemented.

In South Korea, as in Japan, opening the electric power, inland transport, aviation, and distribution industries to free entry by competitors would greatly stimulate economic recovery. The number of officially sanctioned cartels now operating in the South Korean economy—seventy—should be drastically reduced. At the same time, the United States should insist that South Korea strengthen its anti-monopoly law and vigorously pursue the breakup of illegal cartels, particularly when they have an impact on international trade. In this context, the United States should make clear that while it is prepared to keep its markets fully open to South Korean exports, it will closely monitor trade activity and move against any anti-competitive practices that may be harmful to U.S. commerce. The United States should also make clear that it cannot maintain support for open U.S. markets in the face of the continuing formal and informal protection of South Korean markets. Finally, the United States should insist that South Korea adopt measures that will ensure transparency and limits on the discretionary powers of the bureaucracy. Businesses should be required to use internationally recognized standards of accounting and reporting. Bureaucrats should be subject to an administrative procedures act that requires them to open all regulatory proceedings to the public and that provides for an independent appeals system for bureaucratic rulings.

As a way both of consolidating liberalization measures made in the course of the bailout and of building public confidence in South Korea, the United States should consider negotiating a comprehensive free market agreement with South Korea similar to that discussed above in the recommendation on the restructuring of the Japanese economy.

Recommenation 3 represents the consensus of the signatories. Individual signatories do not necessarily endorse every aspect of the statement. The signatories participated in the Study Group in their personal capacity, not as representatives of the institutions with which they are affiliated.

Selig S. Harrison
Clyde V. Prestowitz, Jr.
Co-Chairmen

Rear Adm. Eugene Carroll, Jr.
Lawrence Clarkson
Steven C. Clemons
Bruce Cumings
Susan Dentzer
Richard Elkus
Charles W. Freeman, Jr.
Maurice Greenberg
Gary Hufbauer
Chalmers Johnson
Nicholas Lardy
Charles William Maynes
Rear Adm. Michael A. McDevitt
Walter Russell Mead
Mike Masato Mochizuki
Marvin C. Ott
Robert Perkins
Harold A. Poling
Richard J. Samuels
Susan Schwab
Edson W. Spencer
Ronald Steel
John Steinbruner
William Taylor
Allen S. Whiting
Jeffrey Winters

4. CHINA AND THE WORLD TRADE ORGANIZATION

In view of the rising U.S. deficit in trade with China and the multiplicity of restrictive Chinese trading practices, the Clinton Administration is requesting removal of most of China's import barriers as the price for Chinese membership in the World Trade Organization (WTO). The Study Group concurred that many aspects of Chinese trade policy are not consonant with WTO standards and should be reformed.

In evaluating the critical factors that should govern U.S. policy on the issue of WTO membership, the Study Group pointed to the importance of the privatization of inefficient state-owned industries, which are imposing great strains on the financial system. Given the continuing ripple effects of the 1997 Asian crisis, the Group urged that China should move as rapidly as possible to implement the pledges made by President Jiang Zemin to reform state-owned industries and should translate these pledges into concrete commitments in the WTO negotiations. Since the state sector employs some two-thirds of all urban workers, the pace of market-oriented reforms is a central issue for China's leaders. However, while it recognized the domestic political and social risks involved in such a restructuring process, the Group warned that delays in restructuring could lead to graver dangers in the form of economic stagnation, accompanied by potential social unrest.

The Group felt that, in negotiating the timetable for Chinese entry into the WTO, a distinction should be made between Chinese structural reforms and other changes in Chinese policies. In the case of structural issues, such as the establishment of adequate legal and administrative procedures, the necessity for widespread reorganization means it will be necessary to allow some time for completion. Even if China agreed to make these changes immediately, as a matter of practicality it could not. Therefore the Study Group recommends a phase-in period of no longer than five years for needed administrative and structural reforms. By contrast, with respect to certain other issues, such as the reduction of excessive tariffs and quotas and distribution rights, the Group felt that U.S., European, and Japanese negotiators should insist on immediate Chinese compliance with WTO standards.

Beijing's admission should be conditioned on a transition

process with a special schedule of reforms relating not only to the removal of explicit import barriers, but also to administrative transparency, the implementation of pledges concerning the protection of intellectual property, and the rule of law. During this transition process, China would be granted "most-favored-nation" (MFN) status and full access to the markets of WTO members. It would agree to a surveillance mechanism with specific review stages and benchmark provisions, with a sanctions mechanism to be invoked in case of failure to meet benchmarks. The Study Group noted that while China, as a WTO member, would have full rights of WTO membership during this transition process, including guaranteed access to WTO member markets, WTO members would not have the same access to China's market for some period of time. The Study Group therefore recommends that WTO members insist on retaining the authority to respond quickly to asymmetrical trade situations that threaten to damage WTO member industries. Such authority should be exercised through a formal WTO consultative mechanism and in discussions with appropriate Chinese authorities. It would entail renunciation by member countries of the use of anti-dumping and countervailing measures during the transition process in exchange for fast-action, low-injury-test, no-compensation safeguard measures.

There is a significant danger that once China is a WTO member, it may not be able to fulfill its obligations. As the Presidential Commission on U.S.–Pacific Trade and Investment Policy observed, "China lacks a legal system characterized by a rule of law, due process and transparency, making commercial ventures, especially by foreigners, both difficult and risky." The Group therefore recommends that the United States work with China under the umbrella of the Joint Commission on Commerce and Trade to promote institutional structures that would facilitate compliance with WTO obligations. This would mean development of a joint plan to use U.S. officials from agencies such as the Office of the U.S. Trade Representative (USTR) and the Departments of Justice, Commerce, and State, as well as representatives from the U.S. private sector, to work with the appropriate Chinese officials and businesspeople to identify and redesign procedures and institutions to make possible China's compliance with WTO obligations. While such structures are being developed, it would be unwise to move too quickly, keeping in mind the experience of South Korea. In its eagerness to join the OECD, Seoul, encouraged by the United States, took the liberalization measures necessary to meet OECD obligations before it had prepared the necessary institutional structures and procedures, which contributed to its 1997 economic debacle. A possible approach in the case of China would be to expand its WTO obligations progressively while progressively granting it increased WTO rights as its institutional structures are put in place. In any case, the Group recommends that the protocol governing Chinese membership, when it comes, should provide for periodic progress reviews.

The debate over WTO membership is closely linked to the debate over whether normal trade status for China—"most-favored-nation" status—should be made permanent or should be extended on an annual basis. WTO membership would strengthen China's case for permanent MFN status, because WTO members normally grant each other such status. The Study Group felt that the annual debate over MFN status during the past fifteen years has been a serious irritant to Sino–U.S. relations that has undermined the ability of the United States to negotiate the resolution of economic disputes with China. Membership in the WTO would serve U.S. interests, in the Group's judgment, by enabling the United States to deal with inevitable trade conflicts on a multilateral rather than a strictly bilateral basis. As China comes into compliance with various provisions of the WTO, the United States will be able to use WTO dispute-resolution procedures to challenge Beijing on trade practices that are in violation of the Uruguay Round Treaty.

Recommendation 4 represents the consensus of the signatories. Individual signatories do not necessarily endorse every aspect of the statement. The signatories participated in the Study Group in their personal capacity, not as representatives of the institutions with which they are affiliated.

Selig S. Harrison
Clyde V. Prestowitz, Jr.
Co-Chairmen

Doug Bandow
Ted Galen Carpenter
Rear Adm. Eugene Carroll, Jr.
Lawrence Clarkson
Steven C. Clemons
Bruce Cumings
Susan Dentzer
Richard Elkus
Charles W. Freeman, Jr.
Donald C. Hellmann
Gary Hufbauer
Chalmers Johnson
Nicholas Lardy
Charles William Maynes
Rear Adm. Michael A. McDevitt
Walter Russell Mead
Mike Masato Mochizuki
Marvin C. Ott
Robert Perkins
Harold A. Poling
Richard J. Samuels
Susan Schwab
Edson W. Spencer
Ronald Steel
John Steinbruner
William Taylor
Allen S. Whiting
Jeffrey Winters

5.
THE FUTURE OF THE U.S. PRESENCE IN JAPAN

During the Cold War, the United States subordinated its economic interests to its security interests in relations with Japan, frequently pulling its punches in trade and investment disputes to avoid damage to the security relationship. Now, despite a radically changed security environment in Asia and growing Japanese sentiment for the reduction of U.S. forces stationed in Japan, the United States continues to assign an overriding priority to the indefinite maintenance of an undiminished military presence in Japan while continuing to accept an inequitable economic relationship.

The Study Group believes that the United States can and should vigorously pursue its economic interests vis-à-vis Japan without detriment to its security interests in Asia. A more consistent and persistent U.S. posture is necessary to induce Japan to remove inequitable trade and investment barriers and to reduce reliance on exports by restructuring its economy.

Apart from the economic factors necessitating a reappraisal of U.S. policy in Japan, the United States confronts a steady increase in nationalistic political pressures within Japan for greater autonomy in defense and foreign policy, including the gradual reduction of the U.S. presence not only in Okinawa, where anti-base sentiment is most acute, but throughout Japan. The Clinton-Hashimoto declaration of April 1996, reaffirming the security relationship, papered over differences on both security and trade issues that are likely to intensify in the absence of new U.S. policy initiatives sensitive to Japan's changing climate. Developments since the declaration have called into question whether there is any substance in the provisions of the declaration relating to Okinawa and whether the United States would have effective use of Okinawa in the event of a military emergency.

The Study Group does not rule out the possibility of an expansionist China at some point in the decades ahead should a future Chinese leadership seek to develop significant power-projection capabilities that the defensively oriented Chinese armed forces now lack. At present, however, Chinese conventional military capabilities do not pose a threat to Japan. In the foreseeable future, therefore, the United States and Japan should focus on constructive economic and political engagement with China and accept the growth of Chinese military power as a natural accompaniment of its emergence as the major power in Asia—provided that it does not develop a menacing level of power-projection capabilities. Above all, they should avoid the appearance that the Japan–U.S. security relationship is being redesigned to contain China militarily or to interfere with the evolution of an indigenous Asian balance of power reflecting China's size and power potential. The current effort of Japanese rightist leaders to give the alliance an anti-China rationale, if successful, would only serve to strengthen ultra-nationalist forces in Beijing.

Given the volatility of the regional political climate resulting from the 1997 economic crisis, it could be destabilizing to disturb the existing U.S.–Japan security relationship in the period immediately ahead. However, the Study Group believes that the United States should offer to discuss a change in the nature of the U.S. presence as soon as circumstances permit to minimize its negative impact on Sino–U.S. relations and to broaden its political acceptability in Japan. Instead of waiting for some future Japanese government to ask for the departure of U.S. forces, the United States should declare its readiness to turn over all of its bases and facilities to the Japanese Self Defense Forces within an agreed period, such as five years, and to withdraw all American combat forces from these bases, including bases in Okinawa. Japan, for its part, should be asked to accept two conditions: first, the joint use in peacetime of the Yokosuka and Sasebo naval bases, so that the Seventh Fleet can continue to operate in the Pacific; and second, wartime U.S. access to all Japanese bases in the event of military emergencies in which Japan concurs in the desirability of U.S. intervention.

U.S. naval vessels now homeported in Japan would be returned to U.S. bases in Hawaii or San Diego but would have ongoing access to support facilities in Japan during their periodic deployments in the Pacific Ocean, the South China Sea, and the Indian Ocean. The United States and Japan would establish machinery under their 1960 Treaty of Mutual Security and Cooperation for regular consultation to agree on the levels of logistics personnel and other U.S. noncombat forces that would continue to be stationed in Japan to facilitate joint exercises, peacetime U.S. access to naval support facilities, and wartime U.S. access to Japanese bases. At the same time, the United States would explore the feasibility of upgrading naval support facilities in Guam and of utilizing other existing ports, such as Subic Bay, Camranh Bay, and Singapore, so that the need for reliance on Yokosuka and Sasebo would be reduced.

If Japan accepts this offer, which the Study Group believes is likely, the U.S.–Japan relationship will be on a sounder and more enduring political and military footing. If it rejects this offer and seeks to retain the existing U.S. presence, the nature of the bargaining relationship will be fundamentally altered, with the United States, not Japan, in the driver's seat in negotiations on economic disputes.

In a separate recommendation, the Study Group urges that the United States seek to minimize its involvement in the unlikely event of a war in Korea. Therefore the Group does not accept the argument that the U.S. military posture in Japan must remain unchanged pending a definitive peace in Korea. In the event of a Korean conflict, South Korean forces should bear the brunt of initial resistance, and adequate warning time would exist for the level of U.S. support regarded as appropriate by the Study Group.

The withdrawal of U.S. conventional combat forces from Japan would not alter the applicability of the U.S. nuclear deterrent to Japan under the Security Treaty. The Study Group recognizes the continued value of the U.S. nuclear umbrella in forestalling the possible growth of sentiment in Japan favoring an independent Japanese nuclear weapons capability should China increase its medium-range ballistic missile deployments targeted at Japan. For this reason, the Group believes that U.S. nuclear protection should be accompanied by regional nuclear arms control negotiations embracing China, in which the United States and Russia should participate. Ultimately, if full nuclear transparency can be achieved in North Korea and a northeast Asia nuclear-free zone can be negotiated, the U.S. nuclear umbrella could be withdrawn.

Recommendation 5 represents the consensus of the signatories. Individual signatories do not necessarily endorse every aspect of the statement. The signatories participated in the Study Group in their personal capacity, not as representatives of the institutions with which they are affiliated.

Selig S. Harrison
Clyde V. Prestowitz, Jr.
Co-Chairmen

Doug Bandow
Ted Galen Carpenter
Rear Adm. Eugene Carroll, Jr.
Lawrence Clarkson
Steven C. Clemons
Bruce Cumings
Susan Dentzer
Maurice Greenberg
Gary Hufbauer
Chalmers Johnson
Charles William Maynes
Marvin C. Ott
Robert Perkins
Harold A. Poling
Edson W. Spencer
Ronald Steel
William Taylor
Allen S. Whiting
Jeffrey Winters

6.
THE FUTURE OF THE U.S. PRESENCE IN KOREA

President Clinton has pledged that the United States will "keep American forces in Korea as long as they are needed and the Korean people want them to remain." Challenging this policy, Doug Bandow of the Cato Institute urges in a chapter in this volume (see p. 155) that the United States withdraw its forces and terminate its security treaty with Seoul. In between these two positions are a variety of proposals that would link U.S. force reductions and an eventual disengagement with the pace of reductions in tension on the peninsula.

The idea of linking a U.S. withdrawal with tension reduction is superficially attractive but embodies a dilemma for the United States. South Korean hardliners who want to see the collapse of the North are generally opposed to the arms control measures that would be critical to a reduction in tensions, such as a mutual North-South reduction of forces and a mutual pullback of forces along the DMZ. Thus, while the United States should seek to promote an easing of tensions before removing its forces, achieving success in such efforts would be difficult. A commitment to remain until tensions are reduced could become a commitment to stay indefinitely.

Given the climate of anxiety in South Korea resulting from the 1997 economic crisis, it could be destabilizing to disturb the existing U.S.–South Korea security relationship in the period immediately ahead. However, the Study Group believes that, as soon as circumstances permit, the United States should move to open negotiations with the South on a timetable for the gradual disengagement of U.S. combat forces. The Study Group envisages an agreed transition period not to exceed seven years.

During this transition period, U.S. ground forces should be reduced and repositioned so that South Korean forces would bear the brunt of any fighting. U.S. air and naval forces would participate from the outset, but American ground forces would intervene only as a last resort—in contrast with existing strategy, in which U.S. forces are intended to serve as a "tripwire." However, the reduction and withdrawal of U.S. forces should not lead to a termination of the U.S. security treaty commitment unless China ends its security treaty with Pyongyang and Russia pledges not to restore its former security commitment. Non-combat logistic and communications forces would remain in Korea pending such agreements with China and Russia to facilitate the return of combat forces in the event of an emergency.

The United States should accompany the reduction, repositioning, and withdrawal of its combat forces with active efforts to replace the 1953 Armistice with new peacekeeping machinery in which U.S. forces should participate. These efforts should include not only multilateral diplomacy involving China, Russia, and Japan, such as the four-power talks initiated by the United States, China, and North and South Korea in 1998, but also the bilateral U.S.–North Korea security dialogue long proposed by North Korea.

The fundamental reason for setting a deadline for disengagement is that the economic subsidy provided by U.S. forces and U.S. bases enables the South to have a maximum of security with a minimum of sacrifice. The South's upper- and middle-income minority, in particular, has acquired a vested interest in the status quo. So long as the South has the U.S. military presence as an economic cushion, it is under no compulsion to explore a *modus vivendi* with the North.

Opponents of disengagement have argued that the sense of insecurity in the South resulting from a U.S. withdrawal would foreclose meaningful dialogue with the North. But this line of analysis is not borne out by the South's approach to North-South dialogue in recent years. For example, until the 1997 financial crisis, far from considering mutual force reductions, the South was moving in the opposite direction, expanding its defense budgets and its military-industrial complex. An open-ended American presence is more likely to result in continued tension than would a U.S. departure preceded by ample notice and serious mediation efforts. It is only in the absence of U.S. forces that Seoul will have to face up to post–Cold War realities, choosing between the sacrifices required to match the level of defense strength now provided by the United States and an accommodation with the North based on a loose confederation and the coexistence of differing systems.

To promote stability in Korea, the United States should be more cooperative in responding to North Korea's efforts to deal with its economic problems. In particular, the United States should phase out the economic sanctions imposed during the Korean War in accordance with the terms of the 1994 nuclear freeze agreement, and it should encourage non-strategic U.S. trade and investment. While providing expanded food aid, the United States should press for the expansion of private markets and other agricultural reforms as the key to long-term food self-sufficiency.

Recommendation 6 represents the consensus of the signatories. Individual signatories do not necessarily endorse every aspect of the statement. The signatories participated in the Study Group in their personal capacity, not as representatives of the institutions with which they are affiliated.

Selig S. Harrison
Clyde V. Prestowitz, Jr.
Co-Chairmen

Doug Bandow
Ted Galen Carpenter
Rear Adm. Eugene Carroll, Jr.
Lawrence Clarkson
Steven C. Clemons
Bruce Cumings
Susan Dentzer
Charles W. Freeman, Jr.
Maurice Greenberg
Gary Hufbauer
Chalmers Johnson
Charles William Maynes
Marvin C. Ott
Robert Perkins
Harold A. Poling
Richard J. Samuels
Edson W. Spencer
Ronald Steel
Allen S. Whiting
Jeffrey Winters

7.
U.S. INTERVENTION IN TAIWAN

The United States accepted the principle of "One China" when it recognized the People's Republic of China (PRC) in 1979, withdrew recognition from the Republic of China on Taiwan, and terminated its mutual security treaty with Taipei. This principle guided U.S. policy for the ensuing fifteen years. Beijing tolerated the *de facto* independence enjoyed by Taiwan during this period, expressing confidence that growing economic ties would set the stage for an eventual political accommodation.

Faced with a firm U.S. commitment to the "One China" principle, political elements in Taiwan favoring *de jure* independence gained limited headway. In 1994, however, the Clinton Administration departed from this principle by permitting U.S. Cabinet members to visit Taiwan for the first time. Pro-independence advocates on the island were quick to launch a campaign for United Nations membership and for a U.S. visit by President Lee Teng-Hui. The Clinton Administration's decision to permit the Lee visit led to a rapid escalation of Sino–U.S. tensions that reached a dangerous level in 1996 when U.S. carriers were deployed near the Taiwan Strait during live-fire Chinese military exercises there.

The Study Group concluded that military action by the PRC against Taiwan is improbable in the absence of grave provocation by Taipei in the form of a formal declaration of independence or steps clearly intended to set the stage for such a declaration. Conversely, emphasizing the historically rooted reasons why Taiwan is an overriding nationalist priority for the PRC, the Group warned that China is likely to resort to military force, if necessary, to prevent the establishment of an independent Taiwan.

The Study Group expressed doubt that the high costs and risks of a military conflict with China over Taiwan would be shared with the United States in significant measure by Japan and other Asian powers. More important, continuing tensions over Taiwan involving the implicit threat of U.S. military intervention would poison all aspects of U.S. relations with the PRC, including economic relations, which are likely to become increasingly strained. The Study Group therefore recommended a determined and unambiguous U.S. posture to forestall a confrontation between Taiwan and China. The United States should make clear: that it opposes independence for Taiwan as well as steps by Taiwan designed to assert a separate international identity incompatible with the "One China" principle; that it would not recognize an independent Taiwan; and that it would not intervene militarily to defend Taiwan against an attack by the PRC resulting from a declaration of independence or steps intended to foreshadow such a declaration. At the same time, the United States should make clear to the PRC that it would not rule out the use of force in the event of an unprovoked attack.

U.S. policy toward Taiwan should be designed to promote a climate conducive to a relaxation of tensions between Beijing and Taipei and the continuing growth of economic interdependence. Such a policy would require implementation of the 1982 "Second Shanghai Communiqué," under which the United States pledged to phase out gradually its arms sales to Taiwan.

Recommendation 7 represents the consensus of the signatories. Individual signatories do not necessarily endorse every aspect of the statement. The signatories participated in the Study Group in their personal capacity, not as representatives of the institutions with which they are affiliated.

Selig S. Harrison
Clyde V. Prestowitz, Jr.
Co-Chairmen

Rear Adm. Eugene Carroll, Jr.
Lawrence Clarkson
Steven C. Clemons
Bruce Cumings
Susan Dentzer
Richard Elkus
Charles W. Freeman, Jr.
Maurice Greenberg
Gary Hufbauer
Chalmers Johnson
Nicholas Lardy
Charles William Maynes
Walter Russell Mead
Mike Masato Mochizuki
Marvin C. Ott
Robert Perkins
Harold A. Poling
Richard J. Samuels
Susan Schwab
Edson W. Spencer
Ronald Steel
John Steinbruner
William Taylor
Allen S. Whiting
Jeffrey Winters

8.
JAPAN, CHINA, AND THEATER MISSILE DEFENSE

In the name of deterring possible threats from North Korean and Chinese missiles, the United States is pressing Japan to join in financing and deploying a Theater Missile Defense (TMD) system that could cost as much as $20 billion.

The Study Group has concluded that such a system is not necessary to deal with the missile capabilities likely to be developed by an economically impoverished North Korea in the foreseeable future. Pyongyang has fully honored its verification and other commitments under its 1994 nuclear freeze agreement with the United States. Critics of the freeze agreement suspect that North Korea may have accumulated enough plutonium prior to the freeze for one or two nuclear weapons. However, even if these suspicions prove to be well-founded, the Study Group finds it implausible that North Korea would seek to intimidate Japan with such a small nuclear force, risking U.S. retaliation.

In contrast to North Korea, China does pose a credible missile threat to Japan. However, the Study Group warns that a TMD system, far from reducing this threat, would accentuate Sino-Japanese tensions and provoke the expansion of Chinese missile deployments and other nuclear delivery systems targeted at Japan. The specific type of TMD system envisaged for Japan is designed for defense against missiles with a 3,500-kilometer range, which is the range of the Chinese CSS-2 missile. Thus, to China, a TMD system would signal a Japanese desire to set up a defensive shield under which it could project its military power without fear of retaliation. In particular, Beijing would see a TMD system as new evidence that Tokyo intends to develop a nuclear first-strike capability.

The Study Group recommends that the United States encourage Japan to engage China in a dialogue on the proposed TMD system and other security issues. In such a dialogue, Japan could offer to suspend consideration of the TMD proposal and the development of possible naval power-projection capabilities in exchange for Chinese confidence-building measures such as steps toward greater transparency, limitations on the development of its own power-projection capabilities, and the removal or relocation of medium-range missile deployments that are threatening to Japan.

Whether or not the suspension of the TMD system can be used to obtain Chinese concessions on security issues, the United States should abandon its present plans for a TMD system in Japan capable of defense against long-range missiles. Apart from the impact on China, such a system would be incompatible with the 1972 U.S.–Soviet Anti-Ballistic Missile Treaty and would further undermine the already imperiled START II nuclear arms reduction agreement with Russia and possible efforts to negotiate a START III agreement.

Recommendation 8 represents the consensus of the signatories. Individual signatories do not necessarily endorse every aspect of the statement. The signatories participated in the Study Group in their personal capacity, not as representatives of the institutions with which they are affiliated.

Selig S. Harrison
Clyde V. Prestowitz, Jr.
Co-Chairmen

Rear Adm. Eugene Carroll, Jr.
Lawrence Clarkson
Steven C. Clemons
Bruce Cumings
Susan Dentzer
Richard Elkus
Charles W. Freeman, Jr.
Maurice Greenberg
Gary Hufbauer
Chalmers Johnson
Nicholas Lardy
Charles William Maynes
Walter Russell Mead
Mike Masato Mochizuki
Marvin C. Ott
Robert Perkins
Harold A. Poling
Richard J. Samuels
Susan Schwab
Edson W. Spencer
Ronald Steel
John Steinbruner
William Taylor
Jeffrey Winters

9.
INDONESIAN DEMOCRACY AND LABOR RIGHTS

Recent developments in Indonesia have resulted from a variety of immediate causes unrelated to U.S. policy. Looking back, however, the Cold War role of the United States in Indonesia clearly exemplifies the long-term costs and dangers inherent in support for authoritarian regimes in the name of short-term security objectives. The U.S. Central Intelligence Agency aided the Sumatran rebellion and other efforts to destabilize the regime of President Sukarno. When the army seized power in 1965, the United States was quick to embrace General Suharto and gave uncritical support to his authoritarian rule in the ensuing decades. Suharto's reliance on a narrow clique of military insiders, family members, and favored businessmen encouraged rampant crony capitalism, reckless speculation, inequitable patterns of economic growth, and the ultimate collapse of economic stability in 1997, leading to profound strains in Indonesian society.

As Jeffrey Winters observes in the paper prepared for the Study Group (see Appendix), "The anger pervading Indonesian society is high and increasing . . . The potential exists in Indonesia for a violent breakdown of the political order." By clearly signaling its desire for meaningful political change, the United States would "encourage the next generation of Indonesian leaders to move preemptively to push Suharto and his family out gracefully."

Given the U.S. role for three decades in helping to sustain the Suharto regime, the Study Group believes that it is incumbent on the United States to encourage a stable transition to a more popularly based government. Such a change in the U.S. posture is necessary to forestall a "breakdown of the political order" in the world's fourth most populous country and to achieve economic stability. In dealing with the immediate economic crisis, the United States should adhere to its policy of conditioning economic support to the present government on compliance with International Monetary Fund standards.

A more representative post-Suharto government would mean greater freedom for unions to press for higher wages and better environmental standards. In Indonesia as in many other third world countries, authoritarian rule has meant the repression of labor for the purpose of keeping the price of exports as low as possible. Strengthening labor rights in a more popularly based system is an essential precondition for the improvement of living standards that is necessary to underpin political stability.

Recommendation 9 represents the consensus of the signatories. Individual signatories do not necessarily endorse every aspect of the statement. The signatories participated in the Study Group in their personal capacity, not as representatives of the institutions with which they are affiliated.

Selig S. Harrison
Clyde V. Prestowitz, Jr.
Co-Chairmen

Doug Bandow
Ted Galen Carpenter
Rear Adm. Eugene Carroll, Jr.
Lawrence Clarkson
Steven C. Clemons
Bruce Cumings
David D. H. Denoon
Susan Dentzer
Richard Elkus
Charles W. Freeman, Jr.
Gary Hufbauer
Chalmers Johnson
Charles William Maynes
Walter Russell Mead
Mike Masato Mochizuki
Robert Perkins
Harold A. Poling
Richard J. Samuels
Susan Schwab
Edson W. Spencer
Ronald Steel
John Steinbruner
William Taylor
Jeffrey Winters

10.
A NUCLEAR BARGAIN WITH INDIA

The civilian nuclear power agreement recently concluded between the United States and China should serve as a model for a similar accord designed to defuse growing tensions between the United States and India over nuclear weapons non-proliferation and nuclear arms control issues.

India has dramatically demonstrated its ability to make nuclear weapons with its nuclear tests in 1974 and 1998. Pakistan, too, has shown that it is nuclear-capable. Until three years ago, the United States repeatedly pressed New Delhi and Islamabad to give up their nuclear options. In January 1995, however, then Defense Secretary William Perry announced an important, little-noticed reversal of policy. Perry acknowledged that "the nuclear capabilities of India and Pakistan flow from a dynamic that we are unlikely to be able to influence in the near term. Rather than seeking to roll back—which we have concluded is unattainable in these two countries—we have decided, instead, to seek to cap their nuclear capabilities."

Despite this pronouncement, the United States has failed to give India and Pakistan concrete incentives to cap their nuclear weapons potential at present levels. The agreement with China opens the way for the Clinton Administration to explore a nuclear bargain with India in which New Delhi would make comparable non-proliferation and arms control concessions in return for access to U.S. civilian nuclear technology and U.S. cooperation in nuclear safety. Until an accommodation is reached with India, no agreement with Pakistan is possible.

In the first stage of a realistic new approach to nuclear diplomacy in South Asia, the Administration should offer to seek Congressional approval for civilian nuclear technology transfers to India, now barred by the 1978 Nuclear Non-Proliferation Act, in return for three major concessions by India.

First, India should agree to extend the application of international safeguards, now limited to one U.S.–supplied reactor near Bombay, to all seven of its civilian nuclear power reactors and any new power and medical research reactors supplied by U.S. or other foreign investors. This would prevent the diversion to military purposes of fissile material produced with U.S. cooperation. At the same time, in accordance with the January 1995 U.S. recognition and acceptance of India as a nuclear-capable power, it would not affect the research reactors and reprocessing facilities where India's militarily applicable nuclear stockpile is produced. These facilities would remain exempt from inspections.

Second, India should make some form of binding, *de jure* commitment not to export nuclear technology, formalizing its present *de facto* policy. This would place India in accord with a key provision of the Non-Proliferation Treaty. New Delhi has hitherto been firm in its refusal to export nuclear or missile know-how, turning down multi-billion-dollar offers for nuclear materials from Muammar Qadhafi and Saddam Hussein.

Third, India should compromise with the United States on the issue of a nuclear test ban. New Delhi has refused to sign the Comprehensive Test Ban Treaty, insisting that it be linked with a timetable for the reduction of nuclear weapons by the existing nuclear powers. But India might well agree to sign the treaty after completing the tests it considered necessary to make its nuclear option credible, just as China conducted a series of tests before agreeing to sign the test ban, or to stop testing without formally signing the treaty. The Indian government could make a declaration, endorsed by Parliament, citing the key provisions of the treaty and explicitly pledging that India will comply with these provisions. This could take the form of an undertaking to the United Nations.

Such an agreement would set the stage for broader negotiations in which the United States should seek to persuade India and Pakistan to cap the further accumulation of weapons-grade fissile material and to refrain from deploying nuclear weapons or to limit such deployments. This would be a realistic possibility only if the United States and Russia moved more rapidly to reduce their own nuclear weapons as the prelude to multilateral reductions encompassing China, Britain, and France.

The United States would benefit both politically and economically from such a bargain. Politically, apart from the overall benefits of improved relations with a rising power that has a population of nearly 1 billion, the United States would acquire significant influence in one of the most sensitive sectors of the Indian economy. The political damage to Indo-American relations would be serious if the United States should sell nuclear technology to China, a nuclear weapons power with a record of exporting nuclear and missile technology, while denying it to India, a country that does not deploy nuclear weapons and has never exported nuclear or missile technology.

Economically, it is in the interest of the United States to facilitate a diversification of energy sources in India and China alike, thus curbing a reliance on petroleum imports that will increasingly deplete world supplies and drive prices up. With its energy needs burgeoning, India wants to offset its dependence on petroleum and coal with a massive expansion of its nuclear power capacity. Imports of nuclear reactors from Russia are under discussion. Indian officials are signaling that imports from the United States and other foreign sources would be welcome and that full foreign ownership of nuclear plants would be permitted. India could absorb up to $50 billion in investments by foreign nuclear technology suppliers during the decades ahead.

India's economic growth rate is averaging 5-7 percent, American investment commitments exceed $8 billion, and cultural links between the world's two largest democracies are growing. But in the absence of a nuclear bargain, tensions over non-proliferation are likely to poison all aspects of Indo-American relations.

Recommendation 10 represents the consensus of the signatories. Individual signatories do not necessarily endorse every aspect of the statement. The signatories participated in the Study Group in their personal capacity, not as representatives of the institutions with which they are affiliated.

Selig S. Harrison
Clyde V. Prestowitz, Jr.
Co-Chairmen

Doug Bandow
Ted Galen Carpenter
Rear Adm. Eugene Carroll, Jr.
Lawrence Clarkson
Steven C. Clemons
Bruce Cumings
David D.H. Denoon
Susan Dentzer
Richard Elkus
Charles W. Freeman, Jr.
Maurice Greenberg
Donald C. Hellmann
Gary Hufbauer
Chalmers Johnson
Charles William Maynes
Rear Adm. Michael A. McDevitt
Walter Russell Mead
Mike Masato Mochizuki
Marvin C. Ott
Robert Perkins
Harold A. Poling
Richard J. Samuels
Susan Schwab
Edson W. Spencer
Ronald Steel
John Steinbruner
William Taylor
Allen S. Whiting
Jeffrey Winters

III. CONFLICTING PERSPECTIVES:
U.S. ECONOMIC AND SECURITY INTERESTS IN ASIA

The Impact of U.S.-Asian Economic Relations on the U.S. Economy

U.S. Economic and Security Interests in Japan

U.S. Economic and Security Interests in Korea

U.S. Economic and Security Interests in China

U.S. Economic and Security Interests in Taiwan

U.S. Economic and Security Interests in Southeast Asia

U.S. Economic and Security Interests in South Asia

U.S. Economic and Security Interests in Asia: The Next Decade

THE IMPACT OF U.S.-ASIAN ECONOMIC RELATIONS ON THE U.S. ECONOMY

CLYDE V. PRESTOWITZ, JR.

AFTER THE MELTDOWN: A NEW APPROACH TO ASIAN MARKETS

In July 1997, what the world had come to call the "Asian miracle" suddenly turned into a nightmare. Thailand, straining to meet the claims of foreign creditors and with its foreign exchange reserves dangerously depleted, announced it would no longer defend the exchange rate of its currency, the baht. Cut loose from the dollar to which it had been tied, the baht immediately nose-dived. This unleashed a chain reaction that over the next few months resulted in the collapse of the Malaysian, Indonesian, Philippine, and Korean currencies; it also reduced by half or more the asset values in these countries. As even mighty Japan teetered on the brink of recession and the possible collapse of its banking system, the International Monetary Fund (IMF) mounted a $100 billion–plus series of bailouts aimed at restoring stability in the financial markets and establishing a sound basis for recovery and renewed growth. This effort is continuing, but success is far from assured, and it is clear that restructuring economic ties in East Asia will be one of America's top foreign policy challenges over the next few years. Critical to satisfactorily meeting this challenge will be the development of a comprehensive approach to the region based on a clear understanding of the fundamental nature of the problem. For while the crisis has largely been reported and dealt with as a matter of financial speculation and bank panics, it is, in fact, systemic and deeply rooted.

THE CREATION OF THE "MIRACLE"

The origins of the Asian "miracle" go back over fifty years to the beginning of the Cold War when U.S. economic policies toward the Asia-Pacific region were developed as a component of the broader containment policy aimed at immunizing the area against the spread of communism. While unilaterally guaranteeing the security of much of Asia, the United States also fostered the rapid economic development of its Asian allies and their integration into the U.S. and free world markets; this was considered a means of preventing them from being seduced by communism and undermining U.S. security policy. Initially the focus was on building up the economic power of Japan, which Secretary of State Dean Acheson contended would have to be "the workshop of Asia." National Security Council document 48 spelled out how "Japanese industrial capacity could and should be utilized for the positive purpose of economic recovery of the entire region of Asia."

In practice this meant U.S. collaboration with Japanese economic policymakers whose approach to stimulating growth had evolved out of pre-war and wartime development efforts that relied heavily on government direction of the economy in conjunction with large industrial and banking combines. The Japanese believed that the wealth and power of the United States stemmed from the application of technology to industrial mass production, and their focus was on "catching up" to U.S. levels of industrial and technological capability. Market measures were seen as tools rather than as ends in themselves, and classical economic theories were often turned on their heads.

In the immediate post–World War II period, most Western experts advised Japan to take advantage of its abundant and cheap labor supply to focus on development of labor-intensive industries. They also recommended that, in view of its desperate shortage of capital, Japan open itself to foreign investment. But the Japanese never contemplated this advice for a minute. As Naohiro Amaya, a former Vice Minister of Japan's Ministry of International Trade and Industry (MITI) once said, "We did the opposite of what the American economists said. We violated all the normal concepts." Amaya went on to note that the American view of economics may help business increase current production or reduce current costs, but it does not necessarily take account of the dynamics for future development. "Businessmen are risk averse," said Amaya. "They hesitate to take the gamble. Therefore, if the invisible hand [of Adam Smith's market] cannot drive the enterprise to development, the visible hand [of the government] must." Indeed, not only did the Japanese believe in the general encouragement of the "visible hand," they also believed this hand of government should actively indicate where the gambles should be taken. "How can you go hunting without a target?" asked Amaya. "When you go hunting, you have to shoot at a target. But your [the U.S] neoclassical school of economics says you can fire in all directions at once, and the 'market' will ensure you hit the target. Well, we don't accept that line of reasoning, and our economic model will probably be stronger in the future and have a greater demonstration effect for developing countries."

Under the influence of this kind of thinking, Japan adopted an economic model that focused on rapid development of capital-intensive, mass-production industries. Of course, labor-intensive industries such as textiles and apparel were encouraged too, but the strategy was to force-feed rapid advance away from these businesses toward higher-value-added, higher-technology sectors. Because strong nationalism led to strict restraints on foreign investment, the capital necessary for investment in these heavy and high-technology industries had to come from Japanese savings. Thus the Japanese government introduced a variety of measures such as limitation of consumer credit, artificial elevation of commodity prices, and low taxation of interest earned on savings accounts to restrict consumption and to compel a high level of national savings. The development of stock and bond markets was also restricted, and savings were allocated through the government-guided banking system to government-backed investment in targeted industries such as shipbuilding, steel, autos, consumer electronics, and semiconductors, which were dominated by large combines. Domestic demand was being restrained and was not initially sufficient to justify installation of the world-class manufacturing facilities Japan wanted. Thus great emphasis was placed on exporting to the United States and to other foreign markets. Japan subsidized exports while at the same time using both tariff and non-tariff measures to hermetically seal its market against imports.

The United States encouraged and accommodated these measures. It was the Occupation authorities who initially restricted investment by U.S. industry in Japan to prevent fragile Japanese companies from being overrun by stronger U.S. competitors. Similarly, in an effort to promote Japanese exports, the United States set a ¥360/$US exchange rate that substantially undervalued the yen and continued to underwrite this fixed exchange rate for over twenty years despite rapid gains in Japanese productivity and a rising U.S. trade deficit. Further, the United States championed Japan's membership in the General Agreement on Tariffs and Trade (GATT) and the Organisation for Economic Co-operation and

Development (OECD) while allowing it to postpone adherence to certain obligations such as abolition of export subsidies and reduction of key tariffs and import quotas for a number of years. Thus the United States fostered a system in which Japanese industry was able for a long time to invest with government guarantees and encouragement in a highly protected home market while enjoying relatively open and subsidized access to the U.S. and other world markets.

As a "catch up" machine, this model was an unparalleled success. Beginning in 1952 with a GNP only 5 percent the size of the U.S. GNP, Japan passed Great Britain in 1967; its $5 trillion GNP today is two-thirds the size of the U.S. economy. Indeed, in nominal terms, Japan's per capita income of $37,000 is nearly 50 percent higher than the U.S. figure of $26,000. This success sparked imitation as other Asian countries began to "look East" rather than West for economic inspiration, just as Amaya had said they would. In fact, the concept of the "flying geese" pattern of economic development that was first articulated before the war was resuscitated and elaborated to explain the spread of the Asian economic miracle. The notion was that Japan would be the leader, heading into the wind and leading the advance of the other Asian countries that would follow behind in a flight pattern like that of geese, imitating Japan and pointing the way for others still farther behind. Of course, all the geese didn't imitate Japan exactly. South Korea was probably the closest copy. Like Japan, it vigorously protected the home market, eschewed foreign investment, compelled high savings, and allocated capital to target industries through a state-guided banking system. Indeed, in its encouragement of giant combines called *chaebol*, it even outdid Japan, creating a few giant entities that came to dominate well over half of the South Korean economy. Other Asian countries tended to be more open to foreign investment, and Singapore and Hong Kong were even relatively open to imports. In general, however, the so-called Asian "tigers" were characterized by a high degree of government involvement in economic decision making, high levels of enforced savings, high investment in key targeted industries such as electronics, and great emphasis on exports. (Some may object in the case of Hong Kong, but they should remember that the great fortunes of Hong Kong have been made in real estate and finance, two sectors that are highly regulated and cartelized.) These exports went disproportionately to the U.S. market because the United States, just as in the case of Japan, accommodated the tigers by throwing its markets open to them despite their reluctance to reciprocate. The United States also championed their entry into the GATT and, in 1997, even enabled Korea to join the OECD without immediately being subject to all normal member obligations.

As in the case of Japan, the Asian development model, combined with the unilateral U.S. security guarantee and very accommodative U.S. trade policies, produced an unprecedented era of growth. South Korea became the world's eleventh largest economy while income levels in Singapore and Hong Kong surpassed those of Western Europe. Total Asian production came to constitute over thirty percent of the world's GDP. Thus, by the mid 1990s, the U.S. vision, rooted in the Cold War, of an economically dynamic and free Asia with Japan at its center had been realized, as had the original policy objective of halting the spread of communism. Indeed, the power of the Asian miracle was such that a theory of "Asian values" arose to explain it. According to this view, the Asian reliance on personal relationships, use of bureaucratic "guidance," interlocking commercial ties, and collaborative relations between government and industry were superior to Western market mechanisms and would lead inevitably to Asia becoming the leader and center of the emerging global economy. Such was the pride that went before the fall.

IMPACT ON THE U.S. ECONOMY

Let us pause at this point to assess the impact of the "miracle" years on the United States.

On the positive side of the ledger, the most obvious benefit to the American economy has been the growth in U.S. exports to Asia, which rose in real terms from $10 billion in 1960 to $163 billion in 1995. Until the 1997 crises, the Asian region was the largest market outside of the North American Free Trade Agreement (NAFTA) for U.S. goods and services exports; these exports to Asia supported nearly four million U.S.–based jobs.

A second positive impact on the United States has been the gain in manufacturing productivity achieved by American industry in response to competition from Asia. For instance, between 1980 and 1989, the U.S. steel industry reduced the man hours required to produce a ton of steel from 10.3 (compared to Japan's 9) to 5.7 (compared to Japan's 6) for a productivity gain of nearly 50 percent.[1] The experiences of the semiconductor, machine tool, and other industries have been similar.

Measuring the direct impact of Asian competition on U.S. productivity is difficult because the effects have been both positive and negative. Manufacturing productivity has grown about 0.5 percent faster annually during the past twenty years than it did during the previous twenty years.[2] But not all of this gain can be attributed to Asian competition. At least half of the gain has been from advances in technology that would have occurred even without Asian competition.

Nevertheless, Asian competition has had a small but significant positive impact on U.S. manufacturing productivity. If we assume that half of the gain in manufacturing productivity was a response to Asian competition, the net impact is about 0.25 percent per year in added efficiency. Since manufacturing accounts for about 20 percent of U.S. output, the direct impact of Asian competition on overall U.S. productivity has been about .05 percent per year (0.25% x 20%) over the past fifteen to twenty years.

A third positive impact has been that quality of U.S. output has improved greatly in response to Asian competition. In the auto industry, for example, the average number of defects per one hundred Big Three vehicles has declined from nearly one hundred to about thirty over the past fifteen years.[3] In the semiconductor industry, U.S. producers, who had more than twice as many rejected chips as their Asian competitors fifteen years ago, now have about the same level of rejects. The picture is similar in the steel, machine tool, and a broad range of other industries. Although this is difficult to quantify, it is clear that this rise in quality has improved the American standard of living.

A fourth positive Asian contribution to the U.S. economy has been the region's supply of inexpensive goods. The exact impact of Asian products on U.S. prices is difficult to measure because appropriate price indexes covering a long period of time simply do not exist. Moreover, the secular decline in the value of the dollar may have counteracted the price-dampening effect of Asian-made goods on U.S. inflation by raising their prices in dollar terms. Nonetheless, it is possible to make a rough estimate, using conservative assumptions, of the impact on U.S. prices of Asian imports, which now account for about 10 percent of U.S. goods consumption. Over the past fifteen years, the overall impact of Asian imports has been to lower average U.S. price levels by about 2-3 percent, which amounts to about a 0.1-0.2 percent reduction in annual inflation during the period.

Finally, the Asian economies have made a positive contribution to the U.S. economy by helping to fund the massive U.S. government budget deficits of the past fifteen years. Asian investors and central bankers from countries with high savings rates have been big buyers of U.S. bonds, thereby filling the U.S. savings gap and keeping interest rates lower and investment rates higher than they otherwise would have been. As of end 1995, Japanese private and official holdings of U.S. Treasury securities totaled $223 billion.[4] Holdings of other Asian countries are substantial as well.[5]

Unfortunately, the story is not entirely positive. In addition to their contributions, the Asian economies have also imposed costs on the U.S. economy that have outweighed the benefits. In the first place, the United States for a long time effectively has subsidized the Asian economies in a number of ways. After the exchange rate of the yen was set at 360 yen to the U.S. dollar (¥360/$US) following World War II, Japanese productivity rose more than threefold during the next two decades, compared with a 44 percent increase for the United States. Yet the nominal exchange rate remained fixed at ¥360/$US. Because price levels in Japan rose 2.5 times more than U.S. price levels during the period, the yen did appreciate in real terms, but not by enough to offset Japan's rising productivity. The yen's sudden appreciation after President Richard M. Nixon adopted a tougher economic stance in 1971 was indicative of the yen's undervaluation, but did not fully reflect Japan's productivity gains. There was another spike in the yen's value in 1978, but the dollar soon reversed course, soaring during the early 1980s even as Japan's productivity continued to outpace that of the United States. Thus for most of the post–Cold War period, the dollar has been chronically overvalued versus the yen. Between 1960 and 1985, this overvaluation amounted to an effective subsidy that can be roughly estimated at more than $300 billion.

The same story has been repeated in other Asian economies as well. According to the World Bank, real GNP per capita (a proxy for productivity) in East Asia grew more than 5 percent per year from 1965 to 1990, compared to growth in the United States of 2 percent per year.[6] Yet, as Table 2 shows, despite these productivity differentials and large trade surpluses with the United States, the inflation-adjusted exchange rates of most Asian currencies and the U.S. dollar have not changed much. In fact, some currencies have actually depreciated.

Table 1. Japan's Productivity Lead, the Weak Yen, and its Impact on U.S.–Japan Trade

Years	Average Annual Productivity Differential (%)	Average Annual Price Advantage Due to the Undervalued Real Yen (%)	Average Annual Import Subsidy to Japan (*$ millions*)	Average Annual Potential Increase in U.S. Exports (*$ millions*)
1960-70	6.70	31.69	1,089	904
1970-80	3.56	35.30	4,463	3,048
1980-85	1.73	56.11	27,295	12,254

Sources: Japanese data from the Economic Planning Agency and the Statistics Bureau of the Management and Coordination Agency; U.S. data from the Bureau of Economic Analysis and the Bureau of the Census; Economic Strategy Institute calculations.

Table 2. Fluctuations in Real Exchange Rates, Annual Productivity Differentials, and Cumulative Bilateral Asian Trade Surpluses between the United States and Selected Asian Economies

	Annual Change in Real Exchange Rate, 1965-90 (%)	Annual Productivity Differentials, 1965-90 (%)	Cumulative Trade Surplus, 1980-95 (*$ billions*)
Korea	–3.5	5.5	49
China	+6.4	4.1	137
Malaysia	+0.7	2.3	37
Indonesia	+0.2	2.5	47
Thailand	+0.8	3.6	28
Singapore	–0.4	6.0	16

Note: Malaysian and Indonesian exchange rates and productivity are for 1970 through 1990. A positive sign indicates a depreciating currency; a negative sign indicates an appreciating currency.
Sources: IMF, DRI/McGraw Hill, and Bureau of Census. ESI calculations.

A second subsidy has been provided through the generalized system of preference (GSP), under which the United States has provided special tariff reductions on goods imported from developing countries. Added to this must be military procurement and co-production and offset arrangements amounting to hundreds of billions of dollars that have been directed toward Asia.

Finally, by unilaterally providing security to Japan, Korea, and much of the Western Pacific, the United States has provided large indirect subsidies. The most obvious is in the form of direct military expense. The cost to the United States of providing the security guarantee is about $42 billion annually. At the same time, the value of this to the Asian economies is much greater. Without the U.S. subsidy, Japan's annual defense budget would be closer to $100 billion, or $60 billion above its present $40 billion level. The same order of magnitude of 1-2 percent of GNP holds for most other Asian countries.

Aside from these direct effects, the U.S. security role carries with it another more indirect but very large subsidy, illustrated by events surrounding recent tensions over Taiwan. In response to Chinese missile firings near Taiwan, the United States dispatched one aircraft carrier task force. As a counter to this, China began switching procurement contracts from U.S. to other Asian and European suppliers. It is impossible to quantify the full impact of this phenomenon, but anecdotal evidence suggests it is quite large.

Another way in which the United States has subsidized Asia has been through its acquiescence in Asian trade-related investment measures (TRIMS) and in policies aimed at forcing technology transfer. Beginning with Japan in the 1950s, and continuing to the present, nearly all the Asian governments have intervened in private industry negotiations to make technology transfer and local production a condition of entering their markets. Beyond this, the Asian governments have often further intervened to adjust the conditions of privately negotiated licensing and joint venture agreements. Moreover, these government policies have often been complemented by collusive activity on the part of the Asian companies, which have banded together to insist on local production and technology transfer by foreign business partners.

James Abegglen has estimated the effect such technology transfer requirements have had in the case of Japan.[7] Over a period of thirty years, Japan entered into 42,000 licensing agreements for a total in fees and royalties of about $17 billion, or roughly 17 percent of one year's worth of the annual U.S. R&D budget of $100 billion. These licensees have supported at least 20 percent of Japan's manufacturing sales, although the share has probably declined in recent years. Even a royalty of just 3 percent on these sales—after accounting for Japan's rising level of technological self-sufficiency—would have yielded, on average, $2.7 billion per year. Thus the R&D subsidy of the past thirty years has been in the order of $65 billion.

A recent example demonstrates what has been happening for a long time with regard to investment. In early 1997, the top management of a leading U.S. company met to discuss its investment strategy. For some time, it had been planning a large investment for new production facilities in the United States. The discussion at the meeting, however, concerned whether or not to alter the plan and put the facility in China instead. In the course of discussion, it became clear that the amount of investment required for China would be higher than for the United States. Moreover, the cost of production would be higher while anticipated quality levels would be lower, and most of the product would be exported from China to the United States and elsewhere. So why even consider putting plants in China? The reason was that the Chinese government was applying enormous pressure on the company to invest and produce in China as a condition of being allowed to sell in the Chinese market. The decision was eventually made to put the plant in China. Thus China's policy created a distortion of the normal working of the law of comparative advantage in a way that affected a $1 billion–plus investment subsidy to the Chinese economy. Similar examples could be cited in most other Asian countries.

Another category of negative influence on the U.S. economy arises out of the structure and nature of the trading relationship between the United States and Asia. In nearly all cases, Asian markets have been and remain opaque and relatively closed in comparison to the transparent and relatively open U.S. market. While debate has raged over the causes of the massive U.S. trade deficit with Asia, no one disputes that it is easier to sell in the U.S. market than in most Asian markets, and most experts agree that many Asian countries import less than would be expected under free market conditions. In other words, the structure of the trading relationship tends to inhibit exports to Asia. Over the years, several analysts such as Robert Lawrence and Peter Petri have attempted to estimate to what extent U.S. exports have been inhibited and what impact this has had on the United States. In their view, Japan under-imports globally by $100-$200 billion.[8] The proportional U.S. share of this amount is $20-$55 billion. An additional $55 billion of U.S. exports to Japan would raise U.S. GNP by $115 billion, add 1.5 million jobs, cut the federal budget deficit by $25 billion, raise national savings by nearly a full percent, and raise investment by $20 billion.[9] These estimates can be viewed as the current annual cost to the U.S. economy of not having these exports. To account for the impact of the rest of Asia, these numbers should be increased by about 30 percent. Thus the annual impact on the U.S. economy of goods not exported to Asia is high. It could be as high as $150 billion in GNP lost, 1.9 million jobs not created, $45 billion added to the budget deficit, $26 billion not invested, and a potential increase of slightly more than 1 percent in the national savings rate not realized.

In addition to these quantifiable costs, there is the less easily quantifiable, but certainly large, negative impact on R&D efforts. When companies know that major markets are likely to be blocked to them and that they will not be able to achieve adequate economies of scale as a result, they tend not to make the R&D effort necessary to get into certain lines of business. For example, the flat panel display industry is growing rapidly as the demand for these displays in computers, aircraft, autos, and other products explodes. Although these displays were invented in the United States, there is little domestic production and virtually no R&D in the area because the Japanese producers who dominate this market live in a sanctuary from which they can make preemptive strikes against competitors in other markets.

This leads us to the question of the impact of imports and trade deficits on the U.S. economy. While imports have operated to hold down U.S. inflation, in some instances dumped imports have had far-reaching negative impacts. For example, documents of Japan's Fair Trade Commission (FTC) confirm that from 1955 until at least 1974,[10] the Japanese electronics industry acted collusively through the Tenth Day Group, the Palace Group, and the Okura Group to drive U.S. producers out of business by selling at very low prices in the U.S. market while keeping prices high in Japan. Eventually, the Japanese FTC issued a cease and desist order, but not before most of the U.S. industry was wiped out. Nor was this an isolated case. In fact, the story has been repeated in industry after industry (semiconductors, CB radios, ceramic chip packages, large forgings, machine tools, etc.) over the years.

Robert Blecker has assessed the relationship between the U.S.

trade and budget deficits.[11] By 1990, the real value of the dollar had returned to about its 1980 level, making U.S. products no less competitive in price terms then they were ten years earlier. In addition, over the decade as a whole, foreign incomes grew as or more rapidly than U.S. income. But the U.S. trade deficit in 1990 was $100 billion higher (in current dollars) than it had been in 1980, representing a decline of about 2 percent of GNP. Blecker argues that the United States has a structural trade deficit that requires continued dollar devaluation just to avoid further deterioration. When U.S. national income rises 10 percent, U.S. imports rise by about 25 percent. But when foreign incomes rise by 10 percent, demand for U.S. exports rises only 15 percent. Thus the United States cannot grow as fast as its trading partners without risking a perpetually widening trade deficit.

The nature of U.S.–Asia trade has acted as a drag on U.S. income growth. The combination of dumping, closed markets, and undervalued currencies in Asia has resulted in asymmetrical income elasticities. Blecker's estimates may exaggerate the difference in elasticities, but his estimates are for global trade. Experience over the past twenty years—America has been running huge trade deficits with Asia despite the fact that Asian economies have been growing more rapidly—suggests that the gap between U.S. export and import elasticities for trade with Asia has been growing. Assuming conservatively that a 1 percent increase in U.S. economic growth leads to a 2.5 percent increase in imports from Asia, and that a 1 percent increase in Asian growth leads to a 1.5 percent increase in U.S. exports to Asia, it becomes clear that U.S. income growth would have to be lower than its historical 3.4 percent growth rate to keep its deficit with Asia from expanding.

Finally, a cost that is usually ignored but has enormous ramifications is that of adjustment. When imports result in closed factories and displaced workers much is lost. Most of the capital invested in the factories is lost as a productive asset to the society. Workers lose wages, and often must sell their homes, move, and adjust to new communities. Homes cannot always be sold for what they cost, and new homes in new locales may cost more than old homes were sold for. New jobs may not be found at the old wage levels—or at all. For example, a 1986 U.S. Labor Department survey of 6.3 million blue collar workers displaced between 1979 and 1984 found that only 77 percent had gained new employment and their median income was 87 percent of previous earnings. Beyond this, incalculable costs of broken homes, rising crime rates, and devastated schools are often associated with job loss, dislocation, and shrinking tax bases.

Again, precise quantification is difficult, but the $100 billion structural trade deficit with Asia implies an adjustment affecting about two million U.S. jobs. If the average wage is $30,000 and 23 percent of these people do not find jobs, the annual loss to the economy is about $14 billion. If the remaining 1,540,000 displaced workers all find jobs at 87 percent of $30,000, the annual loss to the economy is about $6 billion. Since it typically takes between $100,000 and $200,000 of invested capital to create one job, the new investment necessary to handle all the displacement would be $200-$400 billion.

FROM "MIRACLE" TO NIGHTMARE

Astounding though it was, the "miracle" contained the seeds of a later nightmare because it depended inherently on rapid and continual growth of exports. This was not a problem at first because trade was a small part of the largely self-contained U.S. economy, and in any case the Asian economies were very small in comparison with the U.S. economy and had little impact on it. Moreover, the industrial and technological dominance of the United States kept its international accounts in rough balance by dint of the fact that overseas customers had no other source for many of the products they had to buy. This picture began to change in the 1970s and shifted dramatically in the 1980s as the Asian economies grew at unprecedented speed and as rapid globalization made the international economy an increasingly central part of the U.S. economy. In 1970, total imports and exports accounted for only 13 percent of U.S. GDP; by 1992, that figure had nearly doubled to 25 percent, and by 1995, only three years later, it had climbed to 30 percent. The bulk of this change was due to U.S. trade with the burgeoning Asian economies. What drew even more attention than the increase in the amount of trade was the fact that it was increasingly lopsided. As Asian industries caught up with and even surpassed their American competitors, exports to the United States began to overwhelm U.S. exports to Asia, and the United States came to experience a chronic and growing current account deficit with Asia.

The asymmetrical pattern of trade across the Pacific was exacerbated by a disparity in saving, investment, and consumption rates between Asia and the United States. While the Asian model compelled high rates of saving and investment and restricted consumption, the U.S. model did just the opposite. Thus Asia came to produce more than it consumed and exported the excess production, while the United States came to consume more than it produced and imported the shortfall in production. The disparity in saving, investment, and consumption was exaggerated by the asymmetry in market openness. Because U.S. industries were hindered from selling at their full potential in Asian markets, they had lower profits, employed fewer workers, paid less in taxes, and invested less in new production facilities than they would have if trade patterns had been more balanced. Again, Asian companies did just the opposite. The result was not only the chronically growing trade deficit, but also substantial dislocation of important U.S. industries and a rising sense on the part of American industry and labor that trade with Asia was unfair.

By the early 1980s, "trade friction," especially with Japan, had become intense and threatened to sour U.S. relations with its Asian allies. Time and again, U.S. industries such as semiconductors, telecommunications, autos, auto parts, soda ash, glass, forest products, and medical equipment complained that they had extreme difficulty penetrating Asian markets while their Asian competitors aggressively attacked them in the U.S. market. A succession of U.S. administrations engaged in endless negotiations to open Japanese and other Asian markets and threatened to impose sanctions if progress was not forthcoming. Each time, however, the United States refrained from actually imposing sanctions because of its free trade doctrine and concern that trade friction not undermine Cold War security and political relationships. Marginal Asian concessions would temporarily assuage U.S. irritation until the next round of complaints. By 1985, this cycle reached a crescendo as the U.S. trade deficit hit $150 billion, of which Japan accounted for $50 billion. After soaring for several years, the dollar began to weaken as the yen rose, pushed up by the inexorable Japanese trade surplus. In November, U.S. and Japanese negotiators met at the Plaza Hotel in New York and thrashed out an agreement to facilitate the move toward a substantially stronger yen. In the wake of this deal, the yen rose from ¥250/$US to a high mark of ¥79/$US.

The "flying geese" theory always assumed that as the lead goose (Japan) caught up to the West and became more prosperous, it would change the structure of its economy, saving and investing less while importing and consuming more. In this way, it was supposed, the lead goose increasingly would provide the market demand that the following geese would need to support their growing export industries. In the wake of the Plaza Accord, most economists supposed that the rapidly rising yen would force Japan to make this structural shift toward domestic-demand-led growth and more open import markets. In fact, however, Japan strove mightily to prevent this shift from occurring. The central bank and the Ministry of Finance moved to pump liquidity into Japan's financial system while reducing interest rates to record low levels. The objective was to reduce the cost of capital for Japanese industry so that it could invest even more than normal to increase its efficiency and remain competitive in export markets despite the impact of the strong yen. At the peak of this effort in 1989-90, major Japanese companies like Toyota were able to raise capital at negative cost. In other words, the markets paid them to take the money. However, the investment boom that was unleashed not only stimulated investment by Japanese exporters, it also led to rampant speculation by real estate and financial interests.

When financial distortions eventually led the Bank of Japan to burst the speculative bubble, it was again supposed that Japan would shift toward a more consumption-led model. Again, these expectations were confounded. The incentives for saving and investment built into the system remained strong, and Japan continued to generate the world's greatest pool of savings while consuming proportionately far less than the United States and the countries of Western Europe. To maintain its position in world markets, Japanese industry began to invest massively in the rest of Asia, particularly in the countries of Southeast Asia. When added to the already high savings and investment levels in these countries, this move produced an unprecedented investment boom and a rapid spurt of growth that was further enhanced by U.S. and European investment attracted by the prospects for rapid growth. Capacity for production of semiconductors, autos, machinery, and a host of other products grew rapidly and was added to capacity already existing and still growing in Japan, Korea, and Taiwan. In addition, China joined the flock as the last goose, investing at high rates and adding production capacity in many of the same target industries as the other Asian countries. As in Japan during the bubble period, the flood of money not only stimulated investment in industrial capacity, it also sparked real estate and financial asset funding on a grand scale.

Because production in the region far exceeded consumption, the whole system depended on the continuing growth of exports. Despite its heavy new investment in Southeast Asia and rising imports from production there, Japan's trade surplus with the region grew to be bigger than ever. There was much talk of intra-Asian trade and of the decreasing reliance of Asia on U.S. markets, but the end consumers remained heavily concentrated in the United States and to a lesser extent in Europe. Over the years, however, an important change had gradually occurred. The growth and proliferation of export-oriented economies had dramatically increased their weight relative to the United States and other import-oriented economies. In fact, the world had excess capacity in a number of important industries such as autos, semiconductors, steel, and consumer electronics. The first indication that this could be a problem occurred in 1994 when China devalued its currency in order to become more competitive in the export markets. In 1995, Japan, concerned about the slow growth of its economy, convinced the United States to support its attempt to stimulate Japanese exports by intervening in the foreign exchange markets to weaken the yen. These moves put enormous pressure on the other export-oriented economies of Asia. For example, a weaker yen caused orders to be switched from Korean to Japanese producers, and a weaker Chinese yuan diverted orders from Southeast Asia to China. The limits of the export-oriented Asian development model were at last becoming evident. With the fall of the Thai baht, the model reached the end of its useful life.

The flaw in the model is that it has a chronic tendency toward excess productive capacity and is overly dependent on exports. It worked when Asia was in catch-up mode, the targets were easily identifiable (i.e., whatever industries existed in the West), and the economies of the exporters were relatively small compared to those of the importers. But as Asia caught up two problems emerged. The targets were no longer self-evident, and the bureaucratic-led insider system tended to mute market signals and allocate investment to the old target industries, thereby creating enormous overcapacity. At the same time, as Asian capacity grew, the import markets could not absorb all the production; competition for limited markets forced the exporters into *de facto* competitive currency devaluations. Although currently discredited, the model produced several miracles and great benefits for Asia. However, nothing lasts forever, and it is now time for both Asia and the United States to adopt new policies in accord with the new environment in which they find themselves.

NEW POLICIES FOR A NEW MILLENNIUM

In retrospect it is clear that U.S. security and geopolitical concerns conditioned economic policies toward Asia that, while well intentioned, actually contributed to the eventual debacle by acquiescing in non-reciprocal trade agreements and failing to carry through market-opening and deregulation initiatives when opportunities for change presented themselves. Thus the first condition for a new U.S. economic policy toward Asia is a determination to put away the Cold War mentality in Asia as well as in Europe. Stability in Asia is important to the United States, but there is no direct threat to the United States in the region. Moreover, economic distortions resulting from indulgent, one-sided economic policies can actually be more of a threat to stability in the long run than firm insistence on the establishment of market mechanisms, open systems, and equitable treatment for U.S. economic interests.

In present circumstances, U.S. economic policies toward Asia must have both short- and long-term elements. In the short run, the emphasis must be on stabilizing financial markets and reestablishing the basis for growth and sound future development in the Asian markets. In doing this, precedents must be set that will ensure against a repeat of the kinds of practices that contributed to the onset of the crisis. This means first of all that those who lent and invested unwisely must share in the pain of reconstruction. Some observers have argued that troubled companies should be permitted to go bankrupt and then be bought out or revitalized by new, more efficient managers.

But it is important to prevent the collapse of currencies, particularly of the larger economies. The collapse of one the larger Asian economies could trigger a chain reaction that would cause serious harm to the United States and the rest of the global economy. Thus the IMF bailout program has been unavoidable. But the bailout must not be open ended or indiscriminate and it must not cushion those who acted unwisely while workers and ordinary citizens absorb all the pain. Thus the United States should support the provision of IMF funds as a bridging mechanism that will enable governments to keep large parts of their economies from closing down for lack of hard currency to pay for imports or to make other essential payments. However, these funds should only be provided to governments that credibly promise to: a) halt the practice of guiding bank lending; b) break up cartels: c) privatize most government-owned corporations; d) deregulate on a broad scale; and e) establish a true rule of law under which bureaucrats lose the discretionary authority that has long enabled them to administer informal "guidance" because of their power to intimidate. Further, funds should only be made available on the condition that private banks and investors restructure their investments and extend existing loans on a financial basis that enables them to recover no more than seventy-five cents on the dollar of any money invested and potentially lost.

To ensure that the contagion spreads no further, it is important that Hong Kong and China not devalue their currencies. The United States should work with authorities of both governments to help them hold the line, including joint intervention in exchange markets if necessary.

The United States must act as the buyer of last resort and prepare to accept a veritable flood of Asian imports while still keeping its markets open. At the same time, it must insist that others take measures to stimulate Asian consumption. This is particularly important in the case of Japan. As the world's largest creditor nation with a chronic trade surplus, enormous foreign currency reserves, and one of the world's highest rates of saving, Japan should have a strong currency and act as a locomotive for the other Asian economies; it should become a major importer and shift from trade-surplus to trade-deficit status. That it is not doing this greatly exacerbates the difficulties of other Asian countries because Japan effectively competes with and crowds them out of the world's export markets. The United States should orchestrate worldwide pressure on Japan to take steps immediately to clean up the bad debts of its banks, cut the regulatory stranglehold of the bureaucracy on the economy, enforce its anti-monopoly laws, and apply a massive stimulus program of tax cuts and public works spending to its domestic economy. The United States should also work to prevent the IMF from imposing excessive austerity on countries being bailed out. Unlike past cases in Latin America, the Asian economies were for the most part not running large budget deficits or engaging in excessive consumption. While interest rates may need to be kept fairly high to induce investors to return to these markets, measures should be taken to reduce cost burdens on domestic consumers. U.S. officials should work with the IMF to assure that its programs are administered with this in mind.

To prevent U.S. industries from being unfairly harmed by the fallout of the Asian turmoil, the U.S. government should closely monitor for illegal dumping in U.S. markets and should initiate anti-dumping actions when violations occur rather than wait for complaints to be filed by private industry. The President should also direct the Federal Trade Commission to use its authority to act against international cartels that burden U.S. commerce by actively investigating and monitoring for possible cartel activity and issuing cease-and-desist orders when warranted by the results of investigation. The U.S. government should also review the provisions of its various treaties of friendship and commerce in the region and assure that they are being completely implemented along with the conditions of all World Trade Organization (WTO) and other multilateral agreements.

For the past several years, the Asia Pacific Economic Cooperation (APEC) forum has been moving slowly toward a goal of realizing free trade in the region by the year 2010 for developed countries and 2020 for developing countries. In the wake of the current crisis, this timetable seems hopelessly outdated. There is now an overwhelming consensus that what Asia needs as quickly as possible is a big dose of increased openness, both domestically and internationally. Therefore, why wait until 2010 or 2020? The U.S. government should begin pressing APEC to implement free trade immediately.

Finally, the United States must substantially upgrade its resources and capabilities to deal with Asia. The position of Ambassador to Asia for Economic Affairs should be created. This ambassador should be based in a major Asian city and be responsible for overseeing all aspects of U.S. economic activities in Asia. In addition, the commercial and economic staffs of U.S. embassies in Asia should be strengthened and U.S. Agency for International Development (AID) funds for the area increased, perhaps by shifting funds from other areas. U.S. Export-Import Bank capabilities and resources in Asia should also be greatly enhanced. Only by giving Asia a truly high priority can we ensure that the long-term future of Asia will be healthy and congenial to American interests.

NOTES

[1] Lawrence Chimerine, Alan Tonelson, Karl von Schriltz, Gregory Stanko. *Can the Phoenix Survive?* (Washington, DC: Economic Strategy Institute, 1994), p. 89.

[2] Bureau of Labor Statistics. *Manufacturing Output per Hour Index*, series prs 30006093.

[3] *The Future of the U.S. Auto Industry: It Can Compete, Can It Survive?* (Washington, DC: Economic Strategy Institute, 1992), p. 8.

[4] Russel B. Scholl. "The International Investment Position of the United States," *Survey of Current Business* (July 1996), p. 43.

[5] An up-to-date, country-by-country, breakdown of ownership of U.S. Treasury securities is not available for Asian countries other than Japan. However, according to the July 1996 issue of *Survey of Current Business*, $211.2 billion in Treasury securities are not allocated by country. Since Asian economies have accumulated hundreds of billions of dollars by running trade surpluses, a large share of these unallocated securities are probably owned by Asians.

[6] *The East Asia Miracle: Economic Growth and Public Policy* (Washington, DC: The World Bank, 1993), p. 2.

[7] James C. Abegglen and George Stalk, Jr., *Kaisha, The Japanese Corporation* (New York: Basic Books, 1985), pp. 126-28.

[8] See C. Fred Bergsten and Marcus Noland, *Reconcilable Differences?* (Washington, DC: Institute for International Economics, 1993); Robert Z. Lawrence, "Closed Markets or Closed Minds?" *Brookings Papers on Economic Activity* 2, pp. 517-54; Robert Z. Lawrence, "How Open Is Japan?" in Paul Krugman, ed., *Trade With Japan* (Chicago: University of Chicago Press, 1991), pp. 9-50; Peter A. Petri, "Japanese Trade in Transition: Hypotheses and Recent Evidence," in Krugman, ed., *Trade With Japan*, pp. 51-84; and Clyde V. Prestowitz, Jr., Lawrence Chimerine, and Paul Willen, *Closing the Trade Gap with Japan* (Washington, DC: Economic Strategy Institute, 1993).

[9] Prestowitz, Jr., et al., *Closing the Trade Gap*, pp. 15-18.

[10] Documents prepared by Dewey Ballantine for Kodak.

[11] Robert A. Blecker, *Beyond Twin Deficits: A Trade Strategy for the 1990s* (Armonk, NY: M.E. Sharpe, 1992).

BARRY BOSWORTH

WHY TRADE WITH ASIA BENEFITS THE U.S. ECONOMY

While there is a long history of negotiations with Japan over access to its markets, the newer issues involve U.S. economic relations with the rest of Asia—particularly the rapidly growing economies of East Asia and China. On the one side are those who see the expansion of the Asian economies as providing large opportunities for increasing trade with the region. They perceive current U.S. foreign economic policy as too preoccupied with trade with other industrialized economies at the cost of missed opportunities to expand the relationship with the dynamic economies of Asia. They also criticize the U.S. policy of linking economic issues with political concerns such as human rights and arms trade, seeing it as ineffective and costly to U.S. trade with the region. Others are more fearful of a perceived competitive threat from low-wage Asian labor; they foresee that many differences over business practices and access to markets that have plagued relations with Japan will dominate the trade agenda with the rest of Asia. They also are not eager to expand economic relations with China, whose internal politics and foreign policies are so contrary to American beliefs and goals.

Many Asian countries are equally unhappy with U.S. policy in the region because the United States is pressuring them to remove remaining restrictions on trade and to provide greater protection of intellectual property rights, and because the United States continues to link political and economic issues in its relations with China. They are angered by the increased emphasis on bilateral negotiations in which the United States plays the roles of both judge and jury and attempts to implement its decisions by threatening smaller economies with loss of access to the U.S. market. Above all, they are concerned about a perceived drift toward greater protectionism in U.S. trade policy.

There has also been a fundamental shift in the balance of economic power that affects the dialogue. For Asia, the United States remains important, but primarily as a market in which to sell products. It offers little that is unique on the production side, and its products are often viewed as inferior to those of other high-technology producers. Trade within Asia, as well as with other regions, has expanded significantly, giving the region one of the most diversified trading patterns in the world. Economic dependency now flows in both directions as the United States needs the savings of Asia to finance its investment needs in the face of ever-declining rates of national saving.

Asia has emerged as the premier center of growth in the global economy since 1980. Excluding Japan, the growth in real GDP has exceeded 5 percent annually since 1980, and the region's share of world trade has tripled to 23 percent. Given its size and growth, the Asian market should be central to U.S. foreign economic policy; suggestions that the United States downplay its linkages to Asia and focus on the stagnating markets of Europe must be in jest. About equal proportions of the region's trade are directed to the United States, Japan, and Europe. The growth of intra-regional trade has far exceeded that with the large industrial centers—Asia is rapidly emerging as a distinct regional economic entity, rather than an appendage of the industrial economies. Complaints of mercantilist behavior seem particularly puzzling given the consistent trade deficits for the region as a whole, the unusually high level of trade for these countries' income levels and geographical distances from markets, and the oft-expressed view of Asia as a center of free-market liberalism.

For the United States, the Asian share of its foreign trade (excluding trade with Japan) has doubled since 1980, and now surpasses the volume of trade with Europe. Combined trade with Japan and the rest of Asia represents about one-third of total U.S. trade. Trade with the region is quite unbalanced, however; in 1995, imports from the region exceeded exports by about $130 billion, or two-thirds of the total U.S. trade deficit. Finally, the role of the developing economies of Asia in the trade of the United States is much different than their role in Japanese trade. The Asian share of total trade is growing for both countries; but it is more pronounced for the United States on the import side, and the magnitude of the trade deficit has steadily grown over time. Meanwhile the opposite is true for Japan: exports to the rest of Asia have grown far faster than imports, and they are an area of rapidly growing trade surplus for Japan.

The basic structure of trade between the developing regions of Asia and the United States is complementary for both economies. The Asian economies produce a range of consumer products—particularly clothing—in which the United States does not have a comparative advantage; and the willingness of the United States to accept these imports from Asia has translated into substantial gains for American consumers. For example, a 1990 survey of purchasing-power parities found clothing prices in the United States to be two-thirds those of Japan and slightly more than half of those in the European Union.[1] These differences are due in no small part to a more liberal U.S. policy toward apparel imports and the general openness of the U.S. market to products from Asia. For the United States, a large proportion of Asian imports reflects the diversion of trade from other alternative low-cost producers.

On the other hand, the high rates of capital formation and the need to expand the transportation and communication infrastructure of the Asian economies should make them ideal markets for U.S. corporations. U.S. firms have not done as well as they might in the area of capital goods exports, but that is not because of lack of access. Other capital good exporters, particularly Japan, have done very well in the Asian market. It seems implausible that Asian governments would discriminate against American firms in competition with Japanese firms. Instead, Japanese exporters appear simply to have outperformed American firms in these markets.

Indeed, the commodity structures of U.S. and Japanese trade with the rest of Asia differ significantly. The large volume of U.S. imports of clothing and miscellaneous manufactures from the region conforms to the expected pattern. At the same time, however, even though more than half of U.S. exports to the region are in the machinery category, machinery imports are even larger—reflecting a high level of intra-industry trade. Japanese exports of machinery products, on the other hand, exceed imports by a factor of five, and trade in miscellaneous manufactures is roughly balanced.

The large differences in the composition of trade appear to reflect the different strategies of U.S. and Japanese multinational firms operating in Asia. The U.S. firms use Asia as a processing base for products that ultimately return for sale in the U.S. market; and they have traditionally been agreeable to local content requirements as a means of obtaining access to markets, operating their affiliates largely independent of any significant purchases from the parent. In contrast, Japanese firms have maintained a focus on local market sales, using the local affiliate as a vehicle to promote exports. For example, exports of U.S. affiliates in the developing economies of Asia back to their parents are about twice as large as their imports from the United States. In the case of Japanese firms, the ratio is reversed.

In summary, Asia is important to the U.S. economy from four different perspectives. It is the fastest growing market for U.S. exports; it has become the center for the labor-intensive assemble portion of the computer and information-processing industries; it is a primary supplier of high-quality, low-cost consumer products; and it has become a major source of financing to cover the shortfall between U.S. savings and domestic investment.

IMPLICATIONS FOR THE UNITED STATES

What are the implications of the U.S.–Asia relationship for the U.S. economy and what should be the goals of American economic policy toward Asia?

The first priority of U.S. policy should be to promote continued rapid growth in the region. It is a severe mistake to believe that the rise of incomes in Asia comes at a cost to Americans. Economic growth is not a zero-sum game—American wealth is not based on the poverty of others and Americans will gain from the expansion of markets for their products. Over any significant time period, the volume of U.S. exports to Asia will be dominated by growth in the total market rather than variations in its market share. For example, since 1980, U.S. exports to Asia have grown twice as fast as trade with other regions despite a small decline in its share of the market. Capital goods, information processing, and communications are areas of substantial American comparative advantage, and they are products with high income elasticities. Thus growth of the market for these products will depend primarily on the rate of overall economic advance in the region; and expansion of the market for American products allows the United States to extend its own comparative advantage.

In theory, U.S. workers could lose from growth in Asia if it diverts capital from the United States, lowering the productivity of American workers. However, since Asian growth has brought with it a high rate of saving, there has been no diversion of capital—in fact, investment in the U.S. has fallen much less than expected given the decline in domestic saving, precisely because investors have been able to borrow from Asia.

Alternatively, some low-skilled American workers could lose from an expansion of trade with Asia just as they lose from a general opening to the global economy. Increased trade, or openness to the global economy, probably plays some role in reducing the domestic demand for, and thus the wages of, low-skilled workers in the United States. Low-skilled workers are relatively more plentiful in the world economy than in the United States, and it is expectable that trade will somewhat equalize wages for workers of similar skill. The decline in the wages of low-skilled U.S. workers, however, is balanced by an increase in the wages of high-skilled workers, who are relatively more scarce in the global economy. Although it is true that the net gains to the winners will exceed the losses to the losers, we should not pretend that everyone in the United States gains from trade. This is a general statement about trade, however, that is of no special import for trade with Asia. Furthermore, the empirical studies suggest that, in practice, trade has had a relatively minor influence on the widening gap in wages—perhaps accounting for 25 percent of the change over the past two decades.[2] The worsening wage distribution reflects more pervasive trends in technology and a general failure on the supply side to upgrade the skills of workers who do not go on to higher education. It would be absurd for the United States to pass up the larger gains from trade in a futile effort to reserve a pool of low-wage jobs for the unskilled. It would be far cheaper to simply bribe the losers.

Second, U.S. trade policy toward Asia should avoid focusing on individual bilateral trade balances. The notion that bilateral trade flows should be balanced reflects a serious misunderstanding of the benefits of a global trading system. While several Asian economies are less open to trade than is the United States, the extent of their openness is not related in a systematic fashion to the U.S. trade deficit. The trade deficit is a macroeconomic phenomenon driven by the domestic imbalance of saving and investment in the United States. In fact, the United States has a trade deficit with every major region of the world. Given the implausibility of a global conspiracy against the United States, the trade deficit should be viewed as a reflection of the domestic economic situation, not other countries' trade restrictions. If the unwillingness of others to accept U.S. exports were a significant problem, the domestic economy would be plagued by unemployment, and the monetary authorities would be seeking to lower domestic interest rates in an effort to stimulate demand. Instead, the United States is essentially operating at full capacity, with the central bank raising interest rates in an effort to hold down demand pressures. Also exports have consistently exceeded the growth in the economy as a whole. In sum, the United States simply does not fit the profile of an economy plagued with insufficient demand for its products; instead it runs trade deficits because of a persistent desire to spend more than it earns.

The emergence of an international financial system is of great benefit to American business firms, which are no longer constrained in their investments by the inadequate level of domestic saving. The reliance on foreign financing to fill the gap between domestic investment and national saving is also good for American workers because the added capital raises their productivity. But the decision to permit foreign capital inflows brings with it a global trade deficit for the United States.

The continued failure of American politicians to understand the relationship between a nation's current account or trade deficit and the domestic imbalance of saving and investment continues to plague U.S. trade policy. Policymakers see the trade deficit as a measure of the extent of the foreign conspiracy against the United States rather than as a reflection of the domestic economy. While it is important to recognize that the current account deficit is indicative of an important national problem—the low rate of national saving—abolishing the indicator does not solve the problem.

Furthermore, given the existence of an aggregate trade deficit, it is unclear that any importance should be attached to how it is distributed among the various trading partners. It is true that a large portion of the trade deficit is reflected in the bilateral balance with Japan and Asia, but it is the only region of the world with the overall surplus of domestic saving over investment required to generate a trade surplus. Both Europe and Latin America now have net saving shortfalls, and the prior surplus of Organization of Petroleum Exporting Countries (OPEC) has disappeared.

Third, the United States should make a general reduction in trade barriers a major goal of U.S. foreign economic policy. The United States clearly would benefit from reductions of trade barriers in the Asian economies but it must clearly understand that a policy that substitutes bilateral negotiations for multilateral fora could have only limited gains and potentially significant costs. In an open, competitive global market the costs of trade restrictions by individual countries fall largely on their own citizens; to the extent that outsiders benefit from trade liberalization, those benefits are spread over all of the trading partners. In the case of Asia, the U.S. share of the market is about 15 percent. Furthermore, since trade liberalization is unlikely to have major effects on the saving-investment balance of either the United States or Asia, the increase in exports will need to be matched by an equal increase in imports. That is, trade liberalization will neither increase nor decrease the total number of jobs, but it will change their distribution. On net balance, the reallocation of employment from import-competing to export industries implies a net efficiency gain for the United States, but the magnitude is not large.

A primary reason for favoring a multilateral framework for trade negotiations is that in bilateral negotiations the United States will experience some costs, even if only in the form of increased ill-will in the other country, yet will only receive a small portion of the benefits. The United States could be more effective by trying to build a consensus in support of its views throughout Asia—what might be described as "the highest common denominator"—rather than acting unilaterally and seeing its actions undermined by allies that do not agree.

Fourth, the claim that Asian governments have used industrial policies to promote their growth in the past does not suggest that it is a good idea for the United States to adopt similar measures under the rubric of "strategic trade policy." Nor is there any reason to suggest that the United States should trade only with countries whose institutions are similar to our own. The current discussion of strategic trade sounds like a recycled version of the concept of "industrial policy" and it raises many of the same problems.[3] There continues to be considerable debate about whether the high rates of Asian economic growth have been due to or in spite of "state-guided capitalism." As illustrated by Japan's current difficulties, governments can often be wrong. In fact, the most significant factor in the Asian countries' success has not been the role of government but the willingness of their populations to save and invest much larger portions of their incomes than other countries.

More fundamentally, however, there is no reason to limit trade to economic systems with similar or identical institutions—to a large extent, nations trade because they are different. And, quite apart from the question of what system is best for Asia, the United States should not change its policy of a minimal role for government in markets unless the alternative is better suited to American society. As pointed out by Charles Schultze, the notion of picking and choosing among American firms and regions based on some efficiency criteria is incompatible with the American political system.[4] Everything we know about our government reinforces the argument against micromanagement of the economy.

Finally, for economic issues of significance, such as increasing the standard of living of Americans and distributing the resulting gains, the debate over trade policy, or more specifically an Asian trade policy, is a diversion. Increases in the incomes of Americans are fundamentally tied to gains in their own productivity and what happens in the domestic economy. Americans produce 85 percent of the goods and services they consume, and increases in the productivity with which we produce exports yield equivalent benefits in the form of more imports. There is no evidence to support the argument that the reduced growth in productivity after 1973 is somehow linked to the trading system. The growth slowdown has been global in its dimensions, as large for nontradables as for tradables, and unrelated to any change in the industry distribution of production. The economic problems of the United States are largely domestic in origin—the lack of physical capital accumulation and a deteriorating system of secondary education and job training for those who do not attend college. Americans need many things, but an Asian trade policy is not one of them.

NOTES

[1] OECD, *Purchasing Power Parities and Real Expenditures* (Paris: OECD, 1992).

[2] Jeffrey Sachs and Howard Shatz, "Trade and Jobs in U.S. Manufacturing," *Brookings Papers on Economic Activity* 1 (1994), pp. 1-84.

[3] In 1982, Robert Reich and Ira Magaziner described their support for industrial policy: "We suggest that U.S. companies and the government develop a coherent and coordinated industrial policy whose aim is to raise the real income of our citizens by improving the patterns of our investments rather than by focusing only on aggregate investment levels." *Minding America's Business: The Decline and Rise of the American Economy* (New York: Harcourt Brace Jovanovich, 1982), p. 4. This sounds very similar to current calls for a coordinated trade policy.

[4] Charles Schultze, "Industrial Policy: A Dissent," *The Brookings Review* (Fall 1983).

CHALMERS JOHNSON

ENDING JAPAN'S PROTECTORATE STATUS

Japanese-American relations today remain almost totally unchanged from the structure forged in 1960, when the Japanese-American Security Treaty was last negotiated and ratified by the legislatures of both countries. Despite the end of the Cold War in Europe, the collapse of the Soviet Union, China's and Russia's recognition of the Republic of Korea (i.e., South Korea), China's shift in development strategy to emulation of the capitalist developmental states of East Asia, Japan's achievement of a more than $5 trillion economy, and the emergence of the Regional Forum (ARF) of the Association of South East Asian Nations (ASEAN) as a truly indigenous institution for the maintenance of security and stability in the Pacific, the *status quo ante* prevails. Nonetheless, the facade of stability in Japanese-American relations has started to unravel.

In the summer of 1995, two things happened. First, the fiasco of the Japanese-American auto agreement, hammered out in the middle of the night in Geneva, signified the need for new American thinking on Japan. The American threat to impose almost $6 billion worth of trade sanctions on imported Japanese luxury automobiles proved to be hollow, and neither the threat nor the agreement that was reached was part of an integrated strategy toward the superpower of the Pacific. The seeming concessions Japan made at the final moment—to manufacture more cars in Japanese-owned plants in North America and perhaps to buy some more American auto parts were already in the works, dictated by the high value of the yen rather than by anything the American negotiators said or did. Japan was the clear victor in this episode between the two increasingly estranged allies.

Meanwhile, on September 4, 1995, two U.S. marines and a sailor kidnapped and raped a twelve-year-old Okinawan schoolgirl.

This incident proved important not because it was unusual—American military personnel, who today make up some 4.2 percent of the Okinawan population, commit 11.5 percent of the murders, rapes, and robberies there—but because it exemplified the sacrifices the Security Treaty set-up demands without anything comparable in terms of benefits. The rape also brought into being a reactionary Pentagon-Kasumigaseki axis determined to do everything in its power to preserve the old American Cold War protectorate over Japan and the vested interests built up around it (particularly American arms sales to Japan). This covert pressure group was at least temporarily successful. Because of inattentive publics and timid leaders in both Japan and the United States, the American military and the Japanese state bureaucracy were able to camouflage their intentions through the pretense of policy initiatives—APEC meetings, promises of reform in Okinawa, and innumerable bilateral "summit" meetings. But the drift toward containment and possible war with China and a structure of Japanese-American relations built on a badly outdated division of labor remain the most likely causes of instability and insecurity in post–Cold War East Asia.

Japan profited more from the Cold War than any other nation. It has every incentive to try to perpetuate its Cold War relationship with the United States as long as possible. During the Cold War, fearing that Japan might be tempted toward neutralism and wanting to use Japan as a model of development to counter the appeal of Chinese communism in Asia, the United States allowed Japan to rig its domestic market in ways that it permitted no other ally. The United States also encouraged Japan to export to the American market, and it facilitated the transfer to Japan of a vast array of American technologies—even though Japan refused to allow the American owners of these technologies to invest in Japan or to sell their products directly to Japanese consumers. This trade-off between security and economic development was part of a fundamental American grand strategy against communism in Asia, but it unintentionally contributed to the enrichment of East Asia, which the Cold War disguised. Whether the Americans acknowledge it or not, that enrichment, today self-sustaining, is the most important problem for U.S. foreign policy.

In return for supporting and tolerating Japanese mercantilism, Japan gave the United States basing rights; close to 50,000 American troops are still stationed in Japan today—more than fifty years after the end of World War II—and another 37,000 in South

Korea. Japan also passively supported American foreign policy in East Asia, even when it disagreed with the United States (as over China and Vietnam). Japan has no incentive to change these relationships. From its own point of view, Japan adjusted to the world created by its conqueror, and it well remembers the long years of American condescension about Japan's economic growth—as well as American suppression of evidence concerning the cartels (called *keiretsu* in Japan), political corruption, extortionate consumer prices, and non-tariff-barriers to imports that helped achieve high-speed economic growth. The classic example of American condescension was John Foster Dulles's Cold War remark that the Japanese might succeed in exporting to the United States shirts, pajamas, and perhaps cocktail napkins.[1]

In short, the Americans helped create and nurture what is today their single most important competitor, and they are still befuddled by what to do about Japan now that the Cold War is over. It was precisely this situation that American voters expected a president elected on the slogan of "It's the economy, stupid" to address. Yet beyond the midpoint of the second Clinton Administration, America's Asia policy is still a muddle. Even though the disastrous U.S. trade deficit is caused almost entirely by imports from Japan, China, and Taiwan, the Clinton Administration still appoints lawyers and economists to deal with it rather than people with language ability and experience in China and Japan. Mickey Kantor and Charlene Barshefsky, Clinton's U.S. Trade Representatives, are in a long tradition of on-the-job trained USTRs that extends back at least to the Carter Administration's Robert Strauss, who ended up working as a lawyer for Japanese investors in the United States. Even though the Clinton Administration proclaimed that it was taking Japan seriously, there has been no coordination among its various policies, no coherence to any individual policy, and no long-term vision of how to adjust to the rise of both Japanese and Chinese power in the Pacific. There was only the illusion of policy, manipulated by media specialists for short-term political effect.

In February 1995, the Department of Defense unilaterally pledged to keep 100,000 U.S. troops in Japan and Korea for the next twenty years. This had the effect of giving up the United States' only real leverage in the area, since it signaled to Japan's trade negotiators that they could hang tough without endangering America's security guarantee. That is exactly what Ryutaro Hashimoto, then Japan's negotiator and now Prime Minister, did in the auto talks.

The administration also fought hard to get the Uruguay Round of trade negotiations completed in the face of dogged Japanese resistance only to see the Japanese use the resulting World Trade Organization against the United States in the auto negotiations. At home, the Republican Party threatened to gut what little support the U.S. government gives its own industries by trying to abolish the Department of Commerce; and the Republican "Contract with America," which in 1994 brought the Republicans to power in Congress, nowhere mentioned international trade or international investment. Such a contract is somewhat like a political platform in 1954 that failed to mention world communism or the Cold War.

Given all these mixed signals, the Japanese could be forgiven for wondering why Trade Representative Kantor threatened them with sanctions on luxury cars and, then, on Kodak film. They explained it to themselves in terms of political payoffs to domestic American industries and not as basic American foreign policy.

Over the past quarter-century the United States has only twice succeeded in changing the environment of Japanese economic decision-making. The first was the "Nixon Shocks," carried out by President Richard Nixon and Treasury Secretary John Connally in 1971 to force Japan to give up its artificially undervalued yen. The second was the semiconductor agreement of 1987. It is worth recalling that in 1987 the American semiconductor industry was headed for the same graveyard in which the whole American consumer electronics industry is buried. This situation was turned around by the semiconductor agreement, which demanded and got 20 percent of the Japanese market for imports, and by domestic company reforms, including the creation of a joint research consortium. Today both Japan and the United States enjoy thriving semiconductor industries, and the competition between them gives rise to innovations and price reductions throughout world.

It is therefore surprising that the Japanese have vowed never again to enter into such an agreement, and American newspapers such as the *Wall Street Journal* and the *New York Times* editorialize against negotiated market shares among different kinds of capitalist systems. This suggests that the Japanese in 1987 actually intended to destroy the American semiconductor industry rather than achieve a healthy trading relationship with the United States, and that Americans are still so deluded by economic ideology they are unable to recognize their own occasional successes.

The fundamental American error in the auto talks of 1995 was to enter into negotiations at all. It would have been better if the Clinton Administration had just imposed tariffs on imported luxury cars. The Japanese have for years been advising the Americans that they consume too much and save too little and that the Japanese-American trade imbalance is caused by poor macroeconomic fundamentals in the United States. Starting to cut consumption of Japanese luxury cars might have been an excellent symbol of what needs to be done in the automotive industry and elsewhere in the American economy. In any case, the auto talks were never really about automobiles, since the Americans gave away more than a quarter of their domestic automotive market to the Japanese twenty years ago. A few more assembly jobs in Japanese factories in the Midwest today will never compensate for the jobs lost when the Midwest was turned into the first American "rust belt."

There is also great danger for Americans in accepting negotiated "deals" that are vague and unenforceable. Discovering that the U.S. government itself had no record in any department or agency of all the trade agreements it had signed with Japan, the American Chamber of Commerce in Japan has recently compiled as many as it could on an informal, private basis. It also discovered that almost none of them were actually implemented.[2] A good example of what frustrated American businessmen are talking about was the construction industry agreement of 1993—one of the more than two dozen agreements for which the Clinton Administration proudly takes credit. Even if one wants to blame the American automobile industry for not building good cars tailored to the Japanese market, there is no question that the American construction, engineering, and architecture industry is among the most experienced and successful in the world. Japan is the site of some of the largest public works projects in the world and will continue to be that well into the next century.

The Los Angeles and Kobe earthquakes of 1994 and 1995, respectively, revealed that the Americans build better freeways than the domestic Japanese construction industry does; and anyone who has ever flown into Tokyo's Narita Airport knows that the Japanese could use some help with airports. And yet, despite the 1993 agreement, the American construction industry has been totally shut out of this market.

In June 1995, the Austin Construction Company announced that it was closing its last office in Japan, having managed to win just one significant project after six years in the market. Only two

American firms remain in Japan—with no work to do. Meanwhile, President Bill Clinton's first ambassador to Japan and his wife were photographed with officials of Obayashi Construction getting ready to reconstruct the ambassador's residence. It seems that the Americans cannot even find an American contractor to build their own embassy buildings. (Actually, this was a fine example of how the Japanese construction industry rigs bids: since Obayashi was the firm that rebuilt the embassy after the war, no firm was allowed to bid against it.)

With the collapse of the auto negotiations, the Clinton Administration abandoned any further pretense of an economic strategy toward Japan and shifted instead toward a renewed emphasis on threats to military security and the Japanese-American Security Treaty. As already noted, in February 1995, the Department of Defense issued a report unilaterally committing the United States to the forward deployment of 100,000 American troops in Japan and Korea until the year 2015. In other words, in the face of all evidence, the Defense Department declared that nothing essential has changed in East Asia over the past thirty-five years and that the United States' policy should be to freeze relations in the Pacific for at least the next twenty years. The Clinton Administration warmly embraced this perspective and turned over the administration of U.S. foreign policy in East Asia to the Pentagon.

To many East Asians, this new emphasis signals that the Americans do not really understand how hollow their superpower pretensions are, and that Japan and China have a few more years to consolidate their ascendancy before letting the Americans know that they are no longer even marginally useful. The Department of Defense's report also ignores the profound shift that is occurring around the world, particularly in East Asia, from military to economic power. The rape incident in Okinawa brought these issues to a boil, but any other incident—the crash of a fighter plane, an oil spill, or further pressure toward making the Asians pay for American troops—would have the same effect.

When the United States signed its first postwar security treaty with Japan in 1951, Japan still had a devastated economy and was in the last stages of American military occupation. Communists had swept into power two years earlier in China; the Korean War was in full swing; and the yen was 360 to the dollar. Today, Japan has the most modern industrial structure in the world; it has not run a trade deficit with the United States for almost three decades; the dollar has lost nearly 80 percent of its original postwar value against the yen; and Japan faces no known military threat.

A more imaginative administration might have re-evaluated America's strategic interests in Japan in light of long-term changes in strategic and economic trends. It might then have concluded that a regional balance of power among China, Japan, and ASEAN, maintained in part by the United States in return for greater American participation in the Asian economy, was needed for the next century. Instead, as the United States attempts to reassure the region with its continuing defense commitment, the economic factors creating a more independent Asia are exposing the frailty of the U.S. position.

The United States should also recognize that its outdated security policy does not encourage a healthier liberal democracy in Japan, but instead strengthens reactionary, narrow-minded political leadership. This type of leadership is by no means a uniquely Japanese predicament. But the collective amnesia of Japan's political class on the subject of the Pacific War—and this cuts across all generational lines—should be as disturbing to the United States as it is to Japan's Asian neighbors. Hashimoto—the man who negotiated with Kantor over automobiles and was subsequently rewarded with the prime ministership of Japan—is neither a friend of the United States nor a liberal. He headed the Liberal Democratic Party (LDP) faction that on the fiftieth anniversary of the end of World War II watered down the official apology that Japan tendered its Asian neighbors for harm done to them. (Instead of apologizing, Hashimoto and his band of 270 parliamentary followers said they would "reflect" (*hansei*) on Japan's conduct. And they continue to insist that Japan's real wartime mission was to liberate Asians from white colonialism while they ignore Japanese colonialism in Korea.)

This sort of public amnesia is in part made possible by Japan's protectorate status. Unlike the Germans, Japan's political leaders have never had to integrate their views into the confines of an alliance based on shared risks with their former enemies. Whereas Germany entered the NATO alliance in May 1955, the United States colluded with Japan's leaders to devote the country exclusively to economic growth—at the expense of developing a system of equal responsibilities in the U.S.–Japan security arrangement.

The legacy of this Cold War arrangement is also seen in Japan's continuing internal debate over what it means to become an "ordinary country" (*futsu no kuni*), in the words of Ichiro Ozawa, leader of the main opposition (but nonetheless conservative) party. To

Ozawa, this means a country with a balanced portfolio of economic, technological, military, and other forms of power, used in concert with its allies and under firm control of the nation's political leaders. In 1993, the end of the thirty-eight years of uninterrupted rule by the (conservative to reactionary) Liberal Democratic Party reopened discussion of the need for Japan to become an "ordinary country" and the hitherto taboo topics of sovereignty, citizenship, and national responsibility. This debate was last attempted and then foreclosed in 1960, when the Security Treaty riots forced President Dwight Eisenhower to cancel his proposed visit to Japan (the first U.S. president ever to visit Japan was Gerald Ford).

The U.S. commitment to maintain troops and bases in Japan well into the twenty-first century short-circuits this renewed internal debate and instead signals America's total lack of confidence in the ability of Japan ever to become an ordinary country. But Japan's failure to do so could produce the very instability that the Defense Department claims it wants to avoid.

If Washington understood East Asia to the same extent that it understands Europe, policies would have been adopted long ago to preclude today's problems. It would have encouraged a more balanced Japanese approach to foreign policy options in East Asia and ensured that Japan was thoroughly integrated into an international alliance system. Over time, this would have encouraged the development of a robust cadre of foreign affairs specialists among Japan's politicians. Instead, the Japanese Diet remains a largely venal and parochial debating club that only rarely takes an interest in influencing Japan's international policies.

Instead of a new strategy, the Defense Department's report is actually a sign of the United States' policy bankruptcy. Americans still do not recognize that Cold War–style military power is today relevant to only a small and narrowing spectrum of policy problems and that it is an illusion to suppose the opposite. The real danger for the United States in the post–Cold War world is armed impotence. Nowhere is this more true than in the new global economic center of gravity, East Asia.

The ticking timebomb in this situation is the massive U.S. military presence in Okinawa. On September 8, 1996, more than 500,000 Okinawans voted that they wanted the U.S. bases on their islands scaled back. This plebiscite was aimed as much at the government in Tokyo as at the Americans, since both bear a large burden of responsibility and blame for a situation that the Okinawans have now endured for over fifty years.

The Battle of Okinawa was the first of four great betrayals that the 1.3 million Okinawans experienced between 1945 and the present. (The Ryukyu Islands were actually an independent kingdom until they were annexed by Japan in 1879.) Even though the Japanese Emperor knew in February 1945 that the war was lost, he ordered one last great battle (not fought on the Japanese mainland) to buy time to negotiate for better surrender terms for the Imperial institution. The strategy worked—Hirohito survived Japan's defeat—but the Okinawans paid the price with over 200,000 killed. It was the bloodiest battle of World War II.

The second great betrayal occurred in 1952, when Japan won an early peace treaty from the United States but with a price attached: the United States wanted to maintain its military occupation of Okinawa indefinitely. The Okinawans therefore remained a stateless people—neither Japanese nor American citizens—and Okinawa itself remained under military rule.

By the late 1960s, Okinawa was being used as the main U.S. launching pad for the Vietnam War. The island bristled with nuclear rockets, nerve gas storage sites, and B-52 bombers. This led to violent Okinawan protests and the third betrayal of the Okinawans by Japan and the United States. In 1972, a deal was struck whereby Okinawa was returned to Japanese rule; but all of the U.S. bases remained—essentially still beyond either Japanese or Okinawan administration.

This situation came to a head in February 1995, when the Pentagon issued the so-called Nye Report, which said that the Americans intended to maintain the status quo in East Asia for yet another twenty years regardless of the disappearance of the threats that had been used to justify it for the previous fifty years. Precisely what this would entail for Okinawans was then dramatically illustrated on September 4 by the rape incident.

This brings us to the fourth and most recent betrayal—the Clinton-Hashimoto summit of April 1996—in which the two countries pretended to offer Okinawa relief. Futenma Marine Corps Air Station would be closed, they said, but only if it could be moved to another location in Japan. Both governments knew that no other place in Japan would take such a facility and that Futenma would simply end up being moved (if at all) somewhere else in Okinawa.

The American military prattles on about the U.S. role as a lone superpower and the importance of maintaining a "presence" in Asia. But presence on the ground is not nearly as important as access.

The United States' greatest military contribution to maintaining peace and stability in East Asia is its ability to project power over long distances with its navy. Ultimately, the United States does not need foreign bases so much as access and ports of call for the Seventh Fleet. This is in fact what former President George Bush arranged with the government of Singapore after the Philippines forced the closing of Subic Bay. Given the growing airlift capacity afforded by the C-17 aircraft, even the Seventh Fleet is a wasting asset. If during the Gulf War the United States was able to move nine infantry divisions halfway around the world, there is no reason today to have U.S. marines still based in Okinawa.

Most of the U.S. facilities in Okinawa should be handed back to the Okinawans: the docks at Naha (already promised to them in 1974), Futenma Marine Corps Air Station (promised to them by Clinton and Hashimoto in 1996), and Camp Hansen and the other bases devoted to ground forces. Kadena Air Force Base should be scaled back to realistic defensive deployments.

At the present time, the U.S. and Japanese governments are colluding in the dangerous pretense that everything is and will be fine. The U.S. Department of Defense contends that the security and stability that East Asia enjoys today were created by the presence of an American military expeditionary force of at least 100,000 troops, and that future security and stability in the area depend on its remaining forward-deployed there. Contrary to this self-serving view, the overwhelming evidence of the past fifty years is that security and stability came to the region because of high-speed economic growth, not the presence of foreign troops.

The United States of course did contribute to the enrichment of East Asia, but not primarily through its wars, armies, or diplomats. The main contribution of the United States was its markets. The United States bought the high-quality, low-cost manufactured goods—first from Japan, then from Japan's first emulators (South Korea, Taiwan, Hong Kong, and Singapore), and most recently from Southeast Asia and Mainland China. What happens when the United States can no longer serve as absorber of other nations' gross surpluses of production or as the market of last resort is in fact much more relevant to the security and stability of East Asia than the presence there of token American ground forces.

What is equally important for those who want to argue that U.S. troops kept the Cold War from spreading in East Asia is that the Cold War in its primary European meaning of democracy versus totalitarianism never truly fit East Asia. The United States in postwar Asia only rarely championed democracy, preferring instead to support anti-communist dictators such as Chiang Kai-shek in Taiwan, Syngman Rhee in South Korea, Ferdinand Marcos in the Philippines, and Nguyen Van Thieu in Vietnam—whereas the communist revolutions in China, North Korea, Vietnam, and Malaya all had their roots in movements for national liberation from European, American, and Japanese colonialism. These wars of national liberation under communist auspices are now over, and in places such as China and Vietnam the Communist Parties that led the revolutions are being forced to replace Marxism-Leninism as their source of legitimacy with nationalism and economic development. Only vestiges of these wars of national liberation in East Asia remain today—the continuing division of Korea, the reversion of Hong Kong to Chinese sovereignty, the anomalous status of Taiwan, and Chinese irredentist claims to Tibet and the South China Sea.

Meanwhile, the big issue confronting the United States and Japan is how to adjust to the emergence of China as a genuine superpower. Both countries object to many aspects of Chinese policy, such as its nuclear testing, lack of respect for human rights, and military intimidation of Taiwan. But neither country is willing to forego the economic gains that come from cooperating with China on China's terms.

Japan's policy is simply to do everything it can to get along with China and leave any disciplining of China to the Americans. It is also prepared opportunistically to exploit any divisions that happen to arise between China and the United States.

A policy of containment toward China, which Japan and the United States give the appearance of forging in practice while denying in public, implies the possibility of war—just as it did during the Cold War vis-a-vis the USSR. The balance of terror may have prevented war between the United States and the USSR, but in the case of China, great asymmetries in military power between China and any single external power or alliance will always exist. Chinese nationalism and the Chinese people's acute sense of having been victimized by both the West and Japan provide the Chinese government with a firm foundation for resistance to external threats. A war with China would almost certainly bankrupt the United States, radicalize China, and either tear Japan apart or find it sitting on the sidelines.

Military containment of China is a particularly dangerous policy for Japan to espouse, since its own emergence on the world's stage began almost exactly a century ago with its invasion and defeat of China and its seizure of China's territory of Taiwan. Moreover, because Japan's devastation of China in the 1930s and 1940s was the key ingredient that brought the Chinese Communist Party to power, no politically sentient Chinese can ever fully forgive the Japanese. Japan's failure to come to grips with this legacy by, for example, not officially acknowledging and apologizing for its killing of thousands of civilians in China's capital, Nanking, in 1937, has not helped matters.

U.S. policy toward China is equally fraught with issues that might explode at any time. The biggest potential international scandal facing the Clinton Administration concerns suspicions that campaign contributions from rich Asian businessmen influenced its policy toward both Taiwan and the Mainland. The lack of an American policy toward China was also revealed in China's heavy-handed pressure on the Disney Company to suppress a movie about the life of the Dalai Lama that China dislikes. Disney claimed to stand up to Chinese pressure and maintained that it would go ahead with the film, but two weeks later it fired its president, who had sponsored the film in the first place.

Japan and the United States desperately need to agree on and coordinate their policies toward China. But thus far there is no sign whatsoever that they are doing so. Instead both countries are drifting, waiting for some incident to set a new agenda for them. This incident could be the aftermath of Hong Kong's reversion to Chinese rule on June 30, 1997. The world waits to see whether China's hand-picked new leader of Hong Kong, the shipping tycoon Tung Chee-hwa, can maintain the trust of both Beijing and the people of Hong Kong.

The incident could also be Taiwan, which remains today what it has been since the late 1940s: the single most potentially explosive issue in international relations in the Pacific. In 1949, the Chinese Communists under Mao Zedong defeated the Chinese Nationalists under Chiang Kai-shek and drove Chiang's Nationalists into exile on Taiwan. Nonetheless, both the Communists and Nationalists insist there is only one China and that Taiwan is a part of it. They disagree on who should rule that one China. In their great strategic initiative to recognize these historical developments in Asia, President Richard Nixon and Secretary of State Henry Kissinger acknowledged this situation. A few years later, President Jimmy Carter recognized Beijing and broke relations with Taipei. From

China's point of view, Taiwan today is sort of like a Chinese Texas—a place that would like to go its own way but knows that if it did so, it would present an unavoidable challenge to the sovereignty of the United States.

Over the years the Taiwanese have become the second richest people in Asia after the Japanese. Many Taiwanese businessmen are also investing heavily in Mainland China. Many others want to break free from the Mainland and declare their independence. With the death of the original Nationalist exiles and the assimilation of their children, a popular democratization movement is occurring in Taiwan.

Unfortunately, any Mainland Chinese regime that acquiesced in the independence of Taiwan would be overthrown. With the collapse of European and Russian communism, China has turned to Chinese nationalism for its legitimacy. "Remember Taiwan" could be as powerful a rallying cry in contemporary China as "Remember the Alamo" was in the United States at a comparable stage of its development. Many Chinese already believe that President Clinton wants a military alliance with Japan (Taiwan's former colonial overlord) in order to contain China and allow Taiwan to declare its independence.

Meanwhile, U.S. domestic politics has offered Taiwan an opportunity to use its wealth to influence American public opinion. In 1995, the Taiwan Lobby spent $4.5 million to engineer virtually unanimous votes in both the Senate and the House of Representatives to invite Taiwan's president, Lee Teng-hui, to visit the United States under the pretext of attending an alumni meeting at Cornell University. The Mainland Chinese government was infuriated that the White House permitted this, and everything that has happened since then—the Pentagon's dominant role in making U.S. policy in East Asia, the mounting evidence of influence-buying by rich Asians—has only deepened Chinese suspicions.

Thus the stage is set for a real mess. The Chinese are willing to give the Taiwanese a great deal of autonomy as long as they do not cause China to lose face by declaring their independence; and Japanese public opinion will never support Japan's entering into a war with China over Taiwan. If the United States allows itself to be entrapped in such a war, it will certainly destroy the Japanese-American alliance. There is no military "solution" to the Taiwan problem, and all sides need to recognize that resort to force is not a serious option.

Nonetheless, on June 7, 1997, in Honolulu, U.S. and Japanese military officials released to the press New Defense Guidelines outlining Japan's role in support of U.S. forces in the next war. They did not say which nation or nations might be their enemy or whether such a war was likely to occur unless they themselves provoked it. But their war planning went ahead anyway. Publication of the Guidelines instantaneously generated crises in Tokyo, Seoul, and Beijing. All three countries wanted to know why the Americans were forcing reluctant Japanese into unwanted and constitutionally illegal military roles. Tokyo papers gave over most of their front and editorial pages to detailing and analyzing the Guidelines. But the American press ignored the story. In a three-sentence "World in Brief" item on June 9, the *Los Angeles Times* noted opaquely that "Top officials from the [Japanese] Foreign Ministry and Defense Agency were scheduled to arrive in Beijing today to explain new security arrangements between Tokyo and Washington that would give Japan its highest military profile since World War II."

These arrangements are the fruit of the Clinton-Hashimoto summit meeting in Tokyo of April 1996, during which the two leaders pretended to respond to Okinawan protests against American bases while committing the two nations to an enhanced military alliance. The new Defense Guidelines are supposed to replace the old Japanese-American strategy drawn up nineteen years earlier against the Soviet Union.

But who is the enemy today? The Guidelines say, "The fundamental framework of the U.S.–Japan alliance will remain unchanged" and "the United States will maintain its nuclear deterrent capacity, its forward deployed forces in the Asia-Pacific region, and other forces capable of reinforcing those forward deployed forces." Given that the American people have been neither informed nor consulted, it is likely that the Guidelines could not withstand a real test.

For example, under the general heading "Cooperation in Situations in Areas Surrounding Japan," the Guidelines propose that "the [Japanese] Self-Defense Forces will conduct such activities as intelligence gathering, surveillance and minesweeping, to protect lives and property and to ensure navigational safety. U.S. Forces will conduct operations to restore peace and security in the areas surrounding Japan." This means that if a threat ever did arise, American lives would be at risk while the Japanese conducted "intelligence activities." Meanwhile, Japanese commentators are anxious that even minesweeping and intelligence activities would go well beyond what their "peace constitution" allows.

China thinks that the agreement is part of an American-Japanese plot to contain it while allowing Taiwan to declare its independence. The South Koreans have said that no matter what happens on their peninsula, they do not want help of any sort from the Japanese. The *Asahi Shimbun* editorialized on June 9 that the agreement reflects a "Cold War mentality," ignores Japan's constitution, and subordinates Japanese interests to U.S. foreign policy.

The United States needs to craft a new, post–Cold War policy toward Japan. Elements in it should include a revision of the Japanese-American Security Treaty (last modified in 1960), strong incentives for the Japanese government finally to make trans-Pacific trade ***mutually*** beneficial, and further attention in the United States to fiscal reform and industrial and educational development. Without that, the relationship will continue to deteriorate, with periods of drift and inattention punctuated by bitter and unproductive disputes such as the auto talks or embarrassing revelations of American colonial pretensions such as the Okinawan rape incident. Since the American public seems totally resistant to attempts to mobilize it to the changed environment in East Asia and American political elites are devoted to achieving short-term political advantages, it is proper to predict that, *ceteris paribus*, the situation in East Asia today will continue to evolve toward relations of conflict.

NOTES

[1] See John Hunter Boyle, *Modern Japan: The American Nexus* (New York: Harcourt, Brace, Jovanovich, 1993), p. 352.

[2] See *Making Trade Talks Work: Lessons from Recent History* (Tokyo: ACCJ, 1997).

MIKE M. MOCHIZUKI

A NEW U.S.–JAPAN SECURITY BARGAIN

To identify America's economic and security interests in Japan and to determine the best way to promote these interests, one must first have an accurate picture of Japan's international orientation and behavior. For five decades, Japan's mercantile realism has treated economics and security as two sides of the same coin.[1] Economically, Japan protected its markets from foreign competition while both taking advantage of U.S. markets to pursue an aggressive export-growth strategy and acquiring American technology to move up the technological ladder. In terms of security, Japan relied upon the U.S. defense commitment and provided the United States access to bases on its territories in return. This arrangement obviated the need to spend huge sums on the military and facilitated Japan's reentry into the international community. It even made the victims of Japanese aggression in East Asia more receptive to Japan's economic revival. Japanese leaders shrewdly saw that, because it was interested in having Japan serve as the main bulwark against the spread of communism in East Asia, the United States would tolerate bilateral asymmetries in market access in order to facilitate Japan's economic reconstruction.

As Japan moved to the economic forefront, its leaders responded in a piecemeal fashion to U.S. pressures and incrementally recalibrated the basic bilateral bargain in order to sustain it. In the economic sphere, Japan lowered tariffs, adopted voluntary export restraints, and accepted voluntary import-expansion agreements. In the security sphere, it gradually built up and modernized its defense capabilities, participated in joint exercises, and increased its host-nation support for U.S. forces. Although economics and security were integrated in a comprehensive strategy, Japanese leaders usually tried to keep these two policy arenas separate when dealing with their American counterparts.[2] They did not want bilateral economic tensions to spill over to the security relationship. Therefore, Japanese negotiators would give in marginally at the eleventh hour to appease U.S. negotiators on the economic front. But these accommodations did not mean that Japan agreed to a wholesale opening of its economy or to a shift away from its mercantilist orientation. The preservation of explicit and implicit social contracts at home as well as an interest in nurturing new technologies motivated Japanese resistance to the U.S. agenda of liberalizing Japan's economy. American ambivalence about getting Japan to play a more prominent military role reinforced the mainstream Japanese view in favor of a minimalist defense policy that focused on homeland defense while relying on U.S. power-projection and offensive capabilities.

However, recent developments have called into question the viability of Japan's approach to managing relations with the United States. Tensions over North Korea's nuclear program in 1993-94 highlighted the possibility that the U.S.–Japan alliance would not function effectively during a severe regional security crisis. The outburst of popular anger after the rape of an Okinawan school girl in September 1995 reminded both Tokyo and Washington that the heavy concentration of U.S. military bases on Okinawa was not sustainable in the long run. Japan's prolonged economic stagnation after its bubble economy began to burst in late 1989 confirmed the inadequacy of traditional policies for spurring growth. And the East Asian financial crisis of 1997 demonstrated not only the region's vulnerabilities in an era of global financial markets, but also the need for Japan to import more goods and services from its neighbors.

In this context, the United States now has an opportunity to forge a more balanced relationship with Japan. In economic terms, such a relationship would give the United States greater access to Japan's markets and technologies and have a more symmetrical bilateral flow of goods and services. In security terms, such a relationship would require Japan to assume more of the diplomatic and military risks and costs for promoting and maintaining international security.

THE ECONOMIC DIMENSION OF JAPAN'S FOREIGN POLICY

Instead of triggering a shift in economic strategy, the sharp appreciation of the yen after its 1985 agreement with the United States to realign exchange rates reinforced Japan's mercantilist tendencies.[3] This realignment provoked fears that Japanese products would lose their price competitiveness in external markets, causing Japanese businesses to lose market share to foreign competitors. To avert a domestic economic recession, Japanese officials opted for a loose monetary policy so firms would have easy access to capital to restructure their businesses and invest in new technologies and production facilities. This policy response had several consequences. First, the abundance of low-cost capital allowed Japanese corporations to hang on to market shares in the United States by temporarily squeezing profits at home. Second, firms used this capital to move up the technological ladder, to develop new products that were not as vulnerable to competitive pricing, and to expand production capabilities.

Third, Japanese corporations dramatically increased their foreign direct investments (FDI). At first, these outward investments expanded in all directions: to the United States in order to get around possible trade barriers and hedge against exchange rate fluctuations; to Europe in order to get in before the formation of a unified European market; and to East Asia in order to take advantage of low labor costs. But by the 1990s, Japan's FDI became increasingly focused on East Asia. East Asian markets were expanding more rapidly than those in the United States and Europe, and the return on investment was generally greater. In 1994, Japan's FDI in manufacturing surpassed comparable investment in North America. The government facilitated the expansion of Japanese production networks in East Asia (especially Southeast Asia and China) by allocating huge amounts of official development assistance for economic infrastructure development in the region. It also provided low-interest loans to small businesses interested in building production facilities abroad. Through this public-private partnership, Japanese firms replicated their *keiretsu* networks in the region.[4]

Contrary to journalistic accounts that this economic shift to East Asia amounted to a hollowing out of Japanese industry, Japan successfully used its FDI to develop new overseas markets for Japanese machinery and technologically advanced intermediate goods and components while modulating the flow of East Asian products back to Japan. East Asia became a much larger outlet for Japanese merchandise exports than North America. Instead of being hit by an East Asian boomerang, Japan racked up significant trade surpluses with virtually all non–oil exporting East Asian countries. By 1995, its trade surplus with East Asian countries totaled $71 billion.

Japanese commentators justified this economic strategy by invoking the so-called "flying geese" model. Japan as the lead goose was helping the economic advance of its neighbors by providing official aid, commercial investments, and production technology. After the so-called newly industrializing economies (South Korea, Taiwan, Hong Kong, and Singapore) succeeded in making their economic breakthrough, Japan turned its attention to less developed countries in the Association of Southeast Asian Nations (ASEAN)—first to the ASEAN Four (Thailand, Malaysia, Indonesia, and the Philippines), and then to those making a transition from planned socialist economies (China, Vietnam, and even Burma). In this manner, Japan facilitated an orderly, stratified pattern of regional development—so it was said.

Although this Japanese response to the 1985 exchange rate realignment certainly yielded economic benefits for both Japan and East Asia, it also had major negative consequences. First, the loose monetary policy generated an economic bubble in Japan. Even after businesses invested heavily in new production facilities and technologies at home and abroad, there was so much cheap capital available that the private sector began to pour money into shady and risky ventures that had little to do with improving the country's long-term economic health. Inflated land prices led banks and other financial institutions to lend recklessly. After the Bank of Japan started in late 1989 to raise interest rates and burst the economic bubble, real estate and stock prices plummeted, leaving many financial institutions with huge non-performing loans. This financial malaise in turn contributed to the economic slowdown of the 1990s.

Second, while loose monetary policies facilitated industrial restructuring and new investments, the *de facto* cartelization of many sectors due to government regulations and collusive business practices kept yen appreciation from having much of an effect on the ability of foreigners to sell in Japan. Moreover, despite repeated efforts to stimulate domestic demand through large public works programs, domestic consumption remained stagnant and household savings continued to stay at high levels. As a result, Japan's current account surplus hovered around $130 billion in both 1993 and 1994.

The combination of the huge current account surplus and the bad loan problem (which led many Japanese corporations to convert their dollar earnings into yen) triggered an appreciation of the yen to the historically high rate of roughly 80 yen per U.S. dollar

(¥80/$US). This new round of yen appreciation stimulated another push to move production overseas. It also put pressure on Japanese companies to move beyond their affiliates and to procure production inputs at lower costs from foreign firms. But before the high yen could work to loosen up the Japanese business networks (*keiretsu*) and boost imports, financial authorities in Tokyo and Washington intervened in foreign exchange markets to bring the dollar's value back up. However, rather than stabilizing the exchange rate at about ¥100-110/$US, government intervention then could not stop the dollar from appreciating further. While Japan's economy stagnated in large part because it could not deal decisively with its bad loan problem, growth in the United States remained robust. The dollar therefore became more attractive relative to the yen in world currency markets.

Although the steady depreciation of the yen in 1996-97 was a boon for Japanese exporters, this shift in the exchange rate could not have come at a worse time for many of Japan's competitors in East Asia. Since most East Asian countries had pegged their currencies to the dollar, their exports had become less competitive in foreign markets relative to products made in Japan. But these countries needed to export to pay for the large volume of capital goods they imported from Japan—much of which went to factories affiliated with Japanese firms. Moreover, a substantial portion of their new plants and equipment had been imported from Japan when the yen was high. Now they faced the impossible task of competing with Japanese and Chinese goods when both the yen and the yuan were relatively low. The resulting deterioration of the current accounts in many East Asian countries contributed to the region's financial crisis of 1997.

Of course, one should not exaggerate Japan's role in the regional crisis. Financial mismanagement and political corruption in individual countries certainly played a large part in causing the economic turbulence. But one cannot deny the Japan factor. While Japan had done a brilliant job of building up the productive capacity of the East Asian economies, it had done all too little to absorb the excess production of this capacity. As a consequence, trade flows in East Asia were grossly asymmetrical. Japan enjoyed large trade surpluses with both the United States and East Asia, while the United States posted huge trade deficits with both Japan and East Asia. With the dollar serving as the key international currency, the United States could get away with chronic current account surpluses. But the developing countries of East Asia could not. As long as access to the Japanese market was limited, these East Asian economies had to export vigorously to the United States in order to maintain a healthy current account balance. Furthermore, Japan's policy of keeping interest rates inordinately low at home encouraged many Japanese financial institutions to join their American and European counterparts in lending recklessly to East Asia. In short, Japan exported its economic bubble to its neighbors, setting them up for the inevitable financial downfall.

Japan's response to the waves of yen appreciation since 1985 was misguided. As many observers in Japan itself have argued, Japan should have stimulated consumer demand by opening its markets to lower-priced foreign competitors. But this option would have threatened the economically weak, uncompetitive sectors. Unfortunately, these sectors had the political clout to block such a consumer-led growth strategy. Therefore, Japan chose the politically easier path of keeping the weaker sectors protected from foreign competition and promoting more business investment in Japan and the region than the market could bear. With high domestic prices dampening consumer demand, Japan converted its excess savings to excess investment. For Japan, this produced a debilitating bubble economy. For the United States, this meant that its trade deficit with Japan continued to be large while its access to the Japanese market remained limited.

THE SECURITY DIMENSION OF JAPAN'S FOREIGN POLICY

Recent Japanese thinking about security policy manifests two somewhat contradictory trends. One is anxiety about a possible weakening of U.S. military commitments in East Asia. This concern has led many Japanese to think about hedging against the possibility of American disengagement. The other trend reflects a desire to break out of the psychology of dependence on the United States. Although these tendencies together can yield different policy prescriptions, they do strike a common theme: the need to enhance autonomy (*jiritsu*). Prime Minister Ryutaro Hashimoto (president of the conservative Liberal Democratic Party) and Representative Yukio Hatoyama (leader of the dovish Democratic Party) have contrasting political philosophies, but both trumpet the autonomy theme. In his first Diet policy address, Hashimoto emphasized his commitment to an "autonomous diplomacy" (*jiritsu gaiko*)—a concept that unnerved

Foreign Ministry officials enough to cause them to translate the term into English as "proactive diplomacy." In an article published in 1996, Hatoyama also stressed his desire to make Japan less dependent on and less deferential to the United States.[5]

It would be wrong to interpret these sentiments as evidence that Japan is about to embark on an independent military strategy with a nuclear arsenal and extensive power-projection and offensive capabilities. American observers too often get so obsessed with this bogeyman that they cannot envision anything other than the status quo. But recent trends in Japan point toward an emerging consensus in favor of revising the strategic bargain with the United States. What is being debated now is not whether this bargain should be altered or whether Japan should terminate its strategic link to the United States, but rather in what manner and at what pace this bilateral bargain should be changed. This debate divides into two schools of thought.

One view holds that the U.S.–Japan alliance should be restructured so that Japan plays a more prominent military role in regional deterrence and crisis management (especially during a Korean contingency). Ultimately, this means that Japan would recognize its ability to exercise the right of collective self-defense by either reinterpreting or revising its constitution. This "normalized" Japan would then expand its defense role beyond its territory and eventually be willing to fight shoulder-to-shoulder with the United States in defense of common interests. But as Japan expands its defense horizon, the bilateral alliance would need to be based on greater equality. The United States would genuinely consult Japan, not merely inform it of decisions already made. And as Japan musters the will to say "yes" to collective defense missions, it would also gain the right to say "no" to the United States when it disagreed with U.S. policy. In short, the U.S.–Japan alliance would evolve toward something akin to U.S. alliances with the major Western European powers. The only source of disagreement within this school of thought is the political methodology for effecting change. Some advocate constitutional reinterpretation and/or revision sooner rather than later; others support an incremental approach by working first within current constitutional constraints to do as much as possible in the collective defensive mode starting with logistical support in the rear.

The other school of thought believes that Japan should build upon its post-war constitution and its special status as a "pacifist state" (*heiwa kokka*) to promote cooperative security and preventive diplomacy. In this view, Japan should emphasize the development of fledgling multilateral dialogues such as the ASEAN Regional Forum (ARF) and the Asia Pacific Economic Cooperation forum (APEC) to foster trust in the region. It should also take greater diplomatic initiative in dealing with pressing regional problems such as uncertainties in North Korea and China's rapid growth. The Self-Defense Forces would stick primarily to the mission of homeland defense. But many embracing this dovish viewpoint recognize that Japan has an obligation to participate in collective security functions of the United Nations such as humanitarian missions, peacekeeping operations, and even peace enforcement and peacemaking. Some even support participating in a U.N. international or regional standby force. In short, Japanese soldiers could ultimately fight side-by-side with Americans under the U.N. banner.

Despite significant differences between these two views, the divide is much narrower than that between "realist" conservatives and pacifists of old. What is striking is what unites them, rather than what divides them. Both schools want to harmonize the three documents that shape Japanese security policy: the Japanese constitution, the U.S.–Japan Security Treaty, and the United Nations charter. Both schools seek a revised bilateral security pact either in form or in substance at some point. Both assume and desire a reduced U.S. military presence in Japan, and both want to restrain increases in host-nation support contributions (*omoiyari yosan*). In other words, the current debate holds the possibility of generating a new strategic synthesis that garners broad public support.

Despite its desire to become more autonomous, Tokyo is far from creating an East Asian strategic alternative to the United States. Although Japan's image in Southeast Asia has improved steadily, its relations with China and South Korea have worsened. Ironically, right-wing nationalists undermine their notions of a re-Asianized Japan by provoking neighboring states with their warped view of history and their crude handling of territorial disputes. Moreover, the spring 1996 tensions between Taiwan and China prompted the Hashimoto government to tighten the security relationship with the United States by committing itself publicly to review and revise the U.S.–Japan Defense Cooperation Guidelines. Japan, however, does not back a policy of containing China. Mainstream political opinion in Japan wants to integrate China into the regional and global community so that China has a greater stake in the existing international order. The differences regarding China are more about the means than the ends. Again there are two views.

One view emphasizes the construction of a balance-of-power system that can effectively check Chinese military expansion and irredentism.[6] By embracing the right to collective self-defense, Japan would be able to cooperate with the United States to secure maritime safety in the region and to prevent China from threatening Taiwan. The two countries should also promote good relations with countries on China's periphery so that a coalition would immediately emerge to counter China if it became aggressive. The other view stresses the security benefits of bringing China into international economic institutions such as the World Trade Organization and of deepening bilateral and multilateral exchanges with China on political and military issues.[7] The most effective way to constrain China's military buildup is to be more sensitive about China's own insecurities and take steps to mitigate these anxieties.

Despite their differences, these two Japanese views on how to deal with the rise of China have much in common. Both support China's economic development and deeper economic ties with China. Neither believes that holding China back economically to prevent it from becoming a threatening military power is a viable strategy. Both oppose using economic disincentives to change China's internal political behavior. Both reject the ambitious notion held by some Americans of trying to shape China's political evolution or remake it into a liberal democracy. China is too large and too proud a country to respond to such pressures. Although Chinese democratization may eventually make China a less threatening neighbor, outside powers should not force China to accept Western political values.[8] They should rather respect China's culture and recognize Beijing's interest in maintaining domestic stability.

Japanese leaders see no need to make a choice between tightening Japan's alliance with the United States and reaching out to China diplomatically and economically. Although China vigorously condemns the "redefinition" of the U.S.–Japan alliance, the problem is not that this redefinition inherently contradicts a policy of engaging and integrating China. The problem lies in the fact that neither Washington nor Tokyo has taken adequate steps to improve relations with Beijing, to work out a *modus vivendi* on the Taiwan question, and to reassure China as they reinvigorate U.S.–Japanese security arrangements. In international politics, much hinges on timing, sequence, and the manner of implementation.

IMPLICATIONS FOR U.S. ECONOMIC AND SECURITY INTERESTS AND POLICY

The United States has a continuing interest in improving its access to Japanese markets, in getting Japan to absorb more imports from the rest of East Asia, and in enlisting Japan's support for its commercial agenda in the region, including trade and investment liberalization and the protection of intellectual property rights. Temporary sharp declines in the U.S. trade deficit with Japan such as the one in 1996 should not be grounds for complacency. The U.S. unemployment rate may be low, but what matters is not just aggregate employment, but also the types of jobs being created and lost due to trade. Increasing exports of manufactured goods and services to Japan, still the world's second largest economy and the United States' most formidable competitor, is critical to preserving and generating high-quality, high-paying jobs. The depreciation of the yen resulting from the Asian financial crisis in 1997 is again shifting the terms of trade in Japan's favor and is likely to worsen the U.S. trade deficit.

In the wake of the East Asian financial crisis, the United States has a keen interest in getting Japan to resolve its bad loan problem as soon as possible, to stimulate domestic demand, and to become a center of economic growth in the region. In addition to cooperating with the United States and the International Monetary Fund to provide financial support to the distressed economies in the region (especially South Korea) while promoting economic reform, Japan must help to pull these countries out of their current economic turmoil by importing more of their products. Greater Japanese absorption of East Asian products will also alleviate some pressure on the United States from East Asian exports as well as improve opportunities for U.S. subsidiaries in East Asia to export to Japan. Of course, American consumers benefit from inexpensive, quality goods from both Japan and East Asia. But consumers must also have well paying and secure jobs in order to consume without going into debt. We should be careful not to make too stark a distinction between consumers and producers.

The United States has a security interest in maintaining access to critical bases in Japan in order to deter and respond to aggression against U.S. allies in the East Asia–Pacific region and in getting Japanese political-military support to deal with regional and international crises.[9] The United States also has an interest in gaining

Japan's cooperation to check the proliferation of nuclear weapons and other weapons of mass destruction, to prevent the emergence of a hostile coalition in the region, and to maintain safe and secure maritime and air navigation. The United States and Japan should nurture a regional environment that minimizes threats to Taiwan, military conflicts over territorial disputes, regional arms races, and the prospects of violence in the context of Korean reunification. In working toward these objectives, the purpose of the bilateral alliance should not be to contain Japan. Rather the task is to encourage a more prominent Japanese political-military role in such a manner so that Japan's emerging role does not itself become a destabilizing factor.

U.S. economic and security interests with respect to Japan do intersect. At a time when Americans are being asked to make hard choices for the purpose of domestic renewal, the political sustainability of U.S. security commitments to Japan will require that Japan not be seen as undermining U.S. economic interests. And to the extent that Japan produces more and more of the important inputs for U.S. defense systems, the United States has a security interest in maintaining stable supplies of such inputs and accessing Japanese dual-use technologies.

Will the pursuit of economic interests undermine security interests? An assertive policy on the economic front will inevitably strain political relations with Japan and may make Japanese leaders somewhat more reluctant to work with the United States on security-related issues. But given the absence of an attractive strategic alternative, Tokyo will not dilute or dismantle the security alliance because of Washington's pressures on trade. Japan will move away from its side of the bilateral strategic bargain not because of U.S. economic policies, but because of developments in the security arena, such as changes in the strategic environment, misgivings about U.S. defense policy, or irritations about the American military presence in Japan. Therefore, within reason, the United States should not hesitate about pursuing its economic interests vis-à-vis Japan for fear of damaging the security relationship.

But what about the reverse? Does the pursuit of U.S. security interests undermine its economic interests? Not necessarily. In defining our security interests in expansive terms, there is the danger that the United States will be saddled with much larger military expenditures as a percentage of GNP than other major powers.[10] The problem is not that big defense budgets might crowd out business investments. Attractive businesses should be able to raise adequate funds in capital markets. But overblown military spending may make it difficult to sustain and develop the public programs necessary to ease the social adjustments to economic globalization. A choice in favor of the former would be unjust and tear America's social fabric and would even weaken U.S. political will for international engagement. The remedy is to restructure the military establishment and foreign deployments in order to enhance efficiency while continuing to perform the critical roles and missions. Japan can help this process by assuming more of the burden and responsibility for regional security.

If security and economics are inextricably linked, then should the United States explicitly leverage its defense commitments to Japan in order to extract Japanese concessions on economic issues? Although this is theoretically enticing, I have serious doubts that Washington can execute such a strategy with the subtlety necessary to obtain the desired result. Moreover, given the current political climate, Japan is just as likely to accept the hollowing out of the security alliance as to submit to American economic pressures. Of course, although an explicit policy of linking security to trade may be unwise, U.S. leaders should always remind their Japanese counterparts that continuing American public support for the alliance depends greatly on whether bilateral economic relations are seen as fair and reciprocal. But in policy terms, the best course is to pursue vigorously both economic and security interests on their own terms.

Many existing Japanese barriers to trade are not explicit protectionist measures like tariffs and quotas, but rather collusive business practices and opaque arrangements between government agencies and the private sector. Consequently, while a rules-based approach to "leveling the playing field" may help in opening Japan, it is woefully inadequate. The Clinton Administration was therefore right in adopting a results-oriented approach and establishing objective criteria to measure progress. But it erred in not mobilizing the Japanese public who would benefit from U.S. efforts to open markets. Instead Administration officials, initially confused about their policy objectives, neglected to wage an effective campaign in Japan and thereby turned the Japanese press and thus most of the public against the United States. It became good politics to say "no" to the unreasonable Americans. The absurd effect was to let Japan become the champion of free trade, while the United States was denigrated for promoting managed trade.

Although the Clinton Administration boasts that it negotiated twenty-two agreements on a range of trade issues with Japan, the task of implementing them will be arduous, especially since the two countries have divergent interpretations of many of them. Washington and the U.S. diplomatic community in Japan must therefore do a better job of informing the Japanese public of the benefits they would receive from liberalization. Indeed Japan's current economic stagnation gives the United States a golden opportunity to convince Japanese citizens that stimulating domestic demand, deregulating the economy to promote entrepreneurship, and opening up the Japanese market to foreign competition serve their long-term economic interests. The best way for Washington to improve commercial access to Japan is to identify and mobilize Japanese allies on behalf of structural reform.

Pushing on the bilateral front does not preclude the use of multilateral mechanisms like the World Trade Organization. In fact, bilateral and multilateral efforts should be complementary; there is no need to choose one over the other.[11] But in light of the more strident nationalism of the new generation of Japanese bureaucrats, multilateral pressures will be more effective than bilateral ones. Europeans and Asians have their horror stories of how hard it is to crack the Japanese market. It is better to enlist them in U.S. efforts to open up Japan than to let Japan form coalitions with them to resist the United States. Regarding trade with China, it would be better to enlist Japan's support in eliciting China's cooperation on such issues as intellectual property rights than to let Japan watch on the sidelines while the United States leads the charge and takes all of the political heat.

On the security relationship, it is time to strike a new bargain. While the Pentagon has temporarily defused tensions on Okinawa by agreeing to return the Futenma Marine Air Corps Station in five to seven years, there is now widespread support in Japan for a gradual but significant reduction in the U.S. military presence in Okinawa and elsewhere. Rather than stubbornly sticking to the 47,000 number for U.S. troops in Japan, the United States should adopt a "roles and mission" approach and determine what forward deployments are absolutely critical for deterrence and crisis response in the context of changes in the strategic environment and technological capabilities. America's most important military assets in Japan are its Air Force and Navy units. Therefore, the United States should make whatever adjustments are necessary to sustain Japan's willingness to host these assets. In return, Japan should take appropriate steps to support U.S. military operations in regional contingencies and to facilitate rapid deployments into and out of Japan during an emergency. The Japanese government moved modestly in this direction when it agreed to new U.S.-Japan Defense Cooperation Guidelines in September 1997. If a new strategic bargain can be struck, then the Marine combat forces in Okinawa could be removed without harming the integrity of U.S. military missions.[12] This would go far in consolidating Japanese political support for the alliance well into the next century.

But the United States must also move beyond a strategy of military presence to develop an effective strategy to reduce tensions and prevent crises in the region. Keeping 100,000 troops in the East Asia–Pacific region is a poor surrogate for a comprehensive Asia policy. More realism is necessary in claims about what this military presence does. Does it really improve U.S. access to East Asian markets, keep East Asian countries from modernizing their militaries, and mediate conflicts among those countries? Only after recognizing the limits of U.S. forward military deployments as a policy tool will U.S. officials see the urgency of integrating the economic, diplomatic, and military dimensions of foreign policy into a coherent East Asian security strategy. The "regional cooperation" section of the April 1996 U.S.-Japan Joint Declaration on Security did nothing more than list in general terms common regional security goals regarding Korea, China, Russia, and Southeast Asia. What is desperately needed now is a concrete, coordinated policy with Japan to achieve these objectives.

NOTES

[1] For an excellent explication of Japan's mercantile realism, see Eric Heginbotham and Richard J. Samuels, "Mercantile Realism and Japanese Foreign Policy," MIT *Japan Program Working Paper* 96-22 (1996).

[2] One exception was the purported linkage during the Nixon-Sato negotiations between Japanese concessions on textile trade and U.S. reversion of Okinawa to Japanese administration.

[3] R. Taggart Murphy, *The Weight of the Yen: How Denial Imperils America's Future and Ruins an Alliance* (New York: W. W. Norton and Company, 1996), pp. 165-218.

[4] Walter Hatch and Kozo Yamamura, *Asia in Japan's Embrace: Building a Regional Production Alliance* (Cambridge: Cambridge University Press, 1996).

[5] Hatoyama Yukio, "Minshuto: Watashi no seiken koso," *Bungei Shunju* (November 1996), pp. 112-30.

[6] Hisahiko Okazaki, former Japanese ambassador to Thailand and Saudi Arabia, has been the most active proponent of this view.

[7] Kazuo Ogura, senior official in the Ministry of Foreign Affairs and former ambassador to Vietnam, articulates this view. See Ogura Kazuo, "21-seiki no Chugoku to Nihon gaiko," *Sekai* (May 1996), pp. 157-70.

[8] Hisahiko Okazaki favors Japanese support for America's human rights agenda vis-à-vis China not because he thinks the policy will work, but because he feels Japan needs to toe the line on this issue in order to maintain good relations with the United States.

[9] In the East Asia–Pacific region, the United States has alliances with Japan, the Republic of Korea, Australia, the Philippines, and Thailand.

[10] Lawrence J. Korb, "Our Overstuffed Armed Forces," *Foreign Affairs* 74, No. 6 (November/December 1995), pp. 22-34.

[11] Jeffrey E. Garten, "Is America Abandoning Multilateral Trade?" *Foreign Affairs* 74, No. 6 (November/December 1995), pp. 50-62.

[12] For a fuller development of this argument, see Mike M. Mochizuki, ed., *Toward a True Alliance: Restructuring U.S.-Japan Security Relations* (Washington, DC: Brookings Institution Press, 1997).

WILLIAM J. TAYLOR

HOW TO STRENGTHEN THE U.S.–SOUTH KOREA ALLIANCE

This paper examines the confluence of officially stated U.S. security and economic interests around the Korean Peninsula and suggests new departures toward achieving U.S. and allied objectives. The end of the Cold War resulted in a mixed bag of challenges in the Northeast Asian region. Although the Soviet threat is gone, the danger of regional instability remains. For the short term, a belligerent Democratic People's Republic of Korea (DPRK, or North Korea) poses the greatest immediate and tangible threat to regional stability. A cooperative security relationship between the United States and the Republic of Korea (ROK, or South Korea) still serves as the cornerstone in addressing this threat and maintaining peace on the Korean Peninsula. Recently, however, tensions, if not fissures, have developed in the close relationship between Seoul and Washington concerning the North Korean problem. But, we have been there before and, somehow, seem to have overcome our disagreements.

The fall of the communist world was a turning point in the balance of power on the Korean Peninsula—most notably, it spelled doom for the DPRK.[1] The subsequent deterioration of North Korea, rather than subduing the DPRK leadership and easing tensions, has made the security situation on the Korean Peninsula increasingly complex. Analysts and policymakers in Seoul and Washington realize that, although the parameters in dealing with North Korea have changed, the dangers remain. North Korea is no longer a strong, relatively stable country with a menacing military; rather, it is an economically unstable, starving and increasingly desperate country with a substantial military that may pose an unavoidable threat if nothing is done to reverse the North's economic deterioration. It is, in other words, a ticking time bomb.

With these shifting conditions on the peninsula and the uncertain future of the DPRK, the governments of the United States and the Republic of Korea are reexamining and restructuring the strategy for dealing with the North. Deterrence is no longer adequate; as former Ambassador James Laney put it, the approach should be deterrence and "constructive engagement." But any engagement requires ROK leadership as well as U.S. leadership. Cooperation and close coordination between Washington and Seoul is perhaps more critical at this juncture than at any previous time. The governments have common strategic interests vis-à-vis North Korea, but they differ in how they rank those interests in importance and in the tactics they wish to use in pursuit of their objectives. Pyongyang has deliberately exploited these differing priorities through "brinkmanship," trying to drive a wedge between Seoul and Washington. The Clinton Administration, in particular, repeatedly has fallen victim to Pyongyang's diplomatic ploys and has sought to placate the North while marginalizing the South. The result has been a gradual erosion of trust between Seoul and Washington, disruption of U.S.–ROK cooperation, and lost opportunities to make progress in pressuring Pyongyang toward responsible foreign policy conduct. The DPRK leadership understands power politics. They have been playing hardball; the United States has been playing softball.

In addition to tensions between the United States and South Korea over how to handle the North, as in the case of a North Korean submarine that infiltrated the South in 1996, other emotion-laden issues in U.S.–ROK relations also have created friction, most notably bilateral trade and investment disputes. This paper analyzes the security and economic areas of contention driving apart Seoul and Washington in a period when cooperation is critical to confront an increasingly desperate Pyongyang and maintain stability on the Korean Peninsula. What is driving this centrifugal force weakening the U.S.–ROK relationship?

BUMPING HEADS OVER NORTH KOREA

Within the last few years, despite repeated public statements in both Washington and Seoul that the two governments are unified in strategy and policy in dealing with Pyongyang, the policy objectives of the two governments have clashed on a number of occasions resulting in mutual ill will.

The Clinton Administration has four broad policy objectives in relation to North Korea:

- First, to implement the specifically nuclear aspects of the 1994 nuclear freeze agreement between the United States and North Korea, known as the Agreed Framework, designed to halt and dismantle North Korea's nuclear program.
- Second, to implement the political component of the Agreed Framework by promoting North-South dialogue and exchange designed to reduce tension on the Korean Peninsula and eventually lead to reunification.
- Third, to increase political, economic, and academic contacts between the United States and the DPRK (e.g., missile talks, MIA discussions) to induce Pyongyang to open up, to embrace market reforms, to join the international economy, and more broadly, to become a more responsible player in the world community.[2]
- Fourth, by achieving the above aims, to meet regional security objectives. These include a) decreasing missile threats; b) reducing the dangers of a conventional arms race; c) maintaining a significant U.S. presence in the Asia-Pacific region; and d) maintaining the integrity of the nuclear non-proliferation treaty in the region.[3]

An unstated objective is the prevention of an implosive or explosive collapse of the DPRK by alleviating its famine and economic crisis.[4] This is the immediate purpose of the four-party (South Korea, North Korea, the United States, and China) negotiations initiated in Geneva in late 1997 for the stated purpose of replacing the Korean War Armistice, the 1953 agreement that concluded the Korean War and is still in force.

The Clinton Administration has reaffirmed these objectives on a number of occasions, but an overview of policy implementation indicates that they do not hold equal value. Rather, the objectives that address broader regional issues in Northeast Asia (e.g., nuclear non-proliferation) carry more weight than more localized interests such as the improvement of the North Korean–South Korean political relationship, which Seoul holds as its top priority. For example, it is clear that compliance with the nuclear component of the Geneva Agreed Framework is the Clinton Administration's top priority, and the Administration goes to great lengths to prevent Pyongyang from developing nuclear weapons and undermining the integrity of the Non-Proliferation Treaty. However, when the non-nuclear components of the Framework are at issue, such as the reduction of tensions on the peninsula through North-South bilateral talks, Washington sidesteps the real issue with new formulations such as the Four-Party Talks proposal. The Four-Party talks should not be a substitute for the North Korean–South Korean bilateral talks to which Pyongyang agreed in the Agreed Framework. This would undercut the basic concept of successive U.S. and ROK administrations, i.e., that the only acceptable way to secure lasting peace and achieve unification of the Korean Peninsula is through direct North-South governmental dialogue.

APPEASING PYONGYANG

In effect, the DPRK leadership has taken control of the agenda and timing in its relations with both its archenemy to the south and the world's sole superpower. Pyongyang has successfully utilized brinkmanship diplomacy and information warfare to cause concern among American officials and has brought U.S. negotiators to the table without their ally to draw U.S. concessions. The DPRK leadership concluded as early as spring 1994 that the Clinton Administration would give away a great deal to avoid a crisis on the Korean Peninsula and to secure its "broader" interests, even to the extent of inadvertently damaging its relationship with Seoul.

In the view of some South Korean officials, the Clinton Administration has turned into a "self-interested ally" at best, and a broker or a "peddler" using Seoul for its own gain, at worst.[5] Korean commentators in Seoul have lashed out at the U.S. government, accusing U.S. officials of using South Koreans as "hod carriers and financiers" who are called to join negotiations with Pyongyang when Seoul's support is vital, such as to pay for the two light water reactors that are to be built for North Korea under the Agreed Framework, but who are sidelined when not needed.[6] Washington has assured the ROK repeatedly that Seoul will not be left out of discussions with Pyongyang, but that appears to be what is happening. While North-South talks have remained at an impasse over the three years since the Agreed Framework was signed, Pyongyang has held talks with the United States over the remains of American soldiers still missing from the Korean War, humanitarian aid, missile exports, and other disputes.

Meanwhile, members of Congress and State Department officials have been traveling to North Korea on a regular basis to discuss various issues. Of course, the purpose of these discussions is to reduce tensions. Nevertheless, Seoul has not been in the picture officially. The Pyongyang leadership considers any opportunity to talk with the United States without South Korea a diplomatic victory and another reason to further delay direct talks with Seoul.

The Clinton Administration needs to understand that any U.S. contact with an opportunistic North Korea must include South Korea. The North Korean leadership's primary objective is to open formal ties with Washington, secure a separate DPRK–U.S. peace treaty, and achieve an end to U.S. economic sanctions. Pyongyang must be made to understand that in order to deal with Washington, it must first deal with Seoul.

Despite the rhetoric of success that has come out of Washington since former President Jimmy Carter's farcical 1994 trip to Pyongyang, the Clinton Administration's policies have failed to improve the security situation on the Korean Peninsula, and a sense of suspicion and resentment exists within Seoul against Washington. None of the ROK or U.S. diplomatic initiatives, including the nuclear Agreed Framework, rice giveaways, or the Four-Party Talks proposal have led to North-South dialogue and the environment required for peaceful North-South unification. In fact, the political environment around the Korean Peninsula has deteriorated. The 1996 submarine incursion and the U.S. grants of amnesty to the DPRK ambassador to Egypt and his brother, who defected from Paris to the United States in August 1997, contributed to increased tensions, which in mid-1998 are high. The Four-Party Talks face yet another impasse.

A *Washington Post* interview of South Korean President Kim Young-Sam after the 1996 North Korean submarine infiltration illustrates the state of U.S.–ROK relations. In the interview, Kim Young-Sam stated emphatically that, "[The North Korean leaders] are even more hostile than ever . . . Their revolutionary strategy for communizing the Korean Peninsula has not changed. Unless North Korea sincerely apologizes for what has happened and guarantees that the same kind of incident will not be repeated, we cannot help North Korea, whether it is rice or other things."[7] In the same article, U.S. government officials undercut Kim's threat not to carry out the Agreed Framework in the absence of a North Korean apology. These officials described the situation as "merely a 'pause' in a process that is still healthy." Deputy Assistant Secretary of State for East Asian Affairs Charles Kartman went further in undermining Kim's declaration by stating: "They [South Korean leaders] feel there needs to be a resolution of the submarine incident before we get back to business as usual. *But everything is still fine*" (emphasis added).[8] South Korean media and politicians attacked the Clinton Administration for its weak response to the submarine incident. Some went so far as to accuse President Clinton of sacrificing South Korean security for the sake of gains in U.S. domestic politics by carrying out a policy of appeasement toward Pyongyang to keep peace on the Korean Peninsula at any cost before the U.S. elections.[9]

Curiously, then-Ambassador Laney unequivocally voiced his support for President Kim's announcement that, before any talks and progress on the Agreed Framework could resume, North Korea would have to offer a since apology for the submarine incursion.[10] In response, Pyongyang, exercising its usual brinkmanship, refused to give a formal apology, threatened to leave the Agreed Framework,[11] then expressed its sincere regret in order to get larger amounts of food aid. This brinkmanship worked as usual, producing increased economic aid.

A FLAWED POLICY OF ENGAGEMENT

Engaging North Korea is akin to hugging a rattlesnake. The question is not whether Pyongyang will strike by going to the brink again, but when, over what issue, and how.

The DPRK's economy is in crisis and collapse is inevitable if there is not significant external assistance. Analysts and policymakers worry that an economic crash combined with widespread famine could provoke any of a number of troublesome scenarios: attack by the North Korean military against the South or violent collapse of the regime followed by civil war or anarchy and heavy outflows of refugees to neighboring countries. As a result, Seoul and Washington agreed some time ago on the importance of delaying an economic crash and promoting a "soft landing." But the near disastrous condition of the DPRK economy, widespread famine in the North, continued North-South tensions in the wake of the September 1996 submarine infiltration, and increasing numbers of North Korean defectors make it difficult to determine the best method of achieving a soft landing and gradual and peaceful unification.

It is clear, however, that a soft-landing scenario must include certain key components: 1) dialogue between Seoul and Pyongyang; 2) substantial investment in and trade with the DPRK by South Korea and her allies and friends; and 3) the adoption of substantial economic reform by North Korea. For these factors to materialize, two elements are essential: first, a concerted decision by Seoul, Washington, and Tokyo to assist North Korea out of its current crisis; and second, a deliberate decision by Pyongyang to reform its system and accept outside assistance.

However, Pyongyang is unlikely to cooperate with a soft-landing policy for three reasons. First, from the North Korean leadership's perspective, the notion of "soft landing" or "hard landing" is moot, since either approach would eventually yield the same result: termination of the current Juche system of North Korea and the demise of the Korean Workers Party (KWP). The soft-landing approach serves only the self-interest of South Korea and the United States, not the DPRK; soft landing would make it less costly for South Korea to pick up the pieces after the current DPRK regime has crumbled.

Second, the DPRK leadership is aware of the fate of other leaders who chose to reform their Leninist states. In the Soviet Union, reforms led to the eventual collapse of the regime and the communist system. Although China is prospering economically, reforms also contributed to political disruption, such as the Tiananmen Square riots, which seriously challenged the leadership and stability of the country. Perhaps most sobering for Kim Jong-Il and his coterie are the trials and sentencing of former ROK presidents Chun Doo Hwan and Roh Tae Woo.

Third, Kim Jong-Il's legitimacy as the next preeminent leader of North Korea is directly linked to his ability to protect the Juche ideology that the "Great Leader" Kim Il-Sung established as the basis of the entire DPRK political system. Introducing substantive reforms and eliminating Juche would result in Kim Jong-Il's own end. Some institutions within DPRK society, such as the three-million member KWP, exist to ensure the viability and integrity of Juche. The party and its leadership have as much stake in maintaining the current political-ideological structure as Dear Leader Kim Jong-Il; they want to preserve their authority and the privileges they enjoy.[12]

Kim Jong-Il is faced with a Catch-22 situation in which the two pillars of his legitimacy are mutually destabilizing. Juche requires him to maintain a strong, centralized, and controlled economic system, while economic tensions logically would pressure him to loosen the government's grip over production and to introduce a free-market system. Either way, he will ultimately undermine his authority and break the link of legitimacy from his father—and Juche will go down.

Pyongyang's unwillingness to reform its society suggests that the Clinton Administration's policy of engagement, dialogue, and unconditional aid will not work. Rather, aid must be coordinated among the United States, South Korea, and Japan and tied tightly to conditions that Pyongyang must accept, such as reactivation of North-South government dialogue. Does this mean carrots and sticks? Yes, but in a different venue. Right now, Pyongyang is using all the sticks and Washington all the carrots. Without conditions, the United States is only rewarding North Korea's belligerence and propping up Kim Jong-Il's dictatorial regime, which has no interest in reforming its system and helping its people. Meanwhile, horrible human rights abuses in North Korea continue.

The North Korean leadership's plan for the time being appears to be twofold. First, Pyongyang is depending on the anxiety and generosity of the international community to address the immediate hunger needs of North Korea. Second, and most important, Pyongyang is aggressively promoting and developing the Rajin-Sonbong Special Economic Zone (SEZ). Seeing the success of China's trade zones, Pyongyang hoped that it, too, could draw foreign corporations to invest billions of dollars into a sealed-off, 288 square-mile SEZ in an isolated northeastern sector of the country. The goal of its planners is to extract technology and capital from foreign enterprises while controlling foreign, infectious, liberal influences within a cordoned off area, and without actually opening its society and reforming its system. Since 1991, the SEZ has failed to draw in any significant investment, and progress has been negligible. Far behind its twenty-year construction schedule, which was to begin in 1992, the Rajin-Sonbong project simply has failed to facilitate commercial activities because it has not secured the $4 billion required to construct an adequate transportation system, expand ports, and establish basic facilities. In 1991, many were skeptical whether the zone would ever succeed; in 1998, almost everyone who pays attention knows that it will not. In the intervening years, Pyongyang has ruined two principal components that would have given the zone any possibility of success: confidence of potential investors in the stability of North Korea, and the cooperation of the South Korean government and South Korean businesses.

There appear to be more disincentives than incentives to invest in North Korea. True, the Rajin-Sonbong SEZ has advantages: cheap, skilled labor; access to raw materials from the Far East; and entry into the dynamic China market. But reports of starvation, economic deterioration, and political instability, compounded by the DPRK's zero credit rating and debt problems, have eroded the confidence of international business in the future stability of North

Korea's investment environment. In addition, the Rajin-Sonbong SEZ is not the only economic zone. It must compete against other zones located in China, Vietnam, Indonesia, and other developing countries that also provide inexpensive labor, tax benefits, and market access.

Who might actually take the chance to funnel capital into North Korea's high-risk zone? Other Koreans. First, some 150,000 Koreans residing in Japan have close ties to North Korea. They sponsor investments in the DPRK based on their loyalty to the North Korean regime. But their investments have been primarily in small and low-technology projects, having negligible value for economic development. Second, large South Korean business conglomerates have developed grandiose plans to construct oil refineries, textile factories, hotels, convention centers, and billions of dollars worth of other projects in the SEZ. In other words, South Korea is the key to getting the SEZ off the ground. The success or failure of South Korean businesses in the SEZ (or elsewhere in North Korea) will be the litmus test determining whether Japanese and Western companies will also go into North Korea.

So far, political tensions have prevented South Korean capital from being channeled into the North Korean economy on a large scale. Though flexible at times, Seoul has limited investments made by South Korean companies to $5 million, mainly on a process-on-commission basis. Only if the political environment on the Korean Peninsula improves will these limitations be loosened. North Korean–South Korean bilateral talks to reduce political tension could help turn North Korea's economy around.

U.S.–ROK TRADE: THE ECONOMICS OF "THE GOOD OLD TIMES"?

Let us turn now to U.S.–ROK bilateral economic relations. The fundamental issues in the bilateral economic relationship between these two countries have not changed despite the financial turbulence that swept the Republic of Korea and other parts of Asia in 1997. Commercial activities between the two countries have grown dramatically over the years. In 1996, the total value of U.S.–South Korea trade was $49.3 billion. However, while the United States fell into a trade deficit with most Asian countries, it ran a surplus with South Korea of $4 billion in 1996.[13] The United States ranks as South Korea's largest export market, while the ROK is the fifth largest purchaser of American goods and services.[14]

U.S.–ROK economic relations, although healthy, have been rocky. Many American businesses have complained that the Korean market is over-regulated and the bureaucracy uncooperative and heavy-handed with foreign businesses. In the United States, Korean exports, including textiles, steel, televisions, and semi-conductors, have been the targets of anti-dumping law suits and subject to tariffs under the Super 301 clause of U.S. trade law. Meanwhile, the U.S. government has placed increasing pressure on Korea to open its markets to American goods, for example automobiles and agricultural products. South Koreans feel that they have in good faith moved to liberalize significantly and to deregulate their markets across the board, especially as South Korea prepared to enter into the Organisation for Economic Co-operation and Development (OECD) in December 1996. But Washington continues to press South Korea for market access and deregulation while strengthening its own protectionist measures by threatening to implement unilateral sanctions. For example, in the area of telecommunications, the U.S. surplus with Korea reached $403 million during the first five months of 1996, nearly double the U.S. surplus in 1995. Despite the ballooning U.S. surplus in telecommunications equipment, the U.S. Trade Representative named Korea a "Priority Foreign Country" for investigation under the 1988 Omnibus Trade Act, charging that the ROK failed to offer sufficient U.S. businesses access into this market.[15] In July 1997, the U.S. charge against the ROK was settled after year-long negotiations on trade in telecommunications goods and services. However, the ROK then filed a complaint with the World Trade Organization (WTO) against the United States. The South Korean government charged the United States with imposing unfair anti-dumping duties on Korean color television sets, in violation of the WTO Anti-Dumping Agreement. The Korean government also plans to file another complaint at the WTO in response to the U.S. Commerce Department's decision in July 1997 to maintain anti-dumping orders on dynamic random access memory (DRAM) chips.[16] South Koreans are exasperated that U.S. trade officials do not seem to understand that, though the ROK is willing to make changes, its domestic political and economic interests must be addressed.

Trade tensions go beyond bilateral trade, even into commercial activities with third countries. The most notable is the Iran and Libya Sanctions Act passed by the United States in 1996. Under this law, the United States imposes sanctions on businesses making certain investments that directly and significantly contribute to the ability of Iran or Libya to develop oil resources. At the end of 1996, South Korea placed itself under U.S. investigation and possible U.S. sanctions by signing an economic treaty with Iran promising to increase trade. These tensions on the economic front have exacerbated ill feelings between the United States and the Republic of Korea.

WHERE DO WE GO FROM HERE?

The United States has vital interests in the stability of Northeast Asia: the security of its ally the Republic of Korea; the security of about 59,000 Americans in South Korea, including military personnel, business people, and their dependents; and the fate of billions of dollars of U.S. private capital investment and trade. Yet there is no missile defense of Seoul (or Japan) against an estimated 85 DPRK Scud and Nodong 1 missiles, and U.S. and ROK proposals to upgrade missile defense and counter-artillery capabilities have repeatedly been deferred, leaving the defenses of Seoul dangerously inadequate.

For a number of reasons—including how little is known about the inner workings of the Juche government and the motivations of DPRK leaders; the high probability that the North Korean government will disintegrate; the repeated highly tense situations created by the DPRK's pattern of brinkmanship; the fact that wars occur more often than not by accident or miscalculation during times of high tension; and the damage that the DPRK could inflict on Seoul if war were to break out by either accident or miscalculation—the United States should make the following policy changes with the concurrence of Seoul:

1. The United States should quickly reach agreement with the ROK on who pays what share for the systems required to protect/limit damage to Seoul. Production of new systems takes too long, so the United States must decide what risks it can take elsewhere in the world by shifting required military systems to the ROK now, especially missile defense systems.
2. The United States should give Pyongyang a definite deadline for the resumption of North–South dialogue on two existing agreements—Denuclearization of the Korean Peninsula and the Agreement on Non-Aggression, Cooperation, Reconciliation and Exchanges (concluded in 1991 but never put into operation).

3. The United States should make further concessions to the DPRK contingent on its participation in North-South dialogue. Continued funding for light water reactors; support for infrastructure development; future supplies of oil under the reactor agreement; and humanitarian food supplies all should be handled with this approach: The DPRK talks with the South, the United States and its allies supply; the DPRK stops talking, the United States and its allies stop the supply.

The bottom line is that, if the United States is to remain the world's sole superpower, which much of the world expects, then Washington must get back to *realpolitik* in relation to Northeast Asia. International politics, like all politics, is a struggle for power. This is one reality that the DPRK leadership understands all too well.

NOTES

[1] In the words of Kim Il-Sung, "Dr. Taylor, we have been hurt badly by the demise of the former Soviet Union. For example, we have lost one million metric tons of oil each year" (first 3.5 hour meeting with Kim Il-Sung, Pyongyang, June 28, 1992).

[2] Winston Lord, "U.S. Policy Toward the Korean Peninsula," Conference speech presented to the Korea/United States 21st Century Committee, February 1996.

[3] Department of State, "Country Report: North Korea," October 1995 in *Department of State Home Page*, available at gopher://dosfan.lib.wic.e

[4] Elaine Sciolono, "An Economic Basket Case: In North Korea the Threat is Total Collapse," *New York Times*, February 18, 1996.

[5] Hyun Hong-choo, "Koreans' Perception of America" *Korea Focus* 3, No. 1 (January-February 1996), pp. 31-37.

[6] Nigel Holloway, "Appointment in Beijing," *Far Eastern Economic Review*, June 13, 1996, p. 15.

[7] Kevin Sullivan, "S. Korea demands Apology for North: Kim Suspends Nuclear Deal After Sub Incident," *Washington Post*, November 8, 1996, p. A19.

[8] Ibid.

[9] Andrew Browne, "U.S. Official Due in Seoul as Tensions Mount," *Reuters*, October 8, 1996.

[10] Unattributed, "Laney: North Korea Must Apologize for Submarine Incursion," *Associated Press*, November 10, 1996.

[11] Unattributed, "N. Korea May Resume Nuke Plan," *Associated Press*, November 15, 1996; Unattributed, "N. Korea Says Nuke Deal with U.S. in Jeopardy," *Reuters*, November 15, 1996.

[12] For more detail, see William J. Taylor, "Is Peaceful Unification Possible?" Conference paper presented at the Seventh Annual International Defense Conference on *The Prospects for Peace and Reunification on the Korean Peninsula Toward the 21st Century* (Seoul, Korea), November 4-6, 1996.

[13] South Korean Embassy.

[14] Unattributed, "Trade Bulletin Board," *Korea Trade Focus*, No. 85 (August 1997), p. 3.

[15] Unattributed, "U.S. Surplus Surges in Telecom Trade with Korea," *Korea Trade Focus*, No. 74 (September 1996), p. 2.

[16] Unattributed, "Korea Challenges Two U.S. Antidumping Orders At WTO," *Korea Trade Focus*, No. 85 (August 1997), p. 2.

U.S. ECONOMIC AND SECURITY INTERESTS IN KOREA

DOUG BANDOW

TIME FOR THE UNITED STATES TO DISENGAGE

For nearly five decades the United States has been at war, or poised to go to war, on the Korean Peninsula. That remains the case today, even after the collapse of hegemonic communism. In fact, the peninsula is today the only place where a major conflict involving forward-deployed U.S. forces is plausible at this time.

What U.S. interests warrant such a serious commitment? The promiscuous manner in which Washington hands out security guarantees suggests that U.S. policymakers appear to believe them to be costless. If they were indeed without cost, there would be little reason not to hand them out promiscuously. After all, a promise by the United States to defend a nation, be it South Korea or another, reduces the likelihood of attack on that country. But security commitments are not costless—at least to the United States. To the contrary, such promises entail both economic burdens and military risks. Thus Washington should preserve its troop presence and underlying treaty guarantee to South Korea not "as long as the Korean people want it," as sundry American officials have promised, but only as long as doing so serves the interests of the United States.

Official Washington claims that the U.S. presence in the Republic of Korea (ROK) does serve American interests. According to the Department of Defense (DOD), the alliance "is a vital component in our national objective of supporting and promoting democracy." [1] Yet that argument—which, notably, does not claim that Korea's protection is vital to the ***security*** of America—appears to be little more than an afterthought. The continuing U.S. commitment largely reflects inertia. DOD declares that, "Our security relationship with the Republic of Korea continues to be central to the stability of the Korean Peninsula and Northeast Asia, as it has been for over forty years."[2] While America's presence probably was central to the maintenance of peace forty years ago, it is not today.

Events in recent years have rendered obsolete every assumption underlying the Mutual Defense Treaty signed by the United States and South Korea in 1954 following the Korean War. First, there is no more Cold War, in which Washington assumed that any local conflict had global implications. Any North Korean invasion—unlikely given the shifting balance of power on the peninsula—would no longer be tied to a larger, global threat to the United States. Second, Pyongyang can no longer expect support from China and Russia, which armed and assisted the Democratic People's Republic of Korea (DPRK) during the Korean War. In fact, South Korea has been forging close relations, including some military ties, with these two states. Third, the ROK is no longer backward economically or politically. Rather, it vastly outstrips its northern antagonist, giving it the ability to amass an overwhelming military advantage if it wishes. Finally, East Asia is no longer filled with weak nations, supposed dominoes vulnerable to communist aggression.

In short, none of the original arguments for the U.S. security commitment, backed not only by the 37,000 soldiers on the peninsula but also the full military faith and credit of the United States, now apply. If there is a case for continuing America's protectorate over the ROK, it must be made anew.

ECONOMICS AND SECURITY

Although economic ties between the United States and South Korea—roughly $50 billion worth of trade in 1996—are not unimportant, they make only a modest contribution to America's overall economic health. South Korea accounts for about 3 percent of total U.S. trade and contributes only slightly more than 0.5 percent to U.S. GDP. As South Korea's largest export market, the United States is a critical factor in Seoul's economic equation. By contrast, the United States is not dependent on access to the South Korean market. South Korea is a significant purchaser of U.S. goods and services, but not on a scale comparable to Japanese imports from the United States.

Even if Seoul's contribution to the financial health of the United States were greater, Washington's security promise would still fail to provide the United States with any tangible economic advantages. Some ROK officials argue that South Koreans prefer U.S.

goods over competing products out of gratitude for American military support. Any such impact is difficult to discern: the ROK does not import a disproportionate number of U.S. products; it had repeated trade surpluses with the United States in the 1980s; and it continues to impose numerous arbitrary barriers against U.S. imports.

The presence of 37,000 U.S. soldiers in South Korea does not materially strengthen Washington's hand in trade disputes. Short of marching on the Blue House, home of South Korea's president, U.S. soldiers can do little to enhance access for U.S. exporters. The knowledge that the United States is protecting a nation that restricts U.S. access to its markets causes Washington negotiators to be more petulant, not more persuasive.

Real influence might result if the United States threatened to bring home its troops, but it would have to be prepared to follow through, which, of course, would give the lie to the argument that the commitment serves important American interests. Washington could ill afford to issue this most serious of threats for ordinary trade disputes; to do so would quickly poison relations with Seoul. Even the usual run-of-the-mill trade pressure currently exerted by the United States causes significant popular indignation.

In contrast, a withdrawal not linked to economic disputes would offer clear economic advantages for the United States. Washington's military expenditures would fall. Moreover, a pullout of U.S. troops would spur political change on the peninsula; the result would likely be either détente between the two Koreas or a South Korean military buildup. The first course would open new markets for the United States in North Korea, while the second would eliminate the artificial trade advantage Seoul has because of Washington's defense subsidy (discussed in greater detail below) and probably lead to additional weapons purchases from U.S. manufacturers.

Of course, bilateral trade would be harmed by the removal of U.S. troops if South Korea was overrun by North Korea, but that is an unlikely prospect for a nation so much more advanced than its adversary. It has also been argued that trade not just with Korea but with all of Asia depends on the stability ensured by U.S. forces. To the extent that this argument has any validity, Washington's relationship with Japan matters more. In any case, although U.S. deployments are comforting to other nations, a general East Asian war is not imminent; and existing regional institutions such as the

Association of South East Asian Nations (ASEAN) could help promote stability. Even if Japan undertakes a modest military buildup, which is probably inevitable anyway, it would act as a constraint on China, the potentially more disruptive power. Although a wild daisy chain can be constructed purporting to demonstrate that U.S. withdrawal from Korea could lead to, say, a war between China and Japan, it is no more persuasive than the claim that Serb-Muslim conflict in Bosnia could trigger World War III.

Another argument sometimes made is that increased military spending by U.S. allies would hurt their economies and thus, ultimately, the U.S. economy. The South Korean government explains that one reason it does not possess a "completely independent military capability" is because it has "considered the burden of [its] defense budget to [its] economy." [3] Some Americans, too, have advanced this argument. Certainly higher military outlays would burden the South Korean economy, but that hardly seems to pose a serious danger, since its GNP now exceeds $400 billion. From a U.S. economic standpoint, it is obviously better for this expense to be borne by Seoul than by Washington.

A SECURITY BLACK HOLE

America's Korean protectorate also does not yield significant benefits for the United States in ***security*** terms. Washington's presence does reduce the likelihood of a North Korean attack on the South. But this is primarily a plus for the ROK, not the United States. Moreover, the U.S. commitment is not necessary for Seoul's defense, since South Korea is capable of creating an adequate deterrent of its own. As a result, the military gains to the United States are largely illusory.

During the 1994 crisis over North Korea's suspected nuclear program, President Bill Clinton promised ROK President Kim Young-Sam that Washington would treat any attack on the South like an attack on the United States. The President apparently forgot that while the South's safety is vital to the ROK, it is far less important to the United States. More realistic was the Joint Strategic Survey Committee, which ranked Korea fifteenth on a list of sixteen nations critical to U.S. security in 1947. Even the unlikely worst case of a North Korean takeover of South Korea would be a human tragedy, but not a military disaster for the United States

In fact, the ROK does not even meet the standard of an important interest—i.e., one whose attack by another country would materially affect the United States, although not threaten its survival as an independent republic. The preservation of a mid-sized trading partner in a distant region surrounded by competing great powers is not strategically important. (Obviously, survival is not only important but vital to South Korea—but that does not make it vital to the United States.) Rather, the ROK is what analyst Ted Galen Carpenter calls a peripheral interest, one of many "assets that marginally enhance America's security but whose loss would constitute more of an annoyance than a serious setback." [4]

U.S. officials obviously reject such an assessment, often portraying South Korea as an advanced base for the United States, allowing the projection of power into East Asia. Former Assistant Secretary of State Richard Holbrooke went so far as to claim that the loss of Korea "would be the end of our position in the entire Pacific." [5] In early 1995, DOD made much the same pitch, promising to maintain the alliance "even after the North Korean threat passes . . . in the interest of regional security." [6]

Notably, these arguments do not claim that any vital interests are at stake. Rather, America's second most important and costly commitment (after Europe) is rooted in the more nebulous concept of regional "stability." But this contention fails to distinguish between U.S. influence in East Asia and its commitment to the ROK. The latter is not necessary for the former.

First, the Mutual Defense Treaty yields little benefit for the United States; the promise to defend Seoul from North Korea helps stabilize the peninsula but, as already noted, this mostly benefits the ROK and its neighbors. Second, a militarily stronger South Korea, the likely consequence of a U.S. withdrawal, would also promote regional stability by deterring aggression by not only Pyongyang, but also China, Japan, or Russia. (Those nations will always be able to overmatch even a united Korea, but a united Korea could make the prospect of war too expensive for any of them seriously to contemplate it.)

U.S. forces in Korea also do not offer any significant practical military benefits to the United States. One infantry division in Korea would play no useful role in a conflict, for example, with China. Access to South Korean bases, which does not require a permanent troop presence, might be useful in a full-scale war in the region, but it is hard to imagine what interests would warrant U.S. participation, especially use of ground forces, in such a conflict. Would Washington, for example, mount an attack on Manchuria in retaliation for China's sinking of a Filipino warship off of the Spratly Islands?

Furthermore, U.S.–ROK cooperation in such a war would depend not upon past American support but on shared interests at the time. Seoul would likely be reluctant to join in a crusade against a nearby power however much the ROK enjoyed being defended by Washington. After all, South Korea has to live with its large neighbors, while the United States can leave whenever it chooses. For similar reasons, Tokyo has been reluctant to promise the United States base access in a conflict with China over Taiwan.

Moreover, neither troops nor bases in the South are likely to do much to suppress nationalistic sentiments and conflicts throughout the region. If Vietnam, the Philippines, and China slide toward war over the Spratly Islands, only a U.S. threat to intervene, and not the U.S. presence in Korea, is likely to deter them. Yet there is precious little evidence either that Washington is better able to solve regional problems than the parties involved or that the United States has sufficient interests at stake to warrant military action if conflict erupted. The United States might have been the key to regional stability forty, thirty, or even twenty years ago, but it is not today.

Withdrawing troops from Korea would not prevent the United States from maintaining its defense treaty with Japan, if it so desired, or from being involved in regional organizations, promoting reconciliation and cooperation among tense neighbors, preserving base access for emergency use, and initiating naval patrols. Indeed, with a strong mid-Pacific presence, Washington would retain the option of becoming re-involved militarily in East Asia if it so desired.

The only plausible scenario under which phasing out an antiquated defense guarantee to a small nation across the Pacific would unhinge the entire area's stability requires the existence of the sort of aggressive, hegemonic threat once posed by communism. But the Soviet Union no longer exits, and the People's Republic of China (PRC) is unlikely to pose such a threat in the near future. Although Beijing's military power is growing, its capabilities remain modest; moreover, so far, the PRC's ambitions appear peaceful, though more assertive than in the past.[7] Even if the ROK, by virtue of its highly symbolic role in the Cold War struggle with Moscow and China, was important in the fight against communism in 1950, it is not today.[8] In the unlikely event that North Korea defeated the ROK, it would be a triumph for an isolated and impoverished Stalinist state, not international communism or anything else.

THE ILLUSION OF PARITY

Even if an independent Korea were strategically important for the United States today, why must the United States provide a treaty and troops to ensure Korean security? Put bluntly, why can't the ROK defend itself?

American policymakers never seem to ask this question. It is true that the North possesses a quantitative military edge. However, such dramatic statistics, in the words of military analyst Stephen Goose, "are usually overstated, almost always misleading, and often meaningless."[9] Seoul, too, has advantages.[10] Moreover, the end of the Cold War has left North Korea essentially friendless, while the ROK is picking up allies. In sum, Seoul is handily winning the inter-Korean competition.

Of course, it would still be foolish to be complacent, and some analysts make legitimate criticisms of aspects of ROK military preparedness. But when Seoul argues that further U.S. force reductions should wait until "after the security environment on the Korean Peninsula has improved and South and North Korea begin to coexist peacefully,"[11] it ignores its own responsibility. Current military disparities between the North and South result not from, say, uncontrollable sunspots, but from conscious policy decisions in Seoul.

For years, ROK and U.S. officials both have projected the South's imminent achievement of parity against the North.[12] But in the mid-1990s, Seoul still lags militarily. Why? Explains the ROK: "North Korea adopted its 'Four-point Military Guidelines' in the early 1960s and has given top priority to building up its military."[13] Yet this is no excuse. With a larger population and exploding GDP, South Korea did not, acknowledges the Ministry of National Defense, begin "its own force improvement program" until "twelve years later than North Korea," after which "the disparity between the military capabilities of South and North Korea [had become] quite severe."[14] In sum, the South chose not to match Pyongyang's military buildup. It has been able to make this choice because of American protection. Seoul admits it "concentrated on its economic and social development" while North Korea emphasized military production.[15]

However much that strategy may have made sense in the past, it is obsolete today. The GDPs of the ROK and the DPRK were estimated to be $455.5 billion to $22.3 billion, respectively, in 1995. The South need only spend 5 percent of its GDP to make its defense budget equivalent to the entire North Korean economy. North Korea is in a race that it simply cannot win.

Yet while ROK military outlays have been rising in absolute terms, they have been falling as a percentage of that government's overall budget (from 35.9 percent in 1980 to 30.4 percent in 1990 to 24.2 percent in 1994) and as a percentage of GNP (from 6.0 percent in 1980 to 4.4 percent in 1990 to 3.5 percent in 1994).[16] Simply returning to the relative defense effort of 1980 would yield an 83 percent budget increase, providing more than enough resources to match those of the DPRK.

THE COSTS OF COMMITMENT

Although the United States gains neither economic nor security benefits from its military guarantee to South Korea, Washington's promise to go to war on the ROK's behalf imposes high security and economic costs. The risk of unnecessary involvement in another conflict, one in which the United States has no vital interest at stake, is the most important expense. True, the presence of U.S. troops in the ROK reduces the likelihood of a North Korean invasion. However, positioning American soldiers between the two potential combatants ensures that the United States would be involved in any second Korean War.

Such a conflict would be bloody, given the concentration of manpower and materiel along the peninsula's 155-mile long border. The military risks would be greatly exacerbated if Pyongyang developed even a small nuclear arsenal, since U.S. forces would provide a tempting target. Indeed, nowhere else are so many Americans so conveniently clustered for attack by a power that might feel it has nothing to lose.

Another military cost of Washington's security guarantee is that it discourages development of the ROK military. The United States is more secure if allied nations are strong enough to contain regional threats. Yet the U.S. presence in Korea not only allows but encourages the ROK to spend less on its military than it otherwise would. In fact, as long as the United States is willing to maintain a tripwire in the region, Seoul would be foolish to become self-sufficient.

At the same time, the Mutual Defense Treaty is economically expensive for the United States. The direct marginal cost of stationing 37,000 troops in Korea is small by Washington standards; however, the most important expense is not deploying troops, but maintaining and equipping military forces sufficient to provide both forward-deployed troops in Korea itself and the back-up units stationed in East Asia and the United States. Although the exact cost to the United States of its Korean guarantee depends upon one's underlying assumptions, it probably ranges between $15 billion and $20 billion annually.[17]

The burden on the U.S. economy runs even deeper, however. Unnecessary military spending causes the United States, in effect, to borrow from its allies to defend them. The result may not be as dramatic as the "imperial overstretch" on the dilapidated empires of earlier centuries, like the Hapsburgs. But it is still significant. The problem is not just the extra spending devoted to Korea and other allies, as such, but the economic impact resulting from the diversion of resources from civilian to economic purposes required to sustain U.S. overseas military commitments, including the U.S. commitment to Seoul.[18]

U.S. subsidies for the defense of other nations, including some of the nations who bargain most tenaciously with the United States on trade issues, like South Korea, have another pernicious effect. Not only do they divert U.S. resources from more economically beneficial pursuits, they also free up funds for other nations that these nations can then use in competition with United States. Every dollar that South Korea does not spend on the military can be used to advance economic or other goals. Over the years, U.S. defense guarantees have thereby created a huge economic wedge between the United States and other nations. In general, cross-national comparisons demonstrate that countries with higher military expenditures invest less, which lowers productivity and slows economic growth. [19] In the case of Seoul and Washington, the per capita military spending gap between South Korea and the United States actually widened between 1981 and 1994. Without the U.S. subsidy, Seoul, which spent $13 billion on defense in 1997, would have had to double or triple its military budget to replace the conventional forces deployed for its defense by the United States.

A NEW AMERICAN STRATEGY

In the aftermath of World War II, America's interventionist foreign policy appeared to have a purpose: containment of the hegemonic threat posed by the Soviet Union and its satellite allies. Today, however, there is nothing left to contain. The United States now reigns utterly supreme—possessing the world's largest and most productive economy, the most effective and sophisticated military, the most pervasive and even overpowering culture, and the largest collection of populous and prosperous allies. Indeed, the United States and its allies and friends account for roughly 80 percent of the globe's military spending. Washington's enemies, such as they are, comprise a handful of dismal, impoverished dictatorships.

In this world, the Defense Department argues that U.S. bilateral commitments remain inviolable and that the end of the Cold War has not diminished their importance."[20] But it has in fact diminished their importance—particularly the importance of the U.S. commitment to South Korea. In 1953, the ROK was a wreck; without a U.S. security guarantee, South Korea would not have survived for long—and not surviving could have had severe international consequences. Today, however, the South is prosperous and democratic; its adversary is poor, famished, and isolated. North Korea talks of avoiding absorption by Seoul, not of conquest. The suggestion that the South needs Washington's help is frankly ridiculous—rather like the United States begging European countries for help in defending against Mexico.

All of this has led to a busy search for new threats against the ROK requiring Washington's attention. The list now includes China and Japan, along with the ubiquitous demon of instability. Seoul's desire for a friendly big brother is understandable, but the ROK could build a military sufficient to make the cost of aggression too high for any of its neighbors. In any case, even if the potential new threats were serious, they would neither make the South any more vital to America's security, nor reduce the cost of offering South Korea a security guarantee. Without a looming threat of hegemonic Soviet communism, South Korea loses its connection to U.S. security, along with the rationale for the United States to maintain an expensive and dangerous military tripwire so far from home.

PROGRAM OF ACTION

The United States should phase out its troop presence and security guarantee for South Korea. Washington should negotiate over the exact details, but it should set a deadline for the departure of the troops and cancellation of the Mutual Defense Treaty. Disengagement should be total—all soldiers, all guarantees. Doing otherwise, following Jimmy Carter's plan of gradual withdrawal, offers little advantage to the United States since it would remain committed to going to war and maintaining the forces necessary to do so. As it pulls out its troops, Washington should assure Seoul that it nevertheless wants to maintain cultural, economic, and political ties; reducing trade barriers should remain a U.S. priority.

At the same time, the United States should encourage cooperation, both bilateral and through regional forums like ASEAN, among like-minded nations, most obviously Japan and the ROK, which have so many common interests despite their strained relations. Serious regional cooperation will not come easily, but it is less likely to develop as long as Washington makes it unnecessary by policing the region.

The United States should also follow a policy of conciliation with North Korea. Although a detailed assessment of Pyongyang's activities and goals is beyond the scope of this paper, it appears that the DPRK, despite continuing provocation and recrimination, is trying to develop improved international ties. Washington should follow through on its 1994 nuclear freeze agreement with Pyongyang, push to expand diplomatic links, and lift restrictions on trade. The goal should be to draw the North into a more responsible regional role. Such an effort may fail, but it is worth trying, irrespective of the latest permutations of South Korean policy. Should Pyongyang instead grow more hostile, or even restart its nuclear program, the United States would have no good options, but maintaining the Mutual Defense Treaty would still be unnecessary, since the South would remain capable of defending itself.[21]

Following this strategy would enhance both the economic and the security interests of the United States. Eliminating unnecessary military commitments and forces would benefit U.S. citizens by cutting federal spending and improving the nation's competitive position. Disengagement would also reduce the risk of war without impairing any vital or even important interests. South Korea, too, would ultimately gain, though the benefits would be more intangible. It would allow South Korea to shed its dependency on a distant superpower, a dependency that is both humiliating and potentially dangerous since the United States could end up dragging the ROK into a confrontation with its neighboring states.

Are there risks from American withdrawal from Korea? Of course—anything is possible, however unlikely. As historian William Stueck observes, the original war was "laden with miscalculation on all sides."[22] But that record is all the more reason to disengage. Mistakes made between 1945 and 1950 left the United States little choice but to fight a three-year war in a country with no connection to U.S. security. With the end of the Cold War, Washington need no longer take such risks.

To advance both its economic and its security interests, Washington should terminate the Mutual Defense Treaty and adopt a policy of strategic independence. Washington should risk the lives and wealth of its citizens only when something fundamental is at stake for their own political community. That is no longer the case on the Korean Peninsula.

NOTES

[1] *United States Security Strategy for the East Asia-Pacific Region* (Washington, DC: Department of Defense, February 1995), p. 10.

[2] *Ibid.*

[3] Ministry of National Defense, *Defense White Paper*: 1994-1995 (Seoul: Republic of Korea, 1995), p. 235.

[4] Ted Galen Carpenter, "South Korea: A Vital or Peripheral U.S. Security Interest?" in Doug Bandow and Ted Galen Carpenter, eds., *The U.S. South Korean Alliance: Time for a Change* (Washington, DC: Cato Institute, 1992), p. 3.

[5] Quoted in David Pitt, "Seoul, U.S. Forces and the North: The Balance Is As Delicate as Ever," *New York Times*, April 8, 1987, p. A10.

[6] *United States Security Strategy for the East Asia-Pacific Region*, p. 10.

[7] Not everyone agrees with this analysis, obviously, but see Doug Bandow, *Tripwire: Korea and U.S. Foreign Policy in a Changed World* (Washington, DC: Cato Institute, 1996), pp. 153-60.

[8] In fact, the Truman Administration, Joint Chiefs of Staff, and Gen. Douglas MacArthur originally did not believe that South Korea's survival was vital even then. See Bandow, *Tripwire: Korea and U.S. Foreign Policy*, p. 66. The Truman Administration shifted course after Pyongyang's invasion because of its belief that the invasion was Soviet-inspired and therefore part of a larger global struggle.

[9] Stephen Goose, "The Military Situation on the Korean Peninsula," in John Sullivan and Roberta Foss, eds., *Two Koreas—One Future?* (Lanham, MD.: University Press of America, 1987), p. 57.

[10] Bandow, *Tripwire: Korea and U.S. Foreign Policy*, pp. 68-69.

[11] *Defense White Paper*: 1994-1995, p. 128.

[12] Bandow, *Tripwire: Korea and* U.S. *Foreign Policy*, pp. 71-73.

[13] Ministry of National Defense, *Defense White Paper*: 1992-1993 (Seoul: Republic of Korea, 1993), p. 31.

[14] Ministry of National Defense, *Defense White Paper*: 1991-1992 (Seoul: Republic of Korea, 1992), p. 31.

[15] Ministry of National Defense, *Defense White Paper*: 1989 (Seoul: Republic of Korea), p. 118.

[16] *Defense White Paper*: 1994-1995, pp. 223-24; Ministry of National Defense, *Defense White Paper*: 1990 (Seoul: Republic of Korea, 1991), p. 154.

[17] Bandow, *Tripwire: Korea and* U.S. *Foreign Policy*, pp. 40-41.

[18] Bandow, *Tripwire: Korea and* U.S. *Foreign Policy*, pp. 46-52.

[19] Robert DeGrasse, *Military Expansion, Economic Decline: The Impact of Military Spending on* U.S. *Economic Performance* (Armonk, NY: M.E. Sharpe, 1983), pp. 47-48.

[20] *United States Security Strategy for the East Asia-Pacific Region*, p. 6.

[21] See, e.g., Bandow, *Tripwire: Korea and* U.S. *Foreign Policy*, pp. 138-42.

[22] William Stueck, *The Korean War: An International History* (Princeton, NJ: Princeton University Press, 1995), p. 353.

U.S. ECONOMIC AND SECURITY INTERESTS IN CHINA

CHARLES W. FREEMAN, JR.

CHINA, TAIWAN, AND THE UNITED STATES

Most Americans now accept that China is destined, early in the coming century, to resume its millennial pre-1850 status as the world's largest economy.[1] They expect that sometime afterward, China will become a world-class military power. There is, however, no agreement about the impact of China's rise to wealth and power on U.S. interests. Many worry that growing Chinese military prowess could overturn the Asian-Pacific balance of power, challenging American leadership, and gradually imposing a Chinese sphere of influence in the region. Others see a modernized and internationally engaged Chinese military as having the potential to contribute to regional stability and the maintenance of global order. Many are apprehensive that China's economic expansion may disrupt the international trading and investment system formed under U.S. leadership over the past fifty years. Still others argue that if Beijing can be assimilated to the norms of the global economy, China's rapid economic development can help lift living standards in the United States.

The United States emerged on the world stage over the course of the century between the Mexican War of 1846-48 and World War II, i.e., 1939-45. This period coincided with the century of China's eclipse (from the Opium War of 1839-42 to the civil war of 1946-49). Fifty years of transition (roughly coterminous with U.S. preoccupation with the Cold War) have set China on the path to re-attaining the "comprehensive strength" it has long sought. The United States is having difficulty adjusting to a non-bipolar world in which China is an assertively independent actor. For its part, China has yet to learn how to behave with the responsible assurance of a strong and confident country rather than the thin-skinned suspicion of a weak and traumatized one.

CHINA AND U.S. SECURITY INTERESTS

Whether the shifts in the balance of power that China's rise entails harm or help U. S. security, they promise to challenge long-vested American interests over the coming decades. Among the U.S. security interests in doubt are:

- The capacity of the United States to regulate global transfers of militarily sensitive technology and to inhibit the transfer of weapons systems ("weapons of mass destruction") that could threaten the military/technological superiority of the United States or U.S. allies and friends in regions like the Middle East and Persian Gulf;
- The unilateral U.S. guarantee that China cannot impose reunification on its lost province of Taiwan by force;
- The freedom of the United States to intervene militarily in East Asia without fear of retaliation against the United States;
- The position of the United States as the dominant external actor and security partner in the Korean Peninsula and Southeast Asia and as the primary influence on the South Asian politico-military balance;
- The post–World War II status of Japan as American auxiliary rather than as independent military actor in the western Pacific;
- The century-old U.S. interest in preventing the domination of either end of the Eurasian landmass (i.e., the eastern Atlantic and Western Europe or the western Pacific and East Asia) by another great power; and
- The post–Cold War status of the United States, in security terms, as the sole world power, i.e., the only nation whose military reach spans the globe.

Whether these challenges to U.S. security interests eventuate depends in the first instance, of course, on the extent to which China's economic resources are directed at building up its military strength. So far, the evidence in this regard is hardly alarming. Despite China's rapid economic growth, its defense budget remains modest in relation to the military challenges facing China's People's Liberation Army (PLA). This reflects the low priority China has assigned to military, rather than other, aspects of modernization.[2]

In almost every direction, a defensively deployed PLA faces forces that are significantly more modern and capable than its best units. (China's defense planners must consider threats to territories China considers its own from Russia, India, Vietnam, other ASEAN members, Taiwan, Korea, and Japan, not to mention the United States.) The PLA has, nonetheless, been on short rations, forced to pursue modernization through downsizing and the retirement of obsolete equipment. For most of the past fifteen years of rapid economic growth in China, the country's defense budget has been flat or declining, after discounting inflation. Meanwhile, the share of GDP available as revenue to the Chinese central government has been declining. This raises doubts about China's capacity to fund a major military modernization program, should its priorities shift in this direction. Both the level of China's military effort and the resources available to fund it may now again be rising, but it will be a long time before Chinese forces can match those of China's neighbors in quality, much less those of the United States.[3]

Security challenges, however, are not decided by the relative size of economies. Nor is the outcome of war decided by levels of technology alone. When Japan reacted to American sanctions (intended to signal Washington's objections to Tokyo's hegemony in East Asia) by attacking Pearl Harbor, Japanese GDP was about a tenth that of the United States. Japan nevertheless proved a difficult enemy for the United States to overcome. Overwhelming American economic and technological superiority did not gain U. S. victory in the Korean War, and it failed to prevent defeat in Vietnam. Clearly, other factors can outweigh economics and technology in war.

Among these factors is the balance of fervor between contending parties. When one side in a conflict believes its supreme interest in national survival or its vital interests (such as territorial integrity) are at stake, while the other has less compelling strategic interests in the outcome of a dispute, the willingness to make disproportionate sacrifices can overcome technical factors like a disparity in economic strength or technology. Will, as well as strategic acumen, counts heavily even in the nuclear age.

In estimating the Chinese challenge, therefore, one must start by considering Chinese national purposes and the degree of fervor attached to them. There is no reason to doubt Chinese sincerity in seeking a "peaceful international environment" so that China can continue its economic reconstruction. To that end, China has settled its territorial disputes with Russia and is forging a broad partnership with it. It has developed mutually beneficial economic cooperation and security dialogue with Japan and Western European nations. China would like a similarly stable relationship with the United States. Many of its regional objectives are congruent with those of the United States. Beijing has sought to avoid chaos or war on the Korean Peninsula, to preserve Pakistan as a counter to Indian hegemony in South Asia, and to promote amicable relations with Southeast Asian nations. China's military objectives remain modest and—in its view—limited to the defense of Chinese sovereignty and territorial integrity.

The PLA has the following mission:

- To defend the borders and territories currently controlled by China against further efforts by foreign nations to alter or detach them;
- To back up Chinese diplomatic efforts to avoid permanent separation and ultimately achieve recovery of territories wrested from China by great-power intervention—the European seizures of Hong Kong and Macao, the Japanese annexation of Taiwan and the Senkaku (Diaoyu) archipelago, and U.S. Cold War efforts to foster a rival Chinese regime on Taiwan;
- To establish secure and recognized maritime boundaries for the Chinese state where long-standing Chinese claims are now subject to challenge, as in the case of post-independence claims by the Philippines, Malaysia, Brunei, and Vietnam to islets and reefs in the South China Sea and by North Korea, South Korea, and Indonesia to continental shelf and other seabed resources;
- To re-take Taiwan by force if Chinese diplomacy fails (unlike Hong Kong and Macao, where it has succeeded);
- To protect other borders if they are subjected to military challenge (e.g., by Russia, India, Vietnam, or other member states of ASEAN);
- To guarantee the Chinese state against external intervention, coercion, or dictation by other great powers; and
- To support ultimate Chinese emergence as a world power with "comprehensive strength."

Notably absent from this list are many of the aspirations and objectives that made the rise of other great powers, such as the United States, Germany, Japan, or the Soviet Union, so disruptive of international peace and security. China asserts no doctrine of "manifest destiny" or hemispheric exclusion. It has no ideology of

Lebensraum to motivate territorial expansion. Its revanchism does not extend to areas inhabited and claimed by non-Chinese. China does not seek to bring additional minority (non-Han) peoples within its borders. Beijing has no universal set of values and beliefs it can explain to its own people, still less an ideology it seeks to impose on others. China appears to believe that access to distant resources is best guaranteed by an open international trading system rather than by power projection.[4] It has no colonies or satellites and no apparent impulse to establish them. China stations no troops beyond its own borders, as it defines them. It vehemently denies its desire to establish an East Asian order similar to that of the pre-Western colonial era, when Beijing's power overawed China's neighbors.

But however limited China's objectives may be, some of them directly affect the interests of the United States and its allies, especially Japan. China's determination to retain its distinctive political system contradicts the American impulse to enlarge the zone of adherence to the liberal values of American constitutional democracy. Ultimately, China's aspirations conflict with the understandable desire of the United States to remain unchallenged as the single global power.

The principal issue between the United States and China arises, however, from China's ambition to undo its dismemberment by past foreign intervention, specifically to reincorporate Taiwan, if only symbolically, under a single Chinese sovereignty. This imperative is at the very heart of modern Chinese nationalism. Despite Beijing's patient preference for a political solution to the problem of Taiwan's relationship to the rest of China,[5] there can be no doubt about its willingness to use force against Taiwan, if it must. Beijing has made clear that it will intervene militarily if Taiwan's politics, aided and abetted by U.S. or other forces (e.g., Japanese sympathy for Taiwanese separatism), seem to be taking Taiwan toward independence or otherwise foreclosing the possibility of Taiwan's ultimate re-association with "China" under a single sovereignty.

That is, unfortunately, precisely where Beijing believes Taipei is now headed. The need to deter Taiwanese separatism and possible U.S. military backing for it has given Chinese military modernization the sense of urgency and focus it previously lacked. Beijing has long had the capability to intimidate Taiwan through military measures short of war, as it showed when it deployed missiles in the Taiwan Strait in 1996. The PLA's post-1996 obsession with building the capability to conquer Taiwan, and with being able to sink American aircraft carriers if necessary, will not produce a credible invasion capability for a decade or so. Eventually, however, it will.

The good news is that China's focus on Taiwan diverts resources that might otherwise have been devoted to building power-projection capabilities and gives Beijing incentives to compose conflicts with its neighbors on less important border issues. (Recent Chinese diplomacy toward Central Asia, India, and Southeast Asia reflects this.) The bad news is that China is preparing for the possible requirement to use force on the one issue that might set off armed conflict between it and the United States and that these preparations involve building a formidable amphibious warfare capability. Aware of the heavy costs military action against Taiwan would entail, Beijing will remain reluctant to use force against the island unless provoked by developments there. Taiwan's drive for an international status separate from "China," however, virtually guarantees that such provocation will be forthcoming.[6]

As the twenty-first century begins, the United States may face an increasingly stark choice: whether to prepare for eventual war with China over Taiwan's international status or to promote a political solution to cross–Taiwan Strait relations that finesses the danger of war and consequent Sino-American conflict. Gearing up for possible war with a steadily strengthening China would require major increases in U.S. defense spending. A Sino-American conflict over Taiwan would not necessarily be local or regional; it could escalate into general, trans-Pacific war.[7] Even in the absence of armed conflict in the Taiwan Strait, however, emotional Sino-American confrontation over the issue of Taiwan has the potential to poison the relationship between Washington and Beijing and to set off a pattern of hostility between them, first in the Asia-Pacific region and then, as China's power grows, globally. However, promoting a political accommodation in the Taiwan Strait to avoid this unpleasant prospect would place heavy demands on presidential leadership. The president would have to create a large measure of domestic U.S. consensus on an issue that historically has divided Americans. The Chinese civil war and its Taiwan legacy have been an especially contentious issue between Congress and the Executive Branch. Promoting peace would require the United States to go beyond the deterrence of war in the Taiwan Strait. It would very likely demand that the president take an ideologically unpalatable stand against Taiwanese aspirations for self-determination that constitute the

Chinese *casus belli* in the Strait, and embrace the cause of Chinese reunification, even as he continued to warn Beijing against the use of force to achieve it.

Even if American diplomacy can somehow restore a *modus vivendi* and credible prospects for a peaceful settlement between Chinese on both sides of the Taiwan Strait, the United States, like China's neighbors, will still face the problem of how to deal with the massive shifts in regional power balances that China's rise implies. The specific matters at issue between China and its neighbors are as small as the uninhabited islands and reefs whose sovereignty they contest. Only minor territorial adjustments would be required to settle these disputes. How such adjustments take place, however, has large implications for the future pattern of politics in the region and for the U.S. role in it.

China has sought to reassure its neighbors by deferring, rather than pressing for, negotiations to establish its maritime borders. Korea, Japan, and Southeast Asian countries may be forgiven, however, for viewing Chinese procrastination with apprehension. China, they calculate, may wish to wait until the balance of power in the region has shifted decisively in its favor. China might then seek to dictate solutions to its neighbors, rather than compromise with them. This risk would exist even with a continuing, active, and assertive U.S. military presence in the region. Without such a presence, however, no combination of Asian-Pacific states could hope ultimately to balance Chinese power. China's neighbors would have no alternative but to appease it. These realities are at the heart of the regional concerns about Chinese hegemony, which have not been allayed by Beijing's denunciations of "the erroneous theory of a Chinese threat."

Whether the United States can maintain the military presence and play the balancing role in the region that its allies and friends desire depends in the first instance on whether the American people are willing to shoulder that burden. It also depends, however, on the character of Sino-American politico-military relations. If these relations are constructive and cordial, Asian-Pacific states will see much benefit and little cost in continued cooperation with the U. S. military. If, however, the Taiwan issue or other factors cause Sino-American relations to settle into tension and hostility, Asian-Pacific states will see continued military identification with the United States as risking embroilment in conflict with China. Few, if any, will wish to assume that risk. This, more than any other reason, is why military "containment" (confrontation and isolation) of China is not a viable option for the United States.

CHINA AND U.S. ECONOMIC INTERESTS

If military containment of China is not a realistic option for the United States, neither is economic containment.[8] For better or ill, China will clearly play an increasingly large part in both the regional and global economies. The question is not whether this can be prevented, but what the consequences of China's larger economic role will be. The issues for the United States are: first, assuring that China's economic growth does not adversely affect U.S. interests or mitigating such adverse effects if they occur; and second, assuring that Americans enjoy open and nondiscriminatory ("most favored nation" or MFN) access to growing Chinese markets.[9]

Among the U.S. economic interests that China's growth might challenge are the following:

- The maintenance of the integrity and effective operation of the global trading and investment system built under the past fifty years of American economic leadership, on whose increasingly open markets and orderly management of economic conflict U.S. prosperity has come progressively to depend;
- The peerless leadership role and bargaining power of the United States within the global economic system, as China's economy grows to be larger than the U.S. economy and, ultimately, larger than the U.S. and Japanese economies combined;
- Stability in sectors (especially labor-intensive sectors) of the U.S. economy (and the jobs associated with them) where China enjoys comparative advantage (e.g., in labor costs or indifference to environmental and other socially dictated production costs);
- U.S. export growth, should political tensions result in U.S. sanctions or Chinese discrimination against U.S. sales to a Chinese economy that will constitute an increasing percentage of the overall global market;
- The long-standing U.S. dominance of certain third-country foreign markets, if China feels free to follow predatory marketing practices;
- The protection of intellectual property rights central to the continued competitiveness of the U.S. economy;

- The continued structural reliance of the U.S. economy on cheap energy from low-priced oil imports, as Chinese demand bids up international energy prices;
- The ability of the United States to finance its budgetary and current account deficits with foreign capital, as China competes for an increasing percentage of global capital flows; and
- The avoidance of threats to the global and American quality of life, through irresponsible Chinese neglect of the environmental consequences of rapid industrialization.

Some of these challenges are unavoidable consequences of the emergence of a major new player on the global trade and investment scene. Painful adjustments in the structure of U.S. industry and agriculture are always taking place in response to changes in patterns of international trade and finance, not just changes produced by the rise of China. Such adjustments, however, have special political consequences when they can be attributed to developments or patterns of behavior in a particular foreign country. Perceived unfair Chinese competition with domestic U.S. industries, the loss of jobs as imports from China rise in particular sectors of the U.S. market, and the highly visible U.S. bilateral trade deficit with China all serve to generate pressure for a tough U.S. stand on short-term trade and investment issues with China. In turn, this can create an atmosphere of bilateral confrontation. The only way to mitigate the effect of trade and investment disputes between the two countries is to assure that other elements of the relationship are sufficiently positive to offset it.

Other possible economic challenges from China, however, will be greatly affected by the character of U.S.–China relations and U.S. policies toward China's role in the global economy. It makes a big difference whether Chinese and Americans see themselves as engaged in a zero-sum game or as interacting to advance the common prosperity. The key, in this regard, is whether the United States acts to include or to exclude China from the international rule-making bodies it helped to create and continues to lead.

It is impossible to imagine that the current global trading and investment system could function effectively if the United States—as the world's largest economy—was not fully part of it and prepared to play by its rules. That system will also be unable to function effectively if China is not fully part of it and playing by its rules, once China's economic weight has grown to match or surpass that of the United States. That is why Americans and other non-Chinese have such a large stake in bringing China into the world's economic institutions and regulatory regimes[10] on terms that buttress rather than distort their operation. The fact that China's bargaining power is growing apace with its economy makes it desirable to negotiate China's inclusion sooner rather than later. This is all the more so because China's idiosyncratic pattern of economic growth is creating a widening range of vested interests by Chinese organizations and individuals against the painful internal adjustments Beijing would have to make to conform to global norms. As China's self-confidence grows, moreover, its willingness to trade substantive concessions for international acceptance is diminishing.

THE INTERPLAY OF SECURITY AND ECONOMIC RELATIONS

If the security relationship between China and the United States becomes consistently adversarial, it is hard to imagine that the economic relationship between the two countries can develop smoothly. Sino-American contention over security matters raises issues of national pride and creates political tensions that make it difficult, if not impossible, for the two sides to engage in the kind of framework setting necessary to promote freer trade and investment between the two economies. Such tensions engender political interference with commercial transactions from both sides.[11] They reduce the willingness of politicians in both countries to risk appearing to make concessions to the other on economic as well as political matters. Conversely, however, a cooperative economic relationship does not guarantee a non-adversarial security relationship or political cooperation. History is full of examples of countries with strong and growing economic ties that nevertheless went to war with each other. Nor does bilateral economic confrontation over trade and investment issues necessarily translate into military tension. That has not been the U.S. experience with allies like Japan or the member states of the European Union (EU).

A bilateral relationship can be damaged by economic tensions, to be sure, but only tensions in the security arena have the potential to destroy the relationship. More than anything else, the difficulty the United States and China have had in conducting their relations to mutual satisfaction stems from the failure of either side to invest much effort in building political understanding with the other. Since the Chinese suppression of the June 1989 student uprising at Tiananmen Square, most Americans have viewed interaction with China as politically incorrect. For much of the period since then, the United States went out of its way to demonstrate its contempt for the Chinese political system and its distaste for and distrust of the Chinese leadership.[12] China responded with a reflexively counterproductive mixture of passivity, protest, suspicion, and reprisal. In 1993, the Clinton Administration adopted a declared policy of comprehensive engagement with China, but failed to carry it out. This has not been a constructive or productive time in Sino-American relations.

TOWARD "COMPREHENSIVE ENGAGEMENT"?

The United States began in 1996 to carry out its declared policy of engagement with China. In a May speech in New York, and in more detail in November in Shanghai, then Secretary of State Warren Christopher signaled an American resolve to replace derogatory diatribe with respectful dialogue between the two countries. He called for regular summit meetings and institutionalization of other high-level exchanges. These speeches, and National Security Council Advisor Anthony Lake's visit to Beijing in July 1996 (the first by an American official since December 1989), began to articulate an organizing principle for Sino-American relations. (Such a framework has long been needed to replace the collapsed Washington-Beijing-Moscow strategic triangle.) The Administration will now work with China to integrate it fully into the international state system as a responsible member of the councils of the great powers. It has, meanwhile, adopted a more cautious approach to the issue of Taiwan. The questions at the time of this writing are: whether the Administration's new policy will survive the change in its foreign policy team; whether China, after nearly seven years of frustration and pique with Washington, will be ready to meet the United States halfway; and whether positive Sino-American engagement can survive the inevitable setbacks and attacks it can expect to face from political forces in both countries and in Taiwan.[13]

If so, there is a chance that the improved political atmosphere between the two countries would allow the United States to:

- Maneuver Taipei and Beijing away from the course of confrontation on which they are embarked and toward a refashioned *modus vivendi* in which they could resume exploration of a mutually acceptable long-term relationship;
- Strike an acceptable Sino-American deal on China's entry into the WTO that phases in China's adherence to the global norms

governing international trade and investment and opens China's economy to greatly expanded American exports;

- End the cycle of U.S. sanctions and Chinese counteractions that has acted to depress bilateral trade, especially U.S. exports to China;
- Work with China to broker a reduction of tensions on the Korean Peninsula and between India and Pakistan;
- Stimulate China and ASEAN nations to begin active negotiations to settle their differences over islands and resources in the South China Sea;
- Bring China into the MTCR and other international bodies that set standards for the international transfer of sensitive technologies, thereby binding China to current and future norms on these matters; and
- Help China to remove blockages to successful modernization (such as the absence of an adequate legal system) and to address problems its rapid economic development is causing for it, its neighbors, and the global community (such as environmental damage to its own territory and uncontrolled contributions to global warming).

Both the security and economic interests of the United States, as well as U.S. relations with Asian-Pacific allies, would be well served by a well-coordinated U.S. policy that aimed at these objectives.

NOTES

[1] Economic historians estimate that, throughout the premodern period, China's economy was between 30 and 40 percent of global GDP, and sometimes more. They dispute whether the Roman Empire, at its height, had an economy larger than China's.

[2] Estimates of the Chinese defense budget range all over the lot. The difficulty arises not only from Chinese secrecy but also from the fact that the PLA's budget is constructed along very different lines from those with which it is compared. The PLA budget omits military pensions and most of the costs of research and development, foreign arms acquisitions, reserves, and militia forces. Many costs are shared by provincial and local governments. Others are financed by profits from PLA-owned industries.

The published Chinese defense budget is about $8.4 billion at nominal exchange rates. Adding in the items usually included in Western defense budgets might triple that figure or more, producing a defense budget as high as $30 billion. That amount would, of course, buy vastly more in China than it would in a Western economy, where labor and other costs are much higher. Consider the level of defense that nominal defense budgets of $554 million and $2.2 billion buy, respectively, for Vietnam and the Democratic People's Republic of Korea.

The problem of estimating China's defense budgets is exacerbated by China's longstanding aversion to transparency. This policy was adopted to conceal China's weakness when it was threatened by attack from the United States and the Soviet Union. It may now serve the purpose of concealing China's growing strength, especially through its investment in capabilities to take Taiwan by force.

Still, all the alarm about Chinese defense spending is hard to take seriously. The World Bank estimates that central, provincial, and local government revenues constitute about 10 percent of China's GDP, with less than 4 percent of GDP available to the central government. If Chinese defense spending takes about a third of the central government budget and a tenth or less of provincial and local government expenditure, it amounts to less than 2 percent of GDP. The most generous estimates of China's GDP in terms of purchasing power parity (PPP) place it at about $3 trillion. In PPP terms, therefore, the Chinese defense budget would be about $50 billion. Estimates of Chinese defense spending higher than that strain credulity.

The best that can be said is that Chinese military spending is significantly larger than $8.4 billion.

[3] In the short term, the qualitative gap between the PLA and its potential adversaries is actually widening, given the pace of military modernization in China's West Asian neighbors, especially Taiwan. The Asia-Pacific region now spends more on defense than all of Europe (excluding the states of the former Soviet Union). East Asia vies with the Middle East as the largest market for international arms exports.

[4] "Power projection" is taught in Chinese military academies as part of the course on foreign military doctrines. China seeks to join existing international organizations on as favorable terms as possible, rather than to overthrow or displace such institutions.

[5] Unlike India, which seized Goa by force, or Indonesia, which did the same with Irian Jaya and East Timor, China was willing to wait for negotiated solutions of both the Hong Kong and Macao issues. Beijing's opening reunification proposal to Taiwan concedes that the island's economic and political systems would remain unchanged by reunification, that Taiwan could keep its armed forces, and that no civilian or military officials from the Mainland would be stationed in Taiwan after reunification. Taiwan would thus enjoy an enhanced version of the "one country, two systems" scheme to be applied in Hong Kong and Macao. Taipei is naturally skeptical about

the sincerity and reliability of these PRC positions, which would symbolically subordinate Taiwan to Beijing.

[6] Beijing's and Taipei's policies now seem diametrically opposed and premised on confrontation rather than accommodation.

Beijing:

- Strives to sustain the principle of "one China" as the basis of policy toward Taiwan in the United States, Japan, Southeast Asia and elsewhere, and to persuade foreigners to refrain from intervention in the quarrel between Chinese on either side of the Taiwan Strait;
- Has put Taipei on probation, indicating that it reserves the right to punish Taiwan for any further efforts Taipei may make to separate itself from "China" or otherwise alter the status quo in the Taiwan Strait;
- Actively promotes economic and cultural interdependence across the Taiwan Strait to ease the path to future reunification;
- Seeks to defer political dialogue with Taipei until Hong Kong and Macao have been absorbed, Lee Teng-Hui has left office, and Taipei has agreed that the basis of discussion will be the idea of "one China, two systems"; and
- Seeks to build a credible military capability to invade and conquer Taiwan should efforts to achieve reunification through cross-Strait negotiations ultimately fail.

Taipei, on the other hand:

- Seeks officially to establish a principle of "one China, two equal political entities" and to enter the United Nations as a state separate from the People's Republic of China under the name "Republic of China." Taiwan's main opposition party, meanwhile, lobbies internationally for support for Taiwan independence and U.N. membership under the name "Republic of Taiwan";
- While keeping a wary eye on Beijing, strives to accumulate the attributes of independent statehood internationally wherever and however it can;
- Officially opposes economic and cultural interdependence with the Chinese Mainland despite the opposition of the Taiwanese business community, which is continuing to develop such interdependence through trade and investment across the Taiwan Strait;
- Demands political dialogue with Beijing as an "equal political entity" to establish its status as separate from the People's Republic of China; and

- Seeks to buy additional advanced weaponry from the United States to strengthen deterrence and to consolidate a U.S. commitment to come to its aid if war breaks out in the Taiwan Strait.

Taipei's determination to alter its status in the direction of *de jure* independence, and Beijing's determination to maintain the "one China" *status quo de jure,* pending negotiations on the terms of reunification, make it certain that the Taiwan issue will continue to flare up from time to time.

[7] The United States three times threatened the use of nuclear weapons against China in the 1950s. The desire to gain immunity from such strategic blackmail was a principal motivating factor in China's construction of its current, modest *force de frappe*. China has no credible first-strike capability and therefore has a nuclear policy of "no first use." China has pointed out, however, that it can now retaliate against nuclear or nonnuclear attacks on its territory with counterstrikes on the U.S. homeland or U.S. bases overseas.

[8] When the United States adopted its policy of containment against the former Soviet Union, U.S. GDP constituted about two-thirds of the global economy. The U.S. economy today is about one-fifth of global GDP. Nor does the United States now enjoy the undisputed technological superiority and monopolies it did fifty years ago. The Soviet Union was dedicated to economic autarky. China, by contrast, is committed to an increasingly open trading economy. Other countries would not follow the United States in curtailing trade and investment relations with China.

[9] Ironically, given the much more open U.S. economy, its commitment to national treatment for foreign firms, its relative immunity to political manipulation, and the legal protections it offers against unfair trading practices, the United States has a much larger stake in receiving MFN from China than China does in receiving it from the United States. The problem of non-discriminatory access to the Chinese market is not new. The concept of MFN was invented and first applied to obviate unfair competition in nineteenth century China trade.

[10] These organizations include the World Trade Organization (WTO), the Group of Seven (G-7), the Wassenaar Arrangements (successor to COCOM), the Missile Technology Control Regime (MTCR), and the nuclear suppliers group (London Club).

[11] U.S. sanctions prohibiting exports to China are met by Chinese restrictions on imports from the United States. U.S. sanctions on imports from China draw counter restrictions on Chinese imports from the United States. In both cases, U.S. exports take a major hit. China can usually (though not always) make up the imports it loses under U.S. sanctions by turning to non-American suppliers of similar products (though sometimes products of lesser suitability or quality, and higher cost). This mutually counterproductive game has made many Chinese wary of reliance on imports or other forms of cooperation with U.S. firms, caused them to view the United

States as an unreliable partner, and placed U.S. firms at a competitive disadvantage. It has also deterred American exporters from long-term commitments to develop a market for their products in China.

[12] Over this period, no American president visited Beijing, nor did a Chinese president visit Washington. Contacts between leaders of the two countries occurred only at the margins of international gatherings, like APEC and the U.N. General Assembly. (An effort to arrange a visit by the Chinese president to Washington foundered over the unwillingness of the United States to offer full protocol honors to him.) No effective working relationship was established between the two foreign ministers, who concentrated on exploring differences rather than points of common ground between the two countries. The United States sought (successfully) to block the staging of the Olympics in Beijing. Washington made annual efforts (unsuccessfully) to achieve international condemnation of China at the U.N. Human Rights Commission and treated the U.N. Conference on Women as an opportunity to stage an on-site protest of Chinese human rights practices. The U.S. Congress sought (unsuccessfully) to compel the president to recognize Tibet as a state separate from China, an act of war under international law. The absence of contact reinforced mutual ignorance, as each country misunderstood and misperceived (or failed to perceive) changes taking place in the other. Ignorance created suspicion. Suspicion led to apprehensions of mutual hostility.

[13] Among the flashpoints ahead: the ever-present possibility of another flare-up over Taiwan, the annual MFN debate in the U.S. Congress, which may focus on blocking Administration efforts to negotiate Chinese entry into the WTO; the July 1, 1997, reversion of Hong Kong to China, which—even in the absence of a televisable public relations catastrophe—will likely produce an outpouring of anti-China media commentary and intemperate retorts in the Chinese media; and a September 1997 summit meeting, convened by the government of Panama, to which both Bill Clinton and Lee Teng-hui invited.

U.S. ECONOMIC AND SECURITY INTERESTS IN CHINA

NICHOLAS R. LARDY

ACCOMMODATING TO CHINA AS AN ECONOMIC GIANT

Economic relations between China and the United States have been marked by substantial conflict in the past decade. This has been reflected in disputes on market access, protection of intellectual property, and textiles, to name just a few of the most prominent examples. In addition, Chinese firms have been subject to a record number of anti-dumping cases brought before the International Trade Administration of the Department of Commerce by private U.S. companies. In the view of many, China is rapidly surpassing Japan to become the most troublesome U.S. trading partner.

This chapter reviews the source of these frictions and analyzes the prospects for alleviating them. It also argues that attempts in the past to link U.S. economic interests and specific security interests, for the most part, have failed. Barring a dramatic change in China's strategic posture, there is little reason to expect a different outcome in the future. Nonetheless, greater economic integration of China into the world economy in the long run may be the most effective instrument for ameliorating conflicting security interests between the United States and China.

TRADE FRICTION BETWEEN THE UNITED STATES AND CHINA

The challenge the United States and other countries face is not simply to deal with the rise of China as yet another major player on the international trade and financial scene. Accommodating the rise of China is more complex than accommodating prior economic transformations in the post–World War II era, such as that of Japan, for at least three reasons.[1]

First, China's role in the international economy in the 1990s is far larger than that of any other transition economy. Its trade volume in 1994 was two and one half times that of the Russian Federation and exceeded, by a substantial margin, the combined trade volume of all of the countries of the former Soviet Union. The disparity between China and other transition economies is even greater in terms of access to international capital markets. China's annual inflows of foreign direct investment, US$ 40 billion in 1996, are twelve to fifteen times those of Russia. China has borrowed significant amounts on international capital markets over the past decade, whereas Russia did not make its initial foray into the Eurobond market until late 1996.[2] To the extent that trade frictions between transition and market economies are a function of transition economies' still-incomplete move to the market, the large volume of China's trade ensures that U.S.–China economic relations are likely to remain contentious.

Second, China to an unprecedented degree combines low per capita income, on the one hand, and large absolute size and high levels of international trade and investment on the other. Indeed, in the post-war period no other country with such a relatively low per capita income has played such an important absolute role in international trade and international capital markets. This disparity has been the source of continuing friction between the United States and China over such central issues as the terms on which China is to join the World Trade Organization (WTO). For years, China has argued that its low per capita income entitles it to be treated as a developing country in the WTO. That status would automatically give China the longest allowable times for coming into compliance with the trade and other standards incorporated in the Uruguay Round and would exempt it entirely from a few standards. But the U.S. Trade Representative (USTR) has argued that, although China's income may be below the cutoff point for developing-country status, such status is reserved for countries that have relatively low income and also need special treatment to help them succeed in international trade. Since China's exports have been growing about 15 percent per year over the past decade—the highest rate of growth in trade of any significant international trading country—the USTR argues that China does not need special consideration.

The third reason for U.S.–China trade frictions stems from China's unique trade position vis-a-vis the United States in the postwar period. China is the only country with which the United States has had a large bilateral trade deficit that has not itself had a global trade surplus. All other countries with which the United

States has run significant trade deficits have been global surplus countries. The best recent example is Japan. Its global trade surplus soared from US$ 2 billion in 1980 to a peak of US$ 120 billion in 1994. Over the same period the U.S. bilateral deficit with Japan went from US$ 10 billion to US$ 67 billion.

The increase in the U.S. bilateral deficit with China, second only to the U.S. deficit with Japan, leads many in the United States to assume that, like Japan, China must be running an ever-growing global surplus. Moreover, they assume that China must be a relatively closed economy that in its international trade does not play by the rules of market economies. Yet this reasoning by analogy obscures two fundamental facts. First, China does not have a systemic global current account surplus but rather a pattern of trade in which its global current account balance swings from several years of deficit to several years of surplus. Cumulatively over the reform period, it has no global current account surplus, and unlike Japan, it has not adopted macroeconomic and exchange-rate policies that would result in growing global current account surpluses.[3] Second, this reasoning by analogy overlooks the fact that China has dramatically reduced trade barriers in recent years. In certain respects China is already far more open than Japan.

Both tariff and non-tariff barriers have fallen rapidly in recent years in China. The average tariff rate (unweighted) fell from 43 percent in early 1992 to about 22-23 percent in early 1996. In 1992, non-tariff barriers such as import quotas applied to about 1,530 tariff product categories, but by early 1996, they had been eliminated on more than two-thirds of these imports.[4] Clearly tariffs remain quite high on some items and China will have to further reduce tariffs as part of its accession to the World Trade Organization, but substantial progress has been made in recent years.

In addition, China has undertaken other trade-related reforms in recent years. After many years of discussion China has given foreign firms somewhat greater access to its domestic market by granting trading rights. Initially this was done on an experimental basis only in Shanghai, but in late 1996 regulations were promulgated allowing foreign firms to establish joint ventures that would be granted trading rights throughout China. Foreign retailing operations, initially restricted to eleven cities, also have been liberalized. Finally, in 1997, foreign banks in Pudong for the first time were allowed to conduct some types of domestic currency business. In short, while China's own domestic economic reforms may have slowed in recent years, the pattern of gradual reform of its foreign trade regime seems to exhibit great continuity.[5]

The significance of China's openness to foreign direct investment also should not be overlooked, particularly in comparison with Japan. China has attracted more foreign direct investment in the 1990s alone than Japan has in the entire post-war period. This openness has allowed U.S. firms to establish significant, and in some cases even dominant, market positions in a broad range of products and services, including fast food restaurants, soft drinks, and toiletries and cosmetics.

The combination of a rapidly growing and increasingly open economy has resulted in a dramatic increase in Chinese imports, from about US$ 40 billion in 1985 to an estimated US$ 137 billion in 1996. The exports of U.S. firms to China, including those sold via Hong Kong companies, have increased from US$ 6 billion in 1990 to an estimated US$ 17 billion in 1996, outpacing the growth of U.S. exports to any other major foreign market.[6]

U.S. imports from China have grown even more rapidly, leading to a growing trade deficit. However, the rapid growth of Chinese exports has been driven overwhelmingly by joint venture companies and indigenous firms that engage in export processing on a contractual basis for foreign firms. And the most important import goods produced by these firms—consumer electronics, toys, games, sporting goods, footwear, and apparel—were previously produced elsewhere in Asia. Indeed the dramatic growth of China's share of world exports of these products has been more than matched by sharp declines in the shares produced in Hong Kong, South Korea, Singapore, and Taiwan. For example, as China's market share of world exports of clothing, toys, sporting goods, and footwear rose from 14 percent in 1984 to 39 percent in 1994, the share produced by the four Asian tigers fell even more, from 55 percent to 24 percent. The combined market share of China and the four tiger economies actually has fallen for clothing, toys, and sporting goods while remaining unchanged for footwear.[7] Thus the argument that the growing U.S. deficit with China has caused a large loss of manufacturing jobs in the United States seems misplaced. Other countries in Asia have moved up the technology ladder, leaving China to concentrate its production on the most labor-intensive goods.

ECONOMIC AND SECURITY LINKAGES

In the recent past, U.S. attempts to link economic and security interests generally have fallen far short of success. In particular, imposition of economic sanctions on China in order to achieve specific security interests appears to have failed. The best example probably is the sanctions the United States has twice imposed on China for violations of the Missile Technology Control Regime (MTCR), which restricts the sale of missile-related equipment and technology to countries that are not signatories to the Regime. In spring 1991 and again in August 1993, the U.S. government announced sanctions restricting the issuance of export licenses for products covered by the MTCR, in both cases after a finding that China had engaged in missile technology proliferation activities in violation of the MTCR. In each case, under U.S. law, the finding required that the sanctions be imposed for a two-year period.

However, in both cases the sanctions were waived for "national security reasons" well prior to the expiration of the two-year period. On the first occasion the sanctions were waived on March 23, 1992, on the grounds that the U.S. government had received assurances that China would comply with the guidelines. The second waiver came in November 1994, a little more than a year after the sanctions had been re-imposed.[8] There was a similar pattern of sanctions and waivers, unrelated to MTCR violations, on export licenses for the launch of U.S.–built satellites. These sanctions were imposed in November 1989, only to be waived less than a month later. They were re-imposed in February 1990, only to be waived in April 1991.

Since it subsequently has been widely reported in the U.S. press that China has continued to violate the terms of the MTCR, it is not obvious that the United States has received credible assurances from the Chinese government in exchange for suspension of the MTCR sanctions. Rather, it would appear that commercial pressure has been an important factor in the issuance of waivers for both the MTCR and the non-MTCR sanctions on the export of missile and satellite technology, including high-speed computers that could be used to test missiles. The principle effect of the sanctions was to restrict the sale of communications satellites, ground stations, and other missile-related technology to China by the Hughes Aircraft Company and other U.S. manufacturers. Even though provisions for multilateral sanctions are included in the MTCR agreement, other Western countries did not join the United States in imposing the sanctions. Both British and French manufacturers had competed for the same business and were not restricted by the sanctions. Thus if the sanctions had not been waived, their principle effect would not have been to deny technology to China but to shift commercial sales from U.S. to European manufacturers. In the face of the potential loss of billions of dollars in export orders, both the Bush and the Clinton administrations issued waivers that allowed commercial sales of communications satellites and ground stations to proceed.

More generally, barring a dramatic change in China's strategic posture, it appears unlikely that future attempts by the United States to utilize economic sanctions to change China's behavior with respect to its core strategic interests will be successful. In short, given the large size and rapid growth of the China market and the almost unprecedented opportunities for direct investment there, U.S. economic interests are likely to continue to override security interests. Moreover, even if there were a change in China's strategic posture, sanctions would likely fail unless they were multilateral and widely subscribed to by industrialized countries. Based on the experience of the past decade, in which no other industrial country has shown any appetite for imposing significant economic sanctions on China, the multilateral approach would be difficult to implement.

Although economic sanctions are not likely to be an effective tool to advance specific U.S. security interests, the strategy of broader economic integration of China into the world economy is likely to be one of the most effective instruments for ameliorating conflicting interests between China and the United States, including to some degree even security interests. A broad review of China's involvement in world affairs over the last quarter century concludes that a great deal of progress has been made in establishing a mutually satisfactory framework for peacefully integrating China into the evolving international security, economic, and political systems. China, in turn, has created domestic institutions, policy communities, and laws and regulations to support the external commitments that it has made in several functional areas. In short, integration has transformed China much more than it has transformed the various international regimes.[9]

NOTES

[1] Nicholas R. Lardy, *China in the World Economy* (Washington, DC: Institute for International Economics, 1994), pp. 4-8 and 27-28.

[2] World Bank, *World Development Report* 1996: *From Plan to Market* (Oxford: Oxford University Press, 1996), pp. 216-217.

[3] The current account is the appropriate measure for China. Since it has the largest stock of foreign direct investment of any developing country, it must earn a trade surplus to be able to help finance the remittance of profits by the foreign partners in joint ventures. These remittances are an item, along with trade, in a country's current account. According to Dai Xianlong, the Governor of the People's Bank of China, these remittances are currently running at US$ 30 billion per annum. *Jinrong shibao* (*Financial Times*), December 12, 1996, p. 1.

[4] World Bank, *The Chinese Economy: Fighting Inflation, Deepening Reform* (Washington, DC: World Bank, 1996), p. 8.

[5] Nicholas R. Lardy, *Foreign Trade and Economic Reform in China*, 1978-1990 (New York and London: Cambridge University Press, 1992).

[6] Nicholas R. Lardy, "China and the WTO," Brookings Policy Brief, No. 10 (Washington, DC: The Brookings Institution, November 1996), p. 3.

[7] World Bank, *World Development Report* 1996, p. 134.

[8] Dianne E. Rennack, *China: U.S. Economic Sanctions*, CRS Report for Congress (Washington, DC: Congressional Research Service, 1996), pp. CRS-21 to CRS-22, CRS-26, and CRS-28.

[9] Michel Oksenberg and Elizabeth Economy, "The United States and China in World Affairs: Past and Future," unpublished manuscript, October 1996.

U.S. ECONOMIC AND SECURITY INTERESTS IN TAIWAN

ALLEN S. WHITING

THE TAIWAN DILEMMA: CAN THE UNITED STATES STOP THE DRIFT TO INDEPENDENCE?

During the Cold War Taiwan was peripheral to U.S. security and economic interests in East Asia. In the 1950s, confrontation with the Sino-Soviet alliance left Taiwan more important in U.S. domestic politics than in U.S. foreign policy. In the 1960s, Taiwan gained importance as a base of support for the Vietnam War. In 1979, U.S. recognition of the People's Republic of China (PRC) required the United States to terminate diplomatic relations and its defense treaty with Taiwan. Over the next decade, the Taipei-Washington tie weakened as the Beijing-Washington tie strengthened.

But since 1995 and President Lee Teng-Hui's visit to the United States, Taiwan has become pivotal in Sino-American relations. If the island tries to become the independent Republic of Taiwan, Beijing has pledged to use force against it. This confronts Washington with a potential dilemma of either defending Taiwan and risking war with China or abandoning Taiwan and risking impairment of the overall American security position in East Asia. The dilemma is worsened by the moral question of balancing support for democracy on Taiwan against the consequences for Chinese on both sides of the Taiwan Strait in the event of Sino-American conflict.

This chapter examines how politics and policy in the Republic of China (ROC) relate to U.S. security and economic interests in Taiwan, on the Chinese Mainland, and in East Asia. It concludes that Washington must prevent Taipei from pushing for independence, and failing this, must not commit U.S. military forces to its defense.

TAIWAN'S SECURITY POLICY

Taipei has declared the following principle in handling future cross-Strait relations:"Taiwan has the first priority; its national security is a must."[1] This policy serves U.S. economic interests in that it involves acquiring U.S. weapons such as F-16s and Patriot missiles. Such missile sales help to redress the U.S. bilateral trade deficit and provide jobs in the United States. The policy also serves the wider U.S. security interest by furthering a balance of power in the Taiwan Strait that deters the PRC from using force and thereby enhances stability in East Asia.

At the same time, the broader U.S. security interest in a peaceful resolution of the Taiwan Strait confrontation is jeopardized by the provision of 150 F-16s, since it violates the 1982 Sino-American agreement limiting the level and amount of U.S. weaponry available to Taiwan. Announcement of this decision in 1992 contributed substantially to antagonism in Beijing and distrust of Washington-Taipei intentions.[2]

Taiwan's acquisition of advanced weaponry from other countries similarly has contradictory effects on U.S. security interests. On the one hand strengthening the island's defense against blockade and air attack complicates Mainland military offensive plans. Ostensibly this maintains a viable balance of power in the Taiwan Strait as mandated by the 1979 U.S.–Taiwan Relations Act. On the other hand, it encourages a continuing arms race between the two sides that can obstruct negotiations toward a settlement based on the mutual advantage of peaceful unification.

Beyond the immediate question of the island's security lies the question of Taiwan's claims in the East China and South China seas. For more than twenty years, the Taiwanese public has periodically demonstrated against Japanese ownership of the Senkaku Islands in the East China Sea. Taipei has been ambivalent about patrolling its claim in the South China Sea, which includes control over the largest of the Spratly Islands. However, it has shown no more inclination for compromise than has Beijing. On the contrary, Taiwan's participants in non-official workshops on the latter problem sponsored by Indonesia have claimed a larger area than that advanced by PRC representatives.[3]

The security dimension is further complicated by Taipei's broader definition of the concept of security to include elevation of its international status as an additional deterrent against Beijing's use of force. In December 1996, a government-sponsored National Development Conference in Taiwan reaffirmed the official policy that "the Republic of China should expand its international space."[4] Applying for U.N. membership was the ROC's most extreme tactic and was provocative to Beijing. Persistent pressure by ROC officials, including President Lee, to attend international conferences has strained PRC relations with other countries, most notably Japan.

TAIWAN'S ECONOMIC POLICY

Taiwan's interest in economic growth has spawned a steady increase in trade and investment with both the PRC and the United States.

Table 1. Bilateral Merchandise Trade
(US$ *billions*)

	1993	1994	1995
ROC–PRC[5]	14,392	16,327	17,882
ROC–U.S.[6]	41,270	43,789	42,965

Table 2. Investment
(US$ *billions*)

ROC–PRC[7]	3,139	3,391	3,165
ROC–U.S.	3,096	3,878	4,391

This increased trade is congruent with U.S. economic interests. Although the United States has a persistent trade deficit with Taiwan, trade is mutually advantageous provided it is conducted according to international rules. Bilateral trade does not need to be absolutely balanced to be advantageous.[8] In the 1980s, trade issues were the source of considerable controversy between Taipei and Washington. Despite 1994 tariff reductions on 483 high-priority items of U.S. exporters, Taiwan tariffs on various fruit and industrial goods range from 15 to 50 percent.[9] Intellectual property rights protection has improved but remains somewhat contentious. Nevertheless the United States has found Taipei responsive to resolving past disputes and sees Taiwan as ready for membership in the World Trade Organization (WTO) on the basis of its general economic behavior.

Taiwan economic policy toward the Mainland is also congruent with U.S. security interests. To the extent that Taiwan and the PRC become mutually advantaged by economic interaction there is slightly less likelihood that the Mainland will use military force. Profitable economic relations strengthen central, provincial, and municipal support on the Mainland for the status quo and its peaceful alteration. In 1996, local protests in the PRC reportedly arose over the negative impact of People's Liberation Army (PLA) military exercises in the Taiwan Strait.[10]

Taipei monitors the level of Taiwan investment on the Mainland, lest too much investment make it vulnerable to PRC pressure for negotiation on Mainland terms. In addition to an informal limit on the individual size and total amount of such investment, Taipei has encouraged investors to "go south."[11] As a result, Taiwan is the second largest source of foreign investment in Vietnam and the fifth largest in Indonesia. Taiwan's policy of diversifying its investments accords with the U.S. security interest in reducing the likelihood that Beijing can use economic pressure indirectly to force acceptance of its terms for unification.

Taipei's interest in expanding and facilitating its economic activity worldwide is advanced by "unofficial" visits where it lacks diplomatic recognition. This activity has successfully increased foreign investment on Taiwan and enlarged Taiwan's exports. However, the publicity associated with such visits has contributed to suspicions in Beijing that Taipei's ultimate goal is international status as a separate state. As such it is part of the larger problem of Taiwan–PRC relations and complicates U.S. security interests in a peaceful resolution thereof.

TAIWAN AND U.S. SECURITY INTERESTS

For the immediate future, Taipei and Washington have identical security interests in maintaining the status quo whereby both sides of the Taiwan Strait interact to mutual economic advantage and avoid military confrontation. This process was expanding before the PRC conducted missile tests in the Taiwan Strait in March 1996, and has since resumed. However, looking ten years ahead, it seems likely that the security goals of Taiwan and the United States will conflict, depending on how each Chinese side defines its interest in the unification of Taiwan with the Mainland.

Successive statements in Beijing imply that there is no immediate urgency to unification. In late 1996, Jiang Zemin reportedly argued against "impetuosity" in handling the Taiwan issue.[12] He allegedly asserted, "By the year 2006, if Taiwan authorities say that conditions for a reunification are not yet ripe, we still can wait; yet if Taiwan authorities still insist they are not provided with necessary conditions by 2010, we will proceed to resolve the issue on our own." In March 1997, Premier Li Peng publicly hailed the retaking of Hong Kong in 1997 and Macao in 1999, while pledging to "gradually achieve the peaceful reunification of the motherland."[13] The lack of a specific deadline for acquiring Taiwan follows the pattern of Deng Xiaoping's successive shifts of this goal from the 1980s to the 1990s and beyond.

Since 1972, U.S. policy has been based on the implicit assumption that unification of Taiwan and the Mainland is compatible with U.S. security interests so long as it occurs peacefully. In short, Taiwan's status quo is not of vital interest to the United States. This premise rests on diplomatic and military calculations. If the issue of Taiwan could be taken off the ongoing agenda of Sino-American problems, other matters of concern might be more readily resolved. So long as this highly nationalistic goal appears to be obstructed by Washington, opponents in Beijing can use it to attack compromise and refuse cooperation on bilateral and multilateral security questions. No basis for trust can ever be established under these circumstances.

Militarily the island would not be a critical component in a potentially hostile PRC military strategy that would threaten the security of U.S. allies in East Asia. By 2010, the Mainland is expected to acquire the capability for air and sea projection of power over all of its extant claims in the Yellow, East China, and South China seas. Adding Taiwan to its possessions will advance the basis for this power projection by only two hundred miles. Moreover, the anticipated revolution in means of warfare in the next century will further reduce the strategic importance of the island to China. The expanded definition of PRC territorial waters could complicate international use of the Taiwan Strait and the Bashi Channel, but this is a relatively minor problem and is unlikely to arise in the absence of a larger conflict.

Taiwan's value in expanding the Mainland's Exclusive Economic Zone (EEZ) is also of secondary weight. Currently both the PRC and the ROC lay claim to ocean resources in disputes with Japan and the Philippines. Beijing and Taipei have begun to discuss possible joint exploration at sea for oil and natural gas in areas north and west of Taiwan. In these areas, the PRC's claim is already based on the extended definition of the continental shelf, as well as on its historically based claim to the Senkaku Islands. Thus acquiring Taiwan would not substantially change the existing Mainland basis for contesting maritime resources. Extending the PRC EEZ eastward of Taiwan into the West Pacific would not significantly augment PRC opportunities for exploiting seabed petroleum deposits, given the existing technical capacity for exploiting these greater depths.

President Lee's avowed commitment to ultimate unification with the Mainland coexists with his adamant refusal to accept Beijing's terms for negotiations. In September 1997, on a tour of Central American countries, Lee repeatedly declared that the Republic of China is "an independent sovereign country," claimed that "there is nothing to be afraid of" from the Mainland, and scornfully dismissed the Beijing leadership as "stupid."[14] He specifically rejects the concept of "one country, two systems" originated by Deng Xiaoping and dutifully reiterated by Jiang Zemin.[15] This concept is supposedly to govern the Chinese administration of Hong Kong as a Special Autonomous Region (SAR), where its credibility will be tested in practice. However, Taipei has ruled it out in advance regardless of how the SAR develops.

Beijing is unlikely publicly to abandon this formula for reunification in the near future, leaving the two sides at an impasse. Privately officials have alluded to variations on the formula but claim Taipei is unresponsive.[16] The longer that substantive political negotiations do not occur, as opposed to economic and cultural exchanges, the greater will be the tendency for Taiwan public opinion and politics to see independence as the preferred option.[17] By 2010, the leadership will be almost wholly island-born with no Mainland memories or personal affiliations. Barring a major transformation of the Chinese communist regime, the political costs of unification will seem unacceptable, even if Hong Kong enjoys a more liberal atmosphere than currently seems likely. The drift toward an independent Taiwan will be encouraged by American public opinion as expressed in the Congress and media. In short, over the next decade or so, Taiwan is likely to choose permanent separation from Mainland China.

At that point U.S. economic interests would be in conflict with security interests. On the one hand, the asymmetry between the Mainland market for trade and investment and that of Taiwan will be extreme. Beijing has employed economic incentives and sanctions in the past to support its position on Taiwan and is certain to do so in the future. Considering U.S. economic interests on the Mainland compared with its interests on the island, there would be no choice but to bow to Beijing.

On the other hand, U.S. security interests in East Asia could be jeopardized if it accepts the use of force by the Mainland to foreclose Taiwan independence as an imminent eventuality. Yet U.S. military intervention against such force would test the alliance with Japan, perhaps to the breaking point. Much would depend on how the Japanese government defines its obligations under the Mutual Defense Treaty and the reaction of public opinion at that time. Also relevant would be the circumstances under which Beijing's use of force occurred, especially Taiwan's prior actions. On balance, Japanese politics would in all probability severely limit support for the United States in a conflict with China over Taiwan. In return, U.S. politics and public opinion would react very negatively if Tokyo did not carry its full share of the alliance burden.

MORALITY AND STRATEGY

The ultimate question lies in the problematic choice between abandoning Taiwan or submitting both sides of the Strait—as well as American lives—to the destructive consequences of a Sino-American war. This situation poses one of the most difficult moral dilemmas U.S. policy faces in the post–Cold War world because of its origins and its evolution over time.

In 1950, the United States intervened in the Chinese civil war. By this act, the Republic of China was enabled to survive to this day, retaining territory that had been taken from China by Japanese aggression at the turn of the century. In 1979, Washington transferred diplomatic recognition from Taipei to Beijing but did not end U.S. support for Taiwan. On the contrary, the Taiwan Relations Act, continued U.S. arms sales to Taiwan, and the dispatch of two U.S. aircraft carriers to the vicinity of Taiwan in March 1996, all continue to challenge the Mainland effort to gain the island and remove the Republic of China as a rival regime.

In the last half century, Taiwan has grown from 14 to 21 million people. It has one of the highest living standards in Asia, is ranked fourteenth in the world's trading countries (sixth in U.S. trade), and has progressed steadily toward democracy in the past decade, climaxed by the first genuine presidential election in the history of China. Many of these accomplishments resulted from the U.S. intervention. None of them would have been realized if Taiwan had been taken by the Mainland.

It is argued that both strategic and moral considerations compel the United States to support Taiwan against the threat of forceful takeover by the Mainland.[18] The strategic argument rests less on the actual military consequences of a takeover than on the belief that a takeover would a) represent a loss of credibility for the U.S. military position in East Asia, and b) enhance Chinese communist political-military influence. But this assessment requires fuller examination of the actual views of East Asian regimes, most of which have territorial disputes with Beijing and all of which must cope with Chinese power in the future. Foreign policy and security officials in the ASEAN countries agree that Taiwan is "an internal affair of China." However, they vary in the extent to which they accept force as a legitimate means of resolving the dispute, especially should this trigger a war between the United States and the PRC.[19] The maritime ASEAN members, for example, fear that such a conflict would disrupt trade and investment in the region.

The American experience in the Vietnam War suggests that moral consideration should not be compelling. One of the arguments for U.S. participation in Vietnam was to make credible the U.S. willingness to spill blood on behalf of an ally.[20] Yet ironically Japan, the most important U.S. Asian ally, quietly opposed the escalation of U.S. involvement in the Vietnam conflict.[21] The human and material costs to South Vietnam of U.S. intervention far exceed what would have resulted had the United States not sought to block Hanoi's drive for unification. In contrast, the Gulf War offers a positive example of a quick victory with minimal damage to Kuwait and complete suppression of aggression. Taiwan Strait scenarios for U.S. military intervention against the PLA range widely in forecasting the geographic extent and duration of conflict. However, in both the best-case and the worst-case projections, human and material casualties would occur on both sides of the Strait and must be weighed as a moral cost against that resulting from U.S. abstention.

By definition, a dilemma has no ready solution. The choice is often between lesser and greater pain, rather than lesser and greater gain, especially for those who must bear the consequences physically. The moral implication of the U.S. decision is made more difficult because it involves the Taiwanese people, with whom close relations have existed over an extended period of time. The U.S. role as guardian of Taiwan for nearly half a century contrasts with the varied, and at times volatile, American relationship with communist

China. An additional irony is the likelihood that democracy on Taiwan, a basic American goal, will result in a demand for independence that risks the PRC use of force to which the United States is basically opposed.

The current policy of "creative ambiguity" buys time to postpone a final choice. This avoids a clear commitment to defend Taiwan, thereby perhaps lessening Taiwan pressure for independence because it risks isolation in the face of Mainland attack. It also avoids a clear commitment to abstention from intervention, thereby perhaps lessening Mainland willingness to use force because it risks war with the United States. These hypothetical consequences on each side of the Strait argue against "destructive clarity" as a viable alternative to present policy. An unambiguous commitment to defend Taiwan would raise Taiwan's confidence in becoming independent, which would probably result in a PRC attack and U.S. military involvement. Unambiguous declaration of nonintervention would undermine Taiwanese morale and enhance the PRC threat of force to compel unification.

There are risks in professed clarity as well as deliberate ambiguity, especially in a triangular game. Each side is trying to influence and predict the behavior of the other two sides and their separate cost calculations. Estimating rational choice in each case is complicated further by the impact of domestic politics on all three sides. The U.S. Congress and media, Taiwan political parties and public opinion, and elite politics on the Mainland compel and constrain policy choices in unforeseeable ways. Finally, crisis decisions are determined by key individuals who are themselves unpredictable from afar.

At some point in the near future, U.S. policy will have to choose between preventing Taiwan from becoming independent or acquiescing in this act and facing the consequent dilemma of fighting China or abandoning Taiwan. To avoid this dilemma, the United States must do whatever it can to dissuade the leadership in Taipei from establishing a Republic of Taiwan. Should it do so nevertheless, the United States should not intervene militarily but accept however the two sides resolve their future relationship. This is not the best of all possible outcomes but it is dictated by the moral imperative in weighing the lesser harm of abstention against the greater damage of intervention.

NOTES

[1] MAC *News Briefing*, Mainland Affairs Council, Executive Yuan, January 6, 1997, reporting consensus at the National Development Conference held in December 1996. For statement and analysis of earlier declarations see John F. Copper, *Words Across The Taiwan Strait*, pp. 93-127.

[2] A. Doak Barnett, "Dangerous Dilemmas: The Unresolved Problem of Taiwan's Future" *American Foreign Policy Interests* (August 1996); this was also expressed to me in Beijing, July 1995.

[3] Interviews with Association of Southeast Asian Nations (ASEAN) officials in 1995-96.

[4] MAC *News Briefing*, op. cit.

[5] PRC Bureau of Statistics, *China's Customs Statistics*, 1992-96.

[6] U.S. Department of Commerce, *Survey of Current Business*, 1990-1996.

[7] Data on Taiwan investment on the Mainland are not reliable. The Republic of China foreign minister informed the European Parliament that Taiwan investment on the Mainland totaled $50 billion by 1997. *China News Digest*, May 24, 1997.

[8] By U.S. calculations, the trade deficit with Taiwan fell from $14.3 billion in 1989 to $7.8 billion in 1992 and subsequently rose to $9.8 billion in 1994.

[9] Ibid., p. 21.

[10] *South China Morning Post*, March 28, 1996, in Foreign Broadcast Information Service (FBIS), March 28, 1996, p. 15.

[11] Gerald Chan, "*Sudpolitik*: The Political Economy of Taiwan's Trade with Southeast Asia," *The Pacific Review* 9, No. 1 (1996). From 1988 to 1994, Taiwanese investment ranked first in Vietnam with nearly $2 billion in 164 projects; in 1993, Taiwan was ninth in aid to Vietnam, with $45 million to Vietnam.

[12] *Cheng Ming*, December 1, 1996. Other Hong Kong reports parallel this one but without the specific time references, which cannot be verified.

[13] Li Peng, "Report on the Work of the Government," delivered at the Fifth Session of the Eighth National People's Congress, March 1, 1997, in *Beijing Review* 40, No.13, March 31-April 6, 1997, p. xv.

[14] *Reuters*, September 18, 1997, Taipei.

[15] Meeting between Lee and Newt Gingrich, House Majority Leader, in Taipei, April 9, 1997. *China Times*, p. 1.

[16] Conversations reported by U.S. officials and scholars.

[17] Polls conducted in Taiwan during 1996-97 by newspapers and the government showed a gradual increase in hostility toward the PRC and a mod-

est increase in support for independence. MAC *News Briefing*, February 3, 1997.

[18] For the fullest exposition of this view, see Martin L. Lasater chapter in this volume.

[19] Interviews with representatives from all ASEAN countries except Brunei, November 1995-January 1996.

[20] McGeorge Bundy, National Security Adviser to President Johnson, remarked in a private exchange with Under Secretary George Ball, "We have to bleed a little in Vietnam to prove to NATO we will bleed a lot for Europe." From an interview with George Ball in 1967.

[21] Ambassador Edwin O. Reischauer in private communication to the author, March 1996.

U.S. ECONOMIC AND SECURITY INTERESTS IN TAIWAN

MARTIN L. LASATER

TAIWAN'S SECURITY AND U.S. CREDIBILITY IN ASIA

This chapter examines U.S. interests in Taiwan, with emphasis on the economic and security aspects of the U.S.–Taiwan relationship. Taiwan is an important partner of the United States because of the island's considerable economic strength, its democratic government, its close cultural ties with the American people, and its role in the maintenance of peace and stability in the western Pacific. The U.S.–Taiwan relationship is sometimes difficult to manage, however, because of the sensitivity of the Taiwan issue in Sino-American relations. There is little conflict between U.S. economic and security priorities with Taiwan, but there are areas of conflict between U.S. political and security interests in Taiwan on the one hand and some U.S. interests in China on the other.

THE AFTERMATH OF U.S. DE-RECOGNITION

Since the shift in U.S. diplomatic recognition from Taipei to Beijing in January 1979, U.S. relations with Taiwan have been governed by the Taiwan Relations Act (TRA).[1] Passed overwhelmingly by both houses of Congress and supported by a large majority of members from both parties, the TRA was signed into law with some reservation by President Jimmy Carter in April 1979. The TRA authorizes "the continuation of commercial, cultural, and other relations between the people of the United States and the people on Taiwan" and enables the United States "to preserve and promote extensive, close, and friendly" relations with Taiwan in the absence of formal diplomatic ties.[2] The TRA explicitly links the peaceful resolution of Taiwan's future to U. S. political, security, and economic interests in peace and stability in the western Pacific. To further these interests, the TRA states that "the United States will make available to Taiwan such defense articles and defense services in such quantity as may be necessary to enable Taiwan to maintain a sufficient self-defense capability."

Although the Republic of China (ROC) is recognized diplomatically by only thirty countries, Taiwan is regarded by most of the international community as a political and economic entity of some importance. Indeed, by most international standards Taiwan can be regarded as a separate country. It is a large island of 14,000 square miles (roughly the size of Massachusetts, Connecticut, and Rhode Island combined) with a population of around 21 million. Its population density is one of the highest in the world, and it has a 93 percent literacy rate. Taiwan has a democratic government with a popularly elected president and legislature, and the ROC government has ruled Taiwan without interruption since 1945. The island's GDP in 1994 was over $244 billion, the world's nineteenth largest, just behind Russia; its per capita GNP in that year was $11,600, the world's twenty-fifth largest; and its foreign trade was over $178 billion, the fourteenth largest in the world.

Despite its economic and political achievements, Taiwan faces diplomatic isolation from most of the international community. The most recent example of this isolation is the decision by the South African government to sever official relations with Taipei at the end of 1997 and to establish them with Beijing. Taiwan's diplomatic isolation is a reflection of its complicated relationship with Mainland China, a relationship that also bedevils Washington in its policies toward the two Chinese governments.[3]

The seat of government of the Republic of China moved to Taiwan in 1949 following the military defeat of the Nationalists (or Kuomintang) by the communists in the Chinese civil war. Taiwan had been under Japanese control from 1895 until 1945, after being seized from China in the Sino-Japanese War of 1894-95. Though populated mostly by ethnic Chinese, Taiwan previously had been only loosely governed by Imperial China.[4] Because of their long separation from Chinese control, the inhabitants of Taiwan evolved a sense of identity separate from Mainland China, many referring to themselves as "Taiwanese" as opposed to "mainlanders" or even "Chinese." The "Taiwanese" constitute about 85 percent of Taiwan's present population, while most of the other 15 percent are "mainlanders" who accompanied Chiang Kai-shek to Taiwan and their descendants. In general, Taiwanese prefer to maintain their distance from China whereas mainlanders aspire to a reunited China. There has been persistent agitation for an independent Taiwan nation over the years, reflected politically today in the principal opposition party to the ruling Kuomintang (KMT), the Democratic Progressive Party (DPP).[5]

During the Cold War, both the ROC and the People's Republic of China (PRC) insisted they were the sole legal government of China, forcing other nations to choose which side to recognize. (This insistence on a single China, incorporating Taiwan, is the so-called "one China" principle. A united China is often contrasted both with "two Chinas," whereby other nations would recognize both Taipei and Beijing as sovereign Chinese governments, and with "one China, one Taiwan," which would recognize Taiwan as a nation-state separate from China.) The PRC emerged the clear winner in this zero-sum diplomatic contest, as more and more countries chose Beijing over Taipei.

THE POLITICS OF AMBIGUITY

In the face of diplomatic isolation, Taipei in recent years has sought to find a way out of this zero-sum game. At present, the government of the Republic of China adheres to a "one China" principle, but insists that China is temporarily divided, with Taiwan being governed by the ROC and the Mainland being governed by the PRC. Taiwan is said to be part of "China" but not part of the "People's Republic of China." The ROC thus claims to be an equal political entity with the PRC, deserving full recognition and privilege as a sovereign government.[6] Beijing, on the other hand, views Taiwan as a breakaway Chinese province. The PRC considers the ruling authority on Taiwan to be a rebellious local government that should be under the jurisdiction of the national Chinese government in Beijing. The PRC refuses to deal with the ROC as an equal government and opposes virtually all attempts by Taipei to increase its international political representation.

Most countries of the world, including the United States, recognize the government of the PRC as the sole legal government of China and acknowledge that Taiwan is part of China.[7] The word "acknowledge" is important here, because it implies ***understanding*** of the Chinese view of Taiwan without committing the United States to ***accepting*** Beijing's jurisdiction over Taiwan. The predominant U.S. interest is that the future of Taiwan be settled peacefully between the two Chinese sides. U.S. policy is not to support a particular ***out-***

come of Taiwan's future—one China; two Chinas; or one China, one Taiwan—but rather to support the ***process*** of peacefully resolving Taiwan's future status. Within this understanding, the United States follows a "dual track" policy of maintaining official relations with the PRC and unofficial relations with Taiwan, a carefully nuanced arrangement that has been in effect since 1979 and is designed to serve U.S. interests in both Chinas. Such a policy enables the United States to adhere to the three Sino-American joint communiqués (1972, 1979, and 1982) and the legal requirements of the TRA, as well as to deal pragmatically with the relative power of the two Chinese sides and the ambiguity of their relationship.[8]

As long as both Chinese governments adhere to a "one China" policy, the United States probably can manage the Taiwan issue. If, however, the Chinese governments disagree over the one-China principle or lose their patience, then the United States will likely face difficulty. This is precisely what seems to be occurring since 1995.

With the democratization of Taiwan, beginning around 1986, the majority population of Taiwanese gradually came to power, as reflected in President Lee Teng-hui's election to the presidency in March 1996. From Beijing's point of view, President Lee (a Taiwanese) and the now Taiwanese-dominated KMT—allied with moderate DPP members—are leading Taiwan toward eventual independence from China. This is something Beijing has vowed to oppose, by force if necessary; in 1996, it demonstrated its resolve through missile tests and large-scale military exercises in the Taiwan area. Thus one condition that can pose problems in the U.S. management of the Taiwan issue may already be emerging: potential disagreement between the Chinese sides over "one China."

President Lee and his government have tried to assure Beijing and Washington that Taiwan remains committed to eventual reunification with the Mainland (albeit under a democratic, not a communist, government). However, the PRC professes not to believe the ROC president and has refused to resume bilateral talks broken off after President Lee's private visit to his alma mater Cornell University in June 1995. Beijing also has been angered by Taipei's efforts to send high-level officials on visits to other countries and by its attempts to regain representation in the United Nations.[9] Although some observers blame Taipei for the downturn in cross–Taiwan Strait relations, the PRC may also be turning up the heat to force Taiwan to enter into political negotiations now that

Hong Kong has reverted to Chinese sovereignty in July 1997. Thus yet another condition may be in place for increased U.S. difficulty in managing the Taiwan issue: Beijing's growing impatience to settle the issue.

Added to these conditions—potential disagreement over "one China" and Beijing's possible impatience—may be the fact that Washington is losing some influence over the Taiwan issue. This loss of influence can be partly attributed to a number of trends: U.S. power in the Asia-Pacific region is perceived to be declining in the post–Cold War period; China's national power and regional prestige are increasing; and Taiwan's people are making increased demands for their government to improve Taiwan's international status. One current trend on Taiwan, for example, is for the KMT and the DPP to cooperate in trying to expand Taiwan's overseas representation.[10] This is sure to anger Beijing and to cause some concern in Washington, but it reflects a stubborn determination on the part of Taiwan to break out of diplomatic isolation, even if it means risking confrontation with the PRC.

Because of fundamental political differences between Beijing and Taipei, Taiwan will likely remain a sensitive issue in Sino-American relations. It also will remain a potentially explosive issue over which the United States and China might confront each other militarily. That successive U.S. administrations have been willing to accept this risk is a reflection of the important interests the United States has in Taiwan, as well as continued American ambivalence toward the government of the PRC.

U.S.–TAIWAN ECONOMIC RELATIONS

The United States has a variety of economic interests in Taiwan. Three are particularly important: the large amounts of U.S. exports purchased by Taiwan, the large volume of total trade between the United States and the island, and the fact that over 50 percent of Taiwan's total foreign exchange reserves are held in U.S.–dollar instruments. A fourth U.S. interest—continued economic prosperity in the Asia-Pacific region—is furthered by Taiwan's considerable trade and capital investments in the region.

According to the American Institute in Taiwan (AIT), the U.S. corporation established by the TRA to manage unofficial relations with Taiwan, Taiwan's GDP in 1995 was $260.2 billion, with a per capita GDP of $12,264.[11] Preliminary GDP and per capita figures for 1996 are $273.8 billion and $12,798, respectively. Taiwan's total trade in 1995 was \$215.3 billion, with \$111.7 billion in exports (FOB) and \$103.6 billion in imports (CIF), giving the island a trade surplus of \$8.1 billion. (Preliminary 1996 trade figures from the ROC Ministry of Finance are: total exports \$116 billion, total imports \$101.3 billion, surplus \$14.7 billion.)[12]

In 1995, Taiwan was the eighth largest trading partner of the United States and the seventh largest market for U.S. goods. On a per capita basis, Taiwan imports more American goods and services than almost any other U.S. trading partner. Trade between the two countries totaled \$48.3 billion, with Taiwan purchasing \$19.3 billion from the United States and exporting \$29 billion, giving Taiwan a \$9.7 billion surplus. (Preliminary Ministry of Finance figures for 1996 ROC–U.S. trade are: exports to the United States, 26.9 billion; imports from the United States, \$20 billion; Taiwan surplus, \$6.9 billion.)

Taiwan has experienced a trade surplus with the United States for many years. That surplus, however, has declined steadily from a high of about \$17 billion in 1987 to its current level of less than \$10 billion. The most important Taiwan exports to the United States are electronic and information goods, metal products, and textiles and garments. Taiwan is the fifth largest agricultural market for the United States and a major market for American electronic components, aircraft and parts, insurance services, computer software, electronic test equipment, and electric power systems. Taiwan has the world's third largest foreign exchange reserves, standing at \$95.9 billion in 1995, of which some 53 percent were held in U.S. dollars. It should be noted that firms utilizing foreign investment produce about 20 percent of Taiwan's GDP. The United States is the largest investor in Taiwan, with cumulative investment approvals of over \$6.3 billion through 1994. Because Taiwan is isolated diplomatically, its economic strength is a vital strategic asset for Taipei.

For the past several decades Taiwan has maintained rapid economic growth and stability, in part because of favorable security, political, and economic relations with the United States. In the past, the United States absorbed a disproportionate amount of Taiwan's exports—providing the principal engine of the island's booming economy. This resulted in a large trade surplus with the United States, which during the 1986-88 period totaled \$40 billion. Under pressure from both the Ronald Reagan and George Bush administrations, Taiwan adopted a "Trade Action Plan" in 1988 designed to redress the trade imbalance through the purchase of more American goods and the diversification of export markets. Since then, Taiwan's trade surplus with the United States has fallen steadily.

Reducing dependence on the U.S. market was part of a larger economic restructuring in which Taiwan liberalized its economy and lifted most trade barriers. This process accelerated in recent years as Taipei sought to accede first to the General Agreement on Tariffs and Trade (GATT) and then to the World Trade Organization (WTO); to develop into an Asia-Pacific regional operations center; and to play an active role in the Asia Pacific Economic Cooperation (APEC) process. As part of Taiwan's WTO accession process, the United States is seeking to improve market access in several areas, including agricultural products, insurance, and motion pictures, and to remove remaining barriers to foreign investment and government procurement of foreign goods and services. For the most part, the United States has found Taiwan to be a cooperative negotiating partner. It is in Taiwan's vital interest to maintain such a cooperative relationship.

One of the far-reaching results of Taiwan's efforts to redress its trade imbalance with the United States was the relocation of many Taiwan-based factories to Southeast Asia and Mainland China, an economic necessity in any case due to rising labor and real estate costs in Taiwan. At first, these production transfers included mostly labor-intensive, small- and medium-sized industries such as apparel and footwear, but now fairly large enterprises are moving part of their production facilities abroad.

Of special interest to the United States has been Taiwan investments in Mainland China, a development made possible by former ROC President Chiang Ching-kuo's limited opening to China in 1987.[13] According to the Mainland Affairs Council of the ROC government, cross-Strait trade was worth $22.5 billion in 1995, with more than 30,000 Taiwanese companies having invested a total of $30 billion on the Mainland to date. Some 900,000 cross-Strait visits had been made through 1995 and more than one hundred million letters and phone calls had been exchanged. The Council noted in one report, "people-to-people exchanges between the two sides of the Taiwan Strait have outpaced our ties with other countries around the world."[14]

The economic effects of cross-Strait exchanges have been considerable. Taiwan investments and entrepreneurial skills have helped the PRC to modernize commercial sectors of its economy and to become one of the largest trading partners of the United States. Since 1991, China has maintained a larger trade surplus with the United States than has Taiwan and, in 1996, even surpassed Japan in that regard. Perhaps most important, people-to-people contacts across the Taiwan Strait have accelerated the process of Taiwan-Mainland economic integration. This is something the ROC government closely monitors, because it is concerned that Beijing might gain too much leverage over Taipei. From a longer perspective, the economic integration of Taiwan, Hong Kong, and Mainland China into the so-called "Greater China" is a development that will have an historic impact on both Asia and the United States.

U.S.–TAIWAN SECURITY RELATIONS

The United States has been involved with Taiwan's security since 1950, when President Harry Truman interposed the Seventh Fleet into the Taiwan Strait in response to the outbreak of the Korean War. The Mutual Defense Treaty with the Republic of China was signed in 1954, and it remained in effect until it was terminated as part of the 1979 normalization agreement between Washington and Beijing.

U.S. military support was given to the ROC during the Quemoy crises of 1954, 1958, and 1962, and Taiwan played an important role during the Vietnam War as a supply base for American forces. The U.S. Seventh Fleet regularly patrolled the Taiwan Strait until 1969, when President Richard Nixon ended the patrol as a gesture to improve relations with the PRC. Since the 1960s, there had not been a major military confrontation between Beijing and Washington over Taiwan until early 1996, when President Bill Clinton sent two aircraft carrier battle groups into waters near Taiwan in response to PRC efforts to intimidate Taiwan with military exercises prior to the island's presidential elections in March.

Since 1970, U.S. security ties with Taiwan have fallen under the auspices of the Taiwan Relations Act. One of the most significant parts of the TRA is authorization to sell U.S. arms and technology to Taiwan to enable that government "to maintain a sufficient self defense capability." U.S. arms sales to Taiwan have been the source of much controversy in Sino-American relations, in part because the PRC views these sales as a major contributing factor to Taipei's refusal to come to terms over reunification. From the perspective of successive U.S. administrations, the arms sales help ensure peace in the Taiwan Strait by deterring PRC adventurism. Taiwan considers the American weapons as essential for its defense, an assessment that is probably correct.

To better manage the controversial arms sales issue, the United States and China negotiated the August 17, 1982, communiqué, in which the Reagan Administration promised to reduce gradually the quantitative and qualitative levels of U.S. arms sold to Taiwan. According to the U.S. interpretation of the communiqué, this promise was contingent upon Beijing continuing to pursue a policy of peaceful unification toward Taiwan. As with many other aspects of U.S. policy toward Taiwan, the communiqué was cloaked in ambiguity to make it palatable to all sides. Since the TRA linked the level of arms sales to Taiwan's defense needs and made no mention of gradual reductions, the Reagan Administration explained to Congress that the TRA, as the law of the land, would take legal precedence over the communiqué, which was a statement of executive branch policy. Beijing, of course, viewed the communiqué as an international agreement and thus binding on Washington, regardless of U.S. domestic legislation.[15]

Although the August 17 communiqué did not resolve differences between Washington, Beijing, and Taipei, it did serve to moderate arms sales to Taiwan while at the same time providing political cover for advanced weapon sales truly needed for Taiwan's self-defense. Since 1982, the United States has sold Taiwan enormous amounts of military hardware, including 150 F-16s authorized by President Bush; advanced air-defense missiles for ground, naval, and air platforms; main battle tanks; guided-missile frigates; Patriot anti-missile systems; Harpoon anti-ship missiles; advanced early warning radars; and so forth. The total value of these systems runs into the billions of dollars, and the sales represent a significant increase in Taiwan's defensive capabilities.[16]

Beijing remains very irritated over U.S. arms sales to Taiwan, and there are indications that the PRC occasionally signals its displeasure through arms sales of its own that complicate U.S. interests, as in the case of Pakistan, and by discriminating against American contract bids for projects in China. The PRC does not at this time possess the capability to launch a successful amphibious invasion of Taiwan, although it could strike the island with ballistic missiles and at least partially blockade Taiwan's ports with submarines, surface vessels, mines, and perhaps aircraft.[17]

U.S. INTERESTS IN TAIWAN'S SECURITY

A peaceful settlement of the Taiwan issue is in the national security interests of the United States. For several decades, this has been expressed mainly in terms of maintaining peace and stability in the western Pacific. One of the best ways to understand this linkage is to consider the negative consequences of a war in the Taiwan Strait.[18]

First, the probability is high that a war would not be confined to the Taiwan Strait. Taiwan's war-fighting strategy is to expand the conflict as widely and rapidly as possible to maximize damage to the PRC. Trade to and from Kaohsiung and Keelung—Taiwan's principal ports—would be disrupted, as well as trade to Chinese ports between Shanghai and Hong Kong. Taiwan would undoubtedly attack some Mainland coastal facilities and mine PRC harbors. The commercial interests of all countries trading with Taiwan and China would be harmed.

Second, the use of PRC submarines to impose a blockade on Taiwan would pose a danger to all merchant ships passing through the Bashi Channel and the Taiwan Strait. These are major sea lanes through which flow vast amounts of cargo moving between Northeast Asia and ports in southern China, Southeast Asia, South Asia, and the Middle East. If China attempted to enforce the blockade, the likelihood is high that the ships of neutral countries would be harmed, since it is difficult for submarines to identify friend or foe on the high seas. Much of the air traffic in the western Pacific likewise would be affected due to the efforts of both sides to control the airspace above and around Taiwan.

Third, a war in the Taiwan Strait would harm the economies not only of the "two Chinas" but also of many other Asian-Pacific countries. Both Taiwan and China are major trading partners with these countries, and Taiwan is a source of vital investment capital in the region. The economic "miracle" of the region would certainly be derailed for a time. Since continued economic growth is a key factor in regional political stability, a war in the Taiwan Strait might have negative political repercussions as well.

Fourth, a war between Taiwan and China would cause deep security concerns throughout Asia. Most countries of the region are wary of Chinese hegemony, and a conflict in the Taiwan Strait would fuel that anxiety. The purchase of advanced weapons by other countries would increase and perhaps, in some cases, extend to missiles and even limited numbers of weapons of mass destruction. U.S. interests in non-proliferation would be greatly harmed by such a development.

Fifth, because of traditional U.S. commitments to the defense of Taiwan, war in the Taiwan Strait would immediately focus attention on the U.S. response. U.S. credibility in the region is tied to how it responds to PRC military threats to Taiwan, and Asian countries are very sensitive to American credibility due to their own security links with the United States. An ineffective U.S. response to a crisis in the Taiwan Strait would diminish the deterrent value of security ties to the United States on the part of many other Asian countries and weaken American influence in the region. If not handled correctly, a crisis over Taiwan could begin to unravel the U.S. security architecture in Asia.

Finally, there is high probability that a war in the Taiwan Strait would involve the United States. The United States has a long history of commitments to the security of Taiwan and a proven record of military support to Taipei during times of crisis. Whatever circumstances might precipitate a conflict between Taipei and Beijing, there would be strong U.S. domestic pressure for American intervention. The 1996 crisis over Taiwan was largely symbolic, since none of the governments involved intended to engage in conflict. An actual shooting war, however, might well result in a military confrontation between Washington and Beijing—a confrontation neither wants but which could prove difficult to avoid.[19]

OTHER U.S. INTERESTS IN TAIWAN

The United States has several other interests involving Taiwan. Three of the most important are: 1) maintenance of a regional balance of power, 2) Taiwan's continued influence on China's modernization, and 3) preservation of a consensus on U.S. China policy.[20]

With regard to the first interest, traditional U.S. strategy in the Asia-Pacific region has centered on the maintenance of a favorable balance of power.[21] In the post–Cold War period, Taiwan plays an important but understated role in this strategy due to uncertainty over the future direction of China. Simply put, no one knows whether China will be an ally, enemy, friend, or rival of the United States over the next several years or decades. Until China's direction becomes clearer, it would be a mistake to abandon U.S. interests in Taiwan for presumed Chinese cooperation on global or regional issues.

As China becomes a modern power—there is uncertainty even about that—areas of conflicting interests between Beijing and Washington will inevitably arise as each country seeks to define and maintain its sphere of influence in the western Pacific (if the United States does not withdraw from the region). As President Clinton has found, these issues are beginning to emerge with considerable urgency. Missile and nuclear proliferation, trade imbalance and unfair trading practices, human rights violations, the rapid modernization of the People's Liberation Army, and Chinese military action in the South China Sea and Taiwan Strait are issues that defy easy solution. A policy of comprehensive engagement improves dialogue between Washington and Beijing, and perhaps can help manage some of these issues; but it will be difficult for dialogue alone to remove the many fundamental issues between the two nations as they collide like tectonic plates in the western Pacific.

If the United States allows the PRC to take over Taiwan by force, or even to intimidate it through threats of force into accommodation, then the balance of power in East Asia will be changed. U.S. credibility, influence, and prestige will be damaged, while that of China will increase. Having access to Taiwan's military ports, airfields, and investment capital would tremendously expand PRC national power. Moreover, China's success in using force or the threat of force against Taiwan might encourage Beijing to use its military instruments to help resolve other regional problems. This concern over possible hegemony by China was one of the primary reasons most Asian nations supported U.S. intervention in the Taiwan Strait crisis. China's neighbors want the United States and China to maintain cooperative relations, but they do not want the PRC to take over Taiwan by force. For their own interests, they prefer a balance of power in the region.

Another U.S. interest is for Taiwan to exert a positive influence on China's modernization. As a Chinese society, Taiwan serves as a valuable testing ground for various approaches to China's modernization, a process with which the Chinese people have wrestled for more than two centuries. Although they are still evolving, Taiwan has successfully developed institutions of democracy and capitalism, experiences that can prove useful to the Chinese nation as a whole.[22] Since it is in the long-term interest of the United States that China become more democratic and market oriented, U.S. support for Taiwan's democracy and free enterprise advances this goal. On a broader front, U.S. support for Taiwan furthers the American goal of strengthening and expanding the community of market democracies around the world.[23]

Third, friendly ties with Taiwan help Washington to maintain a domestic consensus on U.S. policy toward China. Over the past half century, U.S. policy toward China and Taiwan frequently has been a divisive issue in American politics. That China policy remains sensitive is illustrated by the annual debate between the Administration and the Congress over extension of most-favored-nation trading status to the PRC and the non-stop controversy over Chinese human rights violations. Every year, Congress passes numerous bills and resolutions voicing support for Taiwan, including calls for more advanced weapons sales.

At present, the dual-track policy of engagement with China and friendship toward Taiwan serves U.S. interests with both Beijing and Taipei. This policy is ambiguous, but it is pragmatic and workable. It is my belief that the current dual-track policy is supported by a majority of the U.S. foreign policy establishment and that this consensus was reached only after many bruising political battles. Any change in U.S. policy toward Taiwan—or toward China, for that matter—would result in renewed political fighting with an uncertain outcome. From a domestic political viewpoint, therefore, it is best to leave the current policy in place.

THE CASE FOR THE STATUS QUO

The United States has many interests in Taiwan. Although Taiwan is isolated diplomatically, the island is integrated economically with the rest of the Asian-Pacific community and is a significant contributor to regional stability and prosperity. Most Asian nations favor current U.S. relations with Taiwan, if only to ensure continued U.S. engagement in Asia as a counterbalance to the rising and unpredictable power of China.

Taiwan's political, economic, and security policies rarely harm U.S. interests, although they do sometimes pose a challenge due to the sensitivity of the Taiwan issue in Sino-American relations. The greatest challenge arises from the desire of the people of Taiwan for self-determination: to have international respect and recognition and to avoid unification with China under a communist system of government. Still, it is doubtful that resolution of the Taiwan issue along lines favored by Beijing would remove controversy in U.S.–PRC relations. Thus there is no strategic imperative for a change in U.S. policy toward Taiwan in order to improve Washington's relations with Beijing.

The best U.S. policy remains the one currently in place: a dual-track approach that maintains cooperative, official relations with the PRC and friendly, unofficial relations with the people of Taiwan. This approach is ambiguous and prone to controversy, but it does serve the pragmatic interests of the United States in both China and Taiwan, while giving the two Chinese societies time to work out their differences. The principal role for the United States in this prolonged process is to ensure that these differences are worked out peacefully. As reaffirmed by successive administrations since 1979, such a policy serves fundamental U.S. interests in the western Pacific and it should be continued for the foreseeable future.

NOTES

[1] For a discussion of the Taiwan Relations Act, Public Law 968, enacted April 10, 1979, see Lester L. Wolff and David L. Simon, *Legislative History of the Taiwan Relations Act* (New York: American Association for Chinese Studies, 1982). A collection of the most important documents relating to U.S.–Taiwan relations can be found in Stephen P. Gibert and William M. Carpenter, eds., *America and Island China: A Documentary History* (Lanham, MD: University Press of America, 1989).

[2] For a discussion of U. S. relations with the Republic of China on Taiwan through 1978, see Ralph N. Clough, *Island China* (Cambridge, MA: Harvard University Press, 1978). Another useful study is *China: U.S. Policy Since 1945* (Washington, DC: Congressional Quarterly, Inc., 1980).

[3] For a discussion of Taiwan's uncertain international status, see John F. Copper, *Taiwan: Nation-State or Province?* (Boulder, CO: Westview Press, 1996).

[4]Taiwan's nebulous relationship with China can be seen in Mao Zedong's comments to Edgar Snow in 1936 to the effect that Korea and Taiwan should be independent of both China and Japan. Mao said, "We will extend them our enthusiastic help in their struggle for independence." See Edgar Snow, *Red Star Over China* (New York: Modern Library, 1944), p. 96.

[5] Taiwan has several political parties, the most influential of which are the KMT and the DPP. Others include the New Party, formed by a group of KMT members, mostly Mainlanders, and a splinter party from the DPP, the Taiwan Independence Party. Although the KMT is the ruling party, it does not possess a controlling majority in Taiwan's parliament, the Legislative Yuan. As a result of the December 1995 legislative elections, the KMT holds 85 seats in

the 164-seat legislature, with the DPP holding 54, the New Party 21, and others 4. Coalition politics are the rule of the day on Taiwan, with different alliances being formed around specific issues. On the crucial issues of Taiwan's international status and its relationship with Mainland China, the KMT under President Lee Teng-hui favors the status quo with eventual reunification under a democratic China; the DPP under moderate Hsu Hsin-liang favors the status quo and believes that Taiwan already is independent; the New Party favors the status quo with more deliberate movement toward unification; and the Independence Party favors the status quo with more deliberate movement toward independence. Virtually everyone wants the government to be more assertive of its sovereignty in the international community and opposes unification under communist rule.

[6] One Taiwan official described the ROC perspective as follows: "The most pragmatic description of the current crossStraits situation is that Taiwan and the Mainland are two parallel political entities in one country." Mainland Affairs Council Vice Chairman Kao Koong-lian, as quoted in *Free China Journal* (Taipei), December 13, 1996, p. 1. See also "Vice Chairman Kao Koong-lian at the January 3, 1997 News Conference," MAC News Briefing, January 6, 1997.

[7] The precise terminology in the January 1, 1979, joint communiqué on the establishment of diplomatic relations between the United States and the PRC is: "The United States of America recognizes the Government of the People's Republic of China as the sole legal Government of China. . . .The Government of the United States of America acknowledges the Chinese position that there is but one China and Taiwan is part of China."

[8] Many books discuss the ambiguous relationship of Taiwan with the Mainland and the subsequent implications for U.S. policy. See, for example, Robert G. Sutter and William R. Johnson, eds., *Taiwan in World Affairs* (Boulder: Westview Press, 1994); and the author's *Policy in Evolution: The* U.S. *Role in China's Reunification* (Boulder: Westview Press, 1988). One topic at the December 1996 National Development Conference held in Taipei was Taiwan's relations with the Mainland, a subject on which no consensus could be reached. According to one Legislative Yuan member present at the meeting, cross–Taiwan Strait relations are "international relations" to the DPP; "quasi-international relations" to the KMT; and "non–foreign relations" to the New Party; Angela Chou as quoted in *Free China Journal*, December 27, 1996, p. 2. Nonetheless, participants in the conference were able to agree on general guidelines—i.e., that the two sides of the Taiwan Strait are equivalent political entities; that the ROC on Taiwan is sovereign and not a part of the PRC; and that Beijing's "one China, two systems" formula for unification is not acceptable; Weiling Liu, "Consensus Reached on Straits Relations, Economic Development," *Free China Journal*, January 4, 1997, p. 1.

[9] The government of the PRC assumed China's seat in the United Nations in October 1971, at which time the General Assembly also expelled the

ROC. According to reports originating in Hong Kong in late 1996, PRC officials have set four conditions Taipei must meet before talks can resume: stop its attempts to rejoin the United Nations and other international organizations as a sovereign state; stop visits by Taiwan leaders to countries having diplomatic ties with Beijing; stop pursuing a strategy of "dual recognition"; and stop purchasing advanced weapons from other countries. See Virginia Sheng, "Peking Sets Conditions on Talks," *Free China Journal*, December 13, 1996, p. 1

[10] For discussion of KMT–DPP cooperation in other areas, which some observers are calling a significant shift in Taiwan politics, see "National Conference Leaves KMT and DPP Closer and Stronger," *Free China Journal*, January 17, 1997, p. 1.

[11] Most of this economic information has been taken from the "Taiwan Briefing Book" distributed by the AIT office in Taipei and AIT's 1997 *Trade Act Report on Taiwan*. All figures are in U.S. dollars. AIT's parallel organization handling Taiwan's relations with the United States is the Taipei Economic and Cultural Representative Office in the United States (TECRO), formerly known as the Coordination Council for North American Affairs (CCNAA).

[12] Deborah Shen, "Trade Surplus Reaches 9-Year High," *Free China Journal*, January 10, 1997, p. 3.

[13] See Sandra Sugawara, "Taiwan Opens the Taps on Investment in China," *Washington Post*, December 27, 1996, p. G1.

[14] "Promoting Cross-Strait Relations: The Conscious Efforts of the Republic of China Government" (Taipei: Mainland Affairs Council, Executive Yuan, 1996), p. 9. See also Ralph N. Clough, *Reaching Across the Taiwan Strait: People-to-People Diplomacy* (Boulder: Westview Press, 1993) and Hungdah Chiu, *Koo-Wang Talks and the Prospect of Building Constructive and Stable Relations Across the Taiwan Strait* (Baltimore: University of Maryland School of Law, 1993).

[15] The Reagan Administration's formal comparison of the legal standing of the TRA and the August 17 communiqué was given in the prepared statement of Davis R. Robinson, Legal Advisor, Department of State, before the U.S. Senate, Committee on the Judiciary, Subcommittee on Separation of Powers, September 27, 1982, ms. See also U.S. House of Representatives, Committee on Foreign Affairs, *China-Taiwan: United States Policy* (Washington, DC: Government Printing Office, 1982). Much of the behind-the-scenes debate over the communiqué in Washington can be found in Martin L. Lasater, *The Taiwan Issue in Sino-American Strategic Relations* (Boulder: Westview Press, 1984).

[16] A summary of most of these sales can be found in Dennis Van Vranken Hickey, *United States–Taiwan Security Ties: From Cold War to Beyond Containment* (Westport, CT: Praeger,1994). It should be noted that Taiwan has also purchased advanced weapons from several other countries. France, for example, sold Taiwan 60 Mirage fighters and 16 modern frigates. PRC opposition

to such sales, however, usually deters governments from selling weapons to Taiwan.

[17] This is a common assessment by most American analysts. See, for example, Rear Admiral Eric McVadon (USN, ret.),"Strait Shooters," *Far Eastern Economic Review,* January16, 1997, p. 29.

[18] Details on how U.S. interests would be affected by various conflict scenarios between Beijing and Taipei can be found in several of the author's books. For the most recent, see Martin L. Lasater, *The Changing of the Guard: President Clinton and the Security of Taiwan* (Boulder: Westview Press, 1995).

[19] See Parris H. Chang and Martin L. Lasater, eds., *If China Crosses the Taiwan Strait: The International Response* (Lanham, MD: University Press of America, 1993).

[20] For elaboration, see Martin L. Lasater, *U.S. Interests in the New Taiwan* (Boulder: Westview Press, 1993).

[21] For a discussion of alternative U. S. strategies in Asia, see Michael Mandelbaum, ed., *The Strategic Quadrangle: Russia, China, Japan, and the United States in East Asia* (New York: Council on Foreign Relations, 1994); Martin L. Lasater, *The New Pacific Community: U.S. Strategic Options in Asia* (Boulder: Westview Press, 1996).

[22] That Taiwan's political system is still evolving can be seen in the results of the National Development Conference. The KMT and DPP reached a consensus on several key reforms, including the expansion of the power of the presidency and legislature, the diminishing of the rights and responsibilities of the National Assembly, the adoption of a new balloting system for elections, and the downsizing and possible dismantling of the Taiwan Provincial Government. The New Party walked out of the conference and the Taiwan Provincial Governor, the popular and respected James Soong, resigned his post in protest. Susan Yu, "Conference Maps Shift in Presidential, Legislative Power," *Free China Journal,* January 4, 1997, p.1. Also, Julian Baum, "Taiwan: Second Republic?" *Far Eastern Economic Review,* January 9, 1997, p.17; and Julian Baum, "Taiwan: Loyalist Rebel," *Far Eastern Economic Review,* January 16, 1997, pp. 14-15.

[23] According to the Clinton Administration, "Our national security strategy is based on enlarging the community of market democracies while deterring and containing a range of threats to our nation, our allies and our interests. The more that democracy and political and economic liberalization take hold in the world, particularly in countries of geostrategic importance to us, the safer our nation is likely to be and the more our people are likely to prosper." *A National Security Strategy of Engagement and Enlargement* (Washington, DC: The White House, February 1995), p. 2.

JEFFREY WINTERS

THE RISKS AND LIMITS OF A CORPORATE FOREIGN POLICY

A little-noted consequence of the Cold War's end is that the United States has been left with a nakedly corporate foreign policy. Of course, the U.S. government has long sought to advance the interests of powerful corporate players internationally. But in the past the corporate dimensions of U.S. foreign policy were upstaged by (or at least intermingled with) other causes such as freedom, democracy, or anti-communism—goals that were thought to be worthwhile in their own right. Today everything worth pursuing is derivative of or secondary to a corporate agenda of opening markets and strengthening the international regime for transactions in capital, goods, and services. This a sterile and unsustainable situation. Freedom, democracy, liberty, human dignity, and justice—the objectives that move the human soul—have been relegated more than ever to the realm of rhetoric and empty gestures. According to Secretary of State Madeleine Albright, the U.S. posture is one of "comprehensive engagement" with the countries of the world.[1] But having to call it comprehensive engagement only draws more attention to the obverse truth: U.S. foreign policy stands on a narrow foundation. As is argued more fully below, this foreign policy is based on a definition of national security that may have suited the decades following World War II but must now shift in tandem with the sorts of threats contained in today's patterns of globalized production.

Business interests are much too hollow a basis for U.S. foreign policy. If this was true when American extractive and agricultural interests were taking root in Latin America and parts of Asia, it is even more so now when the corrosive impact of global investment and trade on American jobs and welfare is increasingly on the public mind. This is not to suggest that globalization does not provide benefits, for it clearly does. But from the perspective of the conflict between capital owners and controllers on the one hand, and the vast majority of wage laborers on the other, the net effect of globalization has been to shift a tremendous amount of power and wealth upward to the owners and controllers. Although the reasons for this are many, the most important is that wider capital mobility and easier trade flows now allow capital controllers to pit widely varying labor pools and investment climates against each other in ways that greatly favor the interests of capital over those of everyone else.[2] So far only a rogue Republican candidate for president, Pat Buchanan, has dared to tap into the undercurrent of anger and fear that grips the average American facing competition from exploited laborers in Southeast Asia and elsewhere. Reflecting their allegiance to the corporations and wealthy individuals who fund America's electoral process, both Democrats and Republicans made clear in the 1996 campaign that the mantra of free trade would drown out all alternatives and criticisms.

This essay offers two interpretations of U.S. economic and security priorities in Southeast Asia. The first is an orthodox assessment of trends and developments in the region and their impact on U.S. foreign policy. The second is a somewhat less conventional interpretation of U.S. economic and security interests that is rooted in U.S. links to areas like Southeast Asia, but emphasizes how those links require us to broaden our thinking on economic and security interests to include an increasingly important ***domestic*** dimension. By the phrase "bringing national security home," I want to suggest that the prevailing separation between human rights (especially labor rights) and conventional economic and security priorities is artificial and shortsighted. Let us discuss first the orthodox assessment.

REGIONAL COOPERATION IN SOUTHEAST ASIA

Southeast Asia is comprised of ten countries (plus the contested territory of East Timor) with a combined population that will reach 525 million by the turn of the century. The region's total GDP at purchasing power parity (PPP) in 1996 was $1.7 trillion, roughly equal to that of Germany ($1.6 trillion), half as large as China ($3.2 trillion), and one-fourth as large as the United States ($6.8 trillion). Of all the world's regions or groupings, none is more diverse than Southeast Asia. At one extreme are the city-states of Singapore and Brunei, with a combined population equal to that of one Jakarta suburb, but with per capita GDPs (at PPP) of about $21,000 (the U.S.

per capita GDP is about \$26,000 by comparison). At the other extreme are the small but poor countries of Cambodia and Laos, and the large but poor countries of Indonesia, Burma, the Philippines, and Vietnam. In the middle lie Thailand and Malaysia. Indonesia is the fourth largest country in the world and has the world's largest Muslim population, though it is a secular state where a very moderate and accommodating form of Islam predominates.

Geographically the region is divided between insular and mainland states. Although all the countries in Southeast Asia have deeply exclusionary politics, they range from the faintly democratic systems of the Philippines and Thailand, through the civilian authoritarian systems of Malaysia and Singapore, to the more thoroughly military authoritarian systems of Vietnam, Indonesia, and Burma.

Despite all this diversity, and after almost a quarter century of loose integration and relative invisibility internationally, the clear trend in the region in recent years has been toward institutional thickening in intra-regional relations combined with a more assertive posture in international relations. Trade and investment among Southeast Asian countries has been growing at a faster rate than the region's transactions with the rest of the world. The Association of Southeast Asian Nations (ASEAN), which celebrated its thirtieth anniversary in 1997, has grown in importance in the Pacific Rim.[3] A proliferation of other organizations is emerging, building in on an increasingly solid and expanding ASEAN foundation. These include the ASEAN Regional Forum (ARF) and the Asia-Pacific Economic Cooperation (APEC) grouping.

As the institutional connections among the countries in Southeast Asia have increased and strengthened, ASEAN and its spin-offs have begun to assert themselves more forcefully in regional and international issues. ASEAN pushed through a treaty in Bangkok in December 1995 to make the region a Nuclear Weapon Free Zone, but U.S. and Chinese opposition have stalled implementation of the zone. ASEAN also called on China in 1996 to stop nuclear testing. ARF has emerged since 1994 as the single most important context for dialogue and confidence building in the Asian sphere. ASEAN and its leading members are taking increasingly strident stands on issues deemed off limits to outside powers, including non–Southeast Asian powers invited to participate as so-called "dialogue partners."[4] The muddled but highly contentious debate over whether "Asian values" supersedes democracy has been taken up most vocally by Prime Minister Mahathir of Malaysia, former

Prime Minister Lee Kuan Yew of Singapore, and President Suharto of Indonesia. Relations between ASEAN and the European Union have been strained by Portugal's use of its veto within the European Union to press Indonesia for concessions on East Timor. At a broader level, Prime Minister Chavalit of Thailand (who is also Defense Minister) issued a call in February 1997 for changes in the structure of the U.N. Security Council that would allow greater participation for Southeast Asia. He called for the Security Council to be expanded to 20 to 25 permanent and non-permanent members, which would yield a more "equitable geographic representation."

THE ASEAN REGIONAL FORUM AND THE MAJOR POWERS

The creation and activities of the ARF merit elaboration, as this organization represents the only multilateral forum that brings together China, Japan, and the United States for the explicit purpose of dialogue on security. In 1977, Japan first proposed that a security forum be created between ASEAN and its dialogue partners. But the idea was premature and ASEAN rejected it outright. The idea resurfaced, however, in 1993, this time as an ASEAN proposal. Beginning with the first ARF meeting in Bangkok in 1994, the ASEAN countries plus the fourteen other nations that make up the ARF have held annual cabinet-level meetings each summer to keep lines of communication open, build confidence, and discuss the region's contentious issues. "Intercessional meetings" are held throughout the year; the March 1997 meeting was chaired jointly in Beijing by China and the Philippines, the two countries involved in a minor military scuffle in 1995 over the Mischief Reef in the Spratly atoll.

Through the ARF, the ASEAN states are deeply embroiled in the debates over the roles the United States, Japan, and China will play now that the Cold War has ended.[5] When the ARF was launched, China was already concerned that APEC (which gained real momentum at Seattle in 1993) was an effort by the United States and Australia, in particular, to gain an upper hand in setting the terms of Pacific Rim commerce.[6] Aware of concerns in ASEAN about China's growing assertiveness, Beijing initially interpreted the ARF as a counterpart to APEC in the security realm. Important developments in 1995—including the normalization of relations between the United States and Vietnam, Vietnam's admission to ASEAN, and the very unusual security pact between Indonesia and Australia—as well as the strengthening of the U.S.–Japan Security Treaty in 1996 and again in 1997, have all contributed to China's sense that the collapse of communism has done little to diminish the urge of other regional powers to erect an arc of containment from the Indian Ocean to the North Pacific.

The U.S. position on the ARF is that it is an important multilateral supplement to existing arrangements for stability and security in the Pacific, but that it does not supplant U.S. bilateral alliances, particularly with Japan. The ARF received a cool reception from Beijing precisely because it threatened to overlay a multilateral security arrangement (one which the United States could more easily dominate than China) on a foundation of long-standing bilateral alliances that favored the United States and Japan. The new multilateralism in the Asia-Pacific region could only be palatable to Beijing if the old bilateralism established after World War II were dismantled. The trend since 1993 has been in the opposite direction, largely confirming China's initial assessment and justifying its concerns.

Unable to block the rise of the ARF, China has pursued a policy of ambiguity in an effort to keep ARF's impact and development to a minimum. To safeguard the long-term initiative for modernizing China's military, Beijing has resisted the ARF's arms control and transparency agenda. When the subject of the Spratly Islands was broached at the first ARF summit in 1994, China stated flatly that it was committed to peaceful dialogue on its claims to most of the South China Sea, but that the discussions would be strictly bilateral (where China would have a distinct advantage). To undermine what could be accomplished at the annual ARF meetings, China insisted on "intercessional meetings" rather than "working groups" between the annual summit meetings. This was more than just semantics, as only working groups have a mandate within the ASEAN framework to formulate recommendations. Predictably, there has been much more confidence building and chat at ARF meetings than concrete agreements or policies.

The intercessional meeting in Beijing in March 1997 is an interesting case study in how the ARF is both working and stalled. By the time of the full ARF gathering in Jakarta in 1996, China had already softened its rhetoric on the Spratly Islands and seemed to embrace the idea that the conflict must be settled multilaterally. Beijing changed its posture in part because countries in the region were troubled by all the missiles fired in the general direction of Taiwan early in 1997. Symbolically, at least, it was important that China was already hosting an ARF intercessional meeting in 1997, and that it was doing so jointly with a major Spratly rival, the Philippines.[7] This was China's first opportunity to host a multilateral dialogue on security for the region.

Although everyone was at pains to put a positive spin on the talks, the Beijing ARF meeting was a disaster. The opening session was delayed for hours because China objected strenuously to language proposed by the ASEAN states referring to the "constructive role" the bilateral treaty between the United States and Japan plays in maintaining peace and stability in the region.[8] Even before the talks had finished, China's Foreign Minister, Qian Qichen, stated flatly that his country's claims over the Spratly Islands and the South China Sea were unchanged, while other Chinese officials argued that the meeting was not the proper forum even to begin talks on the disputed atoll.[9] In an effort to have more opportunities to observe China's armed forces and military preparedness, the United States and other ARF members argued in favor of including both unilateral and bilateral military exercises under a proposal that would notify and invite military observers from ARF states when conducting war games. China raised the lone voice of dissent, insisting that only joint military exercises should be covered by the measure.

The deepest disagreement during the three-day meeting centered on existing military alliances in the region. At the close of the talks, the only official to speak on behalf of China was Chen Jian, the assistant foreign affairs minister. Attacking the U.S.–Japan alliance, Chen declared, "We do not think it is correct to regard bilateral military alliances as the foundation of military security and the ARF as a supplement." But this did not necessarily indicate China embraced a multilateralism based on the ARF. Chen would only emphasize, "We cannot accept that the ARF play a secondary role as a complement to bilateral military alliances." In part as a counterpoise to the row that broke out over military alliances, the People's Liberation Army allowed a rare inspection by outsiders of its crack 196th Infantry Division of the Tianjin Garrison. According to a top official in Beijing, this was a "confidence building" exercise.[10]

JAPAN'S "HASHIMOTO DOCTRINE" FOR ASEAN

Japan's role in Southeast and Northeast Asia is clearly evolving. If the full contours of that new role remain fuzzy, it is not for Tokyo's lack of trying. In April 1996, the U.S.–Japan Joint Declaration on

Security signaled that both governments would explore how Tokyo could assist Washington in the event of instability or conflict in Japan's "neighboring areas," which appear (with clarification from Tokyo) to stretch from the Korean Peninsula, the Taiwan Strait, the Spratly Islands, and the Strait of Malacca, all the way to the Persian Gulf. Within this expanse, the ASEAN states would be just one component in a broad web of strategic commitments. At the end of 1996, Prime Minister Ryutaro Hashimoto commented on Japan's long-standing role as the junior partner of the United States in regional affairs by saying, "The time has come for Japan to spread its own values and philosophy in the world."

Against this backdrop, Hashimoto unveiled a proposal in a Singapore speech in January 1997 to deepen and broaden Japan's ties with Southeast Asia. The centerpiece of the initiative is a call for regular summit meetings between top leaders from ASEAN and Japan, and for holding bilateral talks with individual ASEAN member countries on security issues. Immediately dubbed the "Hashimoto Doctrine," the proposal was received with polite caution in ASEAN countries, and mostly with scorn in Japan. Unlike his predecessors, Hashimoto neither expressed remorse about Japan's brutality in the region nor affirmed that Japan would avoid becoming a great military power—a key tenet in both the Yoshida and Fukuda doctrines.[11] Although the feelings are not as intense in Southeast Asia as in Korea and China, there is still an undercurrent of suspicion toward Japan and the potential for aggression. It is particularly worrisome to observers in ASEAN that Japan appears unwilling to confront its past fully and honestly.

Leaders in ASEAN are not sure they want to accord Japan the special status and prestige of being the only great power to hold a regular summit with them. The precedent could trigger requests from China and the United States that would be awkward to reject. And so much bilateralism could undermine all the efforts being made in the ARF. Reservations have also been raised about how China would view a regular ASEAN–Japan summit. Thus the response from ASEAN so far to the Hashimoto initiative has been cautious and noncommittal. Malaysia and Singapore suggested that it might be better to include China and South Korea in the summit—partly to calm Beijing and partly to make sure Japan could not dominate the sessions. Based largely on concerns about the added security dimension in relations with ASEAN, reactions in Japan to the proposal have ranged from cool to hostile. Press reports and opinions said Hashimoto was wrong to upstage the ARF and the promise of multilateralism for the region. *Asahi Shimbun* criticized Hashimoto for failing to mention in his Singapore speech either human rights abuses in Burma or Indonesia's occupation of and atrocities in East Timor. Although it is too early to say, the "Hashimoto Doctrine" appears to have little potential.

FLASHPOINTS IN SOUTHEAST ASIA

Although these developments in bilateral and multilateral regional security are important, they are of little use for confronting the most serious sources of instability and conflict in Southeast Asia. Apart from competing claims in the South China Sea and a few other minor territorial disputes (since 1962, for instance, the Philippines has laid claim to the Malaysian state of Sabah), the greatest threats to political and economic security in the region are from conflicts and problems within states, not among them. Indeed, the regional institutions could even prove counterproductive insofar as ASEAN agreements severely constrain the actions member states can take toward each other.[12] The cases mentioned below are by no means an exhaustive list, but they give a sense of the struggles under way. Claims that Asians are less interested in democracy, political participation, and human rights notwithstanding, an important theme in most of the tensions is a desire for self-determination and an end to political and economic exclusion.

Cambodia. With the pullout of Vietnam in 1989, and despite some cross-border activities involving the Thai military, the conflicts in Cambodia have assumed a more inward character. This does not mean, however, that neighboring powers could not get pulled back into the conflict if current instabilities in Cambodia deepen. Until a coup by Hun Sen in summer 1997, Cambodia was ruled by a dysfunctional coalition government. Although Hun Sen and his Cambodian People's Party (CPP) lost the U.N.–supervised elections in 1993, he refused to step aside. Instead he forced a coalition with the winners, the royalist FUNCINPEC party. The CPP dominated the country from the ministries down to the local level. The armies of the coalition partners were joined but never integrated. Small clashes between the rival factions were not uncommon in the lead up to the coup, as both sides tried to attract followers of the Khmer Rouge by offering them amnesty. The political turmoil in Cambodia proved to be too much even for the accommodating ASEAN states;

although they were eager to achieve the goal of the "ASEAN Ten" by having Cambodia be a full member at the organization's thirtieth anniversary in 1997, they decided to postpone Cambodia's membership.

Bangsamoros. In September 1996, it appeared that three decades of armed conflict that claimed more than 100,000 lives had been brought to a close when a pact was finally reached between the Philippine government and the Moro National Liberation Front (MNLF) to establish the Autonomous Region in Muslim Mindanao (ARMM). But another group, the Moro Islamic Liberation Front (MILF), is not on board. The MILF, whose leaders recently declared that "the Koran is our law, not the [Philippine] constitution," wants to restore an independent Islamic state they say dates back to four centuries before the Spanish arrived. The MILF's armed forces are estimated to number between 35,000 and 120,000, and in December 1996 the Bangsamoro People's Consultative Assembly, which has strong links to the MILF, attracted 200,000 supporters. Indonesia, which has battled separatist Muslims in Aceh for decades, is also worried about the growing strength of the MILF. The Philippine government is scheduled to hold talks with leaders of the group, but in light of the ARMM agreement reached with the MNLF, it is unclear how much room is left for compromise.

Burma. The struggle under way in Burma between the military junta SLORC and the democratic movement has already spilled over into regional relations. The country's admission into ASEAN as a member, at a time when international pressure against admission was high, generated tensions among ASEAN, the European Union, and the United States. Burmese refugees (especially ethnic Karens) fleeing across the Thai border are causing difficulties as well. But the biggest tensions surrounding Burma are domestic, and it appears that the country's politics will be marked by deep instability for the foreseeable future.

Vietnam. Internationally, Vietnam has normalized relations with the United States and gained full membership in ASEAN. But domestically it has significant problems. First, the Communist Party is aging and faces imminent succession (generational, at a minimum). Hopes that the process would get under way at the Party Congress at the end of 1996 did not materialize. In September 1997, two younger officials moved up to fill the posts of president and prime minister. But the top position in the Communist Party has yet to be determined. More difficult than these political matters, however, are those of rapid economic transformation. The reforms introduced in the early 1990s produced a strong response from foreign investors. From 1988 through 1997, Vietnam approved over 1,700 private investment projects valued at almost $30 billion. Sixty percent of the projects by number and 66 percent by value came from just five countries, all in Asia.[13] But by 1997, much of the euphoria over investment prospects in Vietnam had waned as foreign investors found the Vietnamese government exceedingly difficult to work with, and as the pace of reforms lost momentum. Because its currency is not convertible, Vietnam was not swept into Southeast Asia's financial crisis in 1997. But serious problems remain as the Communist Party tries to attract investment while clinging to a view of outsiders marked by deep suspicion.

Indonesia. The largest and strategically most important nation in the region, Indonesia is confronted with the irony of rising political uncertainty after three decades of stability under Suharto's New Order. The problem is that Suharto's rule was not institutionalized, but rather highly personalized. The Habibie regime that replaced Suharto has made only token changes, and in the absence of far-reaching reform, the country could be rocked by further upheaval that could have ripple effects throughout Southeast Asia. There is also the question of East Timor. This struggle for independence, which many thought had run out of steam at the end of the 1980s, has gained renewed strength and international prominence in the 1990s. It is apparent to observers both in Indonesia and abroad that Jakarta has lost the international battle of persuasion over Timor. Indonesia pays a very high price internationally for its occupation and atrocities. Ali Alatas, Indonesia's distinguished foreign minister, would have certainly been a leading contender as Secretary General of the United Nations if he were not constantly in the international spotlight apologizing for the invasion and occupation. Similarly, the Indonesian military has paid a high price for its role in Timor—not only in terms of difficult relations with Western militaries (especially the U.S. military), but also in terms of ruined careers of officers who have been implicated in massacres of unarmed Timorese. Indonesia is a country of tremendous economic and political importance in Asia, but it cannot assume its proper role in the region until the question of self-determination for the Timorese is addressed diplomatically rather than with brute force.

Ethnic Chinese. The political and security challenges posed by the ethnic Chinese in Southeast Asia are manifested within the politics of the ASEAN states but have an international and regional character as well. The issue is most salient for Singapore, Malaysia, and especially Indonesia, but also to a lesser degree for Thailand and the Philippines. In Malaysia, ethnic Chinese comprise one third of the population and control almost 75 percent of the wealth. In Indonesia the situation is even more skewed, as the ethnic Chinese comprise just 3 percent of the population but control an estimated 80 percent of the wealth. In Malaysia, the domestic tensions surrounding the ethnic Chinese were smoothed over for years by high growth rates. Now that the economic glow appears to be off the country, it is unclear what will happen politically. In Indonesia the tensions are managed by the armed forces.

Two recent developments could exacerbate latent tensions over the region's ethnic Chinese and their economic prominence. First, these entrepreneurs increasingly are investing internationally, especially in China. This has already sparked outrage in Indonesia and charges that even though the capital is needed back home the ethnic Chinese do not feel nationalist connections to the country.[14] Second, as China rises politically and economically, there is a danger, already seen in Singapore, that a combination of Chinese pride and chauvinism could ignite smoldering resentments in Southeast Asia. Interestingly, Indonesian officials could not decide if they were relieved or alarmed at the shift to a China focus when a scandal arose in the U.S. over Democratic Party campaign contributions from the Indonesian Riady conglomerate, controlled by an Indonesian of Chinese ancestry. The relief is that less attention is being paid to the authoritarian character of Indonesia and what sorts of policy concessions (on labor rights or East Timor) businessmen might have wanted from the Clinton Administration. The alarm stems from Southeast Asia's ethnic Chinese network, including heads of major conglomerates in Indonesia, whose members appear eager to shape U.S. policy toward China.

All of these tensions are deep and their potential for destabilizing individual countries and causing ripple effects across the region is real. Neither the ARF nor the bilateral alliances are of much use, however, in addressing these threats to the region's security.

THE 1997 ECONOMIC CRISIS

For at least a decade, capital has flowed generously into Southeast Asia in the form of direct investment, commercial loans, and portfolio investments in the region's nascent stock markets. Drawn by large populations, rich endowments of natural resources, and authoritarian governments that ensured political stability, these capital flows helped produce high growth rates and expanded manufactures for export. Especially with the explosion in portfolio investments managed by huge institutional investors, the flows of capital to Southeast Asian countries occurred on an increasingly thin information base. At the first sign of economic problems during the summer of 1997, particularly in the banking and property sectors of Thailand and Indonesia, capital controllers turned against the region and almost overnight transformed the vaunted Southeast Asian miracle into a debacle.

The currencies of the region were battered, devaluing by over 28 percent on average in a matter of weeks, with the Thai baht dropping 42 percent and the Indonesian rupiah falling 55.4 percent between June and early October 1997. By the beginning of the fourth quarter, the bourse in Bangkok dropped from its 1997 high by a staggering 53.4 percent. In the Philippines, Malaysia, and Indonesia, the stock markets plummeted in tandem by 41.2 percent, 37.4 percent, and 36.4 percent, respectively. Despite a broad spectrum of policy responses, ranging from orthodox to unorthodox, central bankers and ministers of finance in these countries appeared unable to halt a crisis that seemed to come from nowhere and was based on economic conditions that were not dramatically different from earlier in the year, when the consensus was that these economies were unstoppable "tigers."

This startling economic deterioration will likely have a deep impact on the politics of the countries involved, as well as on the regional equation. Thailand showed early signs that the armed forces might step in to restore both economic and political confidence in the country. Displaying a stronger commitment to stability and profit-making than to the principles of democracy, many of the cell-phone elites who helped push the military back to the barracks began wondering out loud if another interlude with the generals might not be a good idea. In Indonesia, the financial crisis galvanized the long-simmering opposition to President Suharto's rule and hastened its end. In Malaysia, Prime Minister Mahathir bin Mohamad has tried to deflect criticisms of his policies by tapping nationalist sentiments and targeting scapegoats like the financier George Soros. This emphasis on Soros and foreigners in general has prompted journalists and other observers to investigate the active role Malaysian investors themselves played in moving their assets in ways that undermined the national currency and local stock market. The same is true in Indonesia and Thailand. The major industrial countries, meanwhile, were unenthusiastic about calls from within ASEAN to establish an Asian monetary fund that could bail out countries facing serious financial crises. The IMF already exists for this purpose, though its resources are made available only after austerity packages are agreed to and implemented. Given the reluctance of ASEAN states to push each other around (at least in public), it is unlikely that a regional monetary fund would apply a similar degree of conditionality.

BRINGING NATIONAL SECURITY HOME

This essay opened with two claims: first, U.S. foreign policy has a more narrowly corporate foundation than in the past, and second, conventional assessments of security issues, like the one presented here on Southeast Asia, do not adequately represent the range of national security threats posed in the more globalized environment of the late twentieth century. This section develops these themes more fully.

The recent maneuvering by the United States in the Asia-Pacific region must surely be mystifying to most Americans. The United States has strengthened its alliance with Japan and shown its willingness to use aircraft carriers to defend Taiwan. But for what? To contain China for containment's sake? If the system of political exclusion known this century as communism is dead, then on what grounds should we risk the lives of our soldiers to encircle a country like China, but not one like Indonesia? What is the difference, other than that one is authoritarian and unfriendly and the other is authoritarian and friendly? If the Chinese government can suppress its own people and even massacre unarmed civilians, and still not dampen American enthusiasm for doing business and signing contracts, why should any American become indignant enough to go to war when the same thing happens to the people of Hong Kong, Taiwan, or even South Korea?

Americans have figured out that the principles of justice and democracy are playing a much less prominent role in guiding U.S. foreign policy than they did in the first campaign to elect Clinton to the White House. Euphemisms like "comprehensive engagement" do little to mask the reality that business interests and market access have overwhelmed competing considerations. Newspaper cartoons routinely heap scorn on the hollow foundations of late twentieth century U.S. foreign policy.

One consequence of upgrading business priorities and downgrading (or at least muddling) matters of principle is that the range of foreign policy instruments available to U.S. leaders becomes more limited. "Let's win one for the status quo" is as unpersuasive to Americans as "Let's win one for business and free trade." An abiding commitment to principles is not something that can be turned off and on in a country's foreign policy like a light switch. I do not underestimate the capacity of the American government to quickly whip up sentiment for acts of aggression, as in President Bush's war to restore the monarchy of Kuwait. But for the country to engage in anything other than a flash war against so weak an adversary as Iraq, and in the process endure the sorts of casualties Americans experienced in the Vietnam War, a motive that taps more genuinely into the most cherished American values of justice and fairness is required. The emphasis on business and market access around the world, combined with an endless flow of empty rhetoric on matters of freedom and rights, will complicate the job of American officials who want to act in the name of "national security." It is difficult to be threatened by countries with which we conduct so much business. There is, however, a different sort of "national security" concern that looms large when fundamentally dissimilar political systems grow more intimately involved with each other through market transactions.

Markets are the great transmission belt. When products meet in the market, the systems and the people that produced them "meet" as well. And when a purchase is made, factors of cost, efficiency, and quality associated with the producers are assessed. The producer that has the best combination of cost, efficiency, and quality is rewarded and prevails. At the same time, other producers are punished and must adapt to meet or exceed the standards of the first producer. This process of competition pressures "inefficient," "inferior," or "high-cost" producers to adapt and innovate—or they will perish. In this way, "good" practices and techniques are spread and endlessly improved upon, while "bad" systems of production are eventually driven out of existence.

A problem with this image is that the impersonal transactions of the market are indifferent to a whole range of factors that can make one product (or location or business climate) more competitive than another. If the factors that make a product competitive are negative, they will be transmitted just as effectively as the sorts of positive factors cited above. Thus if we assume comparable levels of technology and quality for two producers, but one uses slave labor and the other pays a living wage, the cost of the goods produced by slaves will be lower. The market will reward the producer who uses slaves and punish the producer who pays a living wage. If the second producer does not adapt to or exceed the standards of the first (by achieving a more efficient slavery), it will perish. In this way, "bad" practices and techniques are spread and endlessly improved upon, while "good" ones are undermined and threatened with extinction. Pressures from owners of capital in the living-wage system against the political system that supports slavery will arise only if trans-system investment and production is impossible. A system of maximal free trade and investment will be upheld by all owners of capital if capitalists from the living-wage system are permitted to invest freely in the slave system. Even if they claim their investments will some day help bring an end to slavery, a more immediate competitive impact will be to undermine the benefits laborers enjoy in the living-wage state.

The prevailing ideology is that as markets bring an ever wider range of countries into more intimate contact with each other, the living standards, working conditions, and even political freedoms currently enjoyed by the advanced industrial countries will set the standard for, and eventually spread to, the authoritarian exploitative systems. But if countries with costly welfare cushions, costly safety and environmental regulations, and encumbering political freedoms find it hard to compete with countries that lack these factors, why should we expect markets to do anything but punish and erode the high-cost locations? Richard Robison raises precisely this question for Australia as it adapts to the competitive pressures from its Asian neighbors to the north: "Does the social democratic framework place an untenable burden upon Western economies in their contest with the sleek new industrial predators of the Asian region? Can the West avoid adopting the structures that appear to have underpinned the Asian miracle: a seemingly contradictory world of markets and pervasive state control, where the interest of economic growth is portrayed as the collective public interest and where the state smooths the way for the corporate or family agenda in an ironic reversal of the rhetoric of 'Asian values'?"[15]

One of the biggest changes during the last quarter century in transactions between countries, whether for goods or investment capital, is not in the size of the flows but in the political dissimilarities between the states engaging in the transactions. When countries with relatively similar political freedoms (speech, independent organization, legal recourse) compete economically, market forces are unlikely to put competitive pressure on these political arrangements. But if one country is highly democratic and another is highly authoritarian; if one has high taxes and an extensive social safety net while the other has nothing; and if one allows workers to organize, strike, and play a role in setting the standards of the workplace while the other outlaws all of these things, market forces are far more likely to enter the picture as competitive pressures against the social and political institutions of the more democratic system. In this connection the discussion returns to the subject of national security. The point is not that the conventional approach to national security is no longer useful, but that it must be blended with an accounting of national security that fully appreciates the threats to a country that are associated with linkages abroad, but manifested domestically.

It is beyond the scope of this paper to offer a full characterization of decline and instability in the United States over the last two decades, the period during which competitive pressures from authoritarian states have grown in salience. But a number of factors can be cited. Average unemployment rates went from 4.6 percent in the 1950s and 1960s to 6.8 percent since 1980. The gap in wealth and income in the United States has widened; in 1992, the richest 10 percent of the population owned 62 percent of all assets (if principal residence is excluded, the figure leaps to 77 percent). The United States has the distinction of having the highest gini coefficient of any advanced industrial country.[16] On average, real hourly wages have fallen by close to a percentage point every year since 1973. Job insecurity has increased dramatically, as has the average number of hours worked per week and the number of Americans working more than one job to survive. Union membership has declined in all tradable sectors, though it has increased in services.

Drug use is rampant, the country's jails are overflowing, people in urban and rural areas alike feel unsafe, gated communities abound, bombs are exploding, militia are growing more active, and schools are in decline. Americans now routinely submit to a series of security measures at airports that citizens would not have tolerated in the 1960s or 1970s.[17] The claim being made here is not that global competition is responsible for all of these trends. But given that one of the most important economic developments over the last 25 years is that global production (especially in manufactures) has opened up in predominantly authoritarian countries, it is difficult to fathom that this has occurred without competitive pressures being brought to bear on the social and political relations of production in the United States.

If the scope of national security is broadened to include the downward drag on domestic social and political conditions that are transmitted through economic linkages with authoritarian trading partners and competitive sites for investment, then the U.S. interest in promoting basic rights and freedoms in other countries shifts from the realm of principled idealism to sober pragmatism. Similarly, the current conflict between a focus on human rights and issues of national and economic security, which undergirds the uneasy formulation known as "comprehensive engagement," would collapse as artificial and even counterproductive.

FOR A NEW U.S. POLICY

A number of recommendations flow from this analysis; these range from country-specific recommendations to the more systemic.

With regard to the countries of Southeast Asia, the United States should back up its rhetoric on human rights with concrete action. One way to do this would be to establish closer links with groups and movements inside the ASEAN states that are struggling to broaden political participation. The model for such activity would be the efforts the United States made on behalf of opposition groups and individuals in the former communist states. Progressive movements exist in all the authoritarian states of Southeast Asia, but they operate not only against the intimidation of their own governments but also without a helping hand from such powerful actors as the United States.

To the extent possible, the United States should apply these political pressures through multilateral institutions in order to diminish the negative exposure to Americans. This means the United States will have to take stronger measures to combat the foreign policies of other countries, such as Japan, Germany, France, and Britain, that go along with repressive practices for the sake of economic gain. The World Trade Organization (WTO) would be an ideal forum for such multilateral pressures. This means, above all, that basic conventions on human rights, especially labor rights, need to be negotiated and enforced.

At the time of this writing in 1997, with specific regard to Indonesia, the United States is taking a tremendous risk in its continued support of President Suharto. The anger pervading Indonesian society is high and increasing. The New Order government is fragmenting from within rather than being broken down from without. But this does not mean that when various social forces perceive the state to be badly weakened they will not act to accelerate the decline. The potential exists in Indonesia for a violent breakdown of the political order. The Indonesians are subtle readers of political signals. The United States need not shift its policies dramatically to encourage the next generation of Indonesian leaders to move preemptively to push Suharto and his family out peacefully. Though it may surprise American observers that the U.S. posture carries so much weight in Indonesia, extensive interviews with leading opposition figures in 1996 and 1997, both military and civilian, confirm that they are watching for just such a tilt in U.S. policy toward Indonesia.

On a broader level, the arguments against a corporate foreign policy are relevant to the debate over whether Congress should give fast-track authority to the executive branch for negotiating trade agreements with other countries. The Constitution places the greatest responsibility for foreign treaties squarely in the hands of Congress because the framers understood that the terms agreed to in our relations with other countries necessarily constrains democratic options and freedoms at home. Before Americans surrender rights and prerogatives, the choices and consequences should be debated fully so that there are no shocks or surprises after international agreements are already signed. The conventions against preferential government purchasing included in the WTO are an excellent example of how the public can end up excluded from decisions surrounding trade issues. The United States signed these conventions, and the citizens of Massachusetts found out only belatedly that the conventions conflict with their control over their own state's purchasing choices. When the Massachusetts legislature decided that it would no longer do business with corporations that invested in Burma, Japan and European countries challenged the state policy through the WTO, arguing quite correctly that preferential purchasing policies violated provisions of the international conventions the United States had signed. The federal government had negotiated away State rights and prerogatives in a manner that violated the U.S. Constitution. It was a rude awakening to the people in many sub-national jurisdictions in the United States that agreeing to certain provisions in the WTO meant that they could no longer adopt the same local policies that helped free Nelson Mandela from prison and end apartheid in South Africa.

Fast-track authority is a bad idea because it shifts too much of the democratic, deliberative process regarding international treaties out of the hands of the Congress. There is already too little debate in the United States over the domestic impact of these treaties. Fast track moves the process even further in the wrong direction, epitomizing the costs and dangers of a corporate foreign policy.

NOTES

[1] Aryeh Neier calls this the "new double standard" in American foreign policy. It used to be that the United States was ready to denounce human rights abuses by states aligned with the Soviet Union. Now the United States will do so against the easy targets—countries that are relatively unimportant politically and economically. Aryeh Neier, "The New Double Standard," *Foreign Policy* 105 (Winter 1996-97), pp. 91-101. In a rejoinder to Neier in the same issue, Jeffrey E. Garten makes the familiar call for "pragmatism" in pursuing a human rights agenda, so that important trade and security interests are not undermined.

[2] In the meantime, labor has had much less success in extending their intranational leverage into the international arena. See Jeffrey A. Winters, *Power in Motion: Capital Mobility and the Indonesian State* (Ithaca: Cornell University Press, 1996).

[3] ASEAN was founded in 1967 with five members: Indonesia, the Philippines, Malaysia, Singapore, and Thailand. Brunei was added in 1984, Vietnam in 1995, and Burma in 1997, despite U.S. criticism of Rangoon's human rights violations.

[4] The full list of dialogue partners includes Canada, the United States, Russia, Japan, China, South Korea, Australia, New Zealand, Cambodia, Papua New Guinea, and Taiwan.

[5] Significantly, in ASEAN's view, Japan plays a role in ARF as a "Western" member.

[6] For this reason, Prime Minister Mahathir of Malaysia—who gets considerable political mileage at home for the Asian chauvinism he directs against the United States and Australia—refused to participate in the APEC summit in Seattle and successfully insisted (with a nod from Indonesia and against reservations expressed by Thailand and the Philippines) that Burma, which was granted formal ASEAN "observer" status in 1996, be given full membership in ASEAN at the earliest possible date despite U.S. and European efforts to isolate Burma as a pariah state. (While pressuring against Burma's membership was the right policy, it was also criticized in the West as an easy way to score human rights points while continuing to take no meaningful steps to address the rampant authoritarianism and human rights violations in the countries where Americans and Europeans do most of their business.) In a move to exclude the United States and Australia, Mahathir proposed that the East Asian Economic Caucus (EAEC) be created as an alternative to APEC. The Association endorsed the EAEC in December 1995, but resolved that it should be an East Asian interest group within APEC, not a separate entity.

[7] The Spratly situation rose from a simmer to a boil in 1995, when Philippine planes spotted Chinese structures in an area claimed by both countries. Manila escalated tensions further when it sent troops to destroy Chinese territorial markers in the area. By August 1995, calm was restored and both countries signed a code of conduct committing them to peaceful actions in the disputed areas. This agreement was reaffirmed in February 1997 during a visit by China's defense minister, Chi Haotian, to the Philippines. Parts or all of the Spratlys are claimed by China, the Philippines, Taiwan, Vietnam, Malaysia, and Brunei.

[8] Prior to the meeting, ASEAN officials had already signaled their position by referring to the U.S.-Japan alliance as "the world's most important bilateral relationship," adding that it was the foundation upon which all of the region's other multilateral mechanisms (ARF, APEC, and the nongovernment Council for Security Cooperation in the Asia-Pacific) are built.

[9] Although a major purpose of the ARF talks in Beijing was to move forward on the Spratly dispute, it was evident that government representatives at the meeting were given clear instructions not to press China too hard on the matter. When representatives from the Philippines called on the ARF to endorse the 1992 ASEAN Declaration on the South China Sea, the proposal was met with stone silence.

[10] Though the results are still modest, China has sought to work directly with ASEAN to avoid some of the problems it sees with the ARF. In February 1997, the ASEAN-China Joint Cooperation Committee (ASEAN-JCC) was formed as an umbrella group for all ASEAN-China links. Funded with $700,000 from China and inaugurated in Beijing, the ASEAN-JCC will focus on personnel exchanges, information sharing, and workshops on economic and trade cooperation. It will also coordinate four parallel mechanisms that constitute the key institutional components of the ASEAN-China dia-

logue: the ASEAN-China Senior Officials Political Consultations, the ASEAN-China Joint Committee on Economic and Trade Cooperation, the ASEAN-China Joint Committee on Science and Technology, and the ASEAN Committee in Beijing, made up of the ambassadors from the ASEAN states. An ASEAN-China Business Council is also being formed.

[11] The Yoshida Doctrine, pronounced by Prime Minister Yoshida in 1950, renounced militarism and dedicated the country to economic reconstruction and export-led growth. This policy ran into trouble, in part because of its own success. In 1974, Prime Minister Tanaka's visit to Southeast Asia was met with anti-Japanese riots in Thailand and Indonesia, to the dismay of Japan's foreign policy establishment. In 1977, Prime Minister Fukuda proposed a new doctrine. Japan reiterated its rejection of militarism, but added that Tokyo wanted to maintain a "heart to heart" relationship with the countries of the region. Although it never did it, Japan claimed that it wanted to play a more prominent political role in reconciling the communist and non-communist areas of the region by serving as a "bridge."

[12] All members of ASEAN must uphold the Treaty of Amity and Cooperation, which not only stipulates that members will not act aggressively toward each other, but also that they will not meddle in each other's "internal affairs."

[13] In order of capital invested, the top five are: Singapore (171 projects, $5.3 billion), Taiwan (301 projects, $4.1 billion), Hong Kong (195 projects, $3.7 billion), Japan (212 projects, $3.2 billion), and South Korea (197 projects, $3.1 billion). The United States has 70 projects worth $1.2 billion, ranking it seventh after Malaysia. See "Investment Update," *Vietnam Investment Review*, September 28, 1997, p. 22.

[14] The argument is specious, though this does not diminish its political potency in Indonesia. "Pribumi" (indigenous) investors are just as likely to locate their capital abroad, assuming they have the scale and information to engage in transnational ventures.

[15] Richard Robison, ed., *Pathways to Asia: The Politics of Engagement* (Sydney: Allen and Unwin, 1996), p. xii.

[16] Global income disparities have widened dramatically. The richest 20 percent of the world population had 30 times the income of the poorest 20 percent in 1962. By the mid-1990s, the richest fifth had 60 times the income of the poorest fifth (United Nations Development Programme data).

[17] Not only are we required to show identification to board a plane (a very new and quite shocking development), but we must submit to inane questions such as "Has anyone unknown to you given you anything to carry on the plane?" Inside the terminal passengers are warned every two minutes over a blaring public address system that unattended bags will be investigated and removed by security personnel. Outside the terminal families

loading and unloading bags are treated to similar warnings about unattended bags and vehicles. Most people try to block out the sense of extreme danger and social breakdown these warnings imply. But the reminders gnaw away at the public's subconscious. Two other stories in this same vein made national news in 1997. Rush hour traffic was stalled for hours as explosives specialists cautiously approached a backpack on the side of a highway in Atlanta. When the bag was finally opened, it contained nothing more than clothes and personal effects. A bomb squad was also called to a suburban neighborhood when a man came home and found a small box wrapped with string on his doorstep. He had not ordered anything and there were no postal markings on the box. After several hours of effort and great public expense, the box was finally opened. It contained a chocolate pudding pie left by a neighbor as an old-fashioned gesture of friendship. Such gestures have no place in a society marked by the sort of extreme violence siege mentality that is increasingly seen in America.

U.S. ECONOMIC AND SECURITY INTERESTS IN SOUTHEAST ASIA

JAMES CLAD

THE "PASSING GENDARME": MILITARY POWER AND ECONOMIC ACCESS

The distortions impeding access of foreign goods and services into Southeast Asia became considerably less pressing in the aftermath of the abrupt currency depreciation and resulting liquidity and debt crises afflicting the regional economies after June 1997. In some cases, import barriers rose temporarily, reflecting a need for revenue. But the urgent need to recapitalize the financial sector generally resulted in the hurried removal of hitherto entrenched barriers against foreign ownership and participation in financial firms.

THE 1997 CRISIS

The situation in Thailand, whose powerhouse economy from 1986 to 1996 achieved the fastest sustained growth of any country in the world, illustrated the pragmatic need: under an IMF supervised credit package in August of 1997, ownership and license restrictions in the banking sector were set to largely disappear by 1999. In other afflicted economies, as in Indonesia, reluctance by a long-established regime to remove restrictive licensing and import monopolies, or to end tariff protection for a set of "strategic industries," prompted further disenchantment in external markets and further sell-offs of the local currency.

Despite the immediate intensification of pressures for even faster liberalization of foreign entry into Southeast Asian markets, the longer-term response to the worst financial crisis yet experienced by the region may prove inimical to American interests for two reasons. First, the falling away of rapid growth rates and the continuing currency volatility and foreign exchange risk will result in reduced interest, whether in direct or portfolio investment. Second, the emerging political reaction to the rising unemployment and commercial insolvency will affect the climate for foreign participation.

The abrupt reversal of a decade's heady growth—a reversal prompted by large, short-term, mostly private, and largely unhedged external indebtedness—had already caused, by the beginning of 1998, a gathering resentment against the negative consequences of "globalism," especially unregulated financial flows. Uncertainties about political transitions in some regional countries, notably in Indonesia, will add to the caution.

In this new climate, regional politicians will find new arguments to justify fencing off segments of the economy from competition. Economic nationalism will enjoy new favor. New monopolistic prerogatives and concessions will be accorded to domestic infant and strategic industries, even as demands for continuing entry into American markets become shriller.

Compared with Northeast Asia's high-tariff mercantilism, the Southeast Asian economies will gain a short advantage in terms of their involuntarily cheap currencies. This once-only boost in competitiveness will add to the imbalanced trade figures already creating (after Japan and China) the third largest American merchandise-trade deficit. At the same time, government fiscal retrenchment in Southeast Asia and a curtailment of financing will result in postponed orders for American goods at the higher end of the scale—especially aircraft and capital goods supply contracts.

With rare exceptions, the region's indirect obstruction of trade, and its explicit barriers to trade, has received little public attention in the United States. Yet blatant favoritism and persistent high tariffs make for common characteristics among the nine members of the Association of Southeast Asian Nations (ASEAN). Until recently, the size of aggregated deficits with Southeast Asia mattered little. And in the aftermath of the currency crisis, the need for export revenues has become so pressing that the region, like Japan, will seek salvation in foreign markets.

THE CONSEQUENCES FOR SECURITY

What does this mean for U.S. security interests? The most important consequence of the rolling crisis following the baht's float on July 2, 1997, has been the fracturing of regional unity. Brave words in late 1997 about preserving momentum toward the ASEAN Free Trade Area (AFTA) could not mask the deep fissures in regional cohesion. Internal preoccupations—as in Indonesia's agonizing about the post-Suharto period or Thailand's faltering parliamentary system—stymied efforts to present a united face to the IMF. Calls for a special regional fund to deal with the emergency failed to win Japanese or American endorsement.

The diplomatic equilibrium of Southeast Asia rests on maintaining a minimal consensus about the involvement of outside powers. In a region in which internal preoccupations have arisen, the opportunities for outside gain have increased. Major segments of the region's elite see Western and Japanese interests amply served in, first, the devaluation (by "currency speculation") of their local currencies and, then, in the acquisition by foreign banks and securities houses of domestic financial firms at fire-sale prices.

In both security terms and competitive position, China is best positioned to gain from the region's turmoil. China will gain new appeal as a destination for foreign direct investment, and its competitiveness will be sealed by another round of devaluation of its own currency. In security terms, Beijing can only take satisfaction from the region's preoccupations—which will work against the attainment of common reactive positions on issues such as diplomacy in the South China Sea, where China and five other regional states have often-competing territorial claims.

Since the closure of U.S. naval air facilities in Luzon, the U.S. military presence in Southeast Asia has been diluted, shifting to a "places, not bases" strategy for onward movement of naval vessels and aircraft through Southeast Asia. However, in an era of rising uncertainty and fears of possible new Chinese aggrandizement, the facilities, training, and/or courtesies that Malaysia, Singapore, Thailand, and Indonesia extend to U.S. forces will begin to lose their provisional air. The new "Visiting Forces Agreement" negotiated with the Philippine authorities during 1997-98 will complete the network of cooperation. The air of reluctant acquiescence to the American security presence will yield to more overt expressions of welcome to U.S. forces.

At present the United States can refurbish its ships at commercial rates in Singapore's Sembawang shipyards—a tidy business for the busy docks that receive eighty to ninety visits a year. Malaysia and Indonesia provision U.S. ships and permit overflights in certain contingencies, yet neither has a full status-of-forces agreement with the United States. This may change. As noted, these access linkages have a derivative feel as a patched together, follow-on consequence of the pullouts from Subic Bay and Clark Air Field in 1991. (The Philippine authorities managed to convert Subic Bay into a very successful export-processing zone, arguably the best case of U.S. base "conversion" yet achieved.)

Deputy Assistant Secretary of Defense Kurt Campbell testified before Congress in 1997 about the unilateral, bilateral, and even occasional multilateral rationale behind the desire to maintain defense capability in the Far East. Of these three rationales, a unilateral insistence not to be locked out of the Far East, commercially or strategically, has been evident since the first days of the republic. In addition, we have bilateral security commitments to Thailand and to the Philippines.

U.S. security interests in Southeast Asia thus take the form of a hovering "presence" rather than of fixed facilities placed for fixed, demonstrable purposes. Yet this presence has incalculable value to the balance-of-power calculations underpinning ASEAN diplomacy since that minimalist grouping's inception thirty years ago. As noted, this value rises in times of regional troubles.

Sometimes called the presence of a "passing gendarme," America's forward deployment acts as a relative "constant" in the region: All the regional and extra-regional players realize that the United States, if nothing else, remains serious about unimpeded passage from Guam to Diego Garcia. And they know that this will hold for as long as the United States maintains its global power projection.

This means U.S. defense policymakers take a particularly dim view of maritime territorial claims that may work to block or impede naval and air transit. These claims include putative doctrines of exclusion inherent in the Law of the Sea Convention "archipelagic principle" that Indonesia has embraced most comprehensively (although other Southeast Asian states and even China on occasion flirt with archipelagic "closed sea" doctrines).

U.S. ECONOMIC AND SECURITY INTERESTS IN SOUTHEAST ASIA

How does this general description of the U.S. security presence in Southeast Asia mesh with our economic interests? In sharp contrast to Japan, China, or to the lesser dragon economies in Northeast Asia, "mercantilism" as found in Southeast Asia (and as it affects U.S. exports) has a far less coherent policy countenance.

There are several reasons for this.

First, the Southeast Asians welcome, and compete for, U.S. and other foreign direct investment (FDI). Southeast Asian receptivity to for-export manufacturing FDI—whether in wholly owned or joint ventures, in foreign purchases of local share equity or direct subsidiary operations—enabled rapid growth of light industrial production. In this region, where foreign capital has accomplished a very large share of industrial transformation, the non-obstruction of U.S. (and other foreign) capital creates major dependency.

Unlike the economies of Northeast Asia, the Southeast Asian economies lack an MITI-style mercantilism because of their patrimonial, patron-client political culture. In most of the region's countries, various interests (pampered concessionaires, nepotic free-riders, or strategic industry enthusiasts) have "captured" the state, to use a phrase borrowed from political economy. Where we see large, fenced-off areas in a Southeast Asian economy (as in Malaysia's "national" car or in Indonesia's "national" aircraft factory), we either find arguments favoring the establishment of strategic industries, no matter what the short-term cost, or we find no "principled" argument at all—other than a shrugging of shoulders over insider advantages.

These distortions, offensive to liberalizers, do not prevail uniformly throughout the ASEAN economies. Generally, as stated, the region's key element of "openness" (to foreign, manufacturing-for-export capital) remains an across-the-board phenomenon, one that the financial crisis erupting after June 1997 had the effect of enhancing, at least for the short term. In many ways, this openness rests on pragmatism and on the habit of relying on foreign capital, foreign management, and foreign markets. The vastly larger economies to the north have not taken the same open-door approach to foreign investment in retailing, banking, or management services.

The persistence of stiff tariffs (as high as 40 percent in Thailand, or the 45 percent duty on cement in Malaysia)—rather than industrial policy—serves to protect favored suppliers from neighboring price competition in ASEAN. Heading off U.S. products is usually a secondary consideration. By the 1980s, the disputes over patent rights became a problem for the United States throughout ASEAN. However, the ASEAN states do not "target" U.S. industries as Northeast Asian states do. South Korea, Taiwan, China, and Japan deliberately aim to displace U.S. and other foreign firms from some market segments, but Southeast Asia has few such ambitions.

For example, nothing in Southeast Asian industrial development threatens top-end, defense-related technology provided by the United States. Only in small arms ordnance or in procurement of basic materiel do ASEAN countries discriminate against U.S. suppliers by building up local defense capability—which is most advanced in Singapore (with Indonesia, Malaysia, and Thailand now also seeking greater defense "indigenization"). Yet this attracts very little notice from U.S. aerospace firms chasing strike aircraft procurement deals. Since the early 1990s, the region has been buying new-generation interceptors.

If mercantilist motivation seems less evident in Southeast than in Northeast Asia, the region also has no front-burner security headaches like the Korean Peninsula or the Taiwan Strait. Nothing in Southeast Asia even remotely approaches the satisfying simplicity of the short-fuse threats to U.S. security interests further up the latitudes, where even the physical security of our forces can often hang in the balance.

Indeed, the threat scenarios in Southeast Asia have a very ***contingent*** feel to them. The current, broad trends (the expansion of ASEAN and the continuing low level of formal, intra-ASEAN discord) seem to enhance America's strategic aims in this part of the Far East. For example, the entry of Burma, Laos, and Vietnam into ASEAN since 1995 has largely evoked (leaving aside objections to the Rangoon regime's human rights record) a positive response in Washington (a result, unfortunately, of a rather poorly thought out notion that a bigger ASEAN can better "balance" China). Yet the expansion of ASEAN at a time of political succession and economic reversal reinforces the problem of achieving, and sustaining, regional coherence.

DO SECURITY TIES ENHANCE ECONOMIC LINKAGES?

To what extent does the existing U.S. military presence in the region enhance American economic interests in Southeast Asia? The presence, I stress, remains confined to ships' passage, air force overflights, occasional joint exercises, and modest aid and training programs.

Here lie various subsets of economic "interests," which, after mid-1997, must include concern about the fundamental stability of the region's banking and payments systems. In pursuit of these interests, the United States has sought three things:

- Greater ease of access for portfolio and other capital investment;
- Investment by U.S.–owned manufacturing enterprises in for-export plants in ASEAN, and
- Greater access to domestic markets for U.S. goods and services.

In the passages above, I have suggested that ASEAN has been largely "liberal" and receptive to the forces driving global competitiveness. The countries in the region accept—and, until recently, had the resources to acquire and admire—U.S. services and technology. While patrimonial and essentially non-competitive domestically, ASEAN businesses and ASEAN business culture seek the most attractive deals. In seeking technology and sales partnerships abroad, they work to enhance their profit-bearing potential without very much government intercession.

As for the last element above, the direct entry of U.S. goods and services into ASEAN domestic markets and the totality of the U.S. presence in Southeast Asia—which includes our security relationships—can and should, when linked in a ***coherent, low-key*** manner, work strongly in favor of market entry. In the fractured, uncertain environment following the 1997 financial crisis, this power must be used with considerable subtlety, but it can achieve results.

As and when they encounter local impediments in ASEAN markets, most U.S. firms seek to co-opt or otherwise neutralize their opponents. They are mostly loath to seek official U.S. involvement. U.S. embassy commercial services in ASEAN generally have utility as a cost-cutting, head-start source of basic information, helping first-timers among smaller U.S. firms to find their feet.

For major contractual warfare in ASEAN markets with foreign competitors, the picture is different. Here the cohesion and interlinked totality of U.S. interests in Southeast Asia ***does*** matter a great deal for major issues of commercial entry and competition. In this connection, we may recall a highly effective use to which AT&T seven years ago put former President George Bush's well-known penchant for telephoning foreign leaders. In Indonesia, AT&T had fought for a share of that country's telecommunications upgrade contracts announced in the late 1980s. After three telephone conversations between Presidents Suharto and Bush that dramatized AT&T capabilities, the giant firm pushed Japan's NTT aside to gain bidding rights for half of Indonesia's projected $2.5 billion upgrade business. This instance and many others show that the demonstrable effectiveness, competitiveness, reputation, and capability of major U.S. firms can ride on top of American prestige. Asians value U.S. prestige: At the time of these trans-Pacific phone chats, the Gulf War added to the luster of a U.S. military long at home in Asia. It made a critical difference.

I submit that, in this type of top-level intervention, and in this indirect fashion, the U.S. military presence in Southeast Asia furthers a range of U.S. economic interests. If this is the case, would a more aggressive pursuit of greater equity and reciprocity in trade and investment relations undermine our security interests in Southeast Asia? Here the question of the ***style*** of our diplomacy cannot be avoided.

Congressionally defined trade "thresholds" and legislated tripwires for trade retaliation do us poorer service in Southeast Asia than elsewhere. In this region, the "poor-little-us" mentality remains strong. Putting various items sporadically on yearly and half-yearly watch lists simply plays to a type of "you're big/I'm small" self-pity.

When the high profile U.S. Omnibus Trade Act and its retaliatory devices are wheeled into place, they do indeed serve to alert governments in immensely larger Northeast Asian economies that the United States has become "serious" about a particular issue of access. But in Southeast Asia, this signaling seems absurdly out of proportion to specific access problems.

Low-key, sustained insistence on such matters as transparency in government procurement is more effective. Serious prosecution (which all WTO signatories must do anyway) of Intellectual Property Rights (IPR) patent violations also counts—as does a reversal of patrimonial decisions impeding potentially large U.S. sales, especially where globally demonstrable U.S. competence and competitiveness has no chance beside cozy crony relationships that favor ***other*** overseas suppliers. I refer here to the advantages that Japanese and South Korean public works contractors and those countries' capital goods suppliers enjoy in the region.

In this region, does multilateral diplomacy add much leverage to U.S. bilateral efforts for better access for U.S. service industries, for improved IPR protection, for U.S. agricultural access, and the like? Demonstrably, a "you've got to do it now" mentality now holds in the World Trade Organization, where the Suharto regime faces an unprecedented trilateral complaint (from the United States, the European Union, and Japan) about a "national" car scheme patently cooked up to line the pockets of a Suharto family member. In the International Monetary Fund's conditions for credit provision to Indonesia in September 1997, the deferral of the "national" car project assumed considerable importance; the regime's continuing reluctance to bury the scheme did much to undermine confidence in its ability to implement any new reforms.

The region's own multilateral trade diplomacy is exemplified in communiqués from APEC summit meetings, or from the painstakingly slow expansion of tariff reduction schedules for the ASEAN Free Trade Area (AFTA). Can the United States do some "free-riding" of its own on these trade liberalization devices?

This brings us to another, final consideration. In Southeast Asia, the easier parts of domestic economic liberalization have mostly occurred. Yet the Southeast Asian "marketplace" remains a strange place: the foreign-financed, for-export manufacturing plants competing with all the world work within an older structure of business and politics. The frustrated middle classes of Manila, Bangkok, Jakarta, Kuala Lumpur, Saigon, Cebu, and dozens of other cities increasingly despise this structure—one in which naked favoritism and nepotism apply and in which military cronyism and a (troublingly) ethnic Chinese preeminence in commerce far too often rests on cozy arrangements between officials (both civilian and military) and this vulnerable minority.

In my view, the largest future gain for U.S. economic interests in Southeast Asia will come from a readjustment of this patrimonial commerce that possibly—just possibly—may accompany the looming political transitions in Southeast Asia. As noted, some readjustment will follow, if only for reasons of pragmatic adjustment and recapitalization of bankrupt firms. To put it another way, factors that have almost no connection to liberalized trading regimes, or to the quality and competitiveness of U.S. exports *per se*, will probably determine over the next decade the pace at which the United States gains business in Southeast Asia. As and when the economies there resume the growth rates they once assumed to be immutable, the question of greater transparency of commercial transactions will come to dominate American export prospects in the region.

In each ASEAN state, the internal debate over free-riding monopolies and concessionaires has a daily ebb and flow, intensified a hundredfold by the economic crisis, abruptly rising unemployment, and the declining legitimacy of long-established regimes and personalities. Some downscaling of patron-client relationships (the habit can never be eradicated) in an era of political transition and economic readjustment may occur. But much more inertia than liberalization may result in the coming five to ten years, as transitional uncertainties in the power structures of major ASEAN states become more pressing.

In such a situation—where the U.S. security presence is a state of mind and where the determinants of economic change lie mostly outside the confines of trade diplomacy—the ***size*** of U.S. forces in Southeast Asia becomes irrelevant in our survey. For the very nature of the U.S. security presence—the so-called "passing gendarme" syndrome—means that the region will continue to accept U.S. force configurations that result from factors almost completely outside the region. These factors include the global funding and positioning of our forces in general, and the strength, shipworthiness, and cruising frequency of our submarine and surface combatant ships in particular.

In this respect, this Study Group's emphasis on America's overall Pacific Ocean deployment as an interlinked phenomenon seems sound: In military terms, East, Southeast, and South Asia are contiguous operational areas. Since U.S. strategy depends on the ability to get from the East Asian to the South Asian theaters of potential operations, the countries lying in between recognize that some form of American presence is inevitable. If they choose to question this inevitability, it is usually for effect: Few doubt that an overt, maritime challenge to U.S. naval passage would elicit a decisive response.

Yet such a sense of "inevitability" has an obvious pitfall. It can lead to a certain smugness on the part of Southeast Asia and to a sense that whatever the shortcomings of trade access in the region (a sideshow, surely, to the scale of access issues further north), the Pentagon will insist upon its visits, voyages, and exercises. In Southeast Asian eyes, the U.S. "presence" thus comes free of charge.

This attitude toward the U.S. military presence permeates our relations in Southeast Asia, which means that any U.S. reference in economic diplomacy to the U.S. security presence must be made deftly, to avoid gratuitous offense in countries that are generally well disposed toward Washington.

Just as it did in Northeast and East Asia, the U.S. security presence has provided the "oxygen" for Southeast Asia's development, to borrow the phrasing of the 1995 *Security Strategy for the East Asia-Pacific Region*. A clear affirmation of this view came in Singapore Foreign Minister Shunmugam Jayakumar's Georgetown University address on 22 April 1996, in which he acknowledged a "breathing space" that the American phase of the long Indochina wars provided to the (mostly) fledgling ASEAN states. The U.S. effort, fought partly on grounds of preventing a domino effect, achieved a space in which Indonesia, Thailand, Malaysia, and even Singapore mastered internal, mostly leftist-inspired challenges to state consolidation and state authority.

The question is, should the United States employ its security "asset" to more palpable negotiating effect in Southeast Asia? As noted already, I think this can achieve results, but I fear the diplomatic discipline required may lie beyond our present administrative and policy-coordinating capabilities. We are a single-issue, order-of-magnitude people: The exclusionary effect of the ASEAN countries' mercantilism or crony monopolies is of a far lower order (in terms of foregone exports) and is much more fragmented (in terms of identifying and influencing a deciding authority) than in Northeast Asia.

In any case, what we can "threaten" in the ASEAN region (reduced frequency of ship passage, fewer courtesy and training visits, or a hands-off attitude in the future to "local" territorial squabbles in the South China Sea) does not correlate to what we might lose if the ASEAN states come to believe our threats. There is, in short, a real prospect that the region could bend yet more in China's direction—and do so in a manner disadvantageous to the United States and other outsiders.

China's preeminence could, as often happens with the Japanese at present, result in a creeping situation in which invidious access decisions become the norm. What if it becomes normal to seek China's "approval" before major contractual decisions? What if China takes a dim view of a major U.S. contractor working in a future Mekong River development project?

What keeps the Southeast Asians off-balance is not numbers of U.S. personnel but a sense that the region can never be certain which side of the basic strategic line we might choose—that is, whether the United States might opt to "give China what it wants" in what the United States might view as parochial sideshow disagreements with Southeast Asia. In return, the United States might seek preservation of a bigger accord with Beijing, say, and a comprehensive settlement on the Korean Peninsula.

CONCLUSION

For thirty years, Southeast Asia has presented far fewer problems than Northeast Asia, both in magnitude and in uniformity, for U.S. trade and access. Mercantilist, fenced-off segments of the region's economy exist but so do far larger protected patches of crony commerce, military avarice, and nepotic free-riding—most glaringly in Indonesia but evident elsewhere to a very high order. Signs of major disenchantment over this situation are firing debate in all the major Southeast Asian countries—a consequence of the ruinous state of intra-firm banking, lack of control, and lack of accountability (the so-called "moral hazard" problem). A yearning exists for more merit-based opportunity and for the cheaper prices that result from internal competition and the sundering of monopolies.

In this situation, America's security interests in trade and access diplomacy will have a direct utility only in limited cases. In such instances, the overall spectrum of U.S. interests—one that used to stretch from normal diplomatic representation, consular offices, U.S. development assistance programs, focused U.S. information (USIS) programs, a more preeminent U.S. corporate presence, armed forces cooperation, and the like—can make a difference if marshaled (behind the scenes, consistently, and at senior level) to focus on a specific entry issue.

Apart from this limited direct utility, American security interests will continue to have an independent *raison d'être*, one that arises from the transiting requirements of a global power. But the U.S. presence does not come "free of charge." If the ASEAN countries wish the United States to remain an actively engaged, skillful balancer of the China they fear, they must be prepared for the United States to be equally engaged in the pursuit of its economic interests in the region, applying pressure whenever and wherever that pressure can be most effective.

U.S. ECONOMIC AND SECURITY INTERESTS IN SOUTH ASIA

PAUL H. KREISBERG

NEW HORIZONS FOR AMERICAN TRADE AND INVESTMENT

Although sanctions imposed on India and Pakistan in connection with the 1998 nuclear tests place constraints on U.S. economic relations with the region, these are unlikely to be in effect long enough to affect the current level of, or the future potential for, U.S. economic relations with the countries of South Asia. Evidence of transfer of nuclear technology or materials to non-nuclear states by one of the regional states, or a dramatic deterioration of cooperation on narcotics, terrorism, or the observance of human rights could have potentially serious long-term consequences. None of these seem probable in the near future for India, but Pakistan's situation is more uncertain.

U.S. sanctions against Iran and the unavailability of overseas private investment insurance to Pakistan as a result of current non-proliferation sanctions may limit some forms of U.S. involvement in oil or gas pipeline projects from Iran to Pakistan and onward to India. These could also potentially affect U.S. financing for a pipeline project within Pakistan, although the five current U.S. power-plant projects in Pakistan have moved forward without guarantees from the Overseas Private Investment Corporation (OPIC).

The current de-certification of Afghanistan under U.S. counter-narcotics legislation would prevent OPIC insurance for pipeline construction from Turkmenistan through Afghanistan to Pakistan regardless of the willingness of any U.S. company to do without such coverage in Pakistan. Given the potential risks of pipeline operation in Afghanistan (even should a nominally unified government be established in Kabul in the future), it is uncertain whether U.S. companies would be willing to proceed without such coverage. This obstacle of course could be overcome by a special presidential waiver.

The threat of U.S. non-proliferation sanctions and pressures that appeared to have constrained Indian and Pakistani nuclear and missile activities to some degree up until 1998 broke down with nuclear tests by both countries in late spring. The shift in U.S. policy in the last four years—from attempts to close down regional nuclear programs to a strategy of limiting further expansion of nuclear weapons development—was sensible; even if not ideal from the viewpoint of non-proliferation advocates, it provided both India and Pakistan with needed space within which to accommodate their strategic interests to global pressures. The ultimate response of U.S. policy to the tests remains to be worked out but seems focused on limiting the dimension of development of regional weapon stockpiles and their deployment.

U.S. controls on sales to India and Pakistan of dual-use technology that could be of potential use in nuclear and missile-related programs are a nuisance for the transactions of some U.S. companies in the region. The total value of commercial opportunities actually lost (other than the sale of nuclear reactors and other civilian nuclear-related equipment and material) in terms of denials of export licenses is in the range of $20 million a year. It is difficult to estimate, however, how many transactions are never even considered because of concern about licensing, but U.S. government officials believe it is likely to be much less than $100 million annually.

U.S. military sales are very small in South Asia both because of legislative sanctions, primarily affecting Pakistan, and policy decisions on weapons and manufacturing technology transfers to India. Military sales could amount to well over a billion dollars a year (a) if U.S. policies and laws were changed and (b) if there were sufficient resources in regional states to make such purchases on a commercial basis.

Such sales by the United States have greater political sensitivity in India and Pakistan than sales by any other country. Although some senior Indian strategists privately say that a U.S. policy of selling similar weapons to both India and Pakistan would be acceptable in India, it is far from clear that this would be the domestic political conclusion. It would be a mistake for the United States to change its current policies until there are fundamental changes in political and strategic relations between the two largest South Asian states as well as a resolution of nuclear issues that warrants relaxation of U.S. sanctions.

The most serious "strategic" limitations on U.S. economic relations with the region are those imposed by the economic policies pursued by the countries of the region and the state of their economies. Changes are in process throughout the region, but they have been slow and are unlikely to speed up dramatically.

The United States is the largest commercial partner of and investor in both India and Pakistan. U.S. trade and investment in South Asia, particularly in India—which represents over 60 percent of U.S. trade in the region and an even larger proportion of investment—grew rapidly in recent years. If domestic bottlenecks to investment—infrastructure, fiscal deficits, capital constraints, and populist pressures—are overcome, both trade and investment throughout the region will grow steadily in the coming decade. India in particular could become one of the United States' most important economic partners in Asia.

ECONOMIC RELATIONS

American interests in South Asia are qualitatively different from those elsewhere in Asia. U.S. commodity trade with all South Asian states in 1996 (approximately $15 billion, 60 percent of which was with India) was only marginally greater than with the Philippines alone. It represented roughly 1 percent of total U.S. trade, and less than 0.7 percent of U.S. commodity and service trade.

Although total U.S. exports and imports with the region have grown more than 60 percent since 1992, this rate of growth was lower than that of the United States with China, Hong Kong, and virtually all the countries of Southeast Asia. The gap between U.S. trade with South Asia and with the rest of Asia thus continued to widen during this period.

In recent years, the United States has consistently run a trade deficit with the region as a whole (although trade with Pakistan has generally been roughly in balance). This trade deficit grew to over $5 billion in 1996. If major infrastructure projects (power, telecommunications, construction) that have been on the drawing boards for several years begin to move more quickly, these deficits may reverse for a period as major U.S. equipment sales increase. The long-term trend toward increasing deficits will, however, almost certainly resume as South Asian states rapidly increase exports to the United States as their economies grow.

Regional economies have become steadily more open since 1992: tariff barriers have declined from an average close to 300 percent in 1991 to 45 percent; excise taxes have been reduced; and foreign investment has been encouraged in many areas through the liberalization of economic policies on a variety of fronts. Nevertheless, major segments of local economies continue to be off-limits to foreign investors, and numerous non-tariff barriers and other constraints on both investment and trade continue to be the subject of both bilateral and multilateral negotiation.

Total U.S. investment in South Asia remains small. U.S. foreign direct investment actually transferred to regional states at the end of 1997 was not more than $4 billion, although projected investment was three times as much. Of total estimated private capital flows to all Asian states in 1995—$98 billion (direct and portfolio investments)—the South Asia share was probably no more than 5 percent.

Numerous factors have slowed the economic engagement of the region's countries: the dependence of fiscal systems throughout the region on indirect taxes, particularly tariffs; the continued absence of capital account convertibility; local business fear of international competition; populist resistance to foreign involvement in certain sectors; reservation of certain industries to national state sectors; the absence of adequate intellectual property protection; inadequate infrastructure facilities; administrative delays; and political involvement in prospective projects, including corruption.

Every country in the region is committed to changing these constraints. Real progress is being made—faster in some countries and in parts of those countries than in others, and slower in some sectors than in others. Bangladesh has done surprisingly well. Pakistan has initiated good policies in principle but faces daunting structural problems of debt, resource management, and governance. India has set the right priorities but has encountered difficulties—political and bureaucratic—in implementing with speed and effectiveness many of the policy and infrastructure development programs it knows are essential.

Governments in the region understand that there are global markets in capital, trade, and technology—and if these do not find competitive welcome in one country they will flow elsewhere. There appears to be a consensus across political party lines in both India and Pakistan that economic liberalization is good and that reforms in old patterns of resource allocation are important, but not on the speed of and the priorities for change in individual sectors and programs.

From 1994 to 1996, growth in India was at or slightly above 7 percent; in 1996-97, it was 6.5-7 percent. Early in 1997, the finance minister expressed his hopes for sustained, 8 percent growth by the year 2000; other economic observers are uncertain that even a 6 percent rate can be maintained in the absence of major infrastructure breakthroughs, particularly in power generation.

One of the major international raters of national creditworthiness, Moody's, sees the Indian economic glass as half empty, and in 1997 and 1998 it downgraded Indian credit. Indians differ among themselves over how their economy is doing. It is clear, however, that without enormous inputs of foreign investment—$10 billion a year by the year 2000 or shortly thereafter is the official target—economic development will lag the most optimistic estimates of sustained 8-10 percent growth in the early part of the twenty-first century. Strong U.S. corporate and financial engagement is critical if such flows are to take place, and in 1997 and 1998 there were signs that this was lagging badly.

Despite criticisms by some political elements and wariness by some Indian corporations about vulnerability to takeovers by multinational corporate investors, the current direction of Indian economic policy anticipates a steady rise in economic interaction with the international business and banking community, particularly with the United States.

In the Pakistan economy, the structural problems are more complex. The banking system is very weak, government revenues are falling, the debt/GDP ratio is excessively high, foreign exchange reserves are perilously low, and rhetorical advocacy of critical tax and structural reforms is stronger than actual implementation. Taking into account the smaller size of the Pakistan market compared to that in India, U.S. and other foreign investment in Pakistan has lagged behind that in India; in 1998 it almost disappeared even in the electric power, oil, and gas sectors, where there had earlier been active interest. Nevertheless, in both India and Pakistan and in the smaller South Asian states there are signs of potential interest in greater regionalization of economic development. In late spring 1997, the World Bank indicated it planned to actively encourage this, particularly in areas relevant to the environment. Pronouncements in 1997 by Indian and Pakistani officials of intentions to expand trade in oil and gas, commodities, and a variety of industrial products would have encouraged greater global attention to a "South Asian" market, in addition to national markets in the area, until the nuclear tests in the spring of 1998 stalled the regionalization process.

Barriers to trade and investment will continue to fall in the region, but more slowly than U.S. companies—particularly those in service areas such as insurance and banking—would like. U.S. pressures aimed at accelerating this process may at times be useful but are best pursued in common with other interested states and through coordination in multilateral forums, including the World Trade Organization. Sometimes U.S. legislation may be helpful (e.g., intellectual property watch-lists, special 301 cautions, and Food and Drug Administration as well as U.S. Customs sanctions on improperly handled foods), but it is key that such measures be flexible and applied with discretion, care, and in a carefully targeted way—so that they do not become major political litmus issues between the United States and the states of the region.

SECURITY CONCERNS AND U.S. POLICY OBJECTIVES

General. Interstate political tensions have deep historical roots and will continue indefinitely to produce tensions between states in the region. War is unlikely, however, and the use of nuclear weapons even in the event of conflict remains improbable.

- Throughout the region, the key challenges to political and economic stability are domestic. Political and social unrest—and uncertainties generated by democracy itself through conflicting demands over the allocation of resources and benefits of development—will continue to be the main obstacles to more rapid economic growth, foreign investment, expanded trade, and fiscal integrity.
- Threat of a revival of civil war in Afghanistan continues to paralyze development in that country and potentially threatens stability in both Central Asia and Pakistan. It will be at least another generation before Afghanistan becomes a region in which foreign investors can safely assume the long-term stability of any ventures to which they commit themselves.
- A half-century of regional tensions; three regional wars between India and Pakistan; suspicions remaining from the war between India and China thirty-five years ago; prolonged civil conflict in Sri Lanka; and a heritage of caste, class, ethnic, and religious tensions within every country in the region have all imposed drains on state budgets and national development. Pakistan spends over 6 percent of its GDP, Sri Lanka over 5

percent, and India well over 4 percent on defense and internal security. Internal unrest in northeastern India and in the state of Jammu and Kashmir, and until recently in the Punjab, as well as in northern Sri Lanka—together with less dramatic but persistent political, social, and cultural tensions in other areas of each country in the region—have slowed domestic economic development and to varying degrees discouraged both domestic and foreign investment.

- Democracy in South Asia—desirable as it has been in providing, at least sometimes, for peaceful changes in government, checks on abuses of political power and violations of human rights, and opportunity to reverse failed and initiate new policies—has nevertheless also been paired with stultifying bureaucratic structures, deeply vested political interests in the status quo, and ponderous legal, populist, and emotional barriers to the correction of economic and political policies.
- The strongest democratic and legal structures exist in India and Sri Lanka—the weakest, in Pakistan and Bangladesh. In the two former countries, the military has consistently been subordinate to civil and political power since independence; in the latter two countries, however, the military has repeatedly played an active role within the political structure. Although all the South Asian states at present are under democratically elected governments, it remains uncertain whether this pattern can be preserved in Pakistan and Bangladesh.

India and Pakistan. Pakistan, as the weaker regional power, has looked to foreign powers for military support and for mediation or pressure in resolving its differences with India. With only a few exceptions since it raised the Kashmir issue in the United Nations in 1947, India has resisted such outside roles in the Subcontinent.

If a new crisis in Central Asia, Iran, or elsewhere in the region created another occasion for closer U.S.–Pakistan security collaboration, Indian suspicions would again be inflamed—unless a fundamental change had occurred in Subcontinental relationships or in Indo–U.S. strategic understandings.

The resolution of regional tensions in South Asia will only emerge from decisions and actions of the regional parties themselves. However, economic imperatives and opportunities, changing political generations, and a new regional awareness of the degree to which the region has lagged economically behind East Asia are all gradually bringing awareness throughout the region of the costs of perpetual tensions and the importance of turning all their attention to national and regional development. Recent India-Nepal and India-Bangladesh agreements to cooperate in the development of water, power, and transportation facilities are examples of what is needed.

Good relations with all regional states are in the political, security, and economic interests of the United States. Exclusive or strategic relationships tilted toward individual countries and based on geopolitical threat scenarios will not be reliable building blocks for U.S. policy in South Asia. Military relationships and sales of weapons or military technology transfers are likely to impede the pursuit of U.S. interests and arouse strong new suspicions of American economic activities even in those states that the United States might envisage as potential strategic partners (see all discussion in Military Relations section below).

Anxious to identify how South Asia—which has played a relatively minor role in the geopolitical planning of major global powers—might become more important in the future, many Indian and Pakistani intellectuals and policymakers have often jumped at barely plausible theories of future global interaction. The geopolitical issues they conjure up are not trivial but far from foreordained. As often as not, the rationales look backward at nineteenth century power struggles between contending Russian and British imperialisms. Nor is it clear how India or Pakistan would play significant roles in the hypothetical geopolitical struggles envisaged: contention over oil and gas resources in Central Asia; struggles between an expansionist Islam and the secularizing states of Central Asia; an expanding neo-nationalist Russian power determined to reassert control in Central Asia; Chinese aspirations for hegemony over the new states of Central Asia—or to protect itself from Turkic ethnic minority liberation movements on its own territory; or an Indian role as a political-strategic partner for the states of Southeast Asia, which may come under pressure from China.

All are important issues that U.S. policy must follow closely and which should be included in U.S. political and security discussions with all of the countries of the region—from Russia and China to South Asia and East Asia. But it would be premature (and there are virtually no signs of U.S. policymaker interest in such a move) to commit the United States to act in collaboration or jointly with any of the regional South Asian states in anticipation of such hypothetical developments.

India will continue to be the major economic and military power of South Asia. With its large domestic market, manpower base, business infrastructure, wealthy overseas emigrant population, and growing links with Southeast and East Asia, it offers the greatest potential to U.S. business for foreign trade and investment cooperation. Despite the chill in many aspects of Indo–U.S. relations after the nuclear tests, India is likely to be an important partner for the United States in dealing with a broad range of global concerns. However, the prospects for its joining the Security Council as a permanent member have probably been set back at least a decade by its decision in favor of a nuclear test.

India has a primary responsibility to contribute to strengthening confidence and peace in the region. The United States and other major states should urge India to fulfill this responsibility in ways that do not appear hegemonic. India's former Prime Minister and Foreign Minister, I. K. Gujral, initiated a policy consistent with this view, the so-called "Gujral doctrine." The essence of this policy is that it is in Indian interests to ease Subcontinental tensions without demanding reciprocity, to improve relations with its neighbors, and to develop cooperative relationships throughout the region, including around the Indian Ocean. This policy is congruent with views that the United States has urged on India for decades, but the right-wing Bharatya Janata Party (BJP) that replaced Gujral's coalition with one of its own in early 1998 explicitly rejects such a "non-reciprocal" approach.

A pervasive element in the thinking of the BJP is the perception that the entire region is a zone of potential competition, both with rival states in the region and with powers elsewhere against which India must be constantly vigilant. Those who hold this view see any overly close Indian engagement with the United States, or with other states in the region, as potentially threatening. They are skeptical of prospects for long-term reduction of tensions with Pakistan even in the event of a resolution of the Kashmir issue. Moreover, both those who hold this view and even others who have a more relaxed view of policy toward the United States argue for Indian involvement in Afghanistan and Central Asia in nineteenth century terms of potential threats to India's northwest frontier.

Most Indians, while attracted by the idea that Indian importance in the future might make the United States think of India as a potential geopolitical strategic partner, share a strong nationalist perspective that any ties between India and the United States (other than through the United Nations) focused against any presumed threats elsewhere in the world might endanger Indian policy independence. Thus, although Indian policies in the region are readily welcomed by the United States when they contribute to greater stability and regional cooperation, there is little prospect or desirability of the United States seeking a strategic relationship with India applicable elsewhere in the world.

Nevertheless, an ongoing Indo–U.S. "strategic dialogue" that endeavored to clarify at senior government levels for both states those global and regional issues in which their vital interests may be engaged in the coming years and on which they may have either conflicting or common views would have great value. Such a dialogue began in a very preliminary way in 1997. It should be developed as far as possible, including—at an appropriate time—at the highest levels of government, where there has been little serious interaction for two decades—but without expectations that it will evolve into a new and more intimate genuine strategic cooperative relationship.

Pakistan is also important for the United States as an economic partner. Although this economic relationship has a considerably lower level of potential than that with India, Pakistan has a special relevance to U.S. policy interests in Central and Western Asia as well as on key global issues such as drugs and international terrorism. However, as much as the United States may want Pakistani cooperation in dealing with Afghanistan—in connection with oil and gas resources in Central Asia, or with regard to strategic concerns in Western Asia—it should not replay the failed "special relationship" alliance strategies of the 1950s and 1980s.

U.S. policies dealing with Pakistan are out of date. The current U.S. Administration's attempts to change these, through the Brown Amendment's partial lifting of some sanctions, were partly successful. But new restrictions affecting economic credits were reimposed almost immediately as a consequence of Pakistan's purchase of small quantities of nuclear-reactor-related parts from China and reinforced by Pakistan's nuclear tests.

U.S. non-proliferation policy had marginal success in South Asia but collapsed with the nuclear tests in spring 1998. A roll-back of the Pakistani and Indian nuclear programs is impossible. Prevention of continuing development, and possibly deployment, of short-range missiles is unlikely. The central U.S. interest, as most U.S. officials recognize, is in ensuring that these programs are constrained, in elaborating cooperative arrangements to prevent transfers of technology or weapons or material components to more genuinely threatening and dangerous states, in urging India and Pakistan to continue to move toward bilateral understandings that progressively reduce the likelihood of conflict between them in averting further nuclear testing and in limiting the accumulation of fissile missile material through the conclusion of a cut-off treaty.

Implicit acknowledgment of existing, limited nuclear capabilities and the legitimacy of Indian and Pakistani efforts to maintain these capabilities—and these countries' adherence to international agreements on testing and on safeguards for other nuclear development programs—serve central U.S. interests better than sanctions. Such a strategy would require major decisions in both the executive and legislative branches of the U.S. government to change both policy and laws. Such changes would enable the United States to escape from requirements to impose penalties on regional and American companies that arouse strong political criticism within the region, are likely to achieve their fundamental non-proliferation objectives, and do not contribute to the pursuit of other important cooperative policy initiatives in the non-proliferation area. Experience suggests that such policy changes will be politically difficult, will involve compromises on U.S. non-proliferation policies, and perhaps are impracticable, but they need serious consideration.

Since the end of the 1980s, U.S. security commitments to Pakistan dating back to the 1950s (always ambiguous in any event) have been inoperative—beyond those implicit in the U.N. Charter. If Indo-Pakistani tensions gradually diminish as a consequence of understandings on Kashmir, trade, travel, scientific cooperation in areas of common concern, and above all on security issues—including force levels, assurances relating to nuclear weapons and missiles, and confidence building measures—the United States might reassess its current policies on restricting all but the most limited military sales to the region.

Changes in U.S. policies relating to military sales would have to be made in a context in which there have not only been clear understandings on nuclear issues, but in which defense modernization by either regional state is not seen as a threat to the other. This may be a higher standard than will be achievable in the foreseeable future but it is one to which the United States should adhere before selling any weapon system that provides a critical advantage to one side or the other. Such a standard may mean the United States must continue to opt out of any involvement in weapons developments linked to the so-called "revolution in military warfare" involved in "smart weapons."

At the same time, the kind of strategic interchange envisaged with India above should also be pursued by the United States with Pakistan. A longer-term U.S. objective should aim at a trialogue as well—one conducted in a common forum, with senior representatives of both India and Pakistan.

Afghanistan. Resolution of the civil conflict and the restoration of political stability in Afghanistan is a precondition for the building of a regional infrastructure for economic links between Central Asia and both India and Pakistan. Such an infrastructure would:

- Contribute to the development of oil and gas resources in the Central Asian states and facilitate trans-shipment of these through Afghanistan to the states of the region—all of which have rapidly increasing energy needs—as well as to other markets beyond South Asia;
- Speed economic growth and political stabilization in Central Asia and Afghanistan;
- Contribute toward building common interests among the states of the region involved in maintaining peace and good relations to ensure the flow of oil and gas; and
- Enable both the states of the region and U.S. companies to pursue trade and investment opportunities in Afghanistan and Central Asia.

There is little that the United States can do to influence the murky, ethnically charged Afghan environment, where religion, personal relationships, money, and arms are the real instruments of influence and power—and the United States has few of these to play. The cautious U.S. policy currently being followed—encouraging the formation of a unified government with which the United States might cooperate consistent with its concerns about human rights; encouraging international economic assistance and support for development; urging stronger international cooperation to halt the growth of narcotics production and trade; and seeking to prevent the escalation of military conflict—is close to the limits of what can and should be done.

The likelihood of this being achieved in the near future is slim. Even if a unified government were to emerge in Afghanistan, the ability of such a government to effectively halt the production and shipment of opium and other narcotics would be limited, as it has been so far for the Islamic Taliban government.

Restoring stability in Afghanistan and consolidating stability in Central Asia will also at some point demand re-evaluation of U.S. policy toward and relations with Iran.

Smaller States. U.S. policy interests and public awareness are far less focused on the smaller states of South Asia, and this is unlikely to change. It is difficult to envisage independent U.S. security interests or objectives that might lead the United States to identify any of the smaller states as key foci of attention for U.S. policy in the foreseeable future. The only exception to this might conceivably be some dramatic changes relating to U.S. interests in furthering Tibetan independence, or a fundamental worsening in China's political and security relations with the states of the region or with the United States. The likelihood of such scenarios appears small for the foreseeable future.

Regional Cooperation. Regional incoherence and the absence of structured economic and political cooperation in South Asia has blocked the development of a South Asian regional market. The initiation of a South Asian Preferential Trade Area in 1996 could, in theory, alter this, but the process is likely to be slow.

The absence of a regional market has not been a serious factor affecting corporate judgments relating to investment in individual states of the region. Nevertheless, a regional strategy for telecommunications, power, oil and natural gas exploration and development, transportation and shipping, financing and investment, tariffs, and marketing would make the region increasingly attractive. U.S. officials and business groups and corporations would do well to make this point a consistent theme in their discussions with officials, politicians, and business groups in the region.

A new economic cooperative group, the Indian Ocean Rim Association for Regional Cooperation (IOR-ARC), took shape at a fourteen-nation meeting in Mauritius early in 1997. The concept of the organizers was to encourage an expansion of trade and political cooperation from Africa to Asia. The evolution of the IOR-ARC into an economically significant trading or investment bloc—much less a politically meaningful association—is uncertain. Economic synergies among the members are still few; many of the participating states belong to other preferential trading blocs that are politically and economically more important to them; and transport and communication links among the states involved are limited. IOR-ARC may serve a modest role in awakening interest in potential new markets for members, but it is unlikely to be a new geopolitical or economic center of gravity in the near future.

In recent years, Indian policy has increasingly "looked East," viewing ASEAN and East Asia as having growing importance for it both politically and economically. Japan and South Korea gradually expanded both trade and investment with India, and Japan was for a number of years India's largest bilateral aid donor—until it suspended much of its aid in 1998 after the nuclear tests. India is improving relations with Burma and sees it as a potential land bridge for Indian economic relations with Southeast Asia. India has also become a full dialogue partner of ASEAN and a member of the ASEAN Regional Forum (ARF)—with Singapore taking the lead in pressing for Indian engagement.

Some ASEAN members see India as a political—and potentially strategic—regional counterbalance to China, as well as a growing economic partner. The evolution of this relationship has been slow, however, and it is likely to continue to develop very cautiously. Most Southeast Asian states, however, have been frustrated by the difficulty of doing business with India, and economic recession throughout Asia in 1997-98, the slow pace of key economic reform in India, and cultural differences continue to make all parties cautious about prospects for deepening economic or political relationships at anything but a very slow pace.

Japanese and Korean companies—though few U.S. companies so far, other than those involved in infrastructure project development—had business strategies that envisaged linking investment or marketing decisions in the East and Southeast Asian region to those in South Asia. It is uncertain how these strategies will evolve in the future.

China. In the early 1990s, Beijing began to shift from an anti-Indian, pro-Pakistani strategy that had its roots in the Cold War period and in Sino-Soviet tensions toward a new strategy focused on building regional stability, reducing South Asian tensions, and developing relations with both India and Pakistan.

- Relations with India improved significantly, and exchanges of high-level visits took place in the last three years. Tension along the Sino-Indian border has been sharply diminished by bilateral agreements, and confidence-building measures and Sino-Indian trade approached $1.5 billion in 1996.
- Beijing's support for Pakistan's nuclear and missile programs has been in check, even if U.S. officials are not sure it has halted completely, since mid-1996—at least in part as a consequence of Chinese concern about potential U.S. economic sanctions and the overall impact on Sino–U.S. relations.
- Chinese interests in Central Asia so far are focused on building cooperative economic and political relationships with the regional states—for economic benefit, to constrain regional help for Uighur separatist activities in China's majority Turkic-speaking province of Sinkiang, and to strengthen the independence of Central Asian states against a potential reassertion of Russian hegemonic power.
- Sino-Burmese military cooperation does not appear targeted against India—although many Indians are not convinced of this—and Beijing does not appear to have discouraged Burmese cooperation with India in dealing with both drug and guerrilla movements across the Indo-Burmese border and in improving political relations.

These trends are consistent with U.S. interests in averting instability in the region. Indian concern about a "China threat" (at least in the near future) has declined sharply, and Indian border deployments along the Sino-Indian frontier have been reduced. Nevertheless, India's immediate rationale in May 1998 for its nuclear tests was concern about the China threat. Indian interest in pursuing the development of a longer-range missile (the intermediate-range Agni) as a potential nuclear-armed missile deterrent against China continues high, and, as long as China remains a significant nuclear weapon and missile power, India appears determined ultimately to have a deterrent strategic capability of its own.

Few Indian strategists write off a longer-term strategic competition between India and China. How, they argue, could there not be an inevitable political, economic, and strategic rivalry for power and influence in Asia between the two largest powers in Asia? This hypothesis, closely resembling recent U.S. debate about the future of China, has led some Americans—and some Indians—to wonder if there may be common strategic ground to be struck.

There is in fact no strategic inevitability of Sino-Indian rivalry. Their respective centers of concern and influence are likely to continue to be fairly distinct. An Indo–U.S. dialogue on broad strategic perceptions of the region and the rest of the world would logically include discussion of China's role. But it would be misguided to anticipate that this will soon lead to a congruence of Indo–U.S. perceptions of the threat environment. The United States shows no current sign of moving to facilitate India's swift advance into the new "military technological revolution" that some Indian strategists hope will be the focus of Indian defense planning in the next decade (but for which there is no current sign of Indian budgetary support) and that might attract U.S. technological support if there were a common vision of a prospective "China menace."

MILITARY RELATIONS

None of the states in the region is a current or prospective security threat to the United States. In the next ten to fifteen years, none of the military forces of regional states have or are likely to have conventional force projection capabilities beyond a few hundred miles from their coasts or land borders. India hopes to have a nuclear submarine at sea by 2010, but it is questionable whether it will achieve this goal. And although both India and Pakistan in theory have the capability to transfer both nuclear and missile technologies to other states, both have been extremely cautious in dealing with sensitive technology-transfer issues. There is always the risk that some dramatic change in leadership in either country could increase these dangers, but no evidence that this is likely. In any event, neither India nor Pakistan is likely to abandon its nuclear capabilities—regardless of U.S. pressures or urgings. U.S. relations with both states will have to accommodate this reality, and U.S. policy and ultimately U.S. legislation will have to do so as well. There are numerous potholes on this track. Both states say they do not plan further tests, but whether they sign and ratify the Comprehensive Test Ban Treaty and sign a new treaty on halting production of fissionable material remains to be seen.

There is, moreover, no way to quell entirely fears that nuclear weapons might be used in the event of an India-Pakistan conflict. Military, civilian government, and political authorities in both countries appear aware of the potential dangers. The likelihood of war, or the escalation of a minor conflict into nuclear war, does not seem great—in part as a consequence of tensions on several occasions in the last decade that focused attention in both states on the risks involved. Moreover, nuclear tests have focused international attention on South Asia more intensely than in the past, increasing the potential for pressures to be brought to bear by major powers if the risk of war became high.

Military capabilities of all states in South Asia have in fact deteriorated in the last decade. The cost of new weapon systems is high, and none of the region's countries has been able to bring itself to reduce the size of ground forces significantly. Moreover, although the view that military threats to the region have sharply declined is not widely acknowledged by military planners in either India or Pakistan, political support for upgrading military forces and sharply increasing real levels of defense expenditures is probably lower than at any time since independence from Great Britain.

U.S. weapons sales to South Asian states has poisoned bilateral relationships with them in recent decades—even when, for brief periods, recipient states have welcomed the sales. The United States has no current military commitments to provide significant quantities of military equipment or technology to any of the states in the region, although it has permitted some transfers of electronic and radar equipment and avionic technology—including some for the prospective indigenous, all-purpose "Light Combat Aircraft" that may come into serial production early in the twenty-first century (after nearly a quarter-century in development).

U.S. forbearance in entering the arms market in this region is well worth the political price, even if other states are making such sales and there is some cost to U.S. manufacturers. Above all, the United States should not sell arms to India or Pakistan while tensions between these states remain unresolved. This issue will remain moot with both countries, since U.S. legislation bars such sales while key issues relating to their nuclear tests and weapons programs remain unresolved.

Both states have access to conventional equipment modernization from Russia, China, or various European states, and India has technology and equipment from Israel. It is true this has continued to add to India's comparative advantage given its stronger economic and robust foreign exchange positions. But this is not sufficient ground for the United States to reconsider its arms sales policies.

This is a source of strong frustration in Pakistan and will continue to make Pakistan reluctant to abandon its ultimate reliance on the presumed nuclear deterrent it developed over the last twenty years with Chinese help. But even when the United States was supplying Pakistan with large amounts of conventional weapons assistance in the 1980s there was no evidence of a slackening role of nuclear deterrence in Islamabad's long-term strategic planning.

Only by easing the tensions between them and developing a range of soft and hard security assurances and confidence-building measures can Pakistan and India provide for their mutual security on the Subcontinent. Both sides can then restructure their defense planning to provide for major reductions in force levels while focusing on the modernization of the forces that remain to deal with whatever threats they perceive elsewhere around their borders as well as with their internal security.

This scenario unfortunately involves a certain level of wishful thinking, since Pakistanis continue to see any enhancement of Indian capabilities as threatening. This perception will be slow to change. Nevertheless, the inability of the Pakistani economy to increase defense expenditures without catastrophic economic fiscal consequences is becoming increasingly clear. And even India, which is convinced it will eventually be able to modernize its military capabilities, is likely to find the costs of doing so and the time horizon in which this could occur far greater than some military planners and strategists currently may envisage.

The only significant U.S. military facility in the region is the air and marine logistics base at Diego Garcia, nearly 1,500 miles south of India. This was at one point, but is no longer, a source of considerable friction with India. It remains an important staging facility for U.S. forces throughout the region and is unlikely to be phased out in the foreseeable future. During the Persian Gulf War, U.S. transport aircraft briefly used airfields in India to transit the area before Indian political sensitivities terminated this cooperation. It is conceivable that such issues could arise again, although current U.S. military planning wisely does not rely on access to facilities of any of the states in the region.

U.S. naval ships call intermittently at Indian and Pakistani ports; before the nuclear tests, they engaged in occasional small-scale exercises with regional naval forces. There are regular exchanges of military and civilian defense delegations at a variety of levels, at which broad issues relating to the region and to Asia and global issues of concern to all sides are reviewed.

Unfortunately, as noted earlier, serious exchanges on a continuing basis at high political levels are so infrequent as to underscore the scant political or economic concern in the United States about the entire region. No American president has visited India or Pakistan in nearly twenty years—and Madeleine Albright was the first Secretary of State to visit in the last fifteen. In earlier years, presidential visits occurred at roughly ten year intervals—hardly an expression of great interest then, either. President Clinton has indicated he would like to visit the area, but the events of 1998 have made scheduling a visit difficult.

GLOBAL ISSUES

The states of South Asia, with a combined population of approximately 1.25 billion in 1996, are central to virtually all U.S. global concerns: non-proliferation, narcotics, terrorism, health (communicable diseases and AIDS), the environment (both air and water quality), energy and food availability, and human rights (particularly for women, children, and prisoners).

Cooperation with the United States in all of these areas is either good or improving throughout the region (except in Afghanistan). Moreover, U.S. companies are the most competitive in the world both in consulting and in equipment relating to the above-listed sectors and are energetically active throughout South Asia. There is very close harmony between U.S. security policy on these issues and U.S. economic interests.

India, Pakistan, and Bangladesh are among the largest recipients of World Bank and IMF funding and assistance. Serious reductions in U.S. support for the international financial institutions would have a significant impact on the economies of these as well as the smaller states in the region.

CONCLUSION

There are few contradictions—other than those generated by the nuclear tests in 1998—between current U.S. security and economic interests in South Asia that are not susceptible to resolution or that are likely to seriously impair trade with or investment in the region over the longer run.

U.S. legal bars on governmental insurance and export credits to Pakistan as a result of non-proliferation sanctions have not been serious obstacles so far for U.S. business. Dual-use technology export guidelines have become a more serious source of political friction and have impaired U.S. business dealings with several Indian companies and government agencies, but have not seriously constrained overall U.S. trade with India. The United States continues to have the option of periodically revising export lists to take account of alternative technology availability in other countries, but trade in some dual-use technology will continue to be impaired indefinitely as a consequence of nuclear testing. U.S. export credits to South Asia are also constrained, but this is likely to change in the next year or so.

The major constraint on trade with or through Afghanistan continues to be political stability in that country. Nevertheless, human rights, narcotics, child labor, and a variety of other issues could become more pressing problems even if stability is restored. If these were to complicate major petroleum and gas pipeline development opportunities indefinitely, this would represent a potential area of serious conflict between security and economic interests in the region.

U.S. sanctions against Iran, along with OPIC constraints in providing insurance coverage within Pakistan under the nuclear sanctions regime, are also a major constraint on any U.S. involvement in a potential pipeline from Iran through Pakistan to India or to Pakistan alone.

U.S. ECONOMIC AND SECURITY INTERESTS IN SOUTH ASIA

GEOFFREY KEMP

INDIA, PAKISTAN, AND THE GEOPOLITICS OF ENERGY

How will American security and economic interests be influenced by security and economic developments in South Asia* in the decades ahead? Are U.S. economic and security interests contradictory? How can they best be managed?

A few pertinent facts encapsulate the key themes of this paper:

- Seventy percent of the world's proven oil reserves and 40 percent of its proven natural gas reserves are located in the Persian Gulf and Caspian Basin—a region literally next door to South Asia, which has a population of over 1.2 billion and a growing need for energy.
- Well over two million South Asians work in the Arabian Peninsula. Foreigners make up 76 percent of the population of the United Arab Emirates—over 50 percent of whom are from South Asia.
- China has become a net importer of oil. By 2010 it may require 3 million barrels a day from foreign sources—most likely the Persian Gulf.
- With the exception of North Korea, the most serious problems concerning the spread of weapons of mass destruction are to be found in South and Southwest Asia.

A recent report issued by an independent task force of the Council on Foreign Relations, in which the author participated and that he fully endorsed, listed U.S. interests in South Asia as includ-

*In this paper, discussion of South Asia will be limited to India and Pakistan.

ing: preventing a major war; cooperating to restrict strategic exports; restraining the regional nuclear arms race; expanding economic growth, trade, and investment; promoting internal stability and democracy; expanding political-military cooperation with the United States; and cooperating on a broad array of global issues, including drug trafficking and terrorism. The report recommended that "the United States should significantly expand its bilateral economic, political and military ties with India and Pakistan simultaneously. It is both possible and desirable to delink the two bilateral relationships and transcend the zero-sum dynamics that have often plagued the region (and U.S. policy) in the past." The report goes on to recommend that the United States establish a closer strategic relationship with India and that the United States adopt a declaratory policy that acknowledges India's growing power and importance while at the same time working to restore normal and close working relations with Pakistan.

While these interests and objectives are admirable, the focus in this paper is on security and economic opportunities. To appreciate the current status of U.S.–South Asian relations, as it applies to these two issue areas, it is important to understand the dynamics of the region and the great challenges that both India and Pakistan face in the next century, deriving from their problems of poverty and stagnation as well as the complex new regional environment in which they find themselves. The Subcontinent faces the powder keg of the Persian Gulf in the west, the changing configuration of Central Asia following the breakup of the Soviet Union to the north; and the booming economies and turbulent geopolitics of Southeast and East Asia, particularly the emergence of China as a world power.

NEW REGIONAL DYNAMICS

In recent years, dramatic geopolitical changes have impacted on South Asia and its relations with Southwest and Central Asia and the United States. The most important was the breakup of the Soviet Union; this was the seminal geopolitical event of the second half of the twentieth century, and it had far-reaching consequences for India and Pakistan.

Over time, this event is likely to be seen as an important factor helping to propel India toward modernization. In the short run, however, India was adversely affected by the collapse of the Soviet Union. Indian-Soviet relations were very close, especially in the area of military cooperation. On the other hand, the end of communism in the Soviet Union has had a salutary effect upon Indian economic development. While India has always nurtured great-power ambitions, its decision to bid for such status was not taken seriously until the end of the Cold War and the 1990-91 Persian Gulf crisis, which forced its leaders to modernize the Indian economy.

By June 1991, India was nearly bankrupt, with barely enough foreign currency to pay for a month's worth of necessary imports, such as oil and high-technology items. To meet this crisis, the Indian government had to turn to the International Monetary Fund for emergency assistance; that help, however, was conditioned upon India at last becoming serious about the reform of its antiquated economy. On July 24, 1991, Finance Minister Manmohan Singh unveiled the New Industrial Policy.

Since then, there has been much speculation on the implications of economic modernization for India. Optimists believe that reform is unstoppable—that India is on the way to major-power status and could become a worthy competitor to China early in the next century. Others agree that India has all the attributes needed for success, but that much depends upon what happens in the next few years. Investors must still be convinced that reform will continue and that real profits can be made and taken home. Confirmed pessimists still believe that India is incapable of the necessary modernization and that it is too insular and caste-ridden to adapt to long-term change.

The Soviet Union's demise also has had a most profound effect on Pakistan. With the Soviet defeat in Afghanistan, Pakistan lost its most persuasive leverage with the United States, which had provided Pakistan with political and military support during the Cold War. No longer seen as a strategic asset challenging communism along its common border with Afghanistan, Pakistan has been subject to punitive measures by the U.S. Congress as a result of the implementation of the Pressler amendment, which cuts off major military assistance to Pakistan so long as it continues to produce nuclear weapons-grade fissionable material. Pakistanis feel betrayed by the United States and no longer regard it as a natural ally against communism. Furthermore, Pakistanis are aware that, with the end of the Soviet-Indian relationship, there is a growing body of opinion in the United States that regards India, not Pakistan, as the most important country to woo in South Asia.

During the 1990s, Pakistan has struggled to find new allies to meet the challenges posed by the loss of the United States as a strategic partner and the parallel emergence of India as a potential regional superpower and closer friend of the United States. It has also had to deal with its own internal problems, including structural economic bottlenecks, widespread corruption, a breakdown in public order, domestic terrorism, ethnic conflict, and the growth of radical Islamic movements.

Both India and Pakistan stand to benefit from new, closer ties with newly independent Central Asian states, all of which are eager to distance themselves from Moscow and develop economic and political ties with their southern neighbors. These developments, together with the competition for access to Caspian Basin energy, have led to talks of a new "great game," with the unresolved war in Afghanistan providing an appropriate backdrop.

AMERICAN SECURITY INTERESTS AND SOUTH ASIA

The United States has two overriding security interests that could be affected by developments in South Asia. The first is the continued—indeed, growing—importance of Persian Gulf and Caspian Basin oil energy for the world economy and the parallel U.S. commitment to defend the Gulf Cooperation Council (GCC) countries against potential military threats, especially from Iraq and Iran. The second is the United States' global interest in arresting the proliferation of weapons of mass destruction, including the possibility of a leakage of nuclear and missile technology and know-how from the Subcontinent to countries and sub-state groups hostile to American interests. Beyond these two concerns is a broader U.S. political objective: seeking the global arms control agreements that would ultimately put restraints on the nuclear capabilities of both India and Pakistan. In this context, the United States must take into account that further conflict between India and its neighbors over unresolved issues such as Kashmir could, in the worst case, lead to a nuclear war on the Subcontinent. The unexpected nuclear tests conducted by first India, then Pakistan, in May 1998 have forced the U.S. government to re-examine its global non-proliferation agenda. Although India and Pakistan may eventually become state parties to the Nuclear Non-Proliferation Treaty and the Comprehensive Test Ban Treaty, they will do so as *de facto* nuclear weapons states. The probability that either country will "roll back" and dismantle its nuclear weapons components is remote. Both countries will wish to retain a minimum nuclear capability for deterrent purposes.

While the prospect of nuclear war on the Subcontinent is the most dangerous contingency, the most likely issue to trouble the United States in the decade ahead concerns the security of the Persian Gulf. Although the United States orchestrated the allied victory against Iraq in 1991, the region remains unstable. The United States has developed an elaborate forward presence in the region with bases and access facilities in several of the GCC countries and an extremely sophisticated and expensive military intervention force that is prepared, in very short order, to intervene in the event of another major military confrontation. This capability involves continued basing rights at Diego Garcia in the Indian Ocean as well as numerous new programs for rapidly deploying forces from the United States, East Asia, and Europe to the Gulf.

Given the high growth rates of Asian economies, an important strategic factor in the next century will be Asia's increasing needs for Persian Gulf and Caspian energy in addition to the continued high energy demand from the OECD countries. Consequently, a greater premium will be placed upon the security of energy supplies, with less opportunity than in the past for the United States to unilaterally dominate and control events in the region. In this context, South Asia becomes particularly important. South Asia itself will need increasing amounts of energy (an issue discussed in more detail in the next section), much of which will have to come from the Persian Gulf and Caspian region. Thus, there are both parallel interests in assuring the security of energy supplies and possibilities of political quarrels between the United States, India, and Pakistan over how to handle the political dynamics of the region, particularly relations with Iraq and Iran.

Aside from the challenges to the GCC states posed by Iraq and Iran, the internal situation on the Arabian Peninsula also poses threats to energy security. While the United States at present has the military capability to deter high-level threats from Iran and Iraq, it has little control over the internal problems that the Gulf countries face, which have to do with social and religious factors, including autocracy, corruption, asymmetric income distribution, human rights abuses, Islamic extremism, and (especially relevant in this context) a huge migrant population. For example, the most serious recent internal security threat to the United Arab Emirates occurred when Hindu and Muslim expatriates began rioting in 1992 following the destruction by Hindu extremists of a Muslim mosque at Ayodhya in India. Citizens of the United Arab Emirates had never heard of Ayodhya but were terrified by visions of foreigners rampaging in downtown Dubai. With over 76 percent of its population made up of foreigners and half of these coming from South Asia, the United Arab Emirates and other Gulf countries cannot remain insulated from the long-standing conflict between India and Pakistan.

Indeed, the Subcontinent, with over 1.2 billion people, is virtually on the doorstep of the Gulf. Bombay and Karachi are only 981 miles and 530 miles, respectively, from Musqat. Although India traditionally has been on friendly terms with most of the Gulf states, its long-standing rivalry with Pakistan, the lack of resolution on the Kashmir issue, and the periodic outbursts of incendiary right-wing Hindu fundamentalism (seen as threatening to India's 130-million strong Muslim minority) are serious stumbling blocks to a truly close relationship.

One of the key factors in the relationship is the constant movement of Indian migrant labor to the region. At the time of the Gulf crisis, the six GCC states of the region—Bahrain, Kuwait, Oman, Qatar, Saudi Arabia, and the United Arab Emirates—had a combined total of over 5 million migrant workers, or about 68 percent of their total labor force. According to pre–Gulf War estimates, up to 30 percent (or some 1.5 million) of these foreign workers were Indians. In addition to laborers, the Indian communities in the Gulf included technicians, builders, nurses, traders, and domestic workers.

The sensitivity of South Asia to Gulf affairs has been well appreciated for many decades on the Subcontinent. India was humiliated during the Gulf crisis. As a result of Saddam Hussein's invasion of Kuwait, hundreds of thousands of Indian expatriate workers were stranded, and India was unable to send even a ship into the Gulf to come to their assistance. Finally, the workers were brought out by charter airlines.

In this complex context, several contingencies would get the attention of the United States. First, U.S. differences with India and Pakistan concerning the American presence in the Gulf could escalate should the United States in the future attempt to use major force against either Iraq or Iran. There is strong pro-Iranian sentiment in Pakistan and, to a lesser extent, in India. Certainly there will be no natural endorsement of U.S. policy. On the other hand, at some point in the future, the United States and India could cooperate on maritime operations. This possibility is likely to be enhanced if, as anticipated, China's needs for energy include Gulf oil and if, at some point in the next century, its maritime capabilities begin to spread into the Indian Ocean. There is a growing interest in the implications of a Chinese blue-water navy for regional security. Much of the analysis is focused on the South China Seas, the Taiwan Strait, and the immediate areas surrounding the huge Chinese littoral. But should China develop a long-range fleet to include aircraft carriers, it would give them power-projection and sea-control capabilities far into the Indian Ocean. Such activities would inevitably trigger a response from the local countries, particularly India. In these circumstances—and depending upon the condition of U.S.–China relations—India and the United States might become natural allies.

Where Pakistan would fit into this equation is a key uncertainty. Closer China-Pakistan relations would further raise Indian suspicions and could also conflict with American interests. Such an increasingly explosive scenario might arise if China continues to use its sales of technology to Pakistan and India to boost influence and to raise funds to pay for oil imports. China's nuclear cooperation with Pakistan and its missile sales are bound to further exacerbate the arms race on the Subcontinent, which indirectly has a negative impact on U.S. interests.

This brings up the second key American concern: preventing the illegal flow of weapons of mass destruction technology from the Subcontinent to the Persian Gulf region. While the primary focus of American efforts is to stem the potential flow from the former Soviet Union—where there is much more materiel around and opportunities are considerable for smuggling and illicit activity—there have been periodic fears that Pakistan's military may involve closer contacts with Iran than is comfortable for many Americans. While there is little evidence that this amounts to much, the reality is that both India and Pakistan have the potential to dramatically upset the balance of power in the Persian Gulf should they decide to provide nuclear and missile technology to the countries most bitterly opposed to the U.S. military presence, notably Iran and Iraq.

A related American security concern is that another war between India and Pakistan, triggered by the unresolved crisis in Kashmir, would not be confined to the traditional, short-lived conventional encounters we have seen in the past and could escalate to involve nuclear weapons and draw in China. While the United States would not necessarily become involved—we have no security guarantees with either India or Pakistan—a nuclear confrontation on the Subcontinent would have enormous global consequences and would trigger a major diplomatic initiative to ensure that such an event would never happen again. If China were directly or indirectly involved in the conflict, the repercussions would be even more ominous and would generate an inevitably high-profile U.S. political response.

ECONOMIC DEVELOPMENTS IN INDIA AND PAKISTAN: IMPLICATIONS FOR THE UNITED STATES

Given the disparity in the size of India's and Pakistan's economies (according to the International Institute for Strategic Studies 1996/97 *Military Balance*, in 1995 Pakistan's GDP was $56 billion and India's was $330 billion), what happens to India's structural reform is by far the most important economic issue on the Subcontinent. Two factors have special relevance for the United States and provide major opportunities for American companies: India's growing consumerism and its infrastructure and energy crisis.

Although there is controversy about the precise number, the Indian middle class is estimated to number some 150-250 million out of a total population of 950 million. Regardless of what numbers we choose to believe, it is clear that this new class of Indian consumers is very large in absolute terms.

New purchasing power means that the Indian middle class is now a significant factor in Indian economic and political life. Economic reforms have produced an orgy of consumer spending at the same time that lower customs duties for imported goods have forced domestic producers to reduce prices of consumer items while improving quality and choice. Middle-class Indians, long deprived of the luxury goods enjoyed by their Western counterparts, are on an extended buying spree. The United States—India's largest trading and investment partner—is a major beneficiary of this activity.

This has been paralleled by another important phenomenon: the slow but steady erosion of India's socialist ethos, long the pillar of the country's economic philosophy. Over half of India's population—521 million people—is under the age of 24. Born after the *swadeshi* (self-reliance) rhetoric of Gandhi that brought India its independence in 1947, and long after the subsequent wars with Pakistan and China, this new breed of moneyed, ambitious, and mostly young Indians has few philosophical ties to socialism and is the major force in the retreat from economic isolationism toward notions of the free market and entrepreneurship. Furthermore, the new middle-class young believe that India is destined to be a great power, and they are not shy about saying so. Traditional professions such as medicine and the civil service, long the preferred route up the socioeconomic ladder, are now being spurned in favor of careers in business and finance.

While the Westernized urban Indians may be busy acquiring their fax machines, air conditioners, and cellular phones, the rural underclasses are buying black-and-white television sets and VCRs, albeit one to a village rather than one to a household. In a 1995 *Economist* survey, "India Today" identified an "aspiring class" of about 670 million people, mostly poor and rural. It is this group that is constantly mobilizing upward and feeding into the middle class. Thus, a two-tiered society, once divided into a small class of "haves" and a huge class of "have-nots," has gradually been redefined into a multiple-tier society—one of "haves," "have lesses," "aspiring-to-haves," and "have-nots."

As middle-class consumption rises and industry expands, so too will the pressure on the energy supply. This is especially true of India's economy, which—like those of all fast-growing developing countries—is extremely energy-intensive. Most energy supplies in India remain in the hands of the public sector monopolies, operated and heavily regulated by the state. Individual State Electricity Boards run government-owned power plants, where overstaffing, inefficient operation, and artificially controlled prices have created huge distortions in the energy sector. Government subsidies have kept prices low in order to mollify rural voters; in some states, farmers receive virtually free electricity.

In theory, India could be self-sufficient in the basic requirements for electricity production. It has abundant coal reserves, but the coal is of poor quality and creates serious pollution and huge amounts of slag as it burns. In addition, transporting it makes increasing demands on the already overused and under-capitalized railway system. If coal use is to grow commensurate with the anticipated demand for fuel, there will need to be major new investments in both transportation and environmental protection.

The other principal alternatives for the production of electricity are natural gas, oil, and hydroelectric and nuclear power.

However, India has very little cheaply available oil and gas, and importing these fuels from the Gulf adds dramatically to the balance-of-payments deficit and poses strategic risks. Hydroelectric schemes have been stymied due to environmental complaints, mismanagement, and conflicts with Nepal and Bangladesh over the control of waters from the north. The future of nuclear power is equally controversial.

In a bold move, Prime Minister Narasimha Rao threw the energy sector open to private investment in 1992, permitting 100-percent foreign ownership and wooing investors by waiving the bidding system and negotiating contracts instead of putting them out to open tender. Project proposals for energy development from foreign firms came pouring in, and seven of them were hastily accepted on a "fast track" for clearance and given generous terms that make the investments almost risk-free. Among these is the controversial $2.8 billion gas-fired power station project in Dabhol, Maharashtra, run jointly by the U.S.–based companies Enron Development, Bechtel, and General Electric.

At one point Indian politics threatened to force Enron to abandon the Dabhol project. The domestic furor over the Enron project began with the ruling Congress (I) Party's electoral loss in Maharashtra in March 1995. The victorious BJP–Shiv Sena coalition suspected irregularities in the deal and established a four-member committee to review the terms of the project. Critics argued that the deal had imposed all sorts of one-sided obligations on the Indian government without corresponding obligations on Enron's part: Enron was guaranteed one and a half times the fees received by public-sector power plants, as well as an extremely high return on its equity and guarantees from the state and central governments to backstop any dues that the Maharashtra State Electricity Board (MSEB) might fail to pay. The company in turn argues that these guarantees were necessary, given the woefully inept functioning of the state electricity boards and the high likelihood that they would default on payments. Once in power, the BJP and the Shiv Sena softened their adversarial stances, and there was a fair review of the case. By August 1996, the project was back on track albeit with new arrangements on costs.

No matter how individual energy cases are resolved, what is abundantly clear is that India's energy crisis can only get worse with burgeoning consumer demand from the middle class. Another indicator of increased energy consumption is the growth in sales of automobiles, trucks, and two-wheeled vehicles (motorcycles and scooters). The continuing increase in the number of vehicles in use since the 1991 reforms has exacerbated the strain on India's archaic road transport system. This Indian government has now thrown the entire infrastructure sector open to private and foreign investment, introducing a five-year tax holiday for any enterprises that build, maintain, or operate roads, highways, expressways, bridges, and other transport infrastructure. India has yet to open a modern divided highway on truck routes.

In addition to stimulating a boom in foreign investment and in the construction industry, this added demand for cars will translate into increased demand for gasoline. All of this points inevitably to even more pressure on the country's already limited hydrocarbon supply, as well as to more demand for gasoline imports from the Persian Gulf.

While Pakistan's economic reforms have been less dramatic than India's, it, too, faces huge challenges to modernize, attract foreign investment, and resolve its own energy crisis. This will likely mean increased imports of oil and natural gas from its western neighbors, as well as an expanded nuclear energy program.

THE GULF AND CASPIAN CONNECTIONS

As both India and Pakistan increase their demand for imported energy, remittances from workers in the rich Gulf states become even more important. (At the time of the Gulf War, India alone received $2.5 billion annually from its workers in the Gulf.)

Thus, favorable relations with the Gulf states will be essential in the coming decade. India's Oil and Natural Gas Corporation and the National Iran Oil Company have discussed a joint venture to explore for and produce oil and natural gas. The two have also discussed a $5-billion deal to build a 1,367-mile pipeline from Iran to India. Deals have been signed with Qatar, and India's private Essar Group has signed a memorandum of understanding for 2.5 million tons of Qatari liquefied natural gas for the next twenty-five years. The Bahraini Development and Industry Ministry is also working on an oil and petrochemical agreement with India. India has also investigated the possibility of laying a gas pipeline under the Arabian Sea from Oman to Bombay, although the costs appear to be prohibitive.

Pakistan has been active in the Caspian Basin. Turkmenistan and Pakistan signed a memorandum early in 1995 expressing their intention to build a pipeline to export Turkmen gas to Pakistan via Afghanistan and reached an agreement in principle to do so on June 19, 1995, in Islamabad. The importance of these developments is highlighted by the fact that, at the time, Pakistani Prime Minister Benazir Bhutto personally took charge of the implementation of this project, which could bring 1.6 billion cubic feet of gas a day from Turkmenistan to Pakistan through a pipeline to be built by Unocal. In October 1995, Unocal and the Saudi-owned Delta Oil Company signed a protocol of intentions with the government of Turkmenistan to build the pipeline, which would be linked with a new marine terminal at Gwadar in Pakistan. Construction is set to begin by December 1998, and the first delivery of 1,000 million cubic feet per day of Turkmen gas will be made to Pakistan in 2001.

There has also been talk of cooperation between Pakistan and India on bringing natural gas by pipeline from Iran, which has huge gas resources and is anxious to sell them. Such a proposal would have benefits and costs for both countries. Since they would be dependent upon one another for energy supplies, such an arrangement could be a deterrent to further conflict over Kashmir. Both countries, however, could be held hostage to Iranian control of the supply. In any event, India and Pakistan are going to have to import more oil from the Persian Gulf in the coming decade, and this will make them even more vulnerable than in the past to the effects of another Gulf crisis.

It is also possible that intensified competition rather than cooperation between India and Pakistan will result from the growing importance of their Gulf/Caspian connections. Clearly, as both India and Pakistan attempt to redefine the post–Cold War geopolitics of the region, India has cast its net westward in search of new economic and political allies, leading to what some have called "Indo-Pakistani competition in public diplomacy" in the Muslim world. Political and military ties between Pakistan and Southwest Asia have always been solid, and India has everything to gain by trying to make a dent in Pakistan's traditional influence in the region.

If the Indian economy truly takes off in a fashion that some people believe it capable of, will this have a parallel effect on other South Asian countries, particularly Pakistan? There are equally strong forces in Pakistan urging that reforms be undertaken to bring Pakistan into line with other Asian modernization programs—and Pakistan, while dwarfed in comparison to India, is itself a large country with a population of over 130 million and a potentially significant trading partner for the United States and its allies.

U.S. ECONOMIC INTERESTS

What does this mean for U.S. economic interests? The most obvious point is that India and Pakistan both offer great potential for U.S. business opportunities with the emphasis on the future rather than the present. In 1996, U.S. exports to India totaled $3,318 million, while U.S. imports from India amounted to $6,169 million. Estimates for India's fiscal year April 1995–March 1996 put total Indian exports at $36 billion and imports at $40 billion. Pakistan also provides a growing market for U.S. goods. In 1996, U.S. exports to Pakistan reached $1,277 million, while the United States imported $1,266 million from Pakistan. Pakistan's total exports for July 1996–February 1997 were $5,341 million, while its total imports were $7,665 million.

However, political instability in the region, coupled with continuing constraints on external economic relations, hampers the kinds of highly profitable access that U.S. companies have found in East Asia.

According to the 1996 World Bank *Annual Report*:

> In 1995 the South Asian economies grew by 5.3 percent. India continued to reap substantial benefits from the trade and investment liberalization reforms undertaken after 1991. Helped by favorable monsoons, growth is estimated to be around 6 percent, while manufacturing output growth has averaged 10 percent in the past two years . . . Since 1991, the average annual export growth rate for the region has exceeded 10 percent compared to an average of 5.6 percent for the 1981-90 period. Nevertheless, exports of goods and non-factor services represent less than 15 percent of domestic output, well below the average for developing countries. Although recent reforms have succeeded in lowering trade barriers, South Asian tariffs remain far higher than those in other areas. As a result they remain an impediment to growth because, in conjunction with other trade restrictions, they create distortions and can lead to resource misallocations.

In addition, the 1997 *Index of Economic Freedom*, published by the Heritage Foundation and the *Wall Street Journal*, ranks both India and

Pakistan as "mostly not free" on their scale of such freedoms. They find that India's trade policy continues to have a very high level of protectionism, corporate taxation rates are high, and government intervention, while less significant than in the past, is still considerable. Moderate barriers to foreign investment continue, and restrictions on banking are excessive. There are also high levels of wage and price controls, and only a moderate level of protection for private property. The economy is extensively regulated and has generated a significant amount of black market activity. Pakistan, too, reflects much the same indications of a high level of protectionism—high taxes and a high level of regulation. While Pakistan seems to score better than India on issues such as property rights, wage controls, restrictions on banking, and barriers to foreign investment, both countries rank considerably below other major Asian countries, including Indonesia (though not, incidentally, China).

Nevertheless, in comparison with the past, India and Pakistan, and by extension the rest of South Asia, will become much more important for U.S. business interests. In the event that economic relations continue to grow, will there be the same conflicts that are emerging in the great debate over U.S.–China relations with both Democrats and Republicans divided over the moral correctness of U.S. China policy? In principle, there are far fewer intrinsic contradictions in relations with South Asia. Both India and Pakistan are, by global standards, democratic. Furthermore, the elites in both countries are English-speaking, and the legal system is independent and based on Anglo-Saxon law. Nevertheless, the continuing unresolved crisis over Kashmir could plunge the region once more into war, which, in time, would hamper foreign investment and trade. Furthermore, the social problems of both countries ensure that the priority attention of both governments will be focused on domestic issues and the need to demonstrate to the majority of the population that the benefits of economic growth and the free market do indeed trickle down to their huge underclasses.

The combination of a continuing widening of the economic gap between India and Pakistan and failure to resolve the Kashmir dispute poses a potentially explosive challenge to stability in the Subcontinent. India is not only larger in terms of its population and economy than Pakistan, but it has a more modern industrial sector that will be the "power driver" of its economic growth in the decades to come. Unless Pakistan can establish its own conditions for improving its economy, the gap will widen; this could confirm Indian hegemony and force Pakistan to accommodate the reality of India's strengths, or, alternatively, lead to a further precipitous breakdown in relations and possibly war.

BALANCING U.S. SECURITY AND ECONOMIC INTERESTS

In the overall context of South Asian relations, the United States has emerged with a more favorable hand than in the past. Yet the old balancing act between India and Pakistan is not yet over. India is indeed the prize, and closer security and economic ties with India could be a "win-win" situation *provided* that Pakistan's interests are taken into account. It would be foolish for the United States to ignore or continue to snub Pakistan and drive its leaders into closer ties with Iran, China, and extremist Muslim groups. Pakistan is too important geostrategically to be written off as another "failed state" that the United States no longer has to worry about because the Cold War is over.

American security and economic interests are best served by nurturing better relations with Pakistan, but not at the expense of India. This is not easy, given the zero-sum mentality that still permeates Delhi and Islamabad. In this regard, a resolution of the Kashmir crisis would be a "win-win-win" for all three countries just as another war would be a "lose-lose-lose." There are ways for the United States to play a more constructive role on Kashmir, but this complicated issue should be the subject of another paper.

For the next decade, the United States will view India and Pakistan through the prism of non-proliferation, Gulf security, China, and specific business opportunities. The new nuclear-weapons status of India and Pakistan has raised the profile of the Subcontinent on both the American non-proliferation and broader geopolitical agenda. The most important non-proliferation goal for the United States must be to work with both countries to avoid a major deployment of nuclear weapons and to seek ways to resolve the Kashmir crisis. The China issue will undoubtedly grow in importance. Beijing's policies will be under the microscope in the coming decade whether the concern is energy access and the Gulf, arms supplies, nuclear cooperation with Pakistan, China's blue-water navy, Tibet, unresolved border disputes with India, or relations with Southeast Asia. If U.S.–China rivalries emerge as the new dominant feature of international politics, South Asia will be part of a new U.S. security equation. On the other hand, the big difference between today and the Cold War period is that the United States has growing economic interests in China and South Asia. Whether this will intensify the logic of cooperation or classical geopolitical conflict is one of the great unresolved questions of our times.

REFERENCES

Report of an Independent Task Force. "A New U.S. Policy Towards India and Pakistan." New York: Council on Foreign Relations, 1997.

National Defense University. 1997 *Strategic Assessment*, "India and Pakistan," Chapter 10.

India Survey. *The Economist*, January 21, 1995.

The Heritage Foundation and the *Wall Street Journal*. 1997 *Index of Economic Freedom*, 1997.

Geoffrey Kemp and Robert E. Harkavy, *Strategic Geography and the Changing Middle East*. (Washington, DC: Carnegie Endowment for International Peace in cooperation with the Brookings Institution Press, 1997).

"Work on Pakistan-Turkmen Gas Pipeline to Start December '98," *The Nation* (Islamabad), July 24, 1997, in FBIS-NES-97-205, July 25, 1997.

U.S. ECONOMIC AND SECURITY INTERESTS IN ASIA: THE NEXT DECADE

TED GALEN CARPENTER

FROM INTERVENOR OF FIRST RESORT TO BALANCER OF LAST RESORT

An assessment of U.S. policy toward Asia should acknowledge at the outset that America's interests are not evenly distributed throughout the various subregions. There is little question, for example, that American economic and strategic interests are more directly engaged in East Asia (especially Northeast Asia) than they are on the Subcontinent. That is not to say that the latter area is unimportant. The United States maintains modest but significant economic ties with such nations as India and Pakistan, and the Indian Ocean is a strategic arena for lines of supply and communications, given Washington's determination to be the guardian of the Persian Gulf and its oil supplies.

Nevertheless, the economic importance of South Asia pales in comparison with America's vast economic stake in East Asia. The same is true of strategic importance. Unless U.S. policymakers view India as an eventual military counterweight to China, South Asia's strategic relevance to the United States is almost entirely a byproduct of Washington's existing Persian Gulf policy. But that policy could (and many would argue, should) be changed. A shift to a non-interventionist U.S. posture toward the Gulf would immediately and drastically reduce South Asia's strategic importance to the United States.

Washington has no comparable option regarding East Asia. Various scholars have noted that East Asia is the one region in the world where the interests of four major powers (Russia, China, Japan, and the United States) intersect. America's interests in South Asia are largely discretionary; those in East Asia are much more intrinsic. Geographically, the United States is a Pacific (although not an East Asian) power; economically, it has a large and growing stake in East Asia; strategically, the region has been and remains relevant to U.S. security.

That is why it is crucial for the United States to have a wise and sustainable policy toward East Asia. Yet there are warning signals that all is not well with America's current policy and that the need for a new approach is becoming urgent.

Members of the U.S. political elite have an unfortunate habit of branding all proposals for meaningful foreign policy change as harbingers of "isolationism"—a term they almost never define with clarity. But the issue is not one of engagement versus isolationism. Few knowledgeable people would dispute the point that the United States has important strategic and economic interests in East Asia, and even fewer would suggest the adoption of a Fortress America policy or the creation of a hermit republic. Recognizing that the United States has significant interests in the region, however, is not the endpoint of an assessment of U.S. policy. One must then apply a rigorous cost-benefit analysis to U.S. policy. Only if the benefits outweigh the costs and risks—and do so by a decisive margin—does the policy merit support.

All too many analysts focus on the benefits of Washington's East Asia policy (the fostering of regional stability and prosperity, the dampening of incentives for arms races, etc.) while ignoring or minimizing the financial burdens and the risks incurred by being East Asia's policeman.[1] Former Assistant Secretary of Defense Joseph Nye epitomized such myopia when he stated that Washington's security role was akin to providing life-sustaining "oxygen" to the regional environment. Atmospheric oxygen is largely a free good; security commitments decidedly are not.

In addition to determining whether the benefits clearly outweigh the costs and risks, a serious assessment of America's East Asia policy should ask two other questions: First, is the current policy sustainable, not just in the short term (i.e., the next five years or so), but over the long term? Second, even if it is theoretically sustainable, is it the optimal method of advancing America's regional interests, or are there alternative policies that would provide substantially similar benefits at a lower level of cost and risk?

AMERICA'S STRATEGIC AND ECONOMIC INTERESTS IN EAST ASIA

The United States has three especially important interests in East Asia. The first is to prevent any single power from dominating the region. The nations of East Asia have a large population, significant military forces, and an impressive (and growing) array of economic and technological capabilities. A regional hegemon able to control those vast assets could pose a serious threat to U.S. security and economic well-being.

The second important interest is that a reasonable degree of order and stability exist in the region. An East Asia habitually convulsed by armed conflicts would be a difficult and unpleasant neighbor for America. A reasonable degree of order should not, however, be confused with the need to micro-manage the region's security affairs to ensure complete order. Some instability is inherent in the international system, and East Asia will not be immune from that reality. As long as national rivalries in the region are not excessively violent and disruptive, U.S. interests are relatively secure.

The third important interest is economic. East Asia is now the most significant region for U.S. international commerce, having surpassed Western Europe earlier in this decade. Eleven of America's twenty-four largest trading partners are located in the region (Japan, 2nd; the People's Republic of China, 5th; the Republic of Korea, 7th; Taiwan, 8th; Singapore, 9th; Malaysia, 11th; Hong Kong, 13th; Thailand, 17th; Australia, 20th; the Philippines, 22nd; and Indonesia, 24th).[2] Many of those same entities also provide important arenas for U.S. investment. Maintaining, indeed strengthening, that array of economic ties constitutes an interest that Washington cannot ignore.

AMERICA AS EAST ASIA'S HEGEMON

Since the end of World War II, the United States has sought to protect and advance all three of its major interests in East Asia. But it has not done so (as some policy experts have alleged) by guaranteeing a stable balance of power in the region. Instead, the United States has done so by arrogating the role of regional hegemon. Preserving that position has now become something bordering on an obsession.

A prominent justification for continuing the large-scale U.S. military presence in the region is to prevent a power vacuum that might be exploited by an expansionist state. That is hardly a new rationale for Washington's policy. Throughout the Cold War, U.S. forces guarded East Asia's security against Soviet (and for a time Soviet/Chinese) threats. The removal of Japan as a significant political and military factor (because of the destruction of Tokyo's military forces in World War II and Washington's insistence on a minimalist Japanese military capability in the postwar era) meant that the United States was the only credible strategic counterweight to the USSR and its communist allies.[3]

Despite the collapse of the Soviet Union, the rationale for a dominant U.S. military role in East Asia remains largely the same. The Pentagon's 1995 security strategy report for the East Asia–Pacific region, for example, contended that forward-deployed U.S. forces ensure a rapid and flexible worldwide "crisis response capability," but it also stated that they are there to "discourage the emergence of a regional hegemon."[4] Although U.S. officials are vague about what rival might aspire to that status, a passage in the report offered an enticing hint about the target of Washington's apprehension. "If the United States does not provide the central, visible, stabilizing force in the Asia and Pacific region," the report cautioned, "it is quite possible that another country might—but not in a way that meets America's fundamental interests. . . ."[5] Although it is conceivable that the comment referred to possible Chinese hegemonic ambitions, the reference to a "stabilizing" force points to a different interpretation. Given its territorial claims involving the Spratly, Paracel, and Diaoyo islands (not to mention its claims to Taiwan), China would more likely be a disruptive, "revisionist" power than a stabilizing, conservative power.

There is really only one credible candidate to supplant the United States as regional stabilizer: Japan; and that point is well understood by U.S. policymakers. Washington continues, as it has since the end of World War II, to discourage Japan from playing an activist political-military role in East Asia. Even the outcome of the much-touted April 1996 summit between President Clinton and Prime Minister Ryutaro Hashimoto was consistent with that long-standing policy. The joint declaration that emerged from the summit meeting indicated that U.S. officials had finally accepted the need to modestly increase Japan's involvement in the region's security affairs, but the revised blueprint still conceived of Tokyo as Washington's very junior partner.[6] There is no indication that U.S. leaders want Japan to be an ally with a responsibility equal to America's for preserving stability in East Asia—much less that they want Japan to assume the lead role.[7]

Washington's policy toward Japan is merely the most visible manifestation of overall U.S. East Asian policy. The heart of that policy is to prevent the rise of any political and military rival. In other words, it is a policy to preserve U.S. hegemony. The objective of discouraging other powers from even aspiring to play more active political and military roles was perhaps most candidly expressed in the preliminary draft of the Pentagon's planning guidance document that was leaked to the press in 1992.[8] That document is not the only evidence of a hegemonic policy, however. Statements by various military and civilian officials over the years and the substantive features of Washington's East Asia policy since 1945 point to the same conclusion.

WASHINGTON'S SMOTHERING STRATEGY

American officials have zealously guarded U.S. hegemonic prerogatives in an attempt to smother the political-military ambitions of other powers in East Asia. For example, when Japanese Prime Minister Toshiki Kaifu made a surprise proposal in the summer of 1991 for a "security dialogue"—formal regional meetings on defense issues—between Japan and the members of the Association of Southeast Asian Nations (ASEAN), Washington reacted negatively. In a speech to the annual meeting of ASEAN foreign ministers, Secretary of State James Baker III warned them against adopting new arrangements that would replace "tried and true frameworks" involving the United States. "We have a remarkable degree of stability in this region," Baker said. "We ought to be careful about changing those arrangements and discarding them for something else." Privately, U.S. officials expressed strong opposition to the Japanese proposal because it might weaken the bilateral arrangements between the United States and various nations in East Asia and the Pacific.[9] In other words, Tokyo's modest initiative was seen as a challenge to Washington's political and military primacy.

The Clinton Administration has been less clumsy in implementing the smothering strategy. It has even cautiously encouraged the kind of regional security dialogue that its predecessor so tenaciously opposed. But the Administration has also emphasized that the United States must be an active participant in such initiatives; there is no sympathy whatever for measures that the East Asian countries might pursue without U.S. input. Moreover, Administration officials seize every opportunity to emphasize America's determination to maintain a large military presence in the region and to continue the role of stabilizer. The comments of Secretary of Defense William Cohen during his April 1997 trip to East Asia epitomized that approach.

Another manifestation of Washington's smothering strategy is the ongoing military commitment to South Korea. When the mutual security treaty was approved in 1954, the Republic of Korea (ROK) was a poverty-stricken country that had been devastated by more than three years of war. The population was demoralized, and the military (although somewhat stronger than it had been when North Korean troops invaded in June 1950) was still decidedly inferior to its communist adversary in training, equipment, and morale. Moreover, Seoul had to confront not only the hostility of North Korea but the knowledge that Chinese or Soviet forces might support Pyongyang's units in the event of war. The security treaty with the United States was a tangible guarantee that the ROK would not have to deal with such powerful enemies by itself. Given the geostrategic realities in the mid-1950s and for many years thereafter, South Korea could not have provided for its own defense.

That is no longer true. The ROK has become one of the world's great economic successes, achieving a per capita GDP of more than $10,500 in 1995. That dynamism and rapid growth contrast sharply with North Korea's stagnation and have given the ROK an overwhelming economic advantage over its communist nemesis. South Korea's GDP in 1995 stood at more than $455 billion compared to the North's meager $22.3 billion.[10] In other words, the ROK has an economy more than 20 times as large as that of its enemy. It also has a decisive edge in population—some 45.6 million versus 23.5 million. In addition to such quantitative advantages, the ROK enjoys important qualitative advantages. Technologically, South Korea's economy is light years ahead of the North's. South Korean firms compete successfully in global markets for a variety of products, including automobiles, computers, heavy machinery, and electronics. North Korea meanwhile teeters on the brink of famine.[11]

Most defenders of the security treaty and the U.S. troop presence on the Korean Peninsula now grudgingly concede that the ROK could build the conventional forces needed to defend itself against North Korean aggression. They increasingly cite another justification for Washington's *status quo* policy: that the U.S. military presence is an essential component of Washington's general policy of promoting stability in East Asia, preventing the re-emergence of national rivalries and arms races that could once again plunge the region into conflict. Secretary of State Warren Christopher summarized the thinking of U.S. policymakers when he described the alliance with South Korea and the American troop deployment in that country as "a linchpin of America's engagement in the region."[12] More recently, Secretary of Defense Cohen stated bluntly that U.S. troop levels in both Japan and South Korea would remain unchanged even if the Korean Peninsula were peacefully reunified.[13]

WHY THE SMOTHERING STRATEGY IS OBSOLETE

Washington's post–World War II smothering strategy has been based on the assumption that if the United States took care of the security needs of East Asia, the various countries in the region would forego the option of building large military establishments and acting as normal great powers (or even midsized powers) have acted throughout history to protect their own interests. The resulting environment of stability would not only reduce the chances of armed conflict but maximize the opportunities for economic growth—something that would benefit the United States as well as East Asia.

That may have been a valid assumption during the first two or three decades after World War II, but several factors have been eroding the foundations of U.S. strategy since that time. Until the mid-1970s, the non-communist East Asian powers (including Japan) did not have economies large enough to fund military establishments capable of supporting independent, self-reliant security policies even if the governments had been so inclined. (At least they could not have done so without endangering their newly vigorous economic growth rates—a price none of them wished to pay.) That factor has changed markedly in the last two decades. Japan is by most calculations the world's second largest economic power, and the ROK, Taiwan, Indonesia, and Thailand have all emerged as serious players in the global economy. Several East Asian countries now have the economic wherewithal to fund credible national security forces, and although the growth in their military capabilities has thus far been modest, East Asia has become a lucrative arena for arms sales.

There are other subtle but significant indications that the East Asian states are beginning to hedge against the day when the United States might be unwilling or unable to maintain its position as the regional hegemon. Japan's decision to develop a robust intelligence apparatus instead of continuing to rely on information from U.S. agencies is one example. Tokyo's buildup of plutonium stocks, combined with its development of reprocessing facilities and a sophisticated rocketry program, may also be evidence of a hedging strategy.[14] The willingness of Taiwan and South Korea to make major arms purchases from non–U.S. suppliers (e.g., Taipei's purchase of Mirage fighters from France) and the development of more extensive domestic armaments industries are other signs.

The growth of economic power has been accompanied by more assertive behavior on territorial matters and other issues of national pride. Jingoistic spats such as those between Japan and South Korea over Toktu Island and the three-way quarrel involving Japan, Taiwan, and the People's Republic of China (PRC) over the Senkaku (Diaoyo) islands are only the most visible and recent incidents.

All of this suggests that America's ability to satisfy the security needs of the East Asian states through a smothering strategy is already waning, and that the decline is likely to accelerate in the coming years. It was one thing for weak, poor, and insecure countries to accept the protection of a benign distant protector; the price may have involved the swallowing of national pride on occasion, but U.S. hegemony spared the regional powers from spending large sums on their own military establishments, enabling them to devote scarce resources to their developing economies. It is quite another matter for societies flush with economic prosperity to continue accepting such a humiliating dependency. Sooner or later their behavior is likely to evolve until it conforms to the historical norm of nations that possess serious economic and military capabilities.

There is yet another visible weakness in Washington's smothering strategy. Because it developed during the early years of the Cold War, the danger that there would be serious quarrels between U.S. allies seemed relatively remote. For example, despite the historical legacy of Japanese colonialism and the resulting antipathy of Koreans toward Japan, both Tokyo and Seoul recognized that they confronted the same communist adversary. Without the looming presence of that mutual threat to their security, they have far greater latitude to pursue other grievances—including those against each other. In addition to its confrontation with Japan over the Toktu issue, the ROK's decision to purchase submarines (which are hardly essential for dealing with the North Korean threat) and its vigorous cultivation of political as well as economic ties with China suggest that a confrontational relationship between South Korea and Japan is more than a remote possibility. Pacifying a region and maintaining a hegemonic position will be decidedly more challenging in a volatile environment with shifting agendas and relationships than it was in the bipolar Cold War setting.

A related point is that Washington could previously operate with confidence that its security clients would not have extensive economic ties with America's strategic adversaries. In other words, there would not be a tension between the economic interests of those allies and their security relationships with the United States. The situation is now more ambiguous. For example, a chilly relationship (to say nothing of an armed skirmish) between the United States and the People's Republic of China (PRC) would put the other East Asian countries in an extremely difficult position. Many of them have extensive investments in China and maintain lucrative bilateral trade relations with that country.

Could Washington count on support from its "friends" and allies in the region for a hard-line policy directed against Beijing, when such support might cost them their multi-billion dollar economic stakes? A positive answer is far from certain. Indeed, given the reaction of the East Asian powers to the brouhaha in the Taiwan Strait in early 1996 (discussed below), U.S. policymakers have reason to worry about the prospect of such support. A Japanese scholar's explanation for his country's unwillingness to publicly endorse the U.S. deployment of the Seventh Fleet to waters near Taiwan was most revealing. He did not cite the danger that a military collision between the United States and China might lead to Chinese attacks on Japanese territory because of the U.S. bases there. Rather, he emphasized concerns that an endorsement of U.S. policy might jeopardize Japanese investments in China.[15] (The decision of Japan and Australia to defy U.S. wishes and oppose a U.N. Commission on Human Rights resolution condemning Beijing for its treatment of political dissidents is another, more recent, example of the ambivalence of America's East Asian allies when it comes to dealing with China.) Indeed, those countries might even use a deterioration in U.S.–PRC relations to expand the market share of their companies at the expense of U.S. firms.[16]

A final reason for the increasing inviability of the smothering strategy is that the United States now encounters a power whose security needs and policy objectives Washington is not in a position to satisfy. That power is China. The re-emergence of Japan as a great power (at least economically) has posed problems for the smothering strategy. But Japan's security interests and those of the United States are at least reasonably compatible, and Japan is a *status quo* power. Tokyo has been the principal beneficiary of the existing political and economic system in East Asia. (Indeed, Japan has achieved by peaceful economic penetration and subtle political influence many of the objectives that it unsuccessfully pursued by force in the 1930s and 1940s when it sought to create the Greater East Asia Co-prosperity Sphere.) The Japanese have no incentive to disrupt the current arrangement, nor have they shown any desire to do so.

The situation with respect to China is different in crucial ways. Although Beijing's expanding economic ties with its East Asian neighbors (and with the United States) are an important incentive for *status quo* behavior, there are other factors that produce incentives for aggressive revisionism. Most important, China is still nursing grievances about the territorial amputations that occurred during its period of weakness in the nineteenth century. That is why the return of Hong Kong in the summer of 1997 has acquired an importance that transcends the territory's (admittedly substantial) economic value. It is a powerful symbol of China's restored national pride. The scheduled return of Macao in 1999 is another stage in that process. But it is not at all certain that the process will be completed in the view of China's leaders and population until Taiwan is regained, the land taken by the Russian empire is recovered, and Beijing's claims in the South China and East China seas are vindicated.

Some experts argue that the PRC does not harbor expansionist ambitions.[17] That is possible, but the existence of such an extensive array of unresolved matters points to a less sanguine conclusion. So too does the history of international relations. Rising great powers, especially those with territorial grievances and claims, typically pursue assertive, and often abrasive, policies. One need only recall the behavior of the United States during the nineteenth century, or Wilhelmine Germany during the late nineteenth and early twentieth centuries.

That poses an enormous dilemma for the United States. It is difficult to see how Washington can appease China on any of the outstanding issues without causing massive dislocations to the other components of U.S. policy in East Asia. An attempt to appease China would rapidly undermine the smothering strategy, since the other East Asian powers would conclude that the United States was unwilling to protect—or was incapable of protecting—their vital interests. Yet an attempt to thwart Chinese ambitions would entail its own dangers. As China's economic and military power grew, Beijing would likely see a resistant America as an intolerable impediment to the achievement of legitimate Chinese goals. Again, history suggests that a rising great power sooner or later tries to become the dominant player in its region. Such a power does not generally get on well with the incumbent regional hegemon. The structure of the international system tends to produce bitter, and often violent, rivalries in such situations.

For all of those reasons, the smothering strategy appears to be unsustainable. Indeed, even attempting to preserve it may pose serious dangers to the United States.

THE "DOWNSIDE" TO POLICING EAST ASIA

The United States' dominant position in East Asia has contributed to the region's stability, but the policy also entails mounting costs and risks. The financial burden alone is substantial. It costs at least $35-$40 billion a year to maintain the military forces needed to carry out U.S. security commitments in East Asia in a credible fashion.[18] Yet there is scant evidence that Washington's security commitments give the United States significant leverage in securing access to important East Asian markets. The difficulties encountered in attempting to open the Japanese market have been discussed at length, but the problem is not confined to Japan. Even South Korea, a much smaller client heavily dependent on its alliance with the United States and on the U.S. troop presence, has been surprisingly recalcitrant and exclusionary.[19] The evidence is, at the very least, ambiguous on whether Washington's security policy in East Asia is effectively promoting its economic interests.[20]

The tensions between the PRC and Taiwan in late 1995 and early 1996 illustrated that the policy has an even more disturbing drawback in terms of risk. Although the most recent PRC-Taiwan crisis has receded, there is a serious possibility of similar imbroglios in the coming years. Not only could the United States find itself entangled in a perilous military confrontation, it might have to wage the ensuing struggle virtually alone. Taiwan would undoubtedly contribute to its own defense, but the reaction in various East Asian capitals to Beijing's menacing behavior indicated that assistance from Washington's other "friends" would be problematic, at best.

Indeed, virtually all of the East Asian governments made a concerted effort to distance their policies from that of the United States as the Clinton Administration dispatched two aircraft carriers to the western Pacific to demonstrate concern about the rising tensions in the Taiwan Strait. South Korea and the Philippines both stressed that their "mutual" defense treaties with the United States did not cover contingencies in the Strait. Countries such as Malaysia, Indonesia, Thailand, and Australia contented themselves with the banal response of urging restraint on all sides, conspicuously declining to endorse Washington's moves. Indeed, they echoed Beijing's position that Taiwan is merely a renegade province. Even Japan, the principal U.S. ally in the region, merely expressed "understanding" of the naval deployment.[21]

That lack of support suggests that Washington's encouragement of dependency on the part of the non-communist East Asian countries has created a most unhealthy situation. Those nations seek the best of both worlds: They want the United States to protect them from Chinese aggression or intimidation, if that problem should become acute, but they do not want to incur Beijing's wrath (or even jeopardize their commerce with China) by allying themselves with a hard-line U.S. policy. That may be a good, albeit cynical, strategy for them, but it puts the United States in a precarious position. If China does make a bid for regional hegemony at some point, there is literally no power other than the United States that is positioned to block that bid. That is a blueprint for a U.S.–Chinese war in which China's neighbors conveniently remain on the sidelines.

And it is not just toward the Taiwan issue that Washington's East Asian allies have displayed that attitude. For example, Tokyo rejected a U.S. request at the height of the crisis over North Korea's nuclear program in 1994 to dispatch minesweepers to assist U.S. naval forces should the confrontation with Pyongyang escalate. Again, the "free riding" of the East Asian states on security issues is not merely financial.

The smothering policy has outlived whatever usefulness it may once have had. Instead of creating a situation in which the only alternative to a dangerous power vacuum is America's continuing willingness to be point man in every East Asian crisis, the United States should move toward fostering a reasonably stable balance of power in East Asia. A new policy with that aim would view Japan as the primary strategic counterweight to an increasingly assertive China—a role that the United States will otherwise be pressured to fill by default.[22]

America has important strategic and economic interests in East Asia and cannot be indifferent to the region's fate. But the current strategy, based on the United States' being the regional military hegemon, is proving increasingly difficult to sustain. (The closing of U.S. military bases in the Philippines and the growing friction between American military personnel and the Japanese and South Korean civilian populations are only the most visible symptoms of trouble.[23]) More important, it is neither a necessary nor an optimal method of securing America's interests. The costs and risks of Washington's smothering strategy are beginning to far outweigh the benefits.

Most disquieting are the risks the United States continues to incur because of its role as the guarantor of East Asia's security and stability—risks that would normally be borne primarily by Japan and other regional powers. Japan's unwillingness to play even a supporting military role in regional crises is especially disturbing. Whatever the relevance of Korea, Taiwan, or the Spratlys to the economic and security interests of the United States, their importance to Japan is far greater.

It is highly unusual for a major power to choose to remain catatonic in the face of significant security problems in its own region. But Japanese leaders know that they do not have to incur the costs and risks of playing a more active role to protect their country's interests. The United States has obligingly agreed to incur them. Americans have every reason to ask, however, whether U.S. military personnel should be put in harm's way to deal with problems that are—or at least ought to be—much more important to Japan than they are to the United States. The prospect of American troops dying in an East Asian war, while the Japanese (and other nominal allies) merely provide moral and financial support (if that), is not very appealing. Yet that is the possibility that U.S. security policy in East Asia has created.[24]

TOWARD A SUSTAINABLE STRATEGY

Several steps need to be taken to establish a more sustainable policy. First, the United States should inform Japan and South Korea that it intends to withdraw its forces from both countries within the next few years and that, upon completion of the withdrawals, it will terminate the "mutual" security treaties. At that point, both Japan and South Korea will be expected to provide for their own defense. Washington should implement its withdrawal strategy without rancor and state explicitly that the move is not motivated by traditional complaints about burden-sharing or by the more recent trade disputes. Under no circumstances should

Washington seek to use the security commitments as a bargaining chip. It would be ill-advised to imply that if sufficient concessions are forthcoming on trade matters, the United States will maintain the defense shield, and conversely, if concessions are not made, the shield will be withdrawn. That approach would be a blueprint for resentment, and the damage to America's relations with South Korea and Japan could be substantial and long lasting.

Second, Washington should indicate to Tokyo that it no longer objects to Japan's assuming a more active political and military posture in East Asia. Quite on the contrary, U.S. officials ought to adopt the position that, as the principal indigenous great power, Japan will be expected to help stabilize East Asia, contribute to the resolution of disputes, and contain disruptive or expansionist threats that might emerge. Washington should also use its diplomatic influence to encourage political and security cooperation between Japan and its neighbors, but U.S. policymakers must not let East Asian apprehension about a more assertive Japan dictate U.S. policy and keep the United States in its role of regional policeman. Third, discussions should begin immediately about a new, more limited security relationship between the United States and Japan. Japanese and American security interests are likely to overlap in the coming decades, and it is reasonable to explore avenues of cooperation in those areas where there is sufficient convergence of interests. That cooperation should not, however, take the form of a new alliance. An ongoing security dialogue and occasional joint military exercises would be more appropriate.

Elaborate, formal treaty commitments are a bad idea in general. They are excessively rigid and can lock the United States into commitments that may make sense under one set of conditions but become ill-advised or even counterproductive when conditions change. Beyond that general objection, a U.S.–Japanese alliance would be likely to create special problems in the future. Such an alliance would provide tangible evidence to those in the PRC who contend that Washington is intent on adopting a containment policy directed against China.[25] The United States should retain the ability to work with Japan and other powers if Beijing's ambitions threaten to lead to Chinese dominance of the region, but Washington must be wary of creating a self-fulfilling prophecy. An informal security relationship with Japan would preserve the flexibility to block PRC hegemony, if that danger emerges, without needlessly antagonizing Beijing.

America can still have a potent power projection capability with a reduced military presence based in Guam and other U.S. territories in the central and west-central Pacific.[26] There is no need to have large numbers of forward-deployed forces, much less units to serve as automatic tripwires if even a minor conflict erupts. The United States should be the balancer of last resort, not the intervenor of first resort, in East Asia's security equation. And the most crucial step in adopting that strategy is to transfer primary security responsibilities to Japan, the region's leading conservative, *status quo* power.

There are numerous benefits to such a shift. The first is financial, since a "minimalist" policy would cut the $35-$40 billion annual cost of U.S. security commitments roughly in half. It would also end a lucrative subsidy to economic competitors. Japanese officials have admitted that Tokyo would need to increase its military spending by $25-$50 billion a year to offset the departure of U.S. forces and the end of the security treaty.[27] South Korean officials have conceded that the ROK would have to increase its military spending by $10-$13 billion a year if the United States withdrew its forces and terminated the defense pact.[28] The U.S. security commitment thus provides a financial bonanza to the Japanese and South Korean economies (and a smaller subsidy to other East Asian countries that indirectly benefit from the U.S. military presence). By compelling Washington's security clients to internalize the full cost of their own defense, the United States would achieve a multi-billion-dollar savings for American taxpayers and would help "level the playing field" in the arena of international economic competition.

The second benefit would be to reduce America's risk exposure in the event of an armed conflict in East Asia. As the self-appointed regional stabilizer, the United States is currently on the front lines. Although Washington's hegemonic policy may reduce the overall likelihood of a conflict in Korea, the Taiwan Strait, the South China Sea, or elsewhere, it also virtually guarantees that the United States will be caught up in any conflict that does erupt. The existence of treaty obligations, and especially the deployment of tripwire forces, eliminates the element of choice. At the very least, U.S. policymakers should want to restore America's ability to choose whether or not to intervene.

Finally, a lower profile security policy promises to be more sustainable in the coming decades. America's preponderant position in East Asia arose because of the convergence of unusual circumstances. Japan's total defeat in World War II, China's continuing weakness and political turmoil, and the death throes of decrepit European colonial empires (and the initial economic weakness of the independent successor states) created a vast power vacuum that the United States successfully filled. America's hegemonic status was not without cost; the Korean and Vietnam Wars provide ample testimony to that truth. But America had no credible challengers, and its role as East Asia's pacifier has yielded important benefits.

Whatever the value of that policy in the past, however, conditions have changed radically over the past two decades or so. The United States will find it increasingly difficult to preserve its hegemonic status in a region with not one but two rising great powers. Moreover, the explosive economic growth of the East Asian region as a whole inexorably narrows the advantage that has undergirded America's strategy of preponderance. The United States has been rightly described as the world's sole remaining superpower, and it is indisputably the single strongest nation, both economically and militarily. Nevertheless, as the 1990s draw to a close, the United States has less than 5 percent of the world's population and accounts for barely 20 percent of global economic output. And both percentages are declining. In two decades, America will likely have only 3.5 percent of the world's population and account for no more than 15 or 16 percent of global economic output. By that time, China may well be on the verge of having the world's largest economy and Japan will probably be a strong third in that race. Is it really credible that the United States can continue to dominate a region thousands of miles from its homeland—a region that has an enormous edge in population and is rapidly acquiring the economic clout to match?

Instead of vainly trying to sustain an ebbing hegemony, the United States should restructure its policy to protect its important interests in a new East Asia characterized by multiple power centers. The United States can play a meaningful role in East Asia's affairs indefinitely—if it husbands its strengths and does not attempt to overreach. It will assuredly be more difficult to be merely one major power among several rather than the regional hegemon, but the benefits of relinquishing the burdens of hegemony significantly outweigh the liabilities.

NOTES

[1] A graphic example of that tendency can be found in the comments of Secretary of State Madeleine K. Albright, "1997 Forrestal Lecture: American Principle and Purpose in East Asia," U.S. Naval Academy, Annapolis, Maryland, April 15, 1997.

[2] *U.S. and Asia Statistical Handbook*, 1996, ed. John T. Dori and Richard D. Fisher Jr. (Washington, D.C.: Heritage Foundation Asia Studies Center, 1996).

[3] A similar situation occurred in Europe. The removal of Germany as a political and military player and the drastically weakened positions of Britain and France after World War II meant that there was no European strategic counterweight to the Soviet Union. By default, the United States moved in to fill that power vacuum—in effect playing the balancer role and becoming the leading "European" military power.

[4] Department of Defense, Office of International Security Affairs, *United States Security Strategy for the East Asia–Pacific Region*, February 1995, p. 23.

[5] Ibid., p. 9.

[6] For an extended discussion, see Ted Galen Carpenter, "Smoke and Mirrors: The Clinton-Hashimoto Summit," Cato Institute Foreign Policy Briefing no. 41, May 16, 1996.

[7] Following the summit, U.S. officials stated that, although they hoped for greater Japanese logistical support for U.S. military missions in East Asia, Japan was "far from ready to send troops into battle alongside U.S. forces"—adding that this was "not something the United States wanted anyway." Quoted in Kevin Sullivan and John F. Harris, "Clinton Hails Partnership with Japan," *Washington Post*, April 18, 1996, p. A1.

When asked what help the United States could expect from Japan (in light of the Clinton-Hashimoto summit) if a conflict were to break out in East Asia, former Assistant Secretary of Defense Joseph Nye had extremely limited expectations: "If there were a war in Korea, I'm confident that we would have Japanese support, the use of Japanese bases, and help with supplies and so forth." Nye added that if the conflict were instead in the Taiwan Strait or the South China Sea, Washington would expect—and in his judgment, would need—"considerably less" support from Tokyo. "Treaty Ratification Reassures Region," interview with Joseph Nye, *Washington Times*, April 19, 1996, p. A17.

[8] "Excerpts from Pentagon's Plan: Prevent the Emergence of a New Rival," *New York Times*, March 8, 1992, p. A14.

[9] Philip Shenon, "Baker Asks Asians to Move Warily on New Pacts," *New York Times*, July 25, 1991, p. A14.

[10] *U.S. and Asia Statistical Handbook*, op. cit., pp. 54-57.

[11] For a detailed discussion of how various factors have shifted decisively in favor of South Korea over the past decade, see Doug Bandow, *Tripwire: Korea and U.S. Foreign Policy in a Changed World* (Washington: Cato Institute, 1996), pp. 57-81.

[12] Secretary Christopher, "Strengthening Ties between the United States and South Korea," Remarks at the inaugural reception for the Korean-United States Twenty-First Century Council, Washington, D.C., February 17, 1994. U.S. Department of State *Dispatch*, February 28, 1994, p. 104.

[13] "Japan: Anger As Pentagon Chief Kicks Off Visit," *South China Morning Post*, April 8, 1997.

[14] For a discussion of that issue from diverse perspectives, see *Japan's Nuclear Future: The Plutonium Debate and East Asian Security*, ed. Selig S. Harrison (Washington: Carnegie Endowment for International Peace, 1996).

[15] Hideshi Takeshida, a professor at Japan's Institute for Defense Studies, noted that his country "is always nervous when a problem arises with China." An important root of that nervousness, he contended, is the fear that China will retaliate against Japanese investors on the Mainland. Quoted in Willis Witter, "U.S. Gets No Help from East Asians in Backing Taiwan," *Washington Times*, March 14, 1997, p. A15.

[16] Clyde V. Prestowitz, Jr. "The Impact of U.S.–Asian Economic Relations on the American Economy," Paper presented to the first meeting of the Study Group on "American Interests in Asia: Economic and Security Priorities," sponsored by the Economic Strategy Institute, October 15, 1996, p. 12.

[17] Charles W. Freeman, "American Economic and Security Interests in China," Paper presented to the fourth meeting of the Study Group on "American Interests in Asia: Economic and Security Priorities," sponsored by the Economic Strategy Institute, Washington, D.C., January 16, 1997. p. 5.

[18] Georgetown University professor Earl Ravenal provides an even higher estimate, $82 billion. Earl C. Ravenal, *Defending America in an Uncontrollable World: The Military Budget, 1998 to 2003* (Washington: Cato Institute, forthcoming).

[19] Michael Schuman, "South Korea Acts to Discourage Imports," *Wall Street Journal*, March 7, 1997, p. A8; and Tim Shorrock, "Seoul Opposition Party Leader Slams U.S. Critics for Narrow Trade Focus," *Journal of Commerce*, April 10, 1997, p. 5A.

[20] Chalmers Johnson and E. B. Keehn make a solid case that the notion of America's military presence in East Asia giving the U.S leverage on trade issues is an illusion. Chalmers Johnson and E. B. Keehn, "The Pentagon's Ossified Strategy," *Foreign Affairs* 74 (July-August 1995), pp. 103-14.

[21] Steve Glain Witter, "U.S. Probably Shouldn't Count on Help from Japan in Resolving Taiwan Flap," *Wall Street Journal*, March 11, 1996; "Downer Urges Restraint in China-Taiwan Tension," Melbourne Radio Australia, in *Foreign*

Broadcast Information Service Daily Report—East Asia, March 13, 1996, electronic version, document Odo8cfk040v69n; "Alatas on Tense China-Taiwan Relations," Jakarta Radio Republik Indonesia, in FBIS—*East Asia*, 96-050, March 13, 1996, p. 50; "Further Comment on Assistance to U.S.," *Business World* (Manila), in FBIS—*East Asia*, March 13, 1996, electronic version, document Odoag3j03m9trn; Statement by Tan Sri Ahmad Kamil Jaafar, secretary general of the Foreign Ministry of Malaysia, March 1996, text provided by Malaysian embassy, November 18, 1996.

Such actions contradict the assertion of Martin Lasater (see his chapter in this volume, p. 205ff) that "concern over possible hegemony by China was one of the primary reasons most Asian nations supported American intervention in the recent Taiwan Strait crisis."

[22] Christopher Layne, "Less Is More: Minimal Realism in East Asia," *National Interest* 43 (Spring 1996), pp. 64-77.

[23] For a discussion, see Nicholas D. Kristof, "Welcome Mat Is Wearing Thin for G.I.'s in Asia," *New York Times*, December 3, 1995, p. A14.

[24] For an extended discussion of the undesirable side effects of the U.S.–Japanese alliance, see Ted Galen Carpenter, "Paternalism and Dependence: The U.S.-Japanese Security Relationship," Cato Institute Policy Analysis no. 244, November 1, 1995.

[25] Chalmers Johnson has rightly noted (see his chapter in this volume, p. 109ff) that even the 1995 Nye report and the April 1996 Clinton-Hashimoto summit have created apprehension in China about a U.S.–Japanese effort to contain the PRC. I am less inclined than Johnson, however, to believe that the Chinese interpretation of those events is valid.

[26] That strategy would require the reversal of recent policies that envision the closing of some installations on Guam. It is a measure of the perversity of U.S. strategy in the Western Pacific and East Asia that Washington contemplates drawing down forces stationed in U.S. territories while it maintains, or in the case of South Korea actually strengthens, forces used to subsidize the defense of allies and clients.

[27] Author's conversations with Japanese Foreign Ministry and Defense Agency officials, Tokyo, July 10-14, 1995.

[28] Author's conversations with ROK Defense Ministry officials, Seoul, July 18, 1995.

U.S. ECONOMIC AND SECURITY INTERESTS IN ASIA: THE NEXT DECADE

EZRA VOGEL

STAYING THE COURSE: THE U.S. ROLE IN MAINTAINING A STABLE ASIA

A STRONGER ASIA

In the twenty-first century, the United States will confront an Asia that is not only stronger economically but more confident and influential, politically and culturally, throughout the world.

- At present rates of growth, East Asia will by 2020 account for 40 percent of the world's GDP—measured by Purchasing Power Parity (PPP); North America, for 18 percent; and the 16 countries of Europe, for 14 percent. Trade across the Pacific may in a decade be twice that across the Atlantic, and America's interests in Asia will be far greater than in any other foreign continent.
- While globalism will increase with closer communication, transport, and economic linkages, Asian regionalism, including many diverse regional associations, will also grow.
- Asians expect that, sometime in the twenty-first century, China will become the dominant regional power. Optimistic about China's future behavior, they seek good relations with it and want to avoid alienating it, but—in case China should become menacing—they also want a steady United States to remain strong in Asia.
- As Asian self-confidence grows, the United States must greatly increase its active participation in Asia in many spheres if it is to retain its vitality as an economic power and retain global political and cultural leadership.

COMPLEMENTARITY OF U.S. MILITARY AND ECONOMIC INTERESTS

U.S. military and economic interests after the Cold War complement more than conflict with each other:

- It is in the economic interest of the United States to be deeply involved in the largest and most dynamic economic region of the world. It is in the interest of U.S. consumers to have access to low-cost goods, of U.S. manufacturing and service sectors to have access to markets, and of the U.S. Treasury to have access to bond purchasers. It is also in the interest of the U.S. military to help maintain stability in a region where the United States has deep economic interests and where the risks of conflict have been great enough to involve the United States in the last three major wars.
- To fulfill the mission of maintaining stability and responding to emergencies in the region and elsewhere, the United States needs stable bases in the region, in addition to access to other facilities in time of emergency. Regional stability depends on faith in U.S. commitments, and this faith would be far less without U.S. bases in Japan, South Korea, and other countries. As East Asian nations have grown economically, they have begun to bear an increasingly large share of the overall security burden, so that the stationing of troops and prepositioning of materials will not be an excessive economic burden for the United States.
- U.S. contributions to military security in Asia do not bring a direct, unilinear increase in economic benefits, but an overall positive relationship between the United States and Asian countries provides an atmosphere that improves opportunities for U.S.–based firms to sell products in Asia.
- Unlike the situation in the Cold War, as long as there is no national security emergency, U.S. security interests do not need to constrain U.S. efforts to press vigorously for its commercial interests in opening markets. Other nations recognize that all nations pursue economic interests and, except for rare times when essential supplies or sectors might be involved, do not regard the pursuit of economic interest to be so dangerous as to escalate to conflict. However, military security requires trust between nations, and threatening to abandon a security relationship to achieve U.S. commercial goals would in itself destroy the basis of trust required to maintain a stable security framework.

GUIDING PRINCIPLES FOR U.S. POLICY IN ASIA

To realize its fundamental interests in Asia, the United States should:

- Deepen its economic, political, and cultural linkages with Asia. To gain good will and responsiveness to its articulated interests, the United States should take a positive approach to Asia—demonstrating its commitment to democracy and human rights by positive example rather than by preaching and sanctions, pursuing positive commercial opportunities and linkages rather than complaining. This does not require the United States to refrain from vigorously articulating and pressing for its interests. A positive approach will provide a climate beneficial to U.S. commercial, political, and security interests.
- Continue to take both the lead in getting Asian cooperation for resolving global issues and an active role in regional Asian associations, particularly APEC summit meetings and the ASEAN Regional Forum.
- Provide stable, consistent policies that allow other countries to adjust their expectations in line with U.S. policies.
- Strengthen long-term relationships—governmental and private-sector, institutional and personal—with counterparts in East Asia. A broader portion of U.S. elites should deepen their understanding of the region and linguistic ability to operate in it.

U.S. SECURITY STRATEGY

The United States should:

- Maintain approximately the same level of U.S. military capacity in Asia as at present in order to respond to emergencies and to provide a stable environment—so that no power feels the need to rapidly increase its military power to preserve its security, thereby setting off an arms race. Modest adjustments in force levels can be made to respond to changed circumstances, redefinition of mission responsibilities, and introduction of new technology.
- Maintain bilateral military alliances while beginning to build mutual confidence between Asian nations to prepare for the time beyond 2010, by which time multilateral alliances should be able to supplement and in some areas replace bilateral ones.

- Begin dialogue first with all major partners and then also with smaller powers on the nature of long-range security relationships in the region. In contrast with earlier times, when a small group of elites in Asian countries could resolve issues, today the growth of democracy requires discussions to be carried on with a broad range of key elites, especially young elites, so they can better understand what is required to retain stability.

U.S. COMMERCIAL STRATEGY

The United States should:

- Expand U.S. efforts in trade promotion, providing information and market assistance to U.S.–based firms to help them gain opportunities for business expansion. We should concentrate our efforts not in Washington, but in overseas embassies, where commercial attaches, supported by top embassy officials, have made great progress in recent years. Strategic trade promotion, such as concentrating on the big emerging markets, supported by close cooperation between high-level representatives of business and goverernment agencies, should be continued, but they should be adapted to take account of the size of the market as well as overall growth rate.
- Work primarily through regional and global organizations to continue to open markets for international trade and investment. We should supplement this with bilateral efforts, although the leverage for doing so is constrained by WTO rules.
- Supplement the market-opening efforts of the Office of the U.S. Trade Representative, which tend to reflect political pressures from specific firms, by selecting strategic national market-opening priorities. Such priorities, based on analysis coordinated by the National Economic Council or the Commerce Department, should consider the potential size of a sector, the critical nature of certain technology for military needs or industrial progress, and the necessity of countering special efforts by trading partners.

U.S. CULTURAL STRATEGY

The U.S. government should:

- Increase U.S. public understanding of major issues of concern to Asia in order to provide a domestic U.S. political foundation for appropriate U.S. policy formation. Since U.S. commercial television and print media (and even some foreign policy journals) do not reflect a high level of knowledge about Asia, or responsibility to provide balanced reporting about the region, U.S. senior political leaders should take on a greater role, drawing on former officials and university and think-tank specialists, to help better inform the U.S. public.

- Revamp the U.S. Information Agency (USIA) to assign to U.S. missions overseas officials—comparable to those who serve in key press positions in the White House—whose primary job would be to build relationships with the leading television, print, and electronic media in key Asian countries. Officials should also be assigned specifically to work with the Asian press in Washington. All such officials should have training in Asian languages and regional affairs and have good personal relationships with Asians.
- Make more government funds available to increase the number of people knowledgeable about Asia, expanding the national resource centers and government support for critical language programs. High-level U.S. government functional specialists deeply involved in Asian affairs should be given training about Asia and should have regional specialists as assistants.

CHINA

Because China constitutes two-thirds of East Asia's population and because its growth is having a huge economic and political impact on the rest of Asia, it deserves special attention. The United States should:

- Aim to revive an overall sense of trust between the highest levels of Chinese and U.S. officials to permit the pragmatic resolution of problems (as was achieved between China and the United States from 1971 to 1989, under presidents Nixon, Ford, Carter, Reagan, and Bush). The resolution of key issues such as the environment, nuclear proliferation, arms proliferation, security, and international trade cannot be achieved without China's cooperation. At the same time, the United States should maintain its force levels in the region—so that China's neighbors would not need to yield if China were to apply intimidation to resolve disputes.
- Provide advice and training programs to assist China in preparing for participation in international organizations and regimes

of which it is not yet a member and for fuller participation in organizations where it is short of well-trained personnel.

- Respond positively to Chinese leaders' requests for advice and technology to reduce environmental pollution. Although some Chinese local officials are still reluctant to sacrifice economic growth to maintain the environment, many central government and regional leaders are eager for foreign cooperation.
- Promote a dialogue on security to reduce the chances of conflict from misunderstandings and to promote long-term regional stability. Since Japan's consideration of "theater missile defense" is of such great concern to China, one promising approach might be to launch a multi-year discussion of this issue that would explore whether an agreement could be reached whereby Japan would refrain from building a theater missile defense in exchange for China's agreement to military modernization with greater transparency and restrained force projection capacities, so as not to worry its neighbors. Long-range discussions on the Korean Peninsula should consider how to maintain stability while reducing arms and how to maintain U.S. forces while minimizing China's sense of threat.
- Seek agreements limiting the transfer of weapons of mass destruction to key areas such as Pakistan and the Middle East. Getting China's agreement might require the United States to agree to some restraint on the sale of military weapons systems to Taiwan.
- Hasten the entry of China into the World Trade Organization in exchange for China's agreement to specific dates for progress toward the liberalization of agriculture and of national treatment of foreign enterprises. The United States should continue to press for the protection of intellectual property rights in China and for the opening of the Chinese market to goods and services from abroad. At the same time, the United States must acknowledge that the U.S. trade deficit with China arises mainly because low-paid Chinese workers produce goods that U.S. consumers want to buy. Congress should work toward putting China's most-favored-nation trade status on a continuing basis that does not require annual renewal.
- Seek the cooperation of other countries in urging Beijing to sign and abide by international human rights conventions.
- Seek to improve Chinese-Japanese relations. It is in the inter-

est of the United States to promote joint international research to open up classified documents in all countries in order to get an objective account of World War II. It is also in the U.S. interest for high-level Chinese to gain a fuller and more balanced understanding of the Japanese domestic political and economic situation, particularly Japanese attitudes concerning military issues.

- Act with restraint on **Hong Kong**, which seeks "informed interest" from the United States. Many Asians, critical of the United States for failure to object to the British colonial government's failure to push democracy until the decision was made for reversion to Mainland rule, see current U.S. complaints as reflecting racism rather than principled support for freedom. Given its commitment to democracy and human rights, the United States should show its concern over constraints on a free press and information. But the United States should also accept the willingness of most Hong Kong residents to adapt to Chinese rule. We should continue to deal with Hong Kong as before the reversion.
- Continue broad-gauged relations with **Taiwan** while not encouraging the Taiwan independence movement and not upgrading the type of military equipment that the United States sells to Taiwan. We should encourage Taipei and Beijing to resume dialogue to reduce the risk of conflict and to work toward an agreement that would satisfy Taiwan's insistence on a high level of *de facto* autonomy in exchange for a formula that would satisfy Beijing's need to claim sovereignty.

JAPAN

The United States should continue to deepen the many-sided relationship with Japan, which will remain a major global power with unequaled financial and organizational resources despite its short-term economic adjustment problems. Japan can play a major role in resolving global problems by providing advice and financial assistance for modernization and environmental management in developing countries, and by helping to plan for the availability of global energy capacity to meet needs and to control the spread of weapons of mass destruction. The United States can play a major role in helping China to prepare for fuller participation in the world political and economic order.

In its bilateral relationships in Asia, the United States should:

- Continue working on the redefinition of our security relationships as the Japanese clarify how they will offer support for U.S. forces in emergencies. Now that the U.S.–Japan security relationship has been clearly redefined, Japan and the United States can expand security dialogue with China to promote transparency and build mutual confidence. It is in the U.S. interest to help improve relations between China and Japan.
- Continue to encourage Japan, bilaterally and multilaterally, to reduce regulations that impede market access, cooperating with forces in Japan that have the same goals.

KOREA

The United States, working closely with South Korea, China, Japan, and Russia, should continue to provide leadership in bringing North Korea out of its isolation and into orderly integration in the region.

ASEAN

The United States should deepen its relationships with all ASEAN members, including the new members (Vietnam, Burma, Laos, and Cambodia), in all spheres—economic, political, and cultural. In particular, we should work closely with young elites in Indonesia, who will play a key role in what may well be the most troubling pending succession in East Asia.

SOUTH ASIA

South Asian countries, notably India, Pakistan, Bangladesh, are beginning to show interest in following the examples of East Asia in further opening their economies and industrializing. These developments provide opportunities for the United States to deepen its political relationships in South Asia and to assist economic modernization, which is in U.S. interest.

BACKGROUND PAPER: THE MILITARY ENVIRONMENT IN ASIA

REAR ADM. EUGENE CARROLL, JR.

In order to evaluate opportunities to develop a new U.S. military role in Asia, this paper begins with a brief summary and appraisal of the current military situation in the region. The following appraisal identifies significant military capabilities and trends in each of the nations of Asia and also presents basic factual data concerning the nature of the U.S. presence.

Conclusions based on this summary are presented concerning the critical military danger zones in Asia today as well as probable future military concerns. The potential role for U.S. military forces in addressing this military environment is examined. A new peacetime policy for U.S. military presence and role in Asia is proposed on the basis of these conclusions.

NATIONAL MILITARY FORCE CAPABILITIES AND TRENDS

CAMBODIA

Personnel

Active: 87,700; Reserve: accurate information lacking

Funding

1995: $126 million; 1996: $116 million

Cambodian Army—Active personnel: 36,000

12 small combat divisions

1 combat/combat support division equivalent

110 tanks

Supporting artillery/air defense guns and missiles

Cambodian Navy—Active personnel: 1,200

14 patrol and coastal combatants

3 amphibious warfare crafts

Cambodian Air Force—Active personnel: 500

19 fighter/interceptor aircraft

11 armed helicopters

Assessment. Limited capability to defend homeland against existing and foreseeable threats (China, Vietnam, Laos, Thailand). No force projection capabilities, either air force or naval. Internal instability is rampant as a result of political conflict. Territorial disputes with neighbors exist, but the Cambodian military has no effective offensive forces.

Trends. Military spending is small in comparison with the expenditures of neighbors (Laos, Vietnam, Thailand), and forces are heavily outnumbered. Cambodia is undergoing a military modernization program but is limited by internal political and economic problems. It is expected that any modernization and upgrading will be focused upon maintaining present force levels in a purely defensive posture.

CHINA

Personnel

Active: 2,935,000 (43% conscripts)

Reserve: 1,200,000 (plus provincial militaries)

Funding

1995: $32 billion (estimated)

1996: $35 billion (estimated)

1997: Recent indicators show a 12.7% increase in military spending

People's Liberation Army—Active personnel: 2,200,000

(48% conscripts)

108 combat divisions

12 coastal/border guard divisions

15 combat/combat support division equivalents

9,600 tanks

140 helicopters

Supporting artillery/air defense guns and missiles

People's Liberation Navy—Active personnel: 265,000 (15% conscripts)

2 SLBM firing submarines

61 attack submarines

54 surface combatant ships

830 patrol and coastal defense ships

55 amphibious warfare ships

600 coastal/air defense aircraft

People's Liberation Air Force—Active personnel: 470,000

(34% conscripts)

420 medium/light bomber aircraft

4,400 fighter/attack aircraft

Supporting air defense guns and missiles

Strategic Missile Forces—Active personnel: 90,000

90 ICBM/IRBM nuclear armed missiles

12 SLBM nuclear armed missiles

Assessment. Capable of defending Chinese Mainland against all existing and foreseeable threats (United States, Russia). Capable of offensive land warfare against smaller bordering states individually (Vietnam, Myanmar, Bhutan, and Nepal), but would find logistics daunting even at this level of warfare. Clearly, logistics problems combined with the need to maintain security along borders with Russia, India, and Pakistan are major inhibitions on Chinese offensive operations. China has no naval or air forces capable of projecting effective attacks against Taiwan or Japan and could not sustain a military presence in the South China Sea against U.S. Seventh Fleet. In short, China is impregnable, secure from external attack even by Russia, but has little offensive power to project against other nations.

Trends. In the mid-1980s, China reduced its armed forces by approximately 25 percent and has remained relatively stable at just under 3,000,000 in all military categories. Spending appears to have increased, although reliable information is lacking. In addition, China's remarkable economic growth has been marked by significant inflation, which makes it difficult to determine how much real growth has occurred in military spending.

Nevertheless, it is clear that the primary emphasis is now on the modernization of the existing force, with efforts focused on upgrading aircraft and missiles. None of this to date has produced any significant increase in offensive capabilities. China seems intent on looking to the defense of the homeland, strengthening its domestic economy, and expanding its world trade. All of these objectives would be jeopardized if the leadership were to adopt a more aggressive foreign policy backed by expanded military projection forces.

There is reason also to believe that many power centers in China would resist any such policy in Beijing. For the present, it appears unlikely that Chinese military capabilities will change significantly (quantitatively or qualitatively) in the foreseeable future. Any effort to increase those capabilities would require many years and the diversion of major resources from the domestic economy—thus providing substantial warning of a new approach to security in China.

INDIA

Personnel

Active: 1,145,000; Reserve: 535,000

Funding

1995: $8 billion; 1996: $8 billion

Indian Army—Active personnel: 980,000

36 combat divisions

9 combat/combat support division equivalents

3,500 tanks

199 helicopters

Supporting artillery/air defense guns and missiles

Indian Navy—Active personnel: 55,000

19 attack submarines

26 surface combatant ships (2 carriers)

44 patrol and coastal combatant ships

20 minesweepers

9 amphibious warfare ships

2 fighter attack squadrons (22 aircraft)

Supporting air defense guns and missiles

Indian Air Force—Active personnel: 110,000

17 fighter/ground attack squadrons (370 aircraft)

20 fighter/interceptor squadrons (370 aircraft)

3 attack helicopter squadrons (32 helicopters)

Supporting air defense guns and missiles

Assessment. Capable of defending homeland and adjacent sea lanes against all existing and foreseeable threats (China, Pakistan). India has limited force projection capabilities and an advanced technological and manufacturing base to support large-scale weapons production. The force is primarily defensive in structure, and there is little evidence that efforts are being undertaken to change this. However, tensions between India and Pakistan are high, and the potential for conflict is great. The most pressing threat posed by India as a military force is the possession of nuclear warheads. Although not certain, it is generally accepted as fact that India is capable of waging limited tactical nuclear warfare. This makes the stakes in the territorial dispute between India and Pakistan devastatingly high.

Trends. Over the past ten years, military spending has remained fairly constant in real terms. Personnel numbers in the Indian Army have remained constant as well. Recent developments have indicated that both India and Pakistan are attempting to alleviate some of the confrontational pressure. For the first time in a decade, India and Pakistan are engaged in talks to reduce tensions in the area. It is uncertain what direction their relations will take in the future.

INDONESIA

Personnel

Active: 299,200; Reserve: 400,000

Funding

1995: $3 billion; 1996: $3 billion

Indonesian Army—Active personnel: 235,000

2 combat divisions

15 combat/combat support division equivalents

355 tanks

40 helicopters

Supporting artillery/air defense guns and missiles

Indonesian Navy

2 attack submarines

17 surface combatants

57 patrol and coastal combatants

13 minesweeping ships

28 amphibious warfare ships

38 coastal/air defense aircraft

1 marine combat division (100 tanks/artillery support)

Indonesian Air Force—Active personnel: 21,000

5 fighter/ground attack squadrons (52 aircraft)

1 fighter/interceptor squadron (12 aircraft)

Supporting air defense missiles

Assessment. Capable of defense of islands and internal waters against all existing and foreseeable threats (China, Philippines, Taiwan). Capable of limited protection of sea lanes and surrounding waters against all existing and foreseeable threats (China, Philippines, Taiwan). No ability to project military force abroad.

Trends. Military spending has remained consistent in real terms, with only a slight increase over ten years. Personnel strength has increased slightly over the past ten years. Recent purchases include surface combatant ships from the former East German Navy and two submarines. These purchases are indicative of the concern of the Indonesians regarding territorial and raw-material disputes in the South China Sea. These modernization programs represent no intention to develop force projection capabilities, but they do represent preparations by the Indonesians to defend disputed territories in the South China Sea.

JAPAN

Personnel

Active: 235,000 (all volunteer); Reserve: 48,000

Funding

1996: $45 billion; 1997: $47 billion

Ground Self-Defense Force—Active personnel: 148,000

14 combat divisions

4 combat/combat support division equivalents

1100 tanks

450 helicopters

Supporting artillery/air defense guns and missiles

Maritime Self-Defense Force—Active personnel: 43,000

17 attack submarines

63 surface combatant ships

7 anti-submarine air groups

70 mine warfare ships

Air Self-Defense Force—Active personnel: 44,000

3 ground attack squadrons (50 aircraft)

10 fighter interceptor squadrons (250 aircraft)

Supporting air-defense guns/SAM

Assessment. Capable of defending home islands against all existing and foreseeable military threats (China, Russia). Capable of limited protection of sea lanes out to 1,000 miles against existing and foreseeable naval threats (Russia). No capability to project military force abroad.

Trends. Over the past ten years, spending has increased slightly in real terms, but personnel strength has dropped slightly due to the reluctance of young people to enlist for military service. While Japan continues modest modernization programs, there appears to be no intention to do more than maintain present self-defense capabilities. No indication of efforts to develop any force projection capability with air or naval forces.

DEMOCRATIC PEOPLE'S REPUBLIC OF KOREA (DPKR—NORTH KOREA)

Personnel

Active: 1,054,000; Reserve: 4,700,000

Funding

1994: $6 billion

1995: $5 billion

DPRK *Army*—Active personnel: 923,000

26 combat divisions

87 combat/combat support division equivalents

3,940 tanks
Supporting artillery/air defense guns and missiles

DPRK *Navy*—Active personnel: 46,000
25 attack submarines
3 surface combatant ships
417 patrol and coastal combatant ships
25 minesweepers
260 small amphibious warfare ships (mostly hovercraft)
Supporting coastal air defense artillery/air defense guns and missiles

DPRK *Air Force*—Active personnel: 85,000
3 bomber regiments (82 aircraft)
15 regiments fighter/ground attack/interceptor regiments (529 aircraft)
Supporting air defense guns and missiles

Assessment. Information about the DPRK's military is unreliable and inaccurate. Despite the apparent capabilities of the military in defense of the homeland, the economic situation in the North (particularly with respect to the food supply and petroleum) severely hampers the effectiveness of the DPRK's military. The DPRK is apparently capable of strong initial defense of the homeland against all existing and foreseeable threats (Japan, South Korea, United States) but could not sustain prolonged operations against superior forces. However, although the DPRK has improved missile technology, its primary strength is in the sheer number of personnel and the proximity to the Republic of Korea border. The DPRK would have a difficult time sustaining prolonged warfare on the Peninsula, and its economic situation greatly degrades its ability to wage war on any level.

Trends. Personnel have increased by almost 25 percent over the last ten years, but overall military capability has decreased because of obsolescent equipment and logistic shortages. The one strong exception is in short- and medium-range surface-to-surface missiles, in which the DPRK has developed capability to attack Seoul as part of major initial assault. The strategy is to threaten massive damage in order to mask overall inability to sustain offensive operations against better equipped and trained Republic of Korea forces. The DPRK has no force projection capability and could not defend successfully against a determined attack from combined U.S. and Republic of Korea forces.

REPUBLIC OF KOREA (ROK—SOUTH KOREA)

Personnel

Active: 660,000 (24% conscripts); Reserve: 4,500,000

Funding

1995: $14 billion; 1996: $16 billion

ROK *Army*—Active personnel: 548,000

22 combat divisions
4 combat/combat support division equivalents
2,050 tanks
538 helicopters
Supporting artillery/air defense guns and missiles

ROK *Navy*—Active personnel: 60,000

4 attack submarines
40 surface combatant ships
122 patrol and coastal combatant ships
14 mine warfare ships
15 amphibious warfare ships
3 anti-submarine air groups (23 combat aircraft/47 armed helicopters)
2 marine combat divisions (60 tanks/supporting artillery)

ROK *Air Force*—Active personnel: 52,000

8 ground attack squadrons (155 aircraft)
4 fighter/interceptor squadrons (130 aircraft)
Supporting air defense guns/surface to air missiles/air to surface missiles/air to air missiles

Assessment. Capable of defending homeland against all existing and foreseeable military threats (North Korea). Capable of protection of adjacent waters, and limited protection of sea lanes against all existing and foreseeable threats (North Korea, Japan). No capability to project force abroad.

Trends. There has been a slow increase in military expenditures over the past ten years, as well as a slight increase in number of armed forces—most likely due to uncertainties of internal stability in North Korea. South Korea is undergoing a modernization program at present, with particular focus upon defense with Patriot missiles against North Korean missiles. There appears to be no intention other than the defense of homeland, and no indication of efforts to develop force projection capabilities.

MALAYSIA

Personnel

Active: 114,500; Reserve: 35,800

Funding

1995: $4 billion; 1996: $2 billion

Malaysian Army—Active personnel: 90,000

4 combat divisions

1 combat/combat support division equivalent

26 tanks

10 helicopters

Supporting artillery/air defense guns and missiles

Malaysian Navy—Active personnel: 12,000

6 surface combatant ships

37 patrol and coastal combatants

5 minesweepers

3 amphibious warfare ships

12 armed helicopters

Malaysian Air Force

2 fighter/ground attack squadrons (27 aircraft)

3 fighter/interceptor squadrons (51 aircraft)

Supporting air defense guns and missiles

Assessment. Capable of defending mainland against all existing and foreseeable threats (China, Singapore). Limited ability to defend the sea lanes, using existing naval and air forces against all existing and foreseeable threats (China, Singapore). Naval position is improving with acquisition of missile-equipped frigates and patrol boats, but no force projection capabilities at present.

Trends. Military spending rose in real terms over the past ten years but is now dropping. Personnel have increased slightly. The primary emphasis on military spending at present is obviously geared for coastal and sea-lane defense. No offensive power is being sought. Tensions between Singapore and Malaysia are great, but economic ties are so intricate that any military confrontation is unlikely. Defense of the Straits is integral to both countries, and both countries seem to be shaping their militaries accordingly.

PAKISTAN

Personnel

Active: 587,000; Reserve: 513,000

Funding

1995: $4 billion; 1996: $4 billion

Pakistani Army—Active personnel: 520,000

22 combat divisions

8 combat/combat support division equivalents

2,050 tanks

20 attack helicopters

Supporting artillery/air defense guns and missiles

Pakistani Navy—Active personnel: 22,000

9 attack submarines

11 surface combatant ships

13 patrol and coastal combatant ships

5 minesweeper ships

4 anti-submarine warfare aircraft

Pakistani Air Force

7 fighter/ground attack squadrons (126 aircraft)

10 fighter/interceptor squadrons (243 aircraft)

Supporting air defense guns and missiles

Assessment. Capable of strong defense of homeland against all existing and foreseeable threats (India). Limited ability to defend waters outside direct coastline. No apparent force projection capabilities. In terms of personnel, is half the size of its largest rival (India); however, Pakistan also has nuclear capabilities and the technological and manufacturing base to modernize its military rapidly should active conflict between the two countries develop.

Trends. Over the past ten years, military spending has increased slightly with the bulk of the money going toward military modernization programs. Pakistan has recently purchased weapons and missiles from China. Personnel numbers have increased over the past ten years. The level of Pakistan's nuclear abilities is uncertain because of the lack of reliable evidence—but probably improving.

PHILIPPINES

Personnel

Active: 107,500; Reserve: 131,000

Funding

1996: approximately $1.4 billion*; 1997: approximately $1.4 billion*

* *Supplemented by* U.S. *government for procurement and military modernization programs*

Philippine Army—Active personnel: 68,000

8 combat divisions

1 combat/combat support division equivalents

41 tanks

Philippine Navy—Active personnel: 23,000

1 surface combatant

54 patrol and coastal combatants

9 amphibious warfare ships

8 combat aircraft

Philippine Air Force

1 fighter/attack squadron (7 aircraft)

43 total combat aircraft

104 armed helicopters

Supporting air defense guns and missiles

Assessment. Limited ability to defend mainland against all existing and foreseeable threats (China, Japan, Indonesia). No capability to project military force abroad.

Trends. As the United States withdrew forces from the Philippines, the U.S. government agreed to support procurement and military modernization efforts with small military assistance programs. Personnel levels have remained constant, both in the Philippine military and in paramilitary organizations. The modernization programs amount to little more than updating patrol vessels. No force projection capability.

SINGAPORE

Personnel

Active: 53,900 (62% conscripts); Reserve: 221,000

Funding

1995: $4 billion; 1996: $4 billion

Singaporean Army—Active personnel: 45,000

3 combat divisions

1 combat/combat support division equivalent

410 tanks

Supporting artillery/air defense guns and missiles

Singaporean Navy—Active personnel: 2,900
- 19 patrol and coastal combatants
- 2 minesweeper ships
- 3 amphibious warfare ships

Singaporean Air Force—Active personnel: 6,000
- 4 fighter/ground attack squadrons (82 aircraft)
- 2 fighter/interceptor squadrons (38 aircraft)
- Supporting air defense guns and missiles

Assessment. Capable of defending mainland and immediate sea lanes against any existing and foreseeable threats (China). With purchases of new F-16s, a submarine, and surface combatants, effectiveness of defense of immediate sea lanes will be greatly enhanced. No capability to project force abroad.

Trends. Over the past ten years, spending has increased in real terms. Personnel levels have decreased slightly. Because of its geographic location, Singapore is undergoing a naval and air modernization and upgrade program to enhance its ability to effectively patrol the Straits of Singapore and Malacca. There are no indications that these forces are to be used for force projection, only to improve defense capabilities. Singapore-Thailand military cooperation increasing.

TAIWAN (ROC—REPUBLIC OF CHINA)

Personnel
- Active: 376,000; Reserve: 1,657,500

Funding
- 1996: $14 billion; 1997: $11 billion

ROC *on Taiwan Army*—Active personnel: 240,000
- 12 combat divisions
- 2 combat/combat support division equivalents
- 1,525 tanks
- 207 helicopters
- Supporting artillery/air defense guns and missiles

ROC *on Taiwan Navy*—Active personnel: 68,000
- 4 attack submarines
- 36 surface combatant ships
- 98 patrol and coastal combatant ships
- 16 mine warfare ships
- 21 amphibious warfare ships

ROC *on Taiwan Air Force*—Active personnel: 68,000
- 13 ground attack squadrons/fighter interceptor squadrons (392 aircraft)
- Supporting air-defense guns and missiles

Assessment. Capable of defending home island against all existing and foreseeable military threats (China). Capable of protection of immediate sea lanes, with naval forces supported by technologically advanced air force/naval air against existing and foreseeable naval threats (China). No capability to project military force abroad.

Trends. Over past ten years, military spending has increased slightly in real terms, while personnel have decreased. This is due to increased reliance upon superior technology in the armed services. Taiwan is undergoing a complete modernization program for its armed forces, due to tension in cross-strait relations. In recent years, Taiwan has developed an extensive indigenous military manufacturing capability, producing a variety of high-technology weapons, including fighter aircraft, and is working with the United States to develop more advanced naval forces. Taiwan shows no intention of developing forces other than for defense.

THAILAND

Personnel

Active: 254,000 (conscripts); Reserve: 200,000

Funding

1996: $4 billion; 1997: $4 billion

Thai Army—Active personnel: 150,000

15 combat divisions
1 combat/combat support division
763 tanks (major in are light tanks)
110 helicopters (4 attack helicopters)
Supporting artillery/air defense guns and missiles

Thai Navy—Active personnel: 64,000

12 surface combatants
60 patrol and coastal combatants
5 minesweepers
9 amphibious ships
9 fighter/interceptor aircraft
7 armed helicopters

Thai Air Force—Active personnel: 40,000

3 fighter/ground attack squadrons (83 aircraft)
2 fighter/interceptor squadrons (42 aircraft)
2 helicopter squadrons (39 helicopters)
Supporting air defense guns and missiles

Assessment. Fully capable of defending Thai homeland against all existing and foreseeable threats (Vietnam, Laos, Cambodia, Myanmar, Bhutan, China). Thailand has a large military that is well armed with recent purchases under its military modernization program. As a result of its purchase of a Spanish helicopter/Harrier aircraft carrier, Thailand will soon have the only navy in Asia capable of force projection. Thailand is capable of defending its homeland and coastal areas as well as its borders against all existing and foreseeable threats.

Trends. Over the past ten years, military spending has increased in real terms. Thailand has undergone a major upgrading of forces, and its modernization program is continuing. Personnel levels have remained constant. Thailand's military modernization is primarily designed to increase the capabilities of its naval forces. Several missile-equipped frigates and patrol boats have been purchased recently, and offensive capabilities will be greatly enhanced by acquisition of a small aircraft carrier. The carrier is claimed to be for search and rescue operations, but does support Harrier interceptor jets. Although the modernization program is primarily defensive, the purchase of F-16s and other offensive weapons suggests that Thailand could pose an increasing threat to bordering nations.

VIETNAM

Personnel

Active: 572,000; Reserve: 3-4 million (paramilitary urban and rural units)

Funding

1995: $975 million; 1996: $1 billion

Vietnamese Army—Active personnel: 500,000

53 combat divisions

28 combat/combat support division equivalents

1,900 tanks

Supporting artillery/air defense guns and missiles

Vietnamese Navy—Active personnel: 42,000

8 surface combatant ships

52 patrol and coastal combatants

11 minesweepers

7 amphibious warfare ships

Vietnamese Air Force—Active personnel: 15,000

1 fighter/ground attack regiment (squadron) (71 aircraft)

5 fighter/interceptor regiments (squadrons) (125 aircraft)

Supporting air defense guns and missiles

Vietnamese Air Defense Force—Active personnel: 15,000

14 combat air defense divisions

Supporting air defense guns and missiles

Assessment. Capable of defense of homeland. Military is designed for purely defensive purposes against all existing and foreseeable threats

(Thailand, Cambodia, Laos, China). Limited capability of defense of coastal waters. No force projection capabilities.

Trends. Military spending has increased somewhat in the past ten years in real terms. Vietnam is wary of situation in Southeast Asia, particularly instability in Cambodia and Thailand (territorial and political disputes). Personnel numbers decreased as Vietnamese military became a more formal organization. Vietnam displays no intention of expanding its military to include offensive forces, either naval or air. Economic expansion is the key objective of the Vietnamese government and has been the focal point of foreign policy. Vietnam has been an advocate of the Asian Regional Forum (ARF); under the Association of South East Asian Nations (ASEAN) and is willing to commit troops to any formal multinational military force to maintain regional stability.

U.S. MILITARY CAPABILITIES AND PRESENCE IN ASIA

TOTAL U.S. ARMED FORCES

Personnel

Active: 1,493,391; Reserve:1,542,477

***Funding*:** 1995—$263.5 billion

1996—$257.8 billion

1997—$250.7 billion

U.S. *Army*—Active personnel: 524,900

10 combat divisions

3 combat/combat support division equivalents

12,368 tanks

7,227 helicopters (1,595 armed)

Supporting artillery/air defense guns and missiles

U.S. *Navy*—Active personnel: 441,800

Submarines: 16 strategic submarines; 82 attack submarines

137 principal surface combatants

12 aircraft carriers

21 patrol and coastal combatants

16 mine warfare ships

41 amphibious warfare ships

Aviation: 11 carrier wings; 28 fighter/ground attack squadrons; 20 helicopter squadrons; 34 anti-submarine warfare squadrons (aircraft and helicopters)

U.S. *Marine Corps*—Active personnel: 171,900

3 combat divisions

1 combat/combat support division equivalents

422 tanks

Aviation: 3 air wings; 10 fighter/ground attack squadrons; 7 ground attack squadrons; 34 helicopter squadrons (6 armed)
Supporting artillery/air defense guns and missiles

U.S. *Air Force*—Active personnel: 408,900
24 air wings (air combat command)
51 tactical aircraft fighter/ground attack squadrons
10 air wings (air mobility command)
7 bomber wings
Supporting air defense guns and missiles

Strategic Forces*: U.S. *Strategic Command
U.S. Navy: 384 Submarine-Launched Ballistic Missiles (SLBM); 16 Ballistic-Missile Submarines (SSBN)
U.S. Air Force: 2 strategic missile wings (575 Intercontinental Ballistic Missiles (ICBM)/2075 warheads); 346 heavy bombers; 12 operational bomber squadrons

U.S. FORCES SERVING IN OR AVAILABLE FOR SERVICE IN WESTERN PACIFIC/ INDIAN OCEAN

U.S. *Pacific Command* (PACOM)

Alaska
- U.S. Army: 9,600 troops
- U.S. Air Force: 10,000 troops; 5 tactical air squadrons

Hawaii
- Headquarters: U.S. Pacific Command (PACOM)
- Headquarters: U.S. Pacific Fleet
- U.S. Army: 24,600 troops; 1 combat division
- U.S. Air Force: 4,400 troops; 1 air wing
- U.S. Navy: 19,500 troops

Singapore
- U.S. Navy: 100 troops
- U.S. Air Force: 40 troops

Japan
- U.S. Army: 1 Army Corps Headquarters; 2,000 troops
- U.S. Air Force: 15,200 troops; 2 tactical air wings
- U.S. Navy: 7th Fleet Headquarters in Yokosuka; 7,300 troops (ashore) commanding 20,210 troops (afloat)
- U.S. Marine Corps: 21,000 troops

South Korea
- U.S. Army: 1 Army Headquarters; 27,500 troops; 1 combat division
- U.S. Air Force: 1 Air Force Headquarters; 2 tactical air wings; 8,950 troops

Guam

U.S. Air Force: 1 Air Force Headquarters; 2,200 troops

U.S. Navy: 4,600 troops

Note: 1 naval base scheduled to close in 1997, and 1 naval base scheduled to be realigned in the year 2000.

Diego Garcia

U.S. Navy/U.S. Marine Corps: 900 troops

U.S. West Coast

U.S. Marine Corps: 1 Marine Expeditionary Force

U.S. *Pacific* Fleet (*3rd and 7th* Fleets)

Headquarters—Honolulu, Hawaii

Major base locations: Bangor (WA), San Diego, and Pearl Harbor

6 aircraft carriers (3rd and 7th Fleets)

148 surface ships

32 attack submarines

8 fleet ballistic submarines

Active air unit locations (Pacific Fleet)

14 strike/fighter squadrons

8 fighter squadrons

5 attack squadrons

5 early warning squadrons

6 anti-submarine squadrons

6 anti-submarine warfare helicopters squadrons

6 patrol squadrons

4 fleet air reconnaissance squadrons

1 fleet logistics support squadrons

7 light anti-submarine warfare helicopter squadrons

10 tactical electronic warfare squadrons

4 combat support helicopter squadrons

U.S. *3rd* Fleet

Headquarters—San Diego.

Areas of Operation: Eastern and Central Pacific; Aleutian Islands; Bering Sea

Force Structure: 4 Carrier Battle Groups; 4 Underway Replenishment Groups; 1 Amphibious Group

U.S. *7th* Fleet

Headquarters—Yokosuka, Japan.

Areas of Operation: Western Pacific/Indian Ocean; Japan; Philippines; ANZUS Responsibilities; Indian Ocean

Force Structure: 2 Carrier Battle Groups; 2 Underway Replenishment Groups; 1 Amphibious Ready Group; 1 Marine Expeditionary Unit

Assessment. The United States stands alone in the world as the only military "superpower" today. As the only nation with global reach, the United States keeps nearly 250,000 uniformed service members on foreign soil and foreign seas to provide a continuous military presence in support of U.S. foreign policy. The stated goal is to maintain regional stability through a capability to fight and win nearly simultaneously two major regional wars. No nation threatens the United States militarily. The present spending level of more than $260 billion per year for national defense functions accounts for 17 percent of the federal budget.

Trends. The Quadrennial Defense Review (QDR) report released on May 19, 1997, largely reaffirms the post–Cold War strategy of the United States. It specifically asserts the need to maintain a two-war capability; to retain the present force structure of the four armed services; and to proceed with a broad military modernization program. Small personnel reductions and base closures are proposed as means of saving funds needed to increase spending for this modernization. Overall spending is programmed to rise to $290 billion by the year 2002. In short, the United States will remain a peerless global superpower.

CONCLUSIONS

In a world that has changed fundamentally since 1991, Asia stands out as a region that is reasonably peaceful and stable. Though not without problems and dangers, Asia is relatively tranquil compared to the continuing, ominous violence in the Middle East and the chaos of Africa. India-Pakistan, the Korean Peninsula, Cambodia, Indonesia–East Timor, and China-Taiwan are all of concern but pale in comparison to conditions in the Middle East and Africa.

Two areas of immediate challenge exist in Asia today. The first is the Korean Peninsula, and the second is the long-standing conflict of interests between India and Pakistan. Of longer-term concern and importance are the future roles of China and Japan in Asian affairs. Despite these significant challenges to U.S. policymakers, there is little violence today, and the United States does have time, opportunities, and significant strengths to exploit as it attempts to define new approaches to security in Asia.

Because the Korean Peninsula presents the most immediate active challenge and also because the United States obviously can exert maximum leverage on developments there, let us turn first to that situation.

Korea. The first issue is that both the Republic of Korea (ROK) and the Democratic People's Republic of Korea (DPRK) want the United States to maintain a military presence there for completely different and contradictory reasons. Yet by our continued presence and active influence on both Koreas we inhibit the achievement of the most desirable resolution of the problem: a peaceful, politically unified Korean nation.

ROK officials want us to remain to relieve them of the full burden of maintaining their own security and as an implicit threat to the North that they believe strengthens their hand in negotiations with Pyongyang. DPRK leaders want the United States to remain so that they do not have to deal directly with Seoul—and as *de facto* protection from the influences of China and Japan. Hence our complex role as protector of both while serving as a barrier to effective communications between them.

Recognizing that we cannot continue indefinitely to serve as a crutch for both parties, we should soon make it clear that we intend to set a timetable for withdrawal of U.S. forces from the Peninsula. This policy will serve three purposes: (1) draw both sides into three-way negotiations of the terms and conditions for U.S. withdrawal; (2) give both sides incentives to settle on the elements of a stable military and political relationship between North and South after we leave; and (3) get us out of the middle of an expensive, wasteful, dangerous arrangement where we can be embroiled in a war by the actions of either our present ally or our adversary.

During such negotiations, we should make full use of our leverage to shape the new security arrangements. Our goal should be to create the so-called "soft-landing." Pyongyang should be offered incentives to enter into workable (if loose) cooperative political and economic arrangements with Seoul. The United States can be generous if it spends only part of the billions of dollars it now spends to keep 37,000 troops in the ROK. Seoul can be accommodating because, in the long term, the size and wealth of the South will dominate in any peaceful relationship with the North. ROK patience, food, communications, and good example can only liberalize economic and political conditions in the North over time.

To ensure that there will be time for conditions to evolve favorably, the terms of the U.S. military withdrawal should also include provisions for a substantial pullback and reduction in ROK and DPRK forces as U.S. troops depart. A less threatening military posture will be conducive to political and economic cooperation. A reduction in the crushing military burden now borne by the DPRK will also free up resources to apply to constructive economic development there.

Because the transition from a military confrontational posture along the Demilitarized Zone (DMZ) to a condition of relaxed readiness for conflict will involve the demobilization and movement of substantial forces, all parties will need to be confident that the process is going according to agreed plans. To provide this assurance, a supervisory body should be granted authority to visit and inspect military force dispositions both north and south of the present DMZ. An excellent precedent exists in the U.N.–administered Neutral National Supervisory Commission that was created to supervise implementation of the 1953 Armistice Agreement. This could be the model for a new supervisory body. The completion of the entire U.S. withdrawal process and the reduction and realignment of ROK–DPRK forces might well require five to ten years.

The creation of a Korean nation will not be easy or quickly achieved. Hard-liners in Pyongyang and Seoul will impede unification efforts in many ways. The key, however, is forceful leadership by the United States and an irreversible commitment to the withdrawal of all U.S. forces by a certain date. Then, North and South must face two choices: movement toward a cooperative, constructive relationship; or the stark certainty of a continuing destructive confrontation that will sap both sides and increase the risk of another tragic war on the Peninsula—this time with no intervention by Cold-War rivals to mitigate the outcome.

India and Pakistan. Far more significant than Korea in geopolitical terms, the corrosive conflict between India and Pakistan could prove to be a much greater threat to world peace. There are issues in this conflict that appear as intractable as Arab-Israeli issues. The passage of time and the slow evolution of attitudes seem to offer the only hope for a peaceful resolution.

This is certainly the case in terms of U.S. capabilities to play a direct role on the Subcontinent. A sad legacy of the Cold War is that we believed it necessary to support Pakistan as long as we feared Soviet advances in India, thereby compromising our influence today in India. Similarly, since the end of the Cold War, our concerns about nuclear proliferation have resulted in adversarial relations with Pakistan and the loss of much of our leverage there. Our failure to move with Russia, China, France, and Britain to reduce and eliminate nuclear weapons limits our ability to restrain the emerging nuclear arms race in South Asia.

U.S. military power provides no answer to resolving the India-Pakistan conflict. It is inconceivable that any U.S. government could find justification or public support for military action against either nation. In that sense, our naval supremacy in the Indian Ocean and Arabian Sea is essentially irrelevant, as is our strategic air power. In short, our foreign policy must rest primarily on diplomatic and economic strengths. Nevertheless, our continued naval presence in the Indian Ocean in maintaining access to the Persian Gulf and guaranteeing the freedom of navigation along shipping lanes suggests the wisdom of initiatives to improve military cooperation with both India and Pakistan.

However, because we suffer the consequences of the Cold War on the Subcontinent (as well as in our national budget), we are handicapped both diplomatically and economically. It seems that any influence we may exert on the parties must come with the help of friends in (and through) the United Nations. This is truly a problem for the world community. However difficult, time-consuming, and tenuous the process may be, our leadership with respect to India-Pakistan can only be effective multilaterally, through means other than the threat or exercise of military measures.

China. Here again, U.S. security interests must be pursued primarily through diplomatic and economic channels. The fact is that both China and the United States are very powerful militarily. They effectively cancel out the weight of military considerations in their relationship—because of very different strengths, however.

China is fundamentally impregnable as a land-based power. Within a huge nation (population and space) it maintains a large Army, adequately equipped to defend their territory. If attacked, it can trade space and lives as necessary until it exhausts an invader. Its nuclear capabilities constitute retaliatory capabilities sufficient to inhibit nuclear attack. But China possesses virtually no capability to project force much beyond its borders.

The United States configures, in contrast, its forces almost entirely to project power against external adversaries. This requires heavy investment in air and naval power and relatively less for land forces. Thus, we could conduct an aerial bombardment of China and deny China use of the sea—but to what purpose? We cannot seize or threaten the political control of Chinese territory. The U.S. and China simply are not equipped to fight each other to achieve any valid or credible objective.

But what if China adopts an aggressive foreign policy and develops air and naval forces capable of projecting military power in support of that policy? First, it would take a long time to achieve such a capability—time measured in decades, not years. Second, it would require investment of a national treasure measured in trillions, not billions, of dollars. Although China today is still enjoying rapid economic growth, even under the best of conditions the rate is certain to decrease in the next few years. If China adopts a policy that requires diverting the bulk of savings into military programs rather than economic development, growth will slow or stop entirely, and the recent gains will be jeopardized. This fact would certainly inhibit even an expansionist government in Beijing when considering that it must feed a billion people and improve a marginal twentieth century infrastructure in the twenty-first century.

Another critical question is whether any government in Beijing could impose the sacrifices inherent in a military buildup on the many divergent elements in China today. There would certainly be resistance from many sectors of the Chinese society and economy who have different priorities. For example, political unrest in Xinjiang and Xizang (Tibet) Autonomous Regions and the reluctance of other Chinese provinces to fulfill national tax mandates are indicative of the multitude of internal problems facing China that undermine its ability to act as a truly hegemonic power in Asia. The government acted brutally in Tiananmen Square, but could it enforce compliance throughout China with a policy that threatened the well-being and safety of hundreds of millions of Chinese citizens?

At this moment China cannot even threaten an invasion of Taiwan. It is not the existence of the U.S. Seventh Fleet that blocks an invasion but the defenses available on the island itself. To invade, China would first have to create a massive air and naval force capable of overcoming nearly 2,000,000 active and reserve Taiwanese military defenders.

Achieving that capability would take until the year 2020 by China's own estimates. Given the tremendous investment required just to cross the Taiwan Straits, is it not more likely that in the next twenty years the two Chinas will find a way to co-exist? Despite China's periodic saber-rattling and bombastic rhetoric, it is reported that Taiwan-China trade is expanding and that Taiwanese entrepreneurs and capital are welcome on the Mainland. Where mutual benefits exist, pragmatic accommodations become much more attractive than costly, destructive actions that benefit neither side.

Japan. Japan is today a strong democratic nation that contributes to stability in Asia. The primary objective of U.S. foreign, economic, and military policymakers is to increase incentives for Japan to sustain this positive role. This paper primarily addresses the military security issue as a separate factor in U.S. policy, but because there is a close interrelationship between military and economic policies in the U.S.–Japan relationship, the two facets of policy will be addressed together here.

Harking back to the Cold War, the United States was willing to accept trade imbalances and exclusionary import restrictions in Japan to ensure no rupture of U.S.–Japanese strong joint military opposition to Soviet expansion. Mindful of aggressive Soviet pressure and the continuing dispute over ownership of the "Northern Territories," Japan was happy to have the presence of U.S. forces as both a guarantee of U.S. support and a means to avoid increasing its own defense expenditures.

With the collapse of the Soviet Union, the Cold War rationale for a large U.S. military presence in Japan disappeared—but not the U.S. military's desire to justify a large military budget. In part, this view is linked to promoting the belief that a forward military presence in Europe and Asia is a means of strengthening U.S. political influence in world affairs. The argument that our presence inhibits the expansion of an independent Japanese military force has also again been put forward.

Japanese authorities are happy still to see the United States determined to maintain its military presence, and they use the growing popular spirit (particularly in Okinawa) against the U.S. military presence as an implied threat in trade negotiations. U.S. demands are mitigated by a sense that if we take a hard line on trade issues, the Japanese can respond by reducing or eliminating approximately $5 billion annually in subsidies that defray U.S. military costs in Japan. In the extreme, Japan could even claim that, since the majority of Japanese oppose a U.S. military presence, our forces must withdraw.

In assessing these interrelated military and economic issues, it should first be noted that U.S. forces in Japan are not the inhibitors of Japanese military expansion. Present Japanese interests and policies are self-inhibiting. Japan has become a global power of the first rank through economic power, part of which arises from its very low investment in military programs. Not only does Japan maintain minimal (and shrinking) Self-Defense forces, but it invests virtually nothing in military research and development. In effect, Japan gets a nearly free ride because the United States devotes the majority of federal R & D funds to military programs while Japan invests in the development of products that make it a dominant force in world markets.

Another self-inhibiting factor is the strong anti-military spirit of the great majority of Japanese citizens. There may be some sense in the government of a need to "assume the role of a normal nation" with expanded military forces, but little public support exists. Any proposal to amend Article 9 of the Japanese constitution in order to permit the expansion of the Japanese military and the creation of power projection/offensive capabilities would certainly provoke strong active opposition.

The fact is that U.S. forces are in Japan (for the reasons described above) at the sufferance of the Japanese government. If, and whenever, the mood changed in Japan and a policy of military expansion were adopted, our presence could be ended by a simple order to withdraw. Now, and for the foreseeable future, such an action is highly improbable. Nevertheless, the presence of U.S. forces today is largely irrelevant to such a decision, because Japan faces no external military threat, and there is no reason for it to abandon its reliance on economic strength as the primary element of national security.

Russia. Despite a major presence in Northeast Asia as well as some military installations on the Pacific coast, Russia is not a significant factor in Asian affairs. Its only military efforts in the region met with disaster in 1905 in the Tsushima Straits and with failure in the early 1980s in Vietnam, where the Soviets attempted to maintain a base for naval forces. The Soviet Union did expand its holdings in the Kuril Islands in the aftermath of WW II—a fact that now impinges on Russia's relationship with Japan, but a peaceful resolution of competing claims is likely in the future.

There is no prospect that Russia will initiate any military actions in Asia in the foreseeable future, particularly given the deteriorating condition of its military forces and primary concern with European issues and interests.

A NEW U.S. POLICY IN ASIA

The foregoing review of the military situation in Asia makes it clear that today the United States faces absolutely no significant military threat to its interests in the region. Future threats could arise from either China or Japan, but the present foreign policies and military programs of those nations give no indication of preparations to project military power against the United States or its economic and political interests in Asia. Because of the tremendous investment required and the time needed to develop major military forces capable of force projection in Asia, there would be a long period of warning of any such emerging threat. This would provide the United States ample opportunity to respond.

It is also clear that the United States faces continuing political and economic challenges throughout the region. In none of these circumstances can the U.S. military presence or implied threats make a positive contribution. Examples are Chinese human rights violations, arms exports, China-Taiwan relations, and trade policies; Japanese trade policies; India-Pakistan confrontation; and promotion of Korean unification. In truth, the U.S. military presence and posturing (as in the Taiwan Straits and in Korea) contribute to heightened tensions and inhibit constructive engagement leading to the peaceful resolution of regional issues.

A final factor—one not regional in nature—bears on the role of the U.S. military in Asia. There is nearly total agreement in Washington that overall U.S. military programs today are excessive and unaffordable. The recent Quadrennial Defense Review clearly portends force level and military readiness reductions even if pro-defense advocates are able to sustain current levels of military spending in the face of budget-balancing efforts. Given reduced force levels and readiness, it will become necessary to reduce today's forward military posture.

For all of these reasons—no existing military threat, the need for primary attention to economic and political issues, the counterproductive role of military presence, and the certainty of U.S. force level reductions—the following changes are recommended in U.S. security programs in Asia.

Korea. In tripartite negotiations, set a date certain to commence the phased withdrawal of all U.S. military units from the Korean Peninsula. U.S. withdrawal should be matched by the thinning out and pullback of DPRK and ROK forces into a more stable relationship. Reduced U.S. and ROK military expenditures would permit increased incentives in the form of economic aid for the DPRK to support economic recovery. The United States should facilitate DPRK–ROK political negotiations leading to cooperative relations and development of an incremental plan for unification. The United States should encourage the ROK throughout to avoid attempting to dictate the terms of the relationship in the knowledge that the size and wealth of ROK will ultimately dominate a Korean nation in the twenty-first century. Recent softening of DPRK resistance to negotiations bodes well for incentive-based proposals.

Japan. U.S. military forces in Japan serve no security purpose and are increasingly the focus of anti-American activity, particularly in Okinawa. The public recognizes that they are not needed for the defense of Japan and resents the burden that U.S. forces represent environmentally and financially. Discussions should commence immediately, leading to the phased withdrawal of all land and air forces over the next three years. U.S. warships home-ported in Japan should be returned to U.S. bases, but naval support facilities in Yokosuka and Sasebo should be maintained in active status for joint use by U.S. and Japanese naval units in the future. Small Seventh Fleet detachments should remain at both facilities to assist Japanese work forces in upkeep and repair work there as well as to maintain basic stores of standard repair materials for use by U.S. warships during occasional upkeep periods and voyage repairs. As agreeable to both parties, plans for air and naval exercises on a regular basis should be developed in order to ensure that the combined forces maintain the ability to defend sea lines of communication to and from Japan in the event that a threat develops in the future. The current U.S.–Japan Security Treaty should remain in effect and be observed by both parties.

China. There is no future in relying upon the U.S. military presence or threats to exert constructive pressure on China. Evidence abounds that military signals provoke only negative responses. Accordingly, we should cease all military charades such as the dispatch of carriers to Taiwan when/if China-Taiwan political rhetoric and military threats result in heightened tensions. The United States must focus on key political and economic elements of the U.S.–China relationship, and initiatives should always look at strengthening political cooperation and trade ties. The issue of human rights in China should be addressed only in multilateral channels, primarily through the United Nations. As recent events have shown, the United States can exert only marginal influence on human rights problems in this way, but in the long term constructive engagement offers more promise for improvements than does U.S. unilateral pressure in the form of public criticism or threats.

Chinese arms and nuclear technology transfer policies are of great concern and must be addressed as part of an international problem, not as the primary responsibility of the United States. The most promising venue is in the U.N. Security Council. The five permanent members conduct the overwhelming bulk of international arms trade and technology-transfer actions. Only a cooperative approach in the interests of mutual security can possibly succeed in reducing these negative programs. As the largest trader, the United States clearly must lead by example in setting new standards of restraint if destructive levels of armaments in Asia are ever to be reduced. This problem, like so many others, cannot be resolved by U.S. military force or the threat of unilateral sanctions, military or economic.

Taiwan presents a special problem in the U.S.–China relationship. As a means of reducing the military aspect of that relationship, the United States should privately communicate to Taiwan authorities that there will be no more "shows of force" by U.S. military units during any period of heightened Taiwan-China tensions. We should also ensure that Taiwan is not provided with advanced U.S. weaponry unless and until China has taken positive measures to develop new military means to threaten Taiwan. Then, only defensive weapons needed to balance new Chinese capabilities should be provided. At the diplomatic level, the United States should encourage and support initiatives to strengthen cooperative economic and political ties between the two parties. It must be made clear to Taiwan that we cannot be counted on to support any provocative actions by Taiwan, including a declaration of independence, that threaten peaceful relations between the two Chinas. The recent galling, gratuitous declaration by Speaker Newt Gingrich that "we will defend Taiwan" was a classic example of how not not to improve U.S.–China relations or promote a long-term resolution of the Taiwan issue.

The Subcontinent and the Indian Ocean. There is no place in Asia where U.S. forces have less peacetime utility than this region. The legacy of the Cold War renders U.S. forces unwelcome on land and irrelevant at sea. Any progress in bilateral relationships with India and Pakistan must rest on even-handed political and economic initiatives that contribute to resolution of the India-Pakistan territorial dispute.

In a purely military sense, the United States can properly maintain its presence in Diego Garcia to support its commitments in the Middle East and control of the sea lanes of communication through the Indian Ocean. Intermittent deployments of naval and air units and exercises in the Indian Ocean incident to the transit of naval units to/from the Persian Gulf will be sufficient to demonstrate U.S. capabilities there.

SUMMARY

We are fortunate to be in a stable period of near equilibrium among world powers. The shape of future events cannot be foreseen with confidence nor is there any sense that military power can be used today to foreclose or control developments positively in the twenty-first century. As discussed above, there are even situations in Asia where military presence and actions may well provoke undesirable consequences.

Whatever the future holds, the United States cannot direct and control global events as the world's only military superpower today. We cannot be on guard everywhere, filling so-called "vacuums" with 250,000 American military men and women. We are not that wealthy, and the world will not indefinitely accept U.S. hegemony based upon our military power. Neither will Americans accept the onerous burden forever of attempting to guide the world's affairs by force. The costs in blood and treasure are too great.

Therefore, we should seize this opportunity to reduce our military presence in Asia and withdraw all of our land and air forces to U.S. territory. Such a withdrawal should be conducted in an orderly, phased program based on carefully agreed arrangements with our friends and allies. The U.S. Third and Seventh Fleets should remain the dominant Pacific naval force and demonstrate the assured capability to defend sea lanes of communication throughout the region in order to link together friendly nations in peaceful cooperation. Resources freed by reducing the costs of our forward deployed forces could, in part, be used for constructive economic aid packages in Korea, specifically, and wherever else U.S. support can work for peaceful resolution of local problems.

This approach to security in Asia would greatly reduce the readiness of U.S. forces to intervene militarily in local confrontations where no serious threat to regional stability or U.S. interests is involved. Such a surrender of U.S. responsibility should even extend to the Korean Peninsula after U.S. withdrawal, where (despite all diplomatic and economic efforts) violence might erupt. This change should be made explicit by the elimination of Article 3 of the current Mutual Defense Treaty between the Republic of Korea and the United States, thereby revoking the obligation of the United States to intervene automatically if the ROK is attacked. Article 2 would remain in effect and require consultation in the event of such an attack. Careful reevaluation of reduced military commitments would be required if either Japan or China embarked on an aggressive foreign policy backed by greatly increased offensive military forces in the future—but such actions appear improbable for the foreseeable future.

The words of Walter Lippmann many years ago are highly relevant today:

> A mature and great power will make measured and limited use of its power. It will eschew the theory of a global and universal duty which not only commits it to unending wars of intervention but intoxicates its thinking with the illusion that it is a crusader for righteousness.

The United States is a mature, great power and should eschew the notion that we have the duty to maintain peace everywhere through the use of our military power. Our great political and economic strengths must form the foundation of U.S. leadership efforts in support of a cooperative world order, not our tanks, troops, bombers, and carriers.

THE EDITORS AND AUTHORS

Selig S. Harrison is a Senior Scholar of the Woodrow Wilson International Center for Scholars and a Fellow of The Century Foundation. His many books on U.S. relations with Asia include *The Widening Gulf: Asian Nationalism and* U.S. *Policy.*

Clyde V. Prestowitz, Jr., is President of the Economic Strategy Institute and former Counselor to the Secretary of Commerce.He is the author of *Trading Places: How We Allowed Japan to Take the Lead.*

Doug Bandow is a syndicated columnist with the Copley News Service and former Special Assistant for Policy Development to President Ronald Reagan.

Barry Bosworth is a Senior Fellow of the Brookings Instituttion.

Ted Galen Carpenter is Vice President for Defense and Foreign Policy Studies of the Cato Institute.

James Clad is Professor of Southeast Asia Studies at Georgetown University.

Rear Admiral Eugene Carroll, Jr., is Deputy Director of the Center for Defense Information.

Charles W. Freeman, Jr., is former Ambassador to Saudi Arabia and Assistant Secretary of Defense for International Security Affairs.

Chalmers Johnson is President of the Japan Policy Research Institute.

Geoffrey Kemp is Director of Regional Strategic Programs at the Nixon Center for Peace and Freedom.

Paul H. Kreisberg is a Senior Scholar of the Woodrow Wilson International Center for Scholars.

Nicholas R. Lardy is a Senior Fellow of the Brookings Institution.

Martin L. Lasater is author of *The Changing Of the Guard: President Clinton and the Security of Taiwan.*

Mike Masato Mochizuki is a Senior Fellow of the Brookings Institution.

William J. Taylor is Senior Vice President for International Security Affairs of the Center for Strategic and International Studies.

Ezra Vogel is Director of the John K. Fairbank Center for East Asian Research at Harvard University.

Allen S. Whiting is Regents Professor of Political Science at the University of Arizona.

Jeffrey Winters is a Professor of Political Science at Northwestern University.

THE ECONOMIC STRATEGY INSTITUTE

The Economic Strategy Institute (ESI) was founded in 1989 to develop and promote a comprehensive economic strategy for American economic leadership in the twenty-first century. Because American economic leadership will increasingly be defined in economic rather than military terms, and because the nation will face unprecedented challenges without the benefit of past superiority in industry, technology, and finance, this mission remains one of the highest importance.

In contrast to the conventional economic wisdom, which equates potato chips and computer chips in terms of economic significance, ESI emphasizes that the structure of a country's economy—what it makes—has an effect on the long-term structure, equal in importance to factors such as interest rates, savings rates, and exchange rates.

Thus, ESI emphasizes four key elements: a macroeconomic policy designed to double U.S. savings and investment rates in order to achieve levels comparable to those of other leading countries; policies to enhance the nation's technology and production capabilities; development and maintenance of a broad range of industries and commercial and technological capabilities; and an international trade policy aimed at achieving broadly reciprocal conditions for U.S. traders and investors.

ESI takes its findings and recommendations to a broad range of audiences—to the Congress and the Executive Branch of the U.S. government, to business and labor, and to academia and the press. Many of the studies have had, and continue to have, a major impact on some of the country's biggest economic policy debates.

BOARD OF DIRECTORS

ECONOMIC STRATEGY INSTITUTE
1401 H Street, N.W. • Suite 750 • Washington, D.C. 20005
Tel. 202-289-1288 • Fax: 202-289-1319 • WWW: http://www.econstrat.org